FRIENDS LIKE US

The Unofficial Guide to Friends

By Jim Sangster and Paul Condon:
The Complete Hitchcock

By David Bailey and Warren Martyn:
Goodnight, Seattle

FRIENDS LIKE US

The Unofficial Guide to *Friends*

Jim Sangster & David Bailey

Virgin

This edition first published in 2000 by
Virgin Publishing Ltd
Thames Wharf Studios
Rainville Road
London W6 9HA

First published in Great Britain in 1998 by Virgin Publishing Ltd

A catalogue record for this book is available from the British
Library.

ISBN 0-7535-0439-1

Typset by Galleon Typesetting, Ipswich
Printed and bound in Great Britain by Mackays of Chatham PLC

Acknowledgements

The authors would like to thank the following for their support, love and proof-reading for free:

Eric Aasen, John Ainsworth, Matin Akhtar, Melanie Allan, Liz Ashford, John Binns, Louisianna Boulton-Mudd, Jonathan Burgess, Fido, Fleur Breteau, Helen Buckley, Darryl Butcher, Garven Campbell, Flora Collingwood, Mark Christy, Russell Coburn, Nick Cooper, Paul Cornell, Peter Cooke, Neil Corry, Martin Day, Ellie Eaton, Ian Garrard, Marie-Helene Gauthier, Gary Gillatt, Stephen Griffiths, Marcus Hearn, Clay Hickman, Ian Hodge, Rob Jones, Graham Kibble-White, Katherine Kleeb, Rob & Gemma Lewis, Robin Limmeroth, Steve Lyons, Scott Matthewman, Steven Moffat, Stephen Mouette, Richie Moosbally, Adrianna Mudd-Boulton, Jo Murphy, Tina Nellis, Mark Newton, Carrie O'Grady, Kimberley Piper, Philippa Probert, Geoff Rens, Jim Smith, Bob Stanley, Robin Sturmey, Keith Topping, Lee Travers, Lisa Wardle, Gary Wah, Kevin White, Tony Whitt, Rob Wilson, Mark Wright, Birgit Zich.

Special thanks to Rebecca Levene and Simon Winstone for the original commission, Jo Brooks for giving us another go, and Gary Russell for general advice and inspiration.

David would like to dedicate this book to Andy Brittin, and Jim dedicates his half to Paul Condon, Chris Vanderpijpen and the Goodfellows for (im)moral support.

We would also like to credit Alexander Graham Bell and Tim Berner-Lee, without whom this book could not have been written.

Contents

Introduction To The 2nd Edition

(or 'The One With The Guide To The Guide – Part Two')

When we sat down to write the first edition of this book, it was at a time when the rumour-mags and gossip columns were buzzing with the news that Matthew Perry was about to jump ship and say goodbye to Chandler Bing for good. Two years down the line and at the time of writing, Matthew's still there, but now we hear that it's Lisa Kudrow who'll be leaving. Or maybe it's David Schwimmer. Or it's all of them. Whatever, with two more seasons 'in the can', we thought it was about time we took a look at what's happened since *Friends Like Us* first hit the shelves. We've amended some of the entries, tidied things up and generally overhauled the entire book. This of course means that some things had to go, but we think the sacrifices were worth it to bring you the only pocket-sized guide to *Friends* that actually *does* fit into your pocket.

Just as a reminder, let us tell you what this book is about. It's not a script book or a behind-the-scenes tell-all examination of how to make the most successful comedy on US television. Nor is it an in-depth exposé of the lives of America's six most popular young actors. This is a *fan's* guide to the show, an episode-by-episode *aide-mémoire* to *Friends*, the hit Warner Bros. sitcom shown on Channel 4 and Sky One in the UK.

In some fan cultures, the fans can be caricatured as geeky or nerdish by the way they dress up in costumes and wear T-shirts with slogans such as 'Live Long And Prosper' or 'The Truth Is Out There'. What distinguishes *Friends* fans from the rest is that the characters we all know and love are not some visiting alien or a conspiracy-driven FBI agent. They're people just like us, people who wear T-shirts and jeans when they hang around the house, people who fall in love, people who have crappy jobs and bitch about them to the only people who'll listen – their friends.

How To Use This Guide

Friends Like Us is a reference guide, containing a listing of every episode, grouped into six seasons.* This is for two reasons: first, to make it that bit easier to find your favourite episodes; and second to reduce, as much as we can do, the possibility of spoiling episodes for those fans who have yet to see them.

Anyway, the format goes something like this:

Episode number and title: Each episode has been given a three-figure number – the first digit tells you which season the episode was transmitted in, the next two refer to the episode's transmission order. So for example, 'The One Where Rachel Finds Out' is episode 124, the 24th episode of Season 1. Each episode is listed by episode title, which as every true fan should know is usually prefixed with 'The One Where . . .' or 'The One With . . .' (often abbreviated to 'TOW'). As these titles never appear on screen (they usually appear only in listings magazines), we have had to rely on a number of sources to pin down exactly what each episode is called, but generally we've just stuck to the ones given in the Warner Bros. press releases. There is, as always, an exception to the rule. Whereas the first episode is known to some as 'The One Where It All Began', or even 'The One Where Monica Gets A New Roommate', we've elected to go with the title that Warner Bros. use, which is the rather plain 'Pilot'.

First transmission date: The date the episode was first transmitted on NBC in the USA and on Channel 4 in the UK for series 1–3. The satellite channel Sky One managed to jump in before Channel 4 and show series 4 first so we use these dates for episodes 401 onwards.

Guest Cast: *Friends* has more than its fair share of celebrity guest appearances, but we don't stand on ceremony – they're lumped in with the rest of the supporting cast.

---

* Throughout this book, the term 'season' is used to describe a single transmission block of episodes, with 'series' being used as a description of the programme as a whole.

After all the technical stuff we've included a few categories that may need further explanation. We dip into these pretty much as and when we feel they're appropriate . . .

Poor Ross: Those moments when Ross feels like the world's against him, or when he acts like he's still in the playground. Occasionally, this becomes **Scary Ross**.

Freaky Monica: Every time Monica proves she's that much more obsessive than anyone else.

Spoilt Rachel: Moments when Rachel realises just how protected she was by her daddy's wallet, or when she completely fails to see just why she's being plain selfish.

Phoebisms: Examples of that unique view on life in glorious Phoebe-vision!

Slow Joey: When Joey completely fails to get the point or realise what's going on. Which is, like, always.

Chandleresque / Chandler's Job: Killer one-liners, witty repartee and summations of life in general. Also, there's much debate in the show about Chandler's job. We don't quite know what he does (apart from 'data processing'), and apparently neither does anyone else, but if he gets his ANUS or WENUS out, we'll let you know!

The Ballad of Ross & Rachel: No matter what other plotlines are running, this is one story that just keeps coming back. We chart the highs, the lows and all that bitchiness and point-scoring in between.

Parents / Family – Who Needs 'Em?: From the very first episode we see Rachel having problems with her father. Episode 102 introduces the inimitable Geller parents, each with their own pearls of wisdom and complete lack of insight into their children. Whenever the parent or relative of a Friend pops up, you'll usually find a reference here.

Ugly Naked Guy: The continuing story of the semi-regular character who we really don't *want* to see but still find strangely compelling.

Just Plain Weird: All the strange events and obviously deranged people who pop in and out of the lives of the Central Perk gang.

Generation X: Cultural references and homages are a major part of the whole 'Generation X' (those in their late 20s / early

30s) way of life, and *Friends* is full of them. Of course some of the American culture references are completely wasted on us Brits, so we've tried to explain them whenever possible, as well as catching as many of those 'oh where have I seen him/her before' moments as we can. Effectively, this is our translation section for the culturally or transatlantically impaired.

The Story So Far: *Friends* is unusual in the way the long-term story arc is often as important as the plot for the individual episode. This section helps keep track of all those cross-references to previous episodes and to events that happened before the first episode.

Plus loads of other categories as and when they're relevant. What we've aimed at is a write-up that tells you as much as you need to know to remember what happens, without giving too much away to those who haven't seen every episode (particularly the later ones).

Finally, in **The Last Word**, we offer a brief review of each episode, just a personal comment on the continuing exploits of our favourite TV people. One thing worth noting here, of course, is that on the rare occasions when we might be a little negative, we still think *Friends* is so much better than anything else on TV.

Well, except maybe *Frasier*, at a push. (Did we say that out loud?)

Principal Credits

Regular Cast: Jennifer Aniston (Rachel Green), Courteney Cox-Arquette (Monica Geller), Lisa Kudrow (Phoebe Buffay), Matt LeBlanc (Joey Tribbiani Jr), Matthew Perry (Chandler Bing), David Schwimmer (Ross Geller)

Yasmine and Dick appear courtesy of Benay's Bird & Animals

Executive Producers: Kevin S. Bright, Marta Kauffman and David Crane
Created by: Marta Kauffman and David Crane
Executive Producer: Michael Borkow
Co-Executive Producers: Adam Chase, Michael Curtis and Greg Malins
Co-Producers: Wil Calhoun, Seth Kurland, Jill Condon and Amy Toomin
Producer: Todd Stevens
Executive Story Editors: Shana Goldberg-Meehan and Scott Silveri, Andrew Reich and Ted Cohen
Main Title Theme: Michael Skloff (music), Allee Willis (lyrics), performed by The Rembrandts
Incidental Music: Michael Skloff

Friends is a Bright/Kauffman/Crane Production in association with Warner Bros. Television

The Episodes

First Season

101 The Pilot
102 The One With The Sonogram At The End
103 The One With The Thumb
104 The One With George Stephanopoulos
105 The One With The East German Laundry Detergent
106 The One With The Butt
107 The One With The Blackout
108 The One Where Nana Dies Twice
109 The One Where Underdog Gets Away
110 The One With The Monkey
111 The One With Mrs Bing
112 The One With The Dozen Lasagnes
113 The One With The Boobies
114 The One With The Candy Hearts
115 The One With The Stoned Guy
116 The One With Two Parts, Part 1
117 The One With Two Parts, Part 2
118 The One With All The Poker
119 The One Where The Monkey Gets Away
120 The One With The Evil Orthodontist
121 The One With The Fake Monica
122 The One With The Ick Factor
123 The One With The Birth
124 The One Where Rachel Finds Out

Second Season

201 The One With Ross's New Girlfriend
202 The One With The Breast Milk
203 The One Where Heckles Dies
204 The One With Phoebe's Husband

Third Season

Fourth Season

Fifth Season

501 The One After Ross Says 'Rachel'
502 The One With All The Kissing
503 The One Hundredth
504 The One Where Phoebe Hates PBS
505 The One With All The Kips
506 The One With The Yeti
507 The One Where Ross Moves In
508 The One With The Thanksgiving Flashbacks
509 The One With Ross's Sandwich
510 The One With The Inappropriate Sister
511 The One With All The Resolutions
512 The One With Chandler's Work Laugh
513 The One With Joey's Bag
514 The One Where Everyone Finds Out
515 The One With The Girl Who Hits Joey
516 The One With A Cop
517 The One With Rachel's Inadvertent Kiss
518 The One Where Rachel Smokes
519 The One Where Ross Can't Flirt
520 The One With The Ride Along
521 The One With The Ball
522 The One With Joey's Big Break
523 The One In Vegas

Sixth Season

601 The One After Vegas
602 The One Where Ross Hugs Rachel
603 The One With Ross's Denial
604 The One Where Joey Loses His Insurance
605 The One With Joey's Porsche
606 The One The Last Night
607 The One Where Phoebe Runs
608 The One With Ross's Teeth
609 The One Where Ross Got High
610 The One With The Routine

First Season

1994–1995

24 Episodes

101

'Pilot'
(a.k.a. 'The One Where It All Began' or
'The One Where Monica Gets A New Roommate')

Writers: Marta Kauffman & David Crane
Director: James Burrows
First US transmission: 22.09.94
First UK transmission (C4): 28.04.95

Guest Cast: John Allen Nelson (Paul – The Wine Guy), Clea Lewis (Franny),
Cynthia Mann (Jasmine – credited as The Waitress)

Summary: At the Central Perk Coffee Shop, Monica tells her friends, Phoebe, Joey and Chandler, about Paul, 'The Wine Guy', a guy she's met, but who, she swears, she's not dating. Ross arrives, depressed as his ex-wife has finally moved out of their apartment to live with her lesbian lover. Into this mix of emotions bursts a woman in a wedding dress – it's Rachel, Monica's old school friend, and she's just jilted her groom at the altar. Later, at Monica's apartment, Rachel phones her father and reassures him that she'll be staying with Monica, much to Monica's surprise.

As the guys help Ross put up shelves in his depressingly bare apartment, Joey tries to convince Ross that his belief that there is only one woman for him is ridiculous. Equating women with ice-cream, Joey asserts that Ross should just 'grab a spoon'.

Monica's non-date with Paul 'The Wine Guy' goes well, with Monica offering her support when Paul tells her that since his divorce he's been impotent, oblivious to the fact that this is merely a line he uses to get women into bed. Rachel's attempt to find work fares little better, so she goes on a shopping spree instead, using cards paid for by her father. Monica and the gang urge her to stop relying on others and start fending for herself – and the first step is to cut up all her credit cards. That evening, at Monica's apartment, Ross and Rachel are left alone. Ross confesses that back in High School he'd had a crush on Rachel, though Rachel tells him that she'd known all along. He tentatively asks Rachel if he might ask her out some-time. Rachel seems pleased with the idea, so Ross tells her that maybe he will. As he leaves, he smiles to himself in realisation that he's just 'grabbed a spoon'.

Chandleresque: 'Sometimes I wish I was a lesbian . . . Did I say that out loud?' In one line, Chandler manages to reveal his sexual hang-ups and mixed-up psyche. His dreams, which he insists on sharing, don't help to distract from this: one revolves around a telephone call from his Mother via a phone attached to his groin, another sees him appearing in Las Vegas as Liza Minelli. When Monica says that she's not going on a date with Paul, that it's just two people having dinner and not having sex, Chandler can't help but note that 'it sounds like a date to me'.

Phoebisms: Phoebe tries to cleanse Ross's aura and later tries to calm Rachel by singing her own variation of 'These Are A Few Of Our Favourite Things', but realises she doesn't actu-ally know the words.

Spoilt Rachel: Rachel soon regrets telling her father that maybe she doesn't need his money: 'Wait, I said "maybe!"' she cries as the phone goes dead. After Monica asks if Rachel managed to get a job she joyfully tells her that she'd been laughed out of twelve interviews as she's 'trained for nothing'. She cheers herself up by buying Joan and David boots on sale, fifty per cent off, yet sees no problem in the fact that she used a credit card that her dad pays for. Also, in her first scene, note how Rachel automatically hands the Sweet 'n' Low to Ross . . . and how Ross *automatically* opens it for her and stirs her tea. The guys learn that Rachel has never made coffee in her life – and it shows. [A scene cut from the finished episode shows just how bad her coffee is – it kills the plant that Chandler pours the unwanted coffee into!]

Joey's an Actor?: Joey has appeared in 'regional' productions plus a Reruns Special of *Pinocchio*: 'Look, Geppetto, I'm a real live boy!' chirps Chandler.

The Ballad of Ross & Rachel: Having told the guys that he's afraid he'll never meet another woman again, Ross looks out of his window across the city just as a similar shot of Rachel fades in. A moving and emotional storyline begins with just one shot.

Generation X: Rachel compares Barry to 'Mr Potato Head', a really cool toy from the 70s where you could rearrange the face of a potato. Rachel watches *Joanie Loves Chachi*, one of the spin-off series from *Happy Days*. Ross asks Chandler: 'Do the words "Billy, Don't Be a Hero" mean anything to you?' in reference to the 1974 hit for Paper Lace. Clea Lewis (Monica's co-worker, Franny) is a familiar face to fans of *Ellen*, where she plays Ellen's perky friend Audrey. The song that Phoebe sings to Rachel is a corruption of 'These Are A Few Of My Favourite Things' from *The Sound of Music* (Robert Wise, 1965). In his list of alternative flavours of ice cream, Joey mentions 'jimmies', which are similar to Hundreds and Thousands, apparently. As we see the slow fade from Ross to Rachel, we hear the beautiful 'Sky Blue and Black' by Jackson Browne.

The Story So Far: Monica lives at apartment No. 5 and works at the Iridium restaurant. Monica and Rachel both attended Lincoln High School but lost touch some time since. Ross was a few years above Monica and he once had a crush on Rachel. He is separated from his wife, Carol, who is now living with another woman. Chandler, in a line cut from the final episode, reveals that Ross and Carol were together for four years (see also 'TOW The Thanksgiving Flashbacks'). Rachel would have been going to Aruba on her honeymoon, had she not left Barry at the altar. Phoebe provides her personal history: she was fourteen when she moved to New York, just after her mother committed suicide (see also 'TO At The Beach' and 'TOW Ross's Wedding, Part 1') and her stepfather had been sent to prison again. She ended up living with this albino window cleaner until *he* killed himself and she 'found aromatherapy'. She also once dated a guy named Carl who ate chalk. Cynthia Mann, who appears as a waitress at the Central Perk coffee shop, reappears in Season 3 as Jasmine, Gunther's roommate and Phoebe's co-worker at the Healing Hands Massage Parlour.

The Last Word: 'Welcome to the real world! It sucks. You're gonna love it!' Monica shares her personal philosophy and gives the series inspiration for its first 'bumper sticker' slogan. Many people have commented on the way it seems Chandler is being established as a gay character, especially considering his 'Liza Minelli' dream, though later episodes will explain this away. The regular cast (particularly Perry and Schwimmer) might be trying just a little too hard, but generally this is a good, solid start to the series.

102

'The One With The Sonogram At The End'

Writers: Marta Kauffman & David Crane
Director: James Burrows
First US transmission: 29.09.94
First UK transmission (C4): 05.05.95

Guest Cast: Christopher Miranda (Robbie), Joan Pringle (Dr Oberman),
Merrill Merkoe (Marsha), Anita Barone (Carol Willick)
and introducing: Jessica Hecht (Susan Bunch),
Elliott Gould (Jack Geller), Christina Pickles (Judy Geller),
Mitchell Whitfield (Barry Farber)

Summary: Ross's ex-wife, Carol, tells him that she is pregnant with his child, but that she intends to bring the baby up with her lover, Susan. Monica is freaking out in preparation for a visit from her over-critical parents. It seems that while Ross is their 'prince', Monica can do no right in their eyes. The meal goes as badly as she'd suspected it would, so in desperation, she asks Ross to tell them his news, but even this rebounds on Monica as their mother blames *her* for not telling them.

Rachel finally returns the engagement ring to Barry, her ex-fiancé. She's surprised to see him looking tanned; apparently he decided to go on their honeymoon with Mindy, Rachel's maid of honour, and now they're an item.

Ross accompanies Carol and Susan to the obstetrician, but he and Susan end up bickering. Realising that maybe this whole situation is going to be too much for him, Ross goes to walk out, but then he hears the Sonogram begin to pick up the heartbeat of his unborn child . . .

Freaky Monica: Could those cushions *be* any more fluffed? And don't you just hate the way swallowing when you drink gets in the way of being able to clean the glass? Knowing all this, you'd think Chandler would *know* not to just leave a ball of paper lying where Monica can see it! As Phoebe puts it, Monica's parents have made her all chaotic and twirly, 'and not in a good way!'

Slow Joey: Chandler and Ross's extended metaphor of a Pink Floyd concert being like sex completely loses Joey: 'We still talking about sex?' he asks.

Poor Ross: He's not even over discovering his wife is a lesbian before she tells him that her lover, Susan, will possibly have more say in the way the child's reared than he will. As Chandler notes, it kind of puts Monica's obsessive pillow-fluffing into perspective.

The Ballad of Ross & Rachel: As Ross and Rachel reminisce about when they were at High School, Rachel asks: 'When did it get so complicated . . . didn't you think you were just gonna meet someone, fall in love, and that'd be it?' Ross knows exactly what she means, though not necessarily in the way she means it.

Dinosaurs ROCK!: Ross oversees the assembly of an exhibit at the museum which his co-worker, Marsha, insists is a depiction of Stone Age marital 'issues'.

Parents – Who Needs 'Em?: Monica is convinced that her parents held a ceremony inaugurating Ross as 'The Prince' before she was born. Not surprising really when we actually see them in action; their mum undermines Monica's confidence while claiming that all the girls fancied Ross when they were younger. Their dad insists on calling his daughter 'Our little Harmonica' and reminding her of how fat and lonely she'd been as a teenager. Even when Ross reveals just exactly why Carol left him, their mother blames Monica for not telling them sooner. No wonder Monica says that if she could change her parents, she'd want Ross's. According to Jack Geller, Rachel's parents spent forty thousand dollars on her non-wedding.

Ugly Naked Guy: Uses a Thigh-Master™. Euw!

Generation X: The gang watch *Three's Company* (the American remake of *Man About The House*), a sitcom where there's always some 'misunderstanding' with 'hilarious' consequences. Elliott Gould (Jack Geller) is possibly best known for his roles in the movies *M*A*S*H* (Robert Altman, 1969) and *The Long Goodbye* (Altman, 1973) as well as for being Barbra Streisand's ex-husband. Christina Pickles (Judy Geller) had a long-running stint in *St Elsewhere* as Nurse Helen Rosenthal, played mother to Leonardo Di Caprio's Romeo in *William Shakespeare's Romeo & Juliet* (Baz Luhrmann, 1996) and played 'The Sorceress of Castle Greyskull' in *Masters of the Universe* (Gary Goddard, 1987) opposite a young Courteney Cox! When Phoebe says her twin sister is a waitress it's an in-joke referring to Kudrow's character in the sitcom *Mad About You* (see 'TOW Two Parts'). When Rachel begins, 'I was in the kitchen with . . .' and Chandler jumps in with 'Dinah?', he's quoting from the traditional banjo tune 'I've Been Working on the Railroad'. Ross's objection to the name Helen is no doubt based on the famous Helen *Keller*, the deaf, dumb and blind kid who *didn't* play a mean pinball.

The Story So Far: Ross works at the Museum of Prehistoric History. Chandler is an only child. Carol has a relative (brother?) called Marty and we discover that she left Ross for a woman named Susan. Jack Geller lets slip that Monica was a chubby kid who 'had no friends' (see 'TOW The Prom Video' and 'TOW The Thanksgiving Flashbacks').

The Last Word: Our sympathies are firmly with Monica in this episode – her parents are insufferable (though Elliott Gould is inspired casting – David Schwimmer could *be* his son). We can perfectly understand just why she became so much of a kook, though it's nice to see Ross at least *try* to take some of the attention away from Monica's failures. It's just a shame she still ends up getting the blame.

103
'The One With The Thumb'

Writers: Jeffrey Astrof & Mike Sikowitz
Director: James Burrows
First US transmission: 06.10.94
First UK transmission (C4): 12.05.95

Guest Cast: Geoffrey Lower (Alan), Beth Grant (Lizzy),
Jenifer Lewis (Paula)
and introducing: James Michael Tyler (Gunther – uncredited)

Summary: Monica is keeping her latest boyfriend, Alan, away from her friends, worried that they'll hate him like they've hated her other boyfriends. So she's surprised when they finally meet him and say they really like him – so much so they begin seeing him more than she does.

Phoebe's bank accidentally credits her account with five hundred dollars. Having reported the mistake, the too-honest-for-her-own-good Phoebs is annoyed when she receives an apology for the mix-up, another five hundred bucks and a football-shaped phone! In desperation, Phoebe gives the money to a bag-lady she knows in return for a soda. On opening the soda can, Phoebe sees a human thumb floating to the top. The soda company compensates Phoebe with a cheque for seven thousand dollars!

Much to the gang's disgust, Chandler begins smoking again after a three-year break. No-one can talk any sense into him until Alan phones him and somehow manages to show him the error of his ways. But when Monica finally confesses that she doesn't like Alan as much as her friends do and that she's finished with him, Chandler can't take the pressure any more and resolves to continue smoking. Phoebe's seven-thousand-dollar cheque suddenly comes into use when she bribes him into never smoking again.

Joey's an Actor: Chandler helps Joey rehearse for the part of Damone, a convict on Death Row about to have his last cigarette – but even a non-smoking actor of Joey's fine talents can't fake the joy of inhaling burning leaves deep into your lungs.

Chandleresque: Chandler tries to describe to Joey the feeling of smoking again after a long time without: 'Think of it as the thing that's been missing from your hand.' Chandler claims he doesn't miss smoking, but we know he's faking it (as the rest of the gang later discover when he's smoking while leaning over the back of Central Perk's couch). Chandler's first attempt at explaining how to cushion the blow (about how someone telling you you're such a nice guy can be interpreted as them preparing you for them dating 'leather-wearing alcoholics' and bitching about them to you) could quite conceivably be a reference to an ex-girlfriend . . . or just his dad. The ultimate Chandler line is his rant about the gang's pressure for him to quit smoking again: 'I have had it with you guys and your cancer and your emphysema and your heart disease. The bottom line is, smoking is cool and you know it!'

Phoebisms: Phoebe's delivery of the word 'Statement!!' in relation to her bank shows just how personally she takes her mail. When Rachel suggests Phoebe just spends the money her bank gave her, Phoebe describes how she'd be able to hear the taps of each footstep telling her the shoes were 'not-mine, not-mine'.

Spoilt Rachel: After Phoebe's bank misunderstands her complaint and credits her account with an additional five hundred dollars and sends her a phone as an apology, Rachel asks rather too urgently: 'What bank is this?' She gets excited by the fact that she's finally managing to get everyone's orders right at Central Perk – though when she turns round she doesn't see them swapping drinks with each other so they get what they actually ordered.

Poor Ross: Ross spends most of this episode moping about the sudden discovery that his beloved childhood pet, Chi-Chi, is dead, and not living it up on a farm in Connecticut after all.

Just Plain Weird: In addition to Phoebe's bank (we're with Rachel on that one) and the eponymous thumb, there's Phoebe's friend Lizzie, the bag-lady who asks her to remove all the vowels from her alphabet soup.

There's Gunther!: Gunther makes his first appearance, working behind the counter at Central Perk in the very first scene.

Generation X: Ross recalls the Bugs Bunny cartoon *Baseball Bugs* (Friz Freleng, 1946) where Bugs plays all the positions in a baseball game. Lambchop was an old sock-puppet 'owned' by Shari Lewis. The guys' Laurel and Hardy poster is a still from one of their silent movies, *Leave 'Em Laughing* (Clyde Bruckman, 1928).

The Story So Far: Chandler used to smoke but gave up three years ago, and so sees taking it up again as his 'reward' (see, among others, 'TOW Rachel Smokes'). Monica used to date a guy called Steve who had a speech impediment (but was 'schexy', apparently). We see the guys' apartment for the first time – they live across the hall from Monica at No. 4.

The Last Word: A good episode for Chandler (again), especially when he's alone in his cubicle at work, trying to cover up the fact that he's smoking at his desk. His summation of the gang's individual flaws is spot-on and much needed in a show that is accused of having a too-perfect cast. However, the two main storylines, Phoebe's predicament with her increasing fortunes and Monica's crisis of conscience over her boyfriend, are not nearly as strong as perhaps we'd like and the other three regulars are hardly used at all. It just shows that, even when part of a minor subplot, Matthew Perry can commit petty larceny and steal the show, a recurring felony that continues throughout the series.

104
'The One With George Stephanopoulos'

Writer: Alexa Junge
Director: James Burrows
First US transmission: 13.10.94
First UK transmission (C4): 19.05.95

Guest Cast: Mary Pat Gleason (Nurse Sizemore), Marianne Hagan (Joanne), Michele Maika (Kiki), Leesa Btyte (Leslie), Sean Whalen (Pizza Guy), Benjamin Caya (Bratty Boy), James Michael Tyler (Gunther – uncredited)

Summary: Unable to decide who gets to take a date to the hockey game, Chandler and Joey invite a depressed Ross to use their extra ticket. Today marks the anniversary of the first time Ross and his ex-wife consummated their relationship.

However, rather than cheering Ross up, the game makes him feel even worse when a puck is whacked straight into his face.

The girls are similarly trying to distract Phoebe. She hasn't been sleeping lately because her grandmother has got a new boyfriend and they're very noisy in bed. They decide to have a slumber party. When the pizza delivery boy brings them the wrong pizza the girls learn that politician George Stephanopoulos is staying in an apartment that can be seen from Monica's balcony. The girls move their party to the balcony in the hope that they might get a peek at what George keeps under his towel . . .

Poor Ross: Beginning with his realisation that it's the anniversary of the first time he slept with Carol (and, he later reveals, when he lost his virginity), Ross's day goes from bad to worse. Having spent most of it seeing things that remind him of Carol, he ends up being hit in the face by a hockey puck and left waiting in casualty for over an hour. Earlier, when Ross is less than enthused when the guys offer him a ticket to the hockey game, Chandler sums up Ross's attitude to life: 'Aren't we Mr "The Glass is half empty".'

Slow Joey: Joey misunderstands Monica when she asks him what he'd do if he were omnipotent for a day, and as impotence is the worst thing Joey could imagine, he says he'd probably kill himself. After Ross says he wants to go home and think about his ex-wife and her lesbian lover, Joey tactlessly crows: 'The hell with hockey, let's all do that!' and later points out that a passing woman has an ass like Carol's in the mistaken belief that Ross is just instigating a game of 'I Spy'.

Spoilt Rachel: Her credit card company calls her up because of unusual activity, i.e. she isn't spending like money's about to go out of fashion. Rachel is dismayed to discover that 'FICA' has taken a substantial amount of her first cheque: 'Why's he getting all my money?'

Phoebisms: If Phoebe was omnipotent for a day she says she'd want world peace, an end to hunger, good things for the rainforests . . . and bigger boobs. She also describes Rachel's life as 'floopy', though when Monica suggests she tries to get things 'unfloopy' Phoebe points out that there's no such word.

Boys Will Be Boys: Chandler shows that there's always one person who, if granted a wish, would ask for three more wishes. As Joey accidentally proves, there are some men for whom living is less important than sex.

Just Plain Weird: In all the years Phoebe has had her game of 'Operation' the only piece she's lost appears to be the tweezers.

Generation X: George Stephanopoulos was a senior policy advisor to Bill Clinton and worked as his Deputy Campaign manager during Clinton's first run for presidential candidacy. He is currently a news analyst on ABC and a tutor at Columbia University. Mr Snuffalopagus was Big Bird's best friend on *Sesame Street*. 'FICA' is the Federal Insurance Contributions Act, similar to National Insurance in the UK.

The Story So Far: Ross claims that he and Carol consummated their relationship on October 20th and that his birthday is seven months before this date (it's actually more than that – see 'TOW Joey's New Girlfriend'). He reminisces about how they ate nectarines, that he walked Carol to the bus-stop, how she wore boots that night (and in fact she never took them off), and that there was frost. Phoebe lives with her deaf (and sexually active) grandmother. Joey shows Chandler that Central Perk is less than a hundred paces from their apartment. Phoebe once worked in a Dairy Queen. Monica once dated a guy called Jason Hurley who Phoebe slept with literally hours after they'd broken up. Monica once received a valentine that she'd always believed had been from a guy called Tommy Rollerson, but was actually a prank card from Rachel. When they were in Seventh Grade, Monica once made Rachel laugh so hard that she wet herself.

The Last Word: Our first real 'boys are different from girls' episode, with the hockey match and the slumber party providing a look into how each of the sexes acts when they're apart. Sport at least superficially takes precedence over everything else for the guys (note how Chandler and Joey's patience wears thin after spending an evening with Ross moping about after his lost love), but we feel the girls probably have the better time (and don't they always, guys?).

105

'The One With The East German Laundry Detergent'

Writers: Jeff Greenstein & Jeff Strauss
Director: Pamela Fryman
First US transmission: 20.10.94
First UK transmission (C4): 26.05.95

Guest Cast: Camille Saviola (The Horrible Woman),
Kim Gillingham (Angela), Jack Armstrong (Bob),
James Michael Tyler (Gunther – uncredited)
and introducing: Maggie Wheeler (Janice)

Summary: Chandler is desperate to dump his girlfriend, Janice, but can't find the right way to do it. Having sought advice from his friends, he agrees to go on a double-dumping date with Phoebe – he'll finish with Janice, she'll finish with her current beau, Tony. But while Phoebe manages to free Tony with a mere hug, Chandler's break-up with Janice doesn't go as well. Luckily Phoebe manages to diffuse the situation with another hug – much to Chandler's incredulity.

Joey, meanwhile, is desperate to rekindle his relationship with Angela, a stunningly attractive woman that he once dated. The only problem is that Angela has a new boyfriend called Bob. Telling Monica that Angela's 'brother' needs a date, Joey convinces her to join him and Angela on a double date. But when she sees Angela and Bob together, Monica is repulsed – until she realises that Joey lied to her.

Ross accompanies Rachel to the laundrette to help her continue her quest for independence. But a horrible woman keeps getting in Rachel's way, forcing her to confront her in a suds showdown.

Slow Joey: Joey is fascinated by the way women can see breasts any time they want to: 'How you get any work done is beyond me.' He gives Chandler advice on how to break up with a woman: 'Be a man, just stop calling!'

Spoilt Rachel: She has evidently never done her own washing before and has major difficulties with confrontation: 'I can't even send back soup', she confesses.

Phoebisms: Ever the optimist, Phoebe sees Rachel's ruined clothes and thinks she did it on purpose. 'What a neat idea!' she chirps, vowing to do the same with her own clothes.

The Ballad of Ross & Rachel: What some see as just laundry night is, in Chandler's opinion, Ross and Rachel's first date. Chandler suggests that maybe Ross shouldn't take dirty underwear along. 'This is basically the first time she's gonna see your underwear – do you want it to be dirty?'

Ugly Naked Guy: Monica spies him laying kitchen tiles – euw, *lots* of bending down!

Generation X: As Rachel complains about her father's lack of support, Phoebe breaks into 'That's the Way I Like It' by K.C. and the Sunshine Band. Thanks to Janice, Chandler has two pairs of *Rocky and Bullwinkle* socks, one of each. Monica refers to the previous year's Thanksgiving parade, when they couldn't inflate the giant 'Underdog' balloon (see 'TOW Underdog Gets Away'). As well as appearing in Woody Allen's *Broadway Danny Rose* (1984), *The Purple Rose of Cairo* (1985) and *Shadows and Fog* (1992), Camille Saviola appeared in a few episodes of *Star Trek: Deep Space Nine* as Kai Opaka.

The Story So Far: Monica once dated a cousin of Joey's who could belch the alphabet. Angela dated Joey for quite some time, but he finished with her (we're guessing this is the legendary Angela Delvecchio, mentioned in 'TOW The Dozen Lasagnes', 'TOW The Dirty Girl'). This is Janice's first appearance, and she seems to work in photography (she's just been on a 'shoot').

The Last Word: Phoebe's method of getting rid of unwanted lovers might work for her, but the reality, as shown by Chandler and Janice's predicament, is much more painful. Don't worry, Chandler, you'll get many more chances to dump Janice (most spectacularly in 'TOW All The Rugby'). Ross finally gets to spend some quality time with Rachel, and gets to see her underwear. A sweet moment that really gets The Ballad of Ross & Rachel going.

106
'The One With The Butt'

Writers: Adam Chase & Ira Ungerleider
Director: Arlene Sanford
First US transmission: 27.10.94
First UK transmission (C4): 02.06.95

Guest Cast: Sofia Milos (Aurora)

Summary: Chandler starts dating an incredibly beautiful woman. Of course, she's married, and she already has another lover, but despite his friends' concern, Chandler's unperturbed by such a tricky situation, boasting that he has all of the fun with none of the responsibilities. However, realising Aurora could never be monogamous like he wants her to be, Chandler begrudgingly ends the relationship.

Joey gets the starring role in a musical based on the life of Freud. Unfortunately, the play stinks. Fortunately, an agent sitting in the audience recognises that he was the best thing in it and offers to represent him. Almost instantly his career reaches new heights as he wins the part of Al Pacino's butt double in a movie. But Joey's enthusiasm for the role (and some cheeky method acting) loses him the job.

Slow Joey: Joey is disgusted by Chandler's new girlfriend's promiscuity, claiming that when he's dating a woman, he needs to know he's dating more people than she is.

Freaky Monica: Rachel discovers just how obsessive her roommate can be. Cleaning up (for, presumably, the first time), Rachel moves Monica's ottoman so it can be an extra seat around the table, but Monica insists she return it to its original position. 'Thank God you didn't try to fan out the magazines,' notes an unhelpful Chandler. When Monica defensively claims that she's not *that* picky, Ross reminds her that her 'Raggedy Ann' doll was the only one ever that wasn't raggedy. To prove their point (rather cruelly, we think), the friends present Monica with hypothetical situations guaranteed to freak her out: not paying a bill as soon as it arrives; not buying a detergent with an easy-pour spout; watching as little beads of condensation roll slowly down the side of a glass towards the table top – without a coaster underneath! Obviously Monica can't take the pressure and cracks straight away.

Joey's an actor?: Joey's friends are not impressed by the play. Phoebe claims to be scared of the exclamation mark in the title of Joey's play 'Freud!' while Monica asks the gang if anyone felt like tearing off their skin just for something else to do. Rachel's reaction is short and succinct: 'I feel violated.' Of course, they try to hide their disgust for Joey's sake, focusing on the things they did like . . . such as the fact that he wore a beard and that they didn't know he could dance (quite lame, as support goes). When Joey reveals exactly what he's playing in the Pacino movie, we get the obligatory butt jokes. Chandler congratulates his pal that he's 'finally been able to crack [his] way into show business', while Ross asks if they'll all be invited to 'the big opening'.

Dinosaurs ROCK!: Ross begins to quote a theory about monogamy devised by renowned palaeoanthropologist Richard Leakey, but everyone manages to shut him up by pretending to fall asleep.

Generation X: Al Pacino is one of the best-regarded Italian-American actors of his generation, so it's no wonder Joey becomes all flustered at the thought of playing his arse-lookalike. Joey quotes from Pacino's movies . . . *And Justice for All* (Norman Jewison, 1979) and *The Godfather Part III* (Francis Ford Coppola, 1990). Phoebe explains to Monica just how obsessive she's being by evoking Bernard Hermann's music for Alfred Hitchcock's movie *Psycho* (1960). Joey's song in the play puts Freudian 'Penis Envy' theory to music. When Ross refers to Richard Leakey, it's likely he would have been quoting from Leakey's study 'Origins Reconsidered: In Search of What Makes Us Human', published in 1993.

The Story So Far: Rachel has never seen one of Joey's plays before this episode. He once appeared in a production which featured 'trolls' in which his face was covered up. Joey gets signed up by The Estelle Leonard Talent Agency (see 'TOW Russ'). This episode sees the first appearance of a haircut that, across the world, would become known simply as 'The Rachel'.

The Last Word: Monica's obsessions get another outing, and the end-credits sequence reveals just how deeply she thinks about these things – her 'I need help!' is one of the most telling lines she ever gives. Phoebe's optimistic affirmation of Joey's talents, telling him that one day aspiring actors will long to be his butt double, could *only* work on Joey, but it's a sweet gesture that obviously gives him great comfort.

107
'The One With The Blackout'

Writers: Jeffrey Astrof & Mike Sikowitz
Director: James Burrows
First US transmission: 03.11.94
First UK transmission (C4): 09.06.95

Guest Cast: Jill Connick (Jill Goodacre)
and introducing: Cosimo Fusco (Paolo),
Larry Hankin (Mr Heckles, the Weird Neighbour)

Summary: New York City is hit by a blackout, and the friends end up holed into Monica's apartment for the evening. The moonlight and candles inspire Ross to finally make a move on Rachel, but when he takes her aside to do so, disaster strikes. Out on the balcony, he is about to ask Rachel out when a cat leaps onto his shoulder, digging its claws into him. Rachel searches for the cat's owner, only to find it's an Italian guy called Paolo, who lives in their apartment block. As the evening draws on, Rachel gets more and more infatuated with Paulo until, when the lights come back on, they end up in a passionate clinch. All Ross can do is look on, helpless.

Chandler, meanwhile, is trapped in an ATM vestibule with Jill Goodacre, a Victoria's Secret model! He can't believe his good fortune, but neither can he seem to get past his crippling fear and talk to the woman. Maybe if he choked on someone else's chewing gum, that'd help . . .

Chandleresque: This episode, more than any other, gives us the chance to see exactly how Chandler's mind works. Through a series of scenes where we can 'hear' Chandler's thoughts, we can see his shyness, embarrassment and fear for what it is. When Jill Goodacre offers him some gum, he declines, and almost immediately starts mentally beating himself up about it. A little while later, he tries to open up conversation by backtracking slightly, telling her that, 'On second thoughts, gum would be perfection.' Immediately, he thinks of all the other more naturally phrased things he could have said, concluding, 'I loathe myself.'

Phoebisms: We hear Phoebs composing a new song about the blackout in which she claims that she doesn't find it scary '. . . 'Coz I stay away from dairy.' When she meets Paolo for the first time, he takes her hand and reels off a long and beautiful-sounding sentence in Italian. When he's finished, she just stares at him and says simply, 'You betcha!'

The Ballad of Ross & Rachel: Tonight is the night, as far as Ross is concerned, but Joey warns him that 'It's *never* gonna happen.' It seems Joey believes Ross has waited too long and that now he's 'Mayor of The Friends Zone'. Ross is determined to try anyway, and it's a pity his hopes are dashed by the cat (especially considering who owns him). From the minute Paolo walks into their lives, Ross hates him, but it's clear that the Italian stallion is going to be around for a while.

Just Plain Weird: On the search for the cat's owner, Phoebe and Rachel come across Mr Heckles. He claims the cat is his, and that it's called Bob Buttons, but the animal is obviously so terrified of him that the girls just walk away. As they depart, he calls quietly after them, 'You owe me a cat.'

Ugly Naked Guy: Caught in the blackout himself, Phoebe notices that Ugly Naked Guy has lit some candles. The gang gather at the window, and give an intrigued 'Oooh . . .' at the sight, following it immediately with a loud 'Ow!' as, presumably, his wax begins to drip.

Generation X: Larry Hankin played a truck-driver who offered a lift to John Cusack and Daphne Zuniga in *The Sure Thing* (Rob Reiner, 1985) and has made a few appearances in *Star Trek: Voyager* as Gaunt Gary. Monica, Joey and Phoebe sing a rendition of 'Top of the World' by The Carpenters.

The Story So Far: Mr Heckles lives at apartment No. 8 in the same block as Monica and Rachel. Joey reveals that Chandler's old roommate was Jewish (also 'TOW Russ').

During the discussion about the weirdest place they've ever had sex, Monica claims to have done it on a pool table in her senior year at college. Joey's was the second floor of the New York City Public Library, and Ross remembers he and Carol getting frisky at Disneyland, in the Holland section of the 'It's a Small World After All' ride in 1989. According to Phoebs, Chandler once got bitten by a peacock at the zoo, and Monica had a crush on Joey when he first moved in (see 'TOW The Flashback'). Rachel once spent three weeks in Bermuda with Barry. And finally, Chandler's account number is 7143457.

The Last Word: One of the very best episodes, this tightly scripted, charmingly acted half-hour is pure entertainment from start to finish. Particularly noteworthy are Chandler's internal monologues while trapped in the vestibule and his clumsy attempts to appear normal, let alone cool and attractive. Simply fantastic.

108
'The One Where Nana Dies Twice'

Writers: Marta Kauffman & David Crane
Director: James Burrows
First US transmission: 10.11.94
First UK transmission (C4): 16.06.95

Guest Cast: Elliott Gould (Jack Geller), Christina Pickles (Judy Geller),
Elinor Donahue (Aunt Lillian), Nancy Cassaro (Shelley),
Stuart Fratkin (Lowell), Carolyn Lowery (Andrea), Marilyn Tokuda (Nurse)

Summary: Monica gets a call from her father – her grandmother is in hospital, seriously ill, and it looks like she hasn't got long to live. Rushing to her bedside, Ross and Monica join their mother and father. Before long, the news is broken to them that Nana has died. As Monica and Ross say their final goodbyes, Nana suddenly comes back to life, only to die for a second time a minute later. At the funeral, Mrs Geller describes to Monica how Nana constantly criticised everything she did. Monica begins to wonder whether she should confront her mother with the fact that she does exactly the same to her.

Chandler is approached by his co-worker, Shelley, who

wonders whether he's interested in being set up on a date. Of course, he is. Shelley starts to tell Chandler about the other guy, Lowell, before she suddenly realises that she's got it wrong – she thought Chandler was gay!

Chandleresque: Chandler spends this episode wondering what makes him seem gay and, later, why someone like Brian in Payroll is out of his 'league'. When he returns to his friends at the end of the day, he finds out that all the women thought he might well be gay when they first got to know him (which is interesting, considering Rachel's dream in 'The One With The Ick Factor'). He asks his friends to try and pin down what it is that gives this impression, but they can only say that he has 'a quality'. Later, he asks if it's his hair. 'Yeah,' confirms Phoebe, 'you have homosexual hair.' When he enters Monica's apartment on the morning of the funeral, everyone is in their best sombre outfits. 'Don't we look nice all dressed up?' he says, a note of jollity in his voice, before realising how that sounds. 'It's stuff like that, isn't it?' he concedes. Has he realised that he's just said something stupid and girlie, or has he realised that (as we think the script cues) a daft, trivial comment like that in the face of something very serious and bleak is what makes him seem a little camp?

Phoebisms: Talking about death and missing people, Phoebe tells the gang about her friend Debbie who was struck by lightning on a miniature golf course. Phoebe is convinced that Debbie's spirit now resides inside little stubby pencils, like the ones waitresses use, though not, unfortunately, in the ones that Rachel uses.

Parents – Who Needs 'Em?: Judy Geller is on fine form, taking Monica to task over just about everything. As soon as Monica arrives at the hospital, her mother starts commenting on her hair. Ross tries to calm Monica down, especially as they 'still have boyfriends and your career to cover.' After the funeral, Judy Geller says Monica should be thankful she has a mother who is so 'positive [and] life-affirming'! Jack Geller, who is worried about being predictable, asks Monica to make sure he gets a burial at sea, as he thinks it looks fun and that the family 'could make a day of it'. Monica isn't convinced, but humours him nonetheless.

The Story So Far: Joey claims he never thought Chandler was gay, but see 'TOW The Flashback'. Monica and Ross also had an Aunt Phyllis who died, as well as a pet [?] called Pop-Pop (see also 'TOW The Thumb'). Ross had a brace when he was younger. For some reason, the boys now live at No. 19 and the girls at No. 20 [the block's apartments were recently renumbered?].

The Last Word: Since this episode features two of our favourite things (Chandler, and Monica's relationship with her mother), what can we say other than: this is classic stuff.

109
'The One Where Underdog Gets Away'

Writers: Jeff Greenstein & Jeff Strauss
Director: James Burrows
First US transmission: 17.11.94
First UK transmission (C4): 23.06.95

Guest Cast: Max Wright (Terry), Lara Harris (Obsession Girl),
Jessica Hecht (Susan Bunch)
and introducing: Jane Sibbett (Carol Willick)

Summary: It's Thanksgiving and Rachel is desperate to join her family for their annual skiing holiday, but after asking in vain for an advance on her wages she realises that her new-found independence has its costs. Monica tells a visibly shocked Ross that they won't be seeing their parents either as they've gone to Puerta Rico with friends. Ross is disappointed so Monica offers to cook Thanksgiving dinner the way their mum would and invites Phoebe to join them. As if things couldn't get more emotional for him, Ross also finds out that Carol and Susan are actually talking to Carol's unborn baby in the belief that it can hear every word. Not wishing to be outdone, Ross begrudgingly joins in but is soon glad he did when his singing prompts the baby to begin kicking for the first time.

Joey gets the chance to be the model for a health promotion, but when he realises that the promotion is a V.D. awareness campaign his family ban him from their festivities because they think he actually has the diseases.

Monica gets the others to chip in for Rachel's plane ticket, but just as she's about to leave, Chandler drags the gang up on the roof to see the huge inflatable Underdog balloon, which has come loose from the Thanksgiving parade and is flying across Central Park. When they return to the apartment they are horrified to discover that they are locked out and that dinner is ruined . . . much to Chandler's delight!

Poor Ross: The thought of spending Thanksgiving without his mum really hits Ross hard – and we can perfectly understand why Monica rounds on him when he enters the kitchen and starts moaning that 'it's just not the same without Mom'. Still, you've gotta feel sorry for him when his ex-wife's lover tells him that they've told his unborn child that his name is 'Bobo The Sperm Guy'. Typically, Ross doesn't actually believe that unborn children can hear what happens outside the womb, but he'll speak to his son anyway just to continue his competitive bickering with Susan.

Phoebisms: Phoebs is celebrating Thanksgiving in December because her grandmother's boyfriend is 'lunar'. She suggests Ross stuffs his head inside a chicken so he can experience how babies can hear from inside the womb.

Joey's an Actor/Model?: He once worked at Macy's as an Aramis spritzer (see 'TOW The Breast Milk'). Now that he's between roles he goes after a job as a model for the City Free Clinic's promotions – but they use him on a poster warning all the city's women against Venereal Disease. Stripping off the buy-line on one of the posters, Joey reveals similar messages for bladder control, a campaign to stop wife-beating, haemorrhoids and finally 'Winner of 3 Tony Awards'. Unsurprisingly he leaves the last message with his face on the poster beaming above it.

Chandleresque: When Joey tells him he's now an 'actor-slash-model', Chandler notes the make-up he's wearing and observes that he looks more like 'man-slash-woman'.

Dinosaurs ROCK!: Ross tells his unborn son that he had trouble picking his major when he was preparing to go to college and picked palaeontology on the basis of a dare.

Slow Joey: Splitting a cheese toastie with Monica, Joey makes a wish. When he gets the bigger half, Phoebe asks him what he wished for: 'The bigger half,' states Joey, blankly.

Ugly Naked Guy: Shares his turkey with Ugly Naked Girl and dances with her.

Generation X: Chandler refers to the sickly-sweet teen-angst comedy 'Blossom'. Ross performs his own 'unique' rendition of the theme from *The Monkees* TV show. Underdog, by the way, is the big cartoon dog we see in the parade montage. He was a cartoon superhero hound (with a big 'U' on his chest in the mid-60s, and made by Gamma Productions, creators of *George of the Jungle* and *Rocky and Bullwinkle*. When Joey discovers the effect his V.D. poster has on women, we hear the Police's song 'Don't Stand So Close To Me'. Max Wright (Terry) played the dad, Willie, in the alien sitcom, *A.L.F.*

The Story So Far: Susan tells Ross that Carol is at a faculty meeting, suggesting she's a teacher of some kind. Rachel's family goes skiing in Vail every Thanksgiving. For some undisclosed reason, Joey and Chandler have a copy of Monica's front door key. When Chandler was nine years old, his parents informed him that they were divorcing during their Thanksgiving meal. He was immediately sick and has never celebrated Thanksgiving since ('it's very difficult to appreciate a Thanksgiving dinner once you've seen it in reverse', he claims – and see 'TOW The Thanksgiving Flashbacks' to see what he means). This episode sees Jane Sibbett take over the role of Carol.

The Last Word: Far too often, Monica is shown as a kook, an obsessive freak who tries too hard. In some ways this episode does little to dissuade the audience from this view. But when she finally breaks down as her hard work burns away, we see just a glimpse of the fragile and sensitive woman underneath. She spent so much time working to please everyone, to make her first Thanksgiving perfect, and the fact that it couldn't have been less perfect is devastating for her. This is one episode where we get to appreciate just how difficult it is for her to live up to her own impossibly high standards.

110
'The One With The Monkey'

Writers: Adam Chase & Ira Ungerleider
Director: Peter Bonerz
First US transmission: 15.12.94
First UK transmission (C4): 30.06.95

Guest Cast: Hank Azaria (David), Maggie Wheeler (Janice),
Wayne Pére (Max), Sarah MacDonnell (Sandy),
James Michael Tyler (Gunther – uncredited)
and introducing: Vincent Vintresca (Fun Bobby)

Summary: Ross gets a pet monkey called Marcel. They're not
getting on that well, and Monica's not too keen on Marcel
either. Never mind, it's holiday season, and the gang's New
Year party is fast approaching. Chandler, who is depressed
about facing the celebration alone, makes everyone agree to a
'no date' pact. But then Phoebe meets David, a sexy scientist;
Joey meets a sexy single mum; Paolo's catching a flight back
from Rome to see Rachel; Monica's invited 'Fun Bobby';
Ross wants to bring his monkey . . . and anyway, Chandler's
cracked and got back in touch with Janice. Phoebe's brief
affair with David looks under threat of ending when Max, his
fellow scientist, announces that they've been offered the
chance of a lifetime – to study with their mentors in Russia.
Although David initially agrees to stay, Phoebe manages to
convince him to go and follow his dream, breaking her own
heart in the process. The rest of the gang are similarly unlucky
in love, and as midnight approaches, Chandler becomes
increasingly desperate to be kissed . . .

Freaky Monica: She wants the monkey out of her apartment,
especially after he pees all over her coffee table. 'He was as
embarrassed about that as anyone!' Ross asserts, criticising
Monica for not letting bygones be bygones – after all, Marcel
has swallowed his pride and shown his face again.

Phoebisms: Preparing her set at Central Perk, she says she has
twelve songs about her mother's suicide, and one about a
snowman. Chandler suggests she open with the snowman
song, but unfortunately, this *also* turns out to be about her

mother's suicide. We then hear her singing a song called 'My Mother's Ashes'.

Spoilt Rachel: She brings Joey a big cup of coffee, carrying it very carefully as it's filled right to the brim. When Joey complains that she's not left any room for the milk, Rachel just lifts the cup to her lips, takes a deep slurp, and hands it back to Joey.

Just Plain Weird: The return of Janice's knuckles-through-cheese-grater laugh prompts Chandler to remind Monica, 'You remember Janice?' 'Vividly,' she replies coldly. Later, she hands Ross a camera, and flings her arms around Chandler. 'Smile,' she tells him, 'you're on Janice camera!' Ross keeps snapping away, right through the moment of their second break-up. Strangely, there's not a single 'Oh . . . My . . . God!' in this episode. There's just an 'Oh . . .', a long pause, then an anticlimactic 'Nooo.'

Monkey Business: Ross describes the arguments he has been having with Marcel: 'I said some things that I didn't mean, he threw some faeces.' This sets the tone for Marcel's rebellious nature in the rest of his appearances, and only further enforces the lack of control Ross has on the things that affect his life.

Generation X: Chandler refers to New Year as a 'Dick Clark' holiday in reference to the man's perennial TV 'Specials'. David, the science guy, and his friend discuss whether Phoebe is better-looking than Daryl Hannah, star of *Splash* (Ron Howard, 1984) and *Wall Street* (Oliver Stone, 1987). Phoebe somehow sees a similarity between her relationship with David and the film *An Officer and a Gentleman* (Taylor Hackford, 1982).

The Story So Far: Marcel was rescued from a lab by Ross's friend Bethel. Chandler tells a fellow party-goer about the time he was bitten by a peacock (see 'TOW The Blackout'). Monica and 'Fun Bobby' used to go out with each other (see also 'TOW Phoebe's Husband' and 'TOW Russ').

The Last Word: A hugely touching storyline for Phoebe and a brief but brilliant appearance by the marvellous Maggie Wheeler as Janice make this episode worthy of a big thumbs-up. Keep a careful eye on the camera work during Janice and Chandler's break-up; the way it cuts whenever the flash goes off is subtle but superb.

111
'The One With Mrs Bing'

Writer: Alexa Junge
Director: James Burrows
First US transmission: 05.01.95
First UK transmission (C4): 07.07.95

Guest Cast: Morgan Fairchild (Nora Tyler Bing), Cosimo Fusco (Paolo), David Sederholm (Coma Guy), Jay Leno (himself)

Summary: Phoebe and Monica meet a very cute guy at the news-stand; so cute, that Monica shouts 'Woo-hoo!' to attract his attention. When he turns to look back, a truck drives straight into him. Wracked with guilt, the girls then proceed to become his bedside companions while he is deep in a coma. They bring him gifts and look after him together, until Phoebe discovers that Monica has been visiting him alone. Phoebe chases Monica to the hospital but, when they get there, they discover that the man has come out of his coma and now seems to want nothing to do with them.

Chandler's mother, famous author Nora Tyler Bing, comes to New York to visit her son. She is a stunning blonde bomb-shell of a woman, of whom Chandler is deeply embarrassed: the night before her arrival, she appeared on television to tell the world that she was the one who bought her son his first condoms. At dinner with all the gang, Mrs Bing notices that Ross is getting depressed about all the attention Paolo is lav-ishing on Rachel. When Ross and Mrs Bing meet in a quiet spot in the restaurant, she gives him a peck on the cheek to cheer him up – but the peck turns into a full-blown kiss, which Joey witnesses. Joey tells Ross that he has to admit his indiscre-tion to Chandler, but Ross is fearful of how his friend will react.

Phoebisms: Phoebe and Monica are wondering what Coma Guy's name might be. Monica suggests Glen, but Phoebe decides that it's not special enough, suggesting Agamemnon instead. She even composes a song for the man, which she per-forms at Central Perk. 'You don't have to be awake to be my man,' it begins. 'As long as you have brainwaves, I'll be there to hold your hand.'

Slow Joey: After seeing him kissing Chandler's mother, Joey tells Ross that he broke 'the code'. Apparently, in Joey's eyes, sisters are OK (though you should check out 'TOW Chandler Can't Remember Which Sister'), or even a hot-looking aunt, but 'Never a mom!' And we're sure Joey would know. Ross tries to explain that Mrs Bing is a sexy mum, to which Joey challenges 'You don't think *my* mom's sexy?' Ross, convinced they're heading into dangerously strange territory, walks away from the conversation.

The Ballad of Ross & Rachel: More Paolo jealousy here, but Mrs Bing helps to lighten the load. She asserts that, in her books, a man like Paolo is 'a complication you eventually kill off'. 'When?' pleads Ross.

Parents – Who Needs 'Em?: The secret to Nora Tyler Bing's writing style, she admits, is a mix of half a dozen European cities and thirty euphemisms for male genitalia. Morgan Fairchild plays Chandler's mother to perfection: it's obvious that she really does care about him, but equally obvious that she wants to live and love her own life. It's also quite clear how she managed to attract a gay man as a husband – *Falcon Crest* had a huge gay following, after all!

Generation X: Chandler asks the gang if they'd watch *Weekend at Bernie's* (Ted Kotcheff, 1989) instead of his mother's interview (see 'TOW The Embryos'). Jay Leno is one of America's leading chat show hosts, having inherited *The Tonight Show* from the legendary Johnny Carson. Morgan Fairchild is possibly best-known for just being very glamorous, though she did have regular parts in the melodramatic soap operas *Hotel* and *Falcon Crest*. Phoebe and Monica's adventure with the guy in a coma is a nod to *While You Were Sleeping* (John Turtletaub, 1995). As the girls preen the coma guy, we hear 'My Guy' by Mary Wells.

The Story So Far: Joey's Mother's first name is Gloria and Joey says she's given birth to seven children (he doesn't count himself – see 'TOW The Baby On The Bus' and 'TOW Chandler Can't Remember Which Sister'). Nora Tyler Bing claimed she bought her son his first condoms, much to Chandler's embarrassment. Her books include 'Mistress Bitch',

'Euphoria at Midnight', and her latest, 'Euphoria Unbound'. Rachel's middle name is revealed to be Karen.

The Last Word: God bless Morgan Fairchild! She has an amazing rapport with Matthew Perry, and the two of them manage to bring a realism to what is quite a weird relationship. Monica and Phoebe's infatuation with the coma guy is witty: the way they project all their fantasies of the perfect man on to him, only to be inevitably disappointed when he comes round, is terrific stuff. And Rachel's attempt at a Nora Bing-style book, complete with its comedy typos ('heaving beasts', 'niffle', and 'huge throbbing pens'), is great too.

112
'The One With The Dozen Lasagnes'

Writers: Jeffrey Astrof & Mike Sikowitz and Adam Chase & Ira Ungerleider
Director: Paul Lazarus
First US transmission: 12.01.95
First UK transmission (C4): 14.07.95

Guest Cast: Jessica Hecht (Susan Bunch), Jane Sibbett (Carol Willick), Cosimo Fusco (Paolo), Cynthia Mann (Jasmine, Phoebe's co-worker), Jo Jean Pagano (Customer at Central Perk)

Summary: Rachel prepares to go to Poconos for her first weekend away with Paolo, much to Ross's dismay. Ross considers phoning immigration in one last attempt to get rid of his rival for Rachel's affections. But just before the 'loving' couple leaves, Phoebe tells Rachel that Paolo had turned up at her massage parlour and during the session he'd made a pass at her. Exit Paolo. The guys encourage Ross to swoop in and 'usher in the Age of Ross', but when Rachel tells him she's off men for good he settles for a hug instead.

Ross discovers that Susan and Carol have been told what sex the baby will be, but he decides he doesn't want to know until he/she is born. Trying to avoid finding out becomes increasingly difficult as everybody else soon finds out and eventually Rachel lets it slip that Ross is to have a son.

Chandler and Joey are forced to find a new kitchen table after the old one collapses under the 'immense' strain of Joey's keys. Considering patio furniture for a brief second, the guys finally settle on something much more suitable – a foosball table. Excited by their new purchase, they invite the Gellers to play their first match, only for Monica to thrash them game after game.

Phoebisms: She tells Rachel that she never lies, and that she bakes the best oatmeal raisin cookies in the world. But she doesn't make them very often because she feels it's unfair on the other cookies.

Slow Joey: Joey mimics the way children ask embarrassing questions in a conversation with Ross: 'How come you don't live with Mommy? How come Mommy lives with that other lady? What's a lesbian?' Monica says she's excited about being an aunt. Trying to hide the sex of the baby from Ross, Joey jumps in with: 'or an uncle!'

The Ballad of Ross & Rachel: Realising that Rachel and Paolo are getting closer than he'd like, Ross points out that this was supposed to be just a fling she was having: 'Shouldn't it be . . . flung by now?' After Rachel finishes with Paolo, Ross hugs Rachel to comfort her, but leaves it at that. Ross sums up everyone's hopes for love when he tells Rachel that she deserves to be with someone 'who knows what he has when he has you.'

Generation X: The gang sings the theme tune to the sitcom *The Odd Couple*, but decide against joining Ross in a rousing chorus of the theme from the TV series *I Dream of Jeanie*. Ross compares the photo of Carol and Susan's friend to ageing rocker Huey Lewis, whose biggest hit was 'The Power of Love' (1985). Rachel describes her feelings for Paolo as being like something out of a Danielle Steel book – Ms Steel being synonymous with pulp romantic fiction. Perhaps after meeting Nora Bing ('TOW Mrs Bing'), Rachel's gained a taste for sexploitation novels.

The Story So Far: Ross and Monica have an Aunt Sylvia and an Uncle Freddie (see also 'TOW The Dollhouse'); Rachel has a sister who lives in Poconos; Susan and Carol have friends called Tanya (who looks like Huey Lewis), Deb and Rona. Chandler reminds Joey about when he and Angela Delvecchio had sex on the late, lamented breakfast table (see also 'TOW

The East German Laundry Detergent', 'TOW The Dirty Girl').
Chandler's previous roommate, who was called Kip, moved
out when he got married and Chandler evidently still sees this
as a betrayal. Seeing as Chandler describes Joey as 'my Catholic friend' we can kind of guess his religion.

The Last Word: And so the cat-and-mouse game of Ross and
Rachel continues, with Ross's timing as bad as ever. Looking
back on this it does become frustrating when the outcome is so
inevitable, but at the time this was as captivating as that other
famous 'will-they, won't-they' couple, David and Maddie
from *Moonlighting*. Fortunately, fans of *Friends* are keener
that 'they will' than they were for Mr Addison and Ms Hayes.

113
'The One With The Boobies'

Writer: Alexa Junge
Director: Alan Myerson
First US transmission: 19.01.95
First UK transmission (C4): 21.07.95

Guest Cast: Robert Costanzo (Joey Tribbiani Sr),
Brenda Vaccaro (Gloria Tribbiani), Lee Garlington (Ronni),
Fisher Stevens (Roger)

Summary: Phoebe has a new boyfriend, Roger, who is a
shrink. Over the course of a few days, Roger performs a number
of ad-hoc analysis sessions, causing most of the gang to
unwillingly address their own most personal faults and generally making them all decide that they can't stand him.

Joey doesn't need analysis to tell him what's wrong with
his life: the sudden discovery that his father has been having
an affair with a taxidermist for the last six years. Joey tries
to split them up only to discover that his mother is perfectly
happy with the arrangement – Mr Tribbiani Senior has been
feeling so guilty about being unfaithful that he's been
making the effort to be more attentive and loving to his
wife, and now Joey's ruined everything by trying to put
things right.

After Chandler accidentally walks in on Rachel in the

shower, she becomes determined to get her own back . . . but she's not necessarily prepared for how far this revenge will go.

Phoebisms: Describing her boyfriend, Roger, she claims that for a shrink he's not too 'shrinky'. When she finally finishes with him, she explains that her friends have a 'liking' problem with him – in that they don't!

Slow Joey: Joey compares the discovery of his father's infidelity to finding out that your father's been leading a double life and that he's actually a spy – before realising that in honesty it's completely different. 'That'd be cool,' he notes to himself. 'This blows!'

Chandleresque: Ross suggests that as Chandler saw Rachel's boobies he should show her his 'pee-pee'. Rachel understandably agrees, 'Tit for tat.' But Chandler refuses to show her his 'tat'. When Ronni tells Chandler that she's a taxidermist, he tells Joey that when he dies he wants to be mounted as if he's looking for his keys. After Joey tells everyone about his family's marital problems, Chandler observes how 'Things sure have changed on Waltons' Mountain.'

Spoilt Rachel: In among everyone's past emotional minefields dragged up by Roger's psychoanalysis, Rachel bemoans the lack of a Weeble Play Palace and Weeble Cruise Ship in her formative years.

Parents – Who Needs 'Em?: Rachel sums up Joey's problem: 'Why can't parents just stay parents? Why do they have to become people?'

Generation X: 'Weebles' were egg-shaped people famous for being the toys that wobble but don't fall down. 'Kerplunk' was a game where glass marbles were suspended in a plastic tube, held in place by plastic cocktail sticks; players had to remove one stick at a time, trying to avoid dropping all the marbles. Robert Costanzo (Joey's dad) is perhaps more familiar as the voice of Detective Harvey Bullock in *Batman: The Animated Series*. Fisher Stevens has appeared in loads of films (usually playing an irritating, selfish character just like Roger) including *Short Circuit* (John Badham, 1986) and *Hackers* (Iain Softley, 1995). He currently appears as the irritating, selfish Chuck in the TV series *Early Edition*.

The Story So Far: Thanks to Roger's analytical skills we are reminded that Chandler is an only child whose parents divorced before he hit puberty (see 'TOW The Sonogram At The End' and 'TOW Underdog Gets Away'). He also reminds Monica that cookies are 'just food, they're not love' (see 'TOW The Prom Video'). Mr Tribbiani remembers an ex of Phoebe's who was a 'puppet guy' and asks Ross how his wife is, suggesting that, true to form, Joey hadn't told his dad about Carol being a lesbian. Joey has a little sister called Tina who has just obtained a restraining order against her husband (see 'TOW Chandler Can't Remember Which Sister'). We learn for the first time of one of the reasons for Chandler's parents' divorce – that his father is an alcoholic (dyed?) blond who chases after young boys.

The Last Word: Could we hate Roger more? His outburst about 'dysfunctional dynamics' and 'stupid big cups' towards the end of the episode ('Oh "*define* me! *Love* me"!') may be good psychoanalysis, but who wants to be analysed by a psycho? Considering how many 'twentysomething' shows fall into the trap of turning the parents of characters into sources of comedy or ridicule, it's nice that we see how our gang have some form of understanding of the way things actually are, with Rachel's wry observation that eventually we all turn into our parents, and Joey's dismay at his father's adultery. Of course it's none of this that makes the episode memorable. This is the one which has a nation of red-blooded males going wild at the thought of Jennifer Aniston's 'nipular area' being visible. Who'd have thought the phrase 'open weave' could be in any way erotic?

114
'The One With The Candy Hearts'

Writer: Bill Lawrence
Director: James Burrows
First US transmission: 09.02.95
First UK transmission (C4): 28.07.95

Guest Cast: Maggie Wheeler (Janice), Jane Sibbett (Carol Willick),

Jessica Hecht (Susan Bunch), Heather Medway (Kristen),
Nancy Valen (Lorraine), Larry Pindexter (Fireman Dave),
Jay Acovone (Fireman Charlie), Joel Gretsch (Fireman Ed),
James Michael Tyler (Gunther – uncredited)

Summary: In preparation for Valentine's Night, Ross manages to get a date with a woman from his apartment block, but manages to screw things up when he takes her to the same restaurant that Carol and Susan have chosen for a romantic meal. When Susan is called to work suddenly, Ross invites his ex-wife to join him and a very disgruntled date. Unsurprisingly, the date sneaks out, leaving Carol and Ross alone.

Joey talks Chandler into a double date – with Janice! The night goes well for Joey and progressively worse for Chandler until Joey gives Chandler his credit card as an apology for ducking out with his date. In revenge against their friends, Chandler and Janice order two bottles of the restaurant's 'most overpriced champagne' . . . and wake up in each other's arms, much to Chandler's horror. The girls, meanwhile, decide to perform a 'bad boyfriend cleansing ritual', burning the artefacts left by their exes. Unfortunately, Rachel throws Paolo's Grappa on to the fire, forgetting that it's almost pure alcohol and causing a near inferno.

Poor Ross: He tries to chat up Kristen by returning an egg he borrowed (lame or what!). As Chandler points out: 'You gotta get back in the game here, OK? The Rachel thing's not happening, your ex-wife is a lesbian . . . I don't think we need a third . . .'

Phoebisms: Despite the fact that Roger was 'creepy and mean and a little frightening', Phoebe still considers dating him again. Is she just able to see the good in everyone or is she just that desperate? She's certain that she is somehow magnetic, which is why she never wears a digital watch.

Slow Joey: This possibly sums up every man in the world: 'C'mon man, she's needy, she's vulnerable, I'm thinking "cha-ching"!' After Lorraine offers to slather his body in chocolate, Joey confides in Chandler: 'I don't even know what "slathering" is, but I definitely want to be a part of it.'

Generation X: Chandler orders a Rob Roy just to find out what it is. It's a cocktail consisting of 2 ½ tablespoons of Scotch and 1 ½ tablespoons of vermouth, garnished with lemon.

The Story So Far: Phoebe mentions Abbie, a friend who shaves her head (this might be Bonnie, the friend she introduces to Ross in 'TOW The Ultimate Fighting Champion'). Chandler has dumped Janice twice in the last five months. Phoebe's past boyfriends include Roger (see 'TOW The Boobies') and Nokululu N'K'A-A; Rachel's include Barry (naturally), Pete 'The Weeper' Carney, Adam Ritter and Paolo, while Monica tries to cleanse the memory of the excessively hairy Scotty Jared, plus Howard, the 'I WIN!' Guy who she dated for four months though she herself never got to 'win' once. Ross tells Kristin that Carol teaches sixth grade.

The Last Word: Whereas in her first appearance Janice was just the Worst Girlfriend in the World . . . Ever™, we almost warm to her here. You can see just how badly Chandler hurt her through the way she almost revels in making Chandler uncomfortable (note her jibes about cutting Chandler's head out of every photo she has of him, so he can use them in his 'Theatre of Cruelty'), yet there's something to admire in her absolute certainty that her and Chandler's story isn't over yet: 'You want me. You need me. You can't live without me. And you know it. You just don't *know* you know it.' Who *could* have known how right she'd prove to be.

115

'The One With The Stoned Guy'

Writers: Jeff Greenstein & Jeff Strauss
Director: Alan Myerson
First US transmission: 16.02.95
First UK transmission (C4): 04.08.95

Guest Cast: Jon Lovitz (Steve, the Stoned Guy), Melora Hardin (Celia), Fritzi Burr (Ms Tedlock), James Michael Tyler (Gunther – uncredited)

Summary: When Chandler's boss offers him a promotion, Chandler quits. It seems he'd always thought of his job as being a temporary position and he feels that accepting the position would be an admission that this is what he actually *does*.

He decides to undertake career counselling and spends eight hours undergoing numerous tests only to discover he is already in his 'ideal' job. But when his ex-boss manages to make him an offer he can't refuse, Chandler caves in, and returns to work – to walk straight into his own enormous new office!

Ross manages to get a date with Celia, but Marcel gets in the way. A second date goes slightly better until Celia asks him to talk dirty – he can only think of the word 'vulva'! Joey decides that Ross needs coaching in dirty talk, but while they're practising, Chandler walks in on them, much to his amusement.

Phoebe introduces Monica to one of her new massage clients, Steve, who by a happy coincidence is a restaurateur on the look-out for a new cook. Monica plans an eclectic menu, but Steve arrives at Monica's having smoked a joint and has the munchies. Monica is forced to stand by while her hard work is usurped by gummi-bears and macaroni and cheese.

Chandleresque: Once again leaning perhaps a little too heavily towards his 'feminine side', he asks Rachel if she can see his nipples through his shirt (see 'TOW Phoebe's Husband'). When Phoebe suggests he might want a job as a chef, Chandler says that he doesn't have the right experience: 'unless it's an all-toast restaurant'.

Slow Joey: Joey recommends Tony's restaurant to Ross as a great date place based on the fact that if you can finish a 32-ounce steak there, it's yours for free.

Poor Ross: Despite Joey's assertion that Marcel is a 'chick magnet', Ross's date with Celia goes less than perfectly when the monkey decides to swing from Celia's hair.

Spoilt Rachel: A confused Rachel accidentally leaves a pencil in Monica's coffee, finding the missing swizzle-stick behind her ear. When Monica hires her co-worker Wendy as a waitress because she's a 'professional', Rachel complains sarcastically that she'd only been maintaining her amateur status to allow her to waitress at the Olympics.

Chandler's Job: Chandler denies sending prank memos while hiding a rubber chicken. We finally discover what Chandler does here, though processing supervisor doesn't actually mean that much (he's a data processor, if that helps). The company where he works uses WENUS (Weekly Estimated Net Usage

System). His boss is called Al Kostlick and his P.A. is called Helen.

Generation X: When Monica describes Steve's restaurant as being 'not too big, not too small, just right', Chandler asks if it was 'formerly owned by a blonde woman and some bears' in an obvious reference to Goldilocks. When Ross describes Chandler's moaning as the 'lesser-known "I don't have a dream" speech' he's acknowledging the slightly better known 'I have a dream' speech made by Martin Luther King in 1963. When he finally gets a moment alone with Celia, Ross plays 'Girl, You'll Be A Woman Soon' by Neil Diamond (a song also done by Urge Overkill). Ross compares his dirty talking to James Michener, an author well known for his highly detailed epic novels. Jon Lovitz, a *Saturday Night Live* veteran and voice of *The Critic*, was instrumental in drawing Lisa Kudrow into acting (for which we're all eternally grateful). When Monica says 'I love my life,' Phoebe mistakes it for a quote from *Bryan's Song* (see 'TOW Old Yeller Dies').

The Story So Far: Chandler joined his company five years ago while he was waiting for a better job to come along.

The Last Word: It's a common problem, being stuck in a boring job that we hate. Of course the fact that the job is perfect for Chandler must make the situation so much worse for him. Fortunately, this episode is played strictly for laughs – I doubt the audience would appreciate the cast actually taking such a subject seriously. Of course the high point of this episode is the appearance of Jon Lovitz, who steals the show just by walking through a door. Brilliant.

116
'The One With Two Parts, Part 1'

Writers: Marta Kauffman & David Crane
Director: Michael Lembeck
First US transmission: 23.02.95
First UK transmission (C4): 11.08.95

Guest Cast: Dorien Wilson (Mr Douglas), Jane Sibbett (Carol Willick), Jessica Hecht (Susan Bunch), Larry Hankin (Mr Heckles),

Jennifer Grant (Michelle), Michele Lamar Richards (the Lamaze Teacher),
Helen Hunt (Jamie Buchman), Leila Kenzle (Fran Devanow),
Patty Tiffany (Woman),
James Michael Tyler (Gunther – uncredited)

Summary: Chandler and Joey meet a doppelganger of Phoebe working as a waitress, whom they later discover to be her identical twin sister, Ursula (Lisa Kudrow). Joey is completely smitten with her – which causes Phoebe to begin to worry. Since they were children, she and Ursula have not got on. Ursula, she claims, destroyed everything Phoebe loved: like her 'Judy Jetson' thermos flask and the heart of her boyfriend, Randy Brown. She's now scared that she will do the same to her friendship with Joey. She decides to confront her friend and tell him how she feels, but when she knocks on his door, it isn't Joey who answers, it's Ursula, wearing only Joey's shirt.

Chandler finds himself in a compromising position at work. His boss, Mr Douglas, gives him the job of laying off some of the workforce – starting with the vexingly cute Nina Bookbinder. But Chandler is obviously too taken with her looks and charm to do the dirty deed, so he asks her out for a date instead. When Mr Douglas asks why Nina hasn't been fired yet, Chandler spins a line explaining that she has a serious mental health problem, meaning that she reacted badly to being fired – her psychiatrist ('Dr Fl-, Dr Flennen-, Dr Flan,' Chandler stumbles, brilliantly) 'mentioned the word "frenzy".' When Nina starts to notice that her workmates are hiding scissors from her, she goes to see Chandler to see if he can offer an explanation. Words finally failing him, Chandler first of all offers her a rise, then a proposal of marriage, before admitting to Nina the situation he has landed them both in – only to receive a staple in the hand as thanks.

Ross, meanwhile, has his own problems as he starts to attend Lamaze classes with Carol and Susan (to prepare for the birth of his son). It is only just beginning to dawn on him how deeply a child is going to affect his life – and he feels he may not be ready for it.

Monica is pestering Rachel to take down the Christmas lights, as she promised she would. When Rachel finally relents and crawls out along the balcony to do so, she slips off the wall, catching her foot in the cable. We see her swinging help-lessly outside Mr Heckles' window . . .

Poor Ross: His awkward introduction of Susan at the Lamaze class is wonderfully painful: '. . . and this is Susan Bunch. Susan is Carol's . . . [big pause] Who's next?' When Carol and Susan explain their relationship, Ross merely responds with a feeble, 'You know how women can get.' His realisation of the life-long commitment of parenthood is quite touching; Schwimmer brings a great sense of fear and awe to his performance.

Slow Joey: Joey claims that he sees a difference between the identical Buffay twins. 'Phoebe's Phoebe. Ursula's . . . hot.' This baffling comparison leads Chandler to request: 'You know that thing when you and I talk to each other about things? Let's not do that any more.'

Phoebisms: Phoebs is strangely impressed to discover that 'Urkel' in Spanish is 'Urkel'. Her encounter with Fran and Jamie (who think she is Ursula) is great though. They mistake her for their usual waitress, and try to place an order with her, but when she responds with a simple (and mystified) 'Good choice,' they conclude that it's definitely Ursula.

Chandler's Job: There are plenty of snapshots of Chandler's work, including the return of the WENUS (which now apparently stands for 'Weekly Estimated Net Usage *Statistics*' – see 'TOW The Stoned Guy') and the debut of the ANUS (Annual Net Usage Statistics, obviously). His greatest moments come, though, in his blundering attempts to protect – and seduce – Nina, particularly as his web of lies begins to tighten in around him.

Just Plain Weird: Ursula misunderstands the confused Chandler when he asks her 'How come you're working here?' ''Cause it's close to where I live, and the aprons are really cute.' Mr Heckles complains that the girls' noise is disturbing his cats. When they point out that he doesn't have cats, he says defensively: 'I could have cats.'

Monkey Business: As stressed out as all our friends are by the events of this episode, none of them are prepared for the extra weight put on their shoulders by the mischievous behaviour of Marcel. Marcel steals the TV remote control, forcing everyone to watch television in Spanish. Ross also accuses Marcel of erasing messages from his answering machine, 'supposedly by accident' and of peeing all over the newspaper before Ross can get to the crossword.

Generation X: Phoebe mentions Judy Jetson, from the futuristic Flintstones rip-off, *The Jetsons*. Phoebe's erroneous guesses of who Chandler and Joey saw today include Irish actor Liam Neeson and Morley Safer, journalist, author and presenter of *60 Minutes*. Lisa Kudrow's character Ursula is the ditsy waitress from the sitcom *Mad About You*, which is why the studio audience laugh harder than we did when Helen Hunt and Leila Kenzle (as their *Mad About You* characters) mistake Phoebe for Ursula. Helen Hunt also starred opposite Bill Paxton in *Twister* (Jan DeBont, 1996) and opposite Jack Nicholson in *As Good As It Gets* (James L. Brookes, 1997) for which she won a Best Actress Academy Award. Ross watches a Spanish version of *Laverne and Shirley* and Phoebe watches *Family Matters* (which features the character Steve Urkel – see 'Phoebisms' above).

The Story So Far: Ursula works at Riffs's, and this is the first time she is seen. She's (just) older than Phoebe, started walking (just) before her, and Phoebs claims her sister was always considered the pretty one.

The Last Word: The inclusion of characters from *Mad About You* isn't quite as glaring as the following episode's appearances of George Clooney and Noah Wyle, as there's at least some reason for there to be a crossover with the other series here. Kudrow does a fine job as both a wound-up Phoebe and her equally ditzy sister (and do we detect a darker, more evil tone to Ursula – or do we just hate her for what she is doing to Phoebe and Joey?). Not enough for Aniston and Cox to get their teeth into, but since the rest of the cast do such great work, we don't really mind.

117
'The One With Two Parts, Part 2'

Writers: Marta Kauffman & David Crane
Director: Michael Lembeck
First US transmission: 23.02.95
First UK transmission (C4): 18.08.95

Guest Cast: George Clooney (Dr Mitchell), Noah Wyle (Dr Rosen), Elliott Gould (Jack Geller), Alaina Reed Hall (the Admissions Woman), James Michael Tyler (Gunther – uncredited)

Summary: Rachel has been taken to hospital, but panics when she is forced to tell Monica that she doesn't have medical insurance. Since Rachel was sweet enough to nominate Monica as her 'in case of emergency person', Monica reluctantly agrees to commit fraud and let Rachel use her insurance – but to make it convincing, each of them has to pretend to be the other. They are met by Dr Mitchell and Dr Rosen, two 'very cute' doctors. Continuing with their ruse, Monica and Rachel arrange a date with them, but as the girls get more confused and anxious about adopting each others' personalities, the gloves come off and the claws come out, frightening the doctors away.

There's trouble in paradise for Joey, as Ursula seems to be ignoring him. Phoebe goes to see Ursula and learns that her sister's affections for Joey have waned. Phoebe decides to dump Joey on Ursula's behalf. In a tender scene, Phoebe (wearing a sweater Joey bought Ursula) pretends to be Ursula and gives Joey a kinder goodbye. They kiss, and it is only when Joey sees 'Ursula' chewing her hair that he realises that it's really Phoebe.

Ross, meanwhile, is continuing to fret about his impending fatherhood – he's really not sure he's ready. As he explains to Joey and Chandler, his stress has been expressed in a dream where he is playing football, using the baby as the ball. He decides to meet with his own father to find out when he first felt like a father. Mr Geller tells Ross about the moment he suddenly realised everything was going to be all right: as a new-born, Ross reached out and clasped his father's finger, and squeezed. 'That's when I knew,' he explains. But Ross gets an early dry run of fatherhood when Marcel, choking on a scrabble tile, is rushed to hospital. As the gang waits by his bedside, Marcel comes round, reaches out and grabs hold of Ross's finger. Finally, he realises that maybe he is ready for fatherhood after all.

Poor Ross: His football dream is brilliant, especially with the commentary by Joey (who seems unconcerned – Ross is up against Tampa Bay, who've 'got a terrible team') and Chandler (who seems very concerned – when Ross tells them that he hikes the baby down the pitch, Chandler stutters, 'Are you crazy! That's a baby!'). While the scene with his father is touching, it has to be said that the dreadful re-enforcement by the tacked-on Marcel plot is so sweet it is almost enough to make you throw up.

Spoilt Rachel: Monica, filling in her admission form at the hospital, asks Rachel for details of her insurance. Rachel just responds with, 'Oh, yeah. Check it. Definitely want some of that.' She has no idea (listen up, you lucky Brits) that medical insurance is a necessity in life.

Freaky Monica: When the doctors turn up for their date, Monica and Rachel continue to make a botch of their cover story. Rachel tries to convince Monica that they should just admit their crime, to make the date go more smoothly. But Monica refuses, and an argument ensues. Rachel finally snaps, telling Monica that she's becoming more and more like her mother. That, as far as Monica is concerned, is that. She begins to verbally destroy Rachel in front of the doctors, mentioning that 'she' jilted her husband at the altar (see 'Pilot') – 'I know it's pretty selfish,' she laughs, 'but – hey! That's me!' Rachel, meanwhile, alludes to Monica's bossiness and the fact that she was 'a cow' in high school. The bitching reaches a peak when Rachel, as Monica, claims that she uses her breasts to get people's attention. 'We both do that!' Monica yells. Just then, the phone rings. Dr Mitchell answers and passes the phone to who he thinks is Rachel. In a final act of revenge, Monica tells Mr Green that 'she' and Billy Dreskin (whose father tried to put Mr Green out of business) had sex on his bed – game, set and match to Monica!

Phoebisms: Her reaction to her surprise birthday party is wonderful. Everyone has crowded around the mangled cake that Ross has dropped, and so are completely unaware that Phoebe has walked into the room. When she asks, 'Hey, what's going on?' they all respond with a belated 'Surprise!' And, bless her, she is genuinely surprised. Ursula offers Phoebe some chicken, only to be reminded that she doesn't eat 'food with a face'.

Chandleresque: His mouth runs away with itself yet again as he tries to calm Ross's fears about fatherhood. 'Say you never feel like a father. Say your son never feels connected to you as one. Say all of his relationships are affected by this . . .' Ross asks whether he has a point, to which Chandler – in one of Perry's wonderful trademark 'pinched face' moments – replies, 'You know, you'd think I would.'

Monkey Business: Marcel swallows some letters from a Scrabble game, an 'M', an 'O' and a 'K' – Chandler thinks he was trying to spell 'Monkey'.

Ugly Naked Guy: Over the closing titles, we see a Spanish-dubbed group of friends stare at their nude neighbour as he does . . . something with a hula hoop.

Just Plain Weird: One of the most perplexing scenes in the entire series is where the end sequence of 'TOW Two Parts, Part 2' is overdubbed in Spanish, just like the programmes Marcel has been watching on Monica's TV. We can finally put you out of your misery by telling you what happens. Ross enters with the take-away. Monica asks who ordered General Sal's chicken and Chandler laments the fact that General Sal didn't actually turn up. Rachel spies Ugly Naked Guy playing with a Hula Hoop while Marcel continues to play with the TV remote because he doesn't like what's currently on the TV (i.e. *Friends*?).

Generation X: George Clooney is better known for playing Batman in *Batman and Robin* (Joel Schumaker, 1997). He and Noah Wyle play doctors Ross and Carter in *ER*, Warner Bros.' top-rated show. Dr Rosen claims that his wine is from the vineyards of Ernest and Tova Borgnine (Ernest Borgnine being the crumply faced actor who appeared in, among many other films, *The Dirty Dozen* (Robert Aldrich, 1967)).

The Story So Far: Rachel tells us that Monica's been living in that apartment for about six years. See also 'Monica v Rachel' above.

The Last Word: The main reason for this being a two-parter – the Ursula plot – is rather swiftly dealt with. This leaves more room for the 'very cute, cute, cute doctors' plot, which is classic *Friends*. Monica and Rachel's twisted character self-assassinations are brilliantly scripted, and impeccably delivered – especially that line about the boobies. Wyle and

Clooney handle the comedy very well, with Clooney getting some great lines, reacting naturally to the madness that ensues.

118

'The One With All The Poker'

Writers: Jeffrey Astrof & Mike Sikowitz
Director: James Burrows
First US transmission: 02.03.95
First UK transmission (C4): 25.08.95

Guest Cast: Beverly Garland (Aunt Iris)

Summary: The gang is helping Rachel out, stuffing endless envelopes with copies of her résumé – she is finally sick of being a waitress and decides that it's time to move on. Responses begin to pile in, but no-one is interested in her. No-one, that is, except Ross. As Chandler tries to talk to Ross about his feelings for Rachel, Joey arrives at Central Perk and they are consumed with laughter. It turns out that he broke into tears at their poker game of the previous night, when he confused a three with an eight. The girls, mystified and offended by their all-male games, manage to persuade them to teach them poker. Things don't go smoothly, though. Rachel, Monica and Phoebe (who has particular difficulty with the ethics of 'bluffing') can't get the hang of the game – they're just too nice – and they lose badly. Tensions rise, as the girls realise that the boys take the game way too seriously, so Monica arranges for the girls to receive poker lessons from her Aunt Iris.

The next day, Rachel arrives at the poker game in a terrific mood. She's just had an interview for a job at Saks and feels very confident she'll get the job. Her enthusiasm is dampened, though, when she and the other girls fare badly at their second poker game. By the time of their next game, Monica is even more competitive than ever, while Rachel – who is still waiting to hear about her job – is even more playfully hostile towards Ross. The playfulness ends, though, when the phone rings and Rachel gets bad news – she didn't get the job. Sent spinning into a black mood, she and Ross raise the stakes and face off for the last time . . .

Freaky Monica: After Rachel has taken Ross down a peg or two (with the speech below), she adds, 'We will play you again. And we will win. And you will lose. And you will beg. And we will laugh. And we will take every last dime you have. And you will hate yourselves forever.' Which kind of stamps all over Rachel's lecturing Ross about his obsessive manly need to win.

Spoilt Rachel: Tired of being addressed as 'excuse me' by customers, Rachel compiles a CV, presumably for the first time ever. Reading from one of the copies, Ross notes how potential employers will no doubt be impressed with her excellent 'compu*p*er' skills.

Phoebisms: She really can't get the hang of poker and is seemingly more interested with how the eye of a Jack follows her around wherever she holds it (she eventually throws away two Jacks because they look unhappy). When Joey wins by bluffing, an affronted Phoebe points out that bluffing is merely another word for 'lying'! After hearing about Rachel's job interview at Saks, Phoebs comments: 'It's like the mothership is calling you home.'

Slow Joey: . . . or not. During the Pictionary game over the closing credits, he is the one to guess *The Unbearable Lightness of Being* from Rachel's rather lame drawing of a bean.

Chandleresque: When Phoebe curses the money that Joey wins off her, Chandler offers to take the money instead. Bad things always come his way, he says, but 'this way I can break them up with a movie'.

The Ballad of Ross & Rachel: Ross's need to prove himself to Rachel as a man through playing tough poker is at once brilliant and painful. There are some terrific lines on Ross's part, but Rachel isn't falling for any of it: 'Oh, so typical. Ooh, I'm a man. Ooh, I have a penis. Ooh, I have to win money to exert my power over women.' The final face-off is great – despite the fact he admits he has lost, he doesn't show his hand. Was he just trying to put a smile back on her face after her disappointment over the job? The exchanges between them are excellently sparky. Even the normally wussy Ross shows that he is capable of both anger and genuinely touching compassion.

Dinosaurs ROCK!: According to Chandler, Ross finishes with his latest date, Linda, because of a whole *'The Flintstones* could have really happened' issue.

Just Plain Weird: Aunt Iris is a whirlwind of determination. Her methods to teach the girls bluffing are superb, telling them that 'everything you hear at a poker game is pure crap' before praising a momentarily delighted Phoebe on her choice of earrings.

Generation X: The gang whistle 'Colonel Bogey', the theme tune from *Bridge On The River Kwai* (David Lean, 1957). Marcel's favourite record is 'The Lion Sleeps Tonight', originally sung by The Tokens in 1961, but popularised in the 80s by Tight Fit. Chandler mentions Dee, Danielle Spencer's character from the 70s sitcom, *What's Happening?* Aunt Iris claims to have just killed comedian Tony Randall (from the TV series *The Odd Couple*) in an example of good bluffing. And of course, there are the references in Pictionary to the musical *Bye Bye, Birdie* and to the film *The Unbearable Lightness of Being* (Philip Kaufman, 1987).

The Story So Far: Becoming increasingly angry about losing, the gang remind Monica of an unfortunate enraged plate-throwing incident during a previous 'Pictionary' game.

The Last Word: A fantastic war of the sexes episode, with some brilliant friction between Ross and Rachel. This is the episode where the seeds for Ross's resolve are finally sown, as Chandler and Joey finally point out to him that he really should do something about his feelings for Rachel. The poker games that are the set pieces for the vast majority of the episode are blisteringly good - tense in the right places, but funny all the time. Monica's increasing frustration at being rubbish at poker is brilliant, and the pay-off of her tantrum at the closing Pictionary game is perfect. An all-round spiffing episode.

119
'The One Where The Monkey Gets Away'

Writers: Jeffrey Astrof & Mike Sikowitz
Director: Peter Bonerz

First US transmission: 09.03.95
First UK transmission (C4): 01.09.95

Guest Cast: Mitchell Whitfield (Barry Farber), Larry Hankin (Mr Heckles),
Megan Cavanagh (Luisa Gianetti – the Animal Control Woman),
Angela Visser (Samantha), Elisabeth Sjoli (Tina)

Summary: Rachel's mother callously sends her a magazine that contains an engagement notice for Barry (her ex-fiancé) and Mindy (her ex-maid of honour). Rachel finds this hard to take in, and tells Ross that she suspects she'd be coping better if she had someone of her own to accompany her to the wedding. This sets Ross's hopes to an all-time high. But while he pops out for some wine, Rachel manages to let Marcel escape and a search ensues. When Ross returns he's furious with Rachel, telling her that technically Marcel is an illegal immigrant and that if the authorities catch him he could be deported. Then the authorities turn up in response to Rachel's phone call about a lost monkey.

Ross eventually forgives Rachel and the pair settle down to make a start on the bottle of wine he bought. But just as Ross tries to ask Rachel out, Barry bursts into the apartment declaring his love for Rachel. 'We have *got* to start locking that door!' cries Ross . . .

Spoilt Rachel: Rachel successfully manages to remember all of the different types of tea Central Perk do, only to realise she's telling the wrong customer.

Phoebisms: When she hears that Marcel crapped in Monica's shoes, Phoebs asks which one, because, she claims, the left one is 'lucky'. When Phoebe blows the gaffe to the Animal Control woman about Marcel, Monica warns her, 'You remember how we talked about saying things quietly to *yourself* first?'

Slow Joey: Joey claims he doesn't need violence in movies to enjoy them – just a little female nudity. When Joey spoils Chandler's chances with some incredibly hot babes, Chandler tells him that 'from now on, you don't get to talk to other people!'

The Ballad of Ross & Rachel: Still oblivious to Ross's feelings for her, Rachel asks him if he thinks it's possible to have a best friend who can also 'make your toes curl' with passion.

Ross is about to tell her just why this is possible when the rest of the gang walk in, spoiling his chances. Despite Ross's optimism, Chandler is still doubtful, noting that if something were going to happen it would have by now. Ross declares his intention to 'woo' her, prompting Chandler to advise that maybe he should take her back to the 1890s, 'when that phrase was last used.' After Marcel has been safely returned to Ross, he offers Rachel some wine, asking if she's 'in the mood for, uh, something grape?' But of course Barry gets in the way of things going any further.

Monkey Business: Marcel pleases Ross by finally learning the difference between 'Bring me the rice' and 'Pee in the rice'. However he completely blows it by pooing in Monica's shoe. Heckles dresses him up in a pink frilly tutu.

Just Plain Weird: Everyone's favourite spooky neighbour, Mr Heckles, claims to have left a Belgian waffle in the hallway because he 'wasn't ready for it'.

Generation X: After the gang go to see a film (*Four Weddings and a Funeral* – Mike Newell, 1994), Joey confuses its star, Hugh Grant, for the short, fat and bald Ed Asner, the star of 80s TV series *Lou Grant*. Heckles claims to have seen sports TV/Radio host Regis Philbin.

The Story So Far: Barry and Mindy announce their engagement in the Country Club newsletter (see 'TOW The Sonogram At The End' and 'TOW Barry And Mindy's Wedding'). According to Rachel, Marcel is a capuchin monkey. Ross is forced to tell his friends that Marcel's an illegal immigrant. The woman from Animal Control, Luisa Gianetti, went to Lincoln High at the same time as Rachel and Monica. Rachel was the Homecoming Queen and the class president. Monica was fat (see 'TOW The Prom Video') and appeared in a production of *The Sound of Music*.

The Last Word: What a strange episode, switching from Ross's continued longing for Rachel to a quest to get to Marcel before a big fat woman with a dart gun! Rachel emerges as the star here, both in her genuine apologies to Ross and in the scene where she pleads with Luisa to do the honourable thing and leave Marcel alone and when this fails she blackmails her for shooting Phoebe in the ass. Despite all this, we'd just as

soon have lost Marcel for good if it meant we got more of Mr
Heckles – mad as biscuits!

120
'The One With The Evil Orthodontist'

Writer: Doty Abrams
Director: Peter Bonerz
First US transmission: 06.04.95
First UK transmission (C4): 08.09.95

Guest Cast: Mitchell Whitfield (Barry Farber),
Jennifer Grey (Mindy Hunter), Christopher Miranda (Bobby),
Lynn Clark (Danielle)

Summary: Chandler has had a wonderful date with a woman
called Danielle, but she hasn't called him back yet. He wants
to talk to her, but doesn't want to appear too keen. Eventually,
he leaves a message on her answering machine, but still she
doesn't ring back. He tries her one last time, and finally gets
through – but she's in the middle of a call, so says she'll phone
back. But she doesn't, because Chandler had left the phone
turned off. Eventually, she comes down to Central Perk to see
Chandler – but now he thinks *she* is too needy, so decides not
to pursue it any more.

Barry Farber, the man Rachel left at the altar, is back in town,
and wants to see Rachel. She finds herself having a great time
with him – much to the annoyance of Ross – and the two of
them end up having sex again. Mindy (Rachel's one-time maid
of honour, and now Barry's bride-to-be) then turns up in the
city, wanting to see Rachel. After Rachel has agreed to be
Mindy's maid of honour, she tells Rachel that she thinks Barry
is seeing someone in the city. Mindy says that he might be doing
just what he did when he got engaged to Rachel – and she
should know, as she was the one he was sleeping with! Feeling
quite justified, Rachel admits that she is the one Barry is having
sex with. Both equally disgusted by him, the two decide that
they'll break up with him together. But Mindy can't go through
with it and confesses that she still loves Barry no matter what.

Chandleresque: Having spent the entire episode wondering if

Danielle will call him, she turns up out of the blue at Central Perk to check that he's all right. He watches her leave then asks his friends: 'How needy is *that*?'

Slow Joey: Rachel tells Joey that Mindy taught her how to kiss at summer camp. Joey's interest is immediately piqued. He asks if Rachel and Mindy were wearing 'any kind of little uniform' during the kissing lesson. Later, he walks into Central Perk to see Rachel and Mindy sharing a supportive hug. 'Oh my,' he mutters to himself. Later still, when he sees Monica and Rachel hugging, he just comments, 'Big day!' It's patently obvious where this man travels in his fantasy life.

Freaky Monica: At one point, Chandler rests his feet on a chair while he's using the phone. Monica gets him to lift them up, so that she can drape a tea towel under them to protect the chair.

Phoebisms: She helps Ross out with his crossword. The clue is 'heating device', so she suggests 'radiator'. But it's only five letters, so she amends it to 'rdatr'.

Ugly Naked Guy: The gang find themselves being spied on by a neighbour with a telescope, which they find unsettling, unnerving and plain rude. As they stare out of the window at the peeping tom, Phoebe suddenly pipes up, having noticed that Ugly Naked Guy has bought gravity boots! Obviously a case of double standards, then.

Cruelty to Animals: From Monica's balcony, Phoebe spies a man kicking a pigeon.

Generation X: Jennifer Grey was Patrick Swayze's co-star in *Dirty Dancing* (Emile Ardolino, 1987). The peeper across from Monica's apartment tells Joey that she thinks Mon looks like the legendary actress Ingrid Bergman. When Chandler refers to 'The Real San Francisco Treat', he's quoting the buy-line from Rice-A-Roni, the easy-cook rice meal (fast-food junkies might also like to know there's a 'Noodle-Roni' alternative). The scene where the gang see someone watching them through a telescope spells out just how far the Ugly Naked Guy idea is inspired by Alfred Hitchcock's *Rear Window* (1954).

The Story So Far: Barry refers to his and Rachel's non-honeymoon in Aruba (see 'Pilot', 'TOW The Sonogram At

The End') and Rachel reminds her friends that this was seven months ago.

The Last Word: Chandler's phone-side vigil has to be the stand-out event in this episode. The point where he leaps from one end of the sofa to the other because he thought he heard it ring is brilliant, perfect Chandler. Rachel gets her chance to be strong again, showing how far she's come since leaving Barry: it's just a shame Mindy couldn't do the same.

121
'The One With The Fake Monica'

Writers: Adam Chase & Ira Ungerleider
Director: Gail Mancuso
First US transmission: 27.04.95
First UK transmission (C4): 15.09.95

Guest Cast: Claudia Shears (Fake Monica), Harry Shearer (Dr Baldharar),
Karla Tamburrelli (Dance Teacher),
Marta Kauffman, David Crane and Kevin S. Bright
(the Casting Directors – uncredited)

Summary: Discovering fraudulent payments on her credit card bill, Monica surprises her friends by not being upset about the loss of money, but by the fact that the bogus Monica is evidently having a better time being Monica than she is. Her jealousy prompts her to root out the fake Monica and challenge her. However, the fake Monica is just too likeable and encourages the real Monica to realise just how much fun she can have by living each day as it comes – until the fake Monica is arrested!

The friends are increasingly disgusted with Marcel's habit of trying to hump everything in sight. Unfortunately, the vet tells Ross that this isn't just a phase he's going through – he's reached sexual maturity and that as time goes on he's likely to become aggressive and violent. After searching for a new home for Marcel, Ross finally gives him over to the San Diego Zoo and bids his simian buddy goodbye at the airport . . .

Freaky Monica: As if discovering that someone is using your credit card number wasn't enough, Monica has to come to

terms with them indulging in 'reckless spending' at her
expense. Oh, except for the Wonder Mop, which she actually
bought herself. When she's left without a dance partner,
Monica complains: 'Great, it's gym class all over again!' In an
attempt to assert her new-found personality, Monica declares
that she's not just the person who needs to fluff the pillows and
pay the bills straight away: 'When I'm with [the fake] Monica
I am so much more than that. I'm – I'm Monana!' When
Monica finally confesses to the fake Monica that she's not
even Amish, she asks with genuine surprise: 'Really? Then
why are you like that?'

Phoebisms: Typically 'out there' reaction to Monica's obsession with the woman who stole her credit card: 'This is
madness. It's madness I tell you. For the LOVE OF GOD,
MONICA, DON'T DO IT!' followed by a theatrical curtsey
and a 'Thank you!' Marvellous!

Spoilt Rachel: As Monica looks at the life the fake Monica is
having she asks: 'Let's compare, shall we?' to which Rachel
responds wearily: 'Oh it's so late for "*Shall we . . .*".' The fact
that Rachel picks up the dance teacher's steps so quickly might
lead one to suspect she's had lessons [according to the Warner
Bros. press releases, dance was her minor at university]. Just
watch how Rachel cleans up, by lifting up the magazines,
barely wiping the surface underneath, then plonking the magazines back down. She's obviously never polished a table in her
entire life.

Chandleresque: After Ross explains Marcel's behaviour as
being just a phase, Chandler warns that they said that about
Joey. Chandler's recommendations for Joey's new name are
the highlight of the episode, with suggestions ranging from the
silly Joey Pepponi to the more neutral Joey Switzerland, taking
advantage of Joey's ignorance (Joey – or Joseph – Stalin) and
just taking the piss (Holden McGroin). When Joey asks Ross
how he'd go about getting a monkey into a zoo, a distracted
Chandler pipes up, 'I know that one! No, that's popes in a
Volkswagen.' (For anyone wondering, the joke he half-
remembered was: 'How do you get six popes into a Volkswagen? Take their hats off.')

Joey's an Actor!: When Chandler suggests 'Joseph Stalin' for his new stage name, Joey is later horrified to discover that there already is a Joseph Stalin who was 'this Russian dictator who slaughtered all these people!' God knows what he'll do when he realises the problems inherent in calling himself 'Holden McGroin'. Thankfully, Phoebe's on hand to give him a serious suggestion: 'Flame Boy!'

Just Plain Weird: Dr Baldharar from the 'Interactive Wildlife Experience' tries to persuade Ross to let him look after Marcel, when he's patently trying to gain another victim for his animal gladiator arena.

Generation X: The guys sit in Central Perk in the pose of the Three Wise Monkeys who depicted the edict 'See no evil, hear no evil, speak no evil'. Rachel has a (not so) Curious George doll. Curious George was a monkey created for a series of children's books by Margret and Hans Augusto Rey and first appeared in 1941. Monica tries to explain away her fanatical obsessiveness by claiming she's Amish. The Amish people have shunned modern life, believing that a 'puritan' lifestyle and a strict work ethic will bring them closer to God. As opposed to Monica, who just wants to get closer to clinical cleanliness. The fake Monica suggests that she and Monica audition for Andrew Lloyd Webber's musical 'Cats' by singing 'Memories', the touching and highly emotional song made famous by Elaine Page. Harry Shearer voices numerous characters, including Mr Burns, in *The Simpsons* and appeared in the spoof documentary *This Is Spinal Tap* (Rob Reiner, 1983). The musical 'Fiddler on the Roof' was written by Joseph Stein, inspired by the plays of Arnold Perl. It tells the story of a poor Russian family at the turn of the Century. *Dead Poet's Society* (Peter Weir, 1989) was the tale of a teacher, played by Robin Williams, who inspired a class of unruly pupils and changed their lives. It is much better than the Fake Monica suggests (honest!). *Mrs Doubtfire* (Chris Columbus, 1996) is another film starring Robin Williams. 'Bye Bye, Birdie' (written by Michael Stewart, music by Charles Strouse, lyrics by Lee Adams) is a musical about a 50s rock star, drafted into the army and cajoled into making one final appearance on *The Ed Sullivan Show*. Probably its most famous number is the upbeat 'Put on a Happy Face'. In Joey's audition scene, the shadowy figures the hopefuls perform for are Marta Kauffman, David Crane and Kevin S. Bright, the show's creators.

The Last Word: This is certainly an episode to divide fans. One of us counts this in his favourite episodes of all time; the other hates it. What is notable here is the fact that up until now we've always seen Matthew Perry as the real comic genius and this episode is no exception. Even in the final scene, we as an audience attribute the laughs to Chandler, who isn't even present in the scene, rather than Matt Le Blanc's delivery, which is a tad unfair. Joey's ignorance is played up to the hilt here and Le Blanc has never been so good until now. And the delivery of the name 'Holden McGroin' is simply priceless. Definitely one of the most memorable scenes of the entire series.

122
'The One With The Ick Factor'

Writer: Alexa Junge
Director: Robby Benson
First US transmission: 04.05.95
First UK transmission (C4): 22.09.95

Guest Cast: Stan Kirsch (Ethan), Brian Buckner (Office Worker no. 2),
Darryl Sivad (Office Worker no. 3)

Summary: Monica's got a new boyfriend, Ethan, and he's very young. But it isn't until after they have sex that she realises exactly how young he is – he's seventeen, which means there's a nine-year age difference (not to mention the fact that it makes the sex illegal over most of the United States). Unfortunately, Ethan is crazy about Monica, and Monica thinks she could feel the same way too. What's a girl to do?

Phoebe, who's foolishly lost a lot of clients by teaching a 'Massage Yourself At Home' workshop, is filling in for Chandler's secretary while she has a breast reduction operation. Phoebe finds out from her new co-workers that Chandler is no longer the popular guy now he's the boss. In fact, no-one likes him any more, and they even make fun of the way he speaks behind his back.

Ross has a beeper, so he can be called the second Carol starts to go into labour. But his number (55-JIMBO) keeps being rung by people who are after someone called André, whose number turns out to be 55-JUMBO. André appears to be a male escort, seeking male customers, and Ross and Carol eventually have to agree that she'll punch in '911' as a message to ensure Ross knows it's her.

Chandleresque: Chandler discovers that everyone at work enjoys doing impersonations of the way he speaks. When he asks Ross and Joey whether it's that noticeable, they laugh and do their own impressions: 'Could that report *be* any later?' Chandler insists, 'That is so *not* true,' before realising, much to his frustration, that it is.

Slow Joey: Looking for a new job, Phoebe finds an ad in the paper and asks, 'Can you see me operating a drill press?' Joey's warped little imagination needs a bit of prompting: 'I don't know. What are you wearing?'

Phoebisms: Her turn as Chandler's secretary is wonderful, especially as she has no real work to do. Her phone voice is cool and collected – about as far away from the real Phoebe as you can imagine. When Chandler ushers her out of his office so he can get on with his work, seconds later she buzzes him on the intercom to ask, like a bored child, 'Whatcha doin'?' She seems very concerned not to let her new colleagues know that she's a friend of Chandler, suggesting that they don't go to a work party together. While she seems comfortable with siding against Chandler, it obviously seriously gets on his nerves. Her insensitivity to this, as a person who so wholly believes in honesty, is brilliant: when Chandler asks exactly who doesn't like him, she says, 'Everyone. Except for, er . . . No, everyone.' This episode also features a marvellously Phoebe moment: she stands up from a chair to leave and immediately feels dizzy, saying, 'Woah! Head-rush!' She then sits down and says, 'One more, and then I have to go.'

Freaky Monica: If she already feels like she's about to go over-the-hill, her relationship with Ethan can't help. When she realises just how young he is, she concludes, 'I'm Joan Collins!' Ethan, mystified, asks, 'Who?'

Dinosaurs ROCK!: When the gang discover Ross has a

pager, they wonder what someone in his line of work would need it for. '. . . Dinosaur emergencies? Come quick! They're still extinct!'

The Ballad of Ross & Rachel: Throughout this episode, Rachel admits to having erotic dreams firstly about Chandler and then about Chandler and Joey. Ross, of course, is terrifically jealous. Right at the end of the episode, Ross is watching television at Monica's, and Rachel is asleep on the sofa next to him. As he gets up to go, he drapes a blanket over her and she starts to moan in her dreams. Immediately, he is disgruntled, but he cheers up when he hears her groan, 'Oh, Ross . . .' He leaps on to the coffee table and does a little dance of triumph, before tripping on the fruit bowl and crashing onto the sofa, waking Rachel. She just stares up at him, confused, and for a second it looks like they just might . . . But then his beeper goes off – and this time, it's for real. This is a brilliant moment, and the first inkling that Rachel could possibly find Ross attractive.

Generation X: Ross illustrates Chandler's speech patterns by quoting *The Sound of Music*. Monica compares herself to Joan Collins, based presumably on the role she played in *Dynasty*. The guys mock Monica by pretending to be *Mighty Morphin Power Rangers*. Chandler apparently sang 'Ebony and Ivory', the old Stevie Wonder/Paul McCartney classic, at a karaoke.

The Story So Far: Monica is 26 by this episode (or '25 and thirteen months' as she tells Ethan).

The Last Word: A fun little episode, let down slightly by the unconvincing nature of the Ethan plotline. Are we really to believe that Monica could think that someone who behaves (and looks) so young could be as old as he says? Nevertheless, the 55-JUMBO scenes, and Chandler's realisation that he really is a boss more than make up for it.

123
'The One With The Birth'

Writers: David Crane & Marta Kauffman (story),
Jeff Greenstein & Jeff Strauss (teleplay)

Director: James Burrows
First US transmission: 11.05.95
First UK transmission (C4): 29.09.95

Guest Cast: Jonathan Silverman (Doctor Franzblau),
Jane Sibbett (Carol Willick), Jessica Hecht (Susan Bunch),
Leah Remini (Lydia), June Gable (Nurse), Carlo Imperato (Roy),
Jackie Bright (Janitor)

Summary: As Carol prepares to give birth, Ross and Susan find that they still can't stand each other. In an attempt to keep Carol calm, Phoebe drags the quarrelsome two into a store cupboard, pointing out that their negativity is not what new-born babies need to be greeted with. Unfortunately, Phoebe then discovers that somehow the door to the store cupboard has locked, trapping them inside.

In the waiting room, Monica becomes broody while Chandler offers his support. Rachel meets a cute doctor and Joey meets a young, single mother-to-be and stays around to help her through the birth (shame she's a Celtics fan, though). The trapped trio manage to escape and rush to Carol's side just as she begins to give birth. Thanks to a name tag on an overall they found in the store-room, Ross and Susan finally agree on a name for 'their' son – Ben.

Slow Joey: As he supports Lydia in her hour of need, Joey is horrified when she 'explodes' and has to be told that it was just her water breaking: 'What's that? Water . . . breaking?' It's not surprising that Chandler is spooked by Joey's new-found knowledge of the birthing process when it's Carol's turn.

Chandleresque: As Ross worries that Carol might give birth in a cab, Rachel makes a (quite frankly, hilarious) joke about it costing only two dollars for the first contraction and fifty cents for each additional. When everyone glares at her and she asks why it's OK when Chandler does it, he teaches her a valuable lesson in timing. Rachel can't believe one of them actually has a child: 'I know, I still *am* one of these,' admits Chandler.

Freaky Monica: Monica's persecution complex extends as far as wondering why a woman can have twins when she can't even get a man to help her have just one baby. She even rounds on Chandler when he kindly offers to marry her if, hypothetically, they're both single by the time they're forty: 'OK, hypothetically . . . *why* won't I be married when I'm forty?'

Phoebisms: Phoebe brings a guitar to a birth in case 'things get musical'. When they're trapped inside the store cupboard, she composes an inappropriate song that goes: 'They found their bodies the very next day . . .' until she notices Ross and Susan glaring at her.

Spoilt Rachel: Rachel tries to chat up Carol's obstetrician without much success – she even goes home to *change*! She also drinks the ice-chips that were meant for Carol.

Poor Ross: Complaining that Carol never threw him out of a room before Susan came along, Susan rubs it in: 'There's a lot of things Carol never did before I came along!' As he tries to break down the door to the store-cupboard, Ross steps in a steel bucket, falls over and delivers the lamest 'Ow' ever. He unwittingly comes up with the ultimate liberal bumper-sticker: 'Every day is Lesbian Lover Day!'

Generation X: Jonathan Silverman starred in *Weekend at Bernie's* (Ted Kotcheff, 1989), and appeared in quite a few film adaptations of Neil Simon plays, including *Brighton Beach Memoirs* (Gene Saks, 1986) and *Broadway Bound* (Paul Bogart, 1991).

The Story So Far: Joey is a Knicks fan and at this point is 25 years old. Rachel's father is a doctor, leading Chandler to jump to an oedipal conclusion as to why medical men hold such a primal fascination for Rachel. Susan's first girlfriend was called Jamie, which is why she doesn't want that particular name for 'their' first child.

The Last Word: A story about both the fear of becoming a parent and the fear of maybe never getting the chance to; Ross finally sees his son (and after the whole 'Jessie, Cody, Dylan fiasco' they choose a really nice name for him so that's cool), while Monica's broodiness and closeness to Chandler foreshadow certain future episodes (see 'TOW The Jam', 'TO At The Beach', 'TOW Ross's Wedding, Part 2'). We defy anyone to watch the end-credits sequence (where Ross tries to explain to his new-born son that he might not be around all the time) without getting a lump in their throat.

124

'The One Where Rachel Finds Out'

Writer: Chris Brown
Director: Kevin S. Bright
First US transmission: 18.05.95
First UK transmission (C4): 26.10.95

Guest Cast: Tommy Blaise (Carl),
Corinne Bohrer (Melanie, Joey's Girlfriend),
Kerrie Klark (Flight Representative)
and introducing: Lauren Tom (Julie)

Summary: Joey's been helping out with a science project at the NYU Med School by donating his sperm in exchange for $700. The only catch is he mustn't undertake any 'personal experiments' for the duration of the project, a bit of a drag considering his new girlfriend, Melanie, is gagging to sleep with him. Monica suggests that he could 'be there for her', a concept Joey finds difficult to grasp – until he sees the rewards this approach reaps.

Ross, meanwhile, has problems of his own. He is once again mulling over his unrequited love for Rachel. During preparations for her birthday barbecue, he talks over his feelings with the guys. Having finally accepted that maybe Rachel will never want him, Ross prepares to leave for a trip to China – it's a 'big bone' thing for the museum. While Ross is en route to the airport, Rachel unwraps her presents and is stunned to discover that Ross has bought her a cameo brooch that she'd once pointed out to him. Overwhelmed, she wonders what provoked such a generous and thoughtful act. Chandler's over-active mouth once again blunders in, reminding Monica of the time Ross was in love with Carol and bought her an expensive crystal duck. Rachel pauses, while Chandler desperately tries to back-pedal. But it's too late, Ross's feelings are out and life can never be the same.

Rachel tries to dismiss this revelation from her mind, but on a date with a boring guy, her mind wanders to thoughts of Ross. Leaving her date behind, she rushes to greet Ross at the airport – unaware that he's brought back a surprise from China . . .

Chandleresque: Who'd have thought a reminiscence about a crystal duck could be so shocking? But of course it's not the 'crystal duck' part that alerts Rachel to Ross's feelings for her and saying 'flah . . . flennin' won't get Chandler out of a very embarrassing situation. When the obviously smitten Melanie notes how there's a 'little man' inside of Joey, Chandler notes: 'Yes, and the doctors say if they remove it he'll die.' Phoebe's ranting on about the Rachel/Ross situation and how Chandler insensitively blew the gaff provokes Chandler to retort: 'OK, is there a mute button on this woman?' hinting that maybe sometimes Phoebe is more tolerated than actually liked.

Phoebisms: Weirdness once again rules over propriety. Asked by Ross to show his son Ben a photo of his father every day, Phoebe takes the picture, holds it over her own face and intones in a deep voice, 'Hi, Ben. I'm your father. I am . . . the head! Ahhh!' Chandler's mute button comment suddenly seems very apposite. And only Phoebe could encourage Joey's work with the fertility study by noting he'll be making money 'hand over fist' and *not* realise what she's said.

Slow Joey: Once again we can only wonder what kind of strange and tortured childhood created the beast we call Joey. Giving Rachel a children's book for her birthday, he explains with undue gravitas, 'That book got me through some tough times.' And you know he means it.

Dinosaurs ROCK!: His trip to China may be in search of a discovery of amazing significance to the dinosaur world, but if even Ross can reduce it to just a 'big bone thing', then it's no wonder no-one else is interested.

The Ballad of Ross & Rachel: Love, when it comes down to it, is about two people and not their friends. As Ross says in the wonderful daydream sequence, what's stopping Rachel going out with him? 'Because it might get weird for everyone else? Who cares about them? This is about us.' Thankfully, Rachel finally gets the message . . .

Generation X: Joey's gift to Rachel is a book by Dr Seuss. Dr Theodor Seuss Geisel was hailed a pioneer against illiteracy thanks to his children's books, which include the classics *The Cat In The Hat* and *Green Eggs and Ham*. Melanie's company name (the Tree Basketeers) is of course inspired by Alexander

Dumas's *The Three Musketeers*. As Rachel reaches the airport in search of Ross we hear Madonna's 'Take a Bow'.

The Story So Far: When asked if Ross has shown any interest in her before, a dazed Rachel reminds us of events in the first episode when he broached the subject of the two of them going on a date. And it turns out that Chandler attended the same college as Ross and Carol (where, presumably, the unhappy couple met).

The Last Word: Again, while this episode is ostensibly about Ross and Rachel, it's the peripheral characters that make it what it is. Chandler in particular seems to have more than his fair share of quotable lines, and Joey is showing signs of evolving into the star player he'll become in subsequent seasons. But if ever we doubted just how romantic a person Ross actually is, this is the episode that confirms it, when we finally know that Ross and Rachel MUST get together, making the episode's denouement even more heart-breaking. As we watch Ross seduce Rachel (in what turns out to be a dream sequence) we all know this is a good thing – it just feels *right*. So Rachel races to the airport, (literally) not knowing what awaits her just around the corner, and *Friends* fans across the world drown out the end credits with their sniffles and sobs. For many of us, this is the episode we stopped simply watching the show and realised we'd become fans. One of the defining moments of the series.

Second Season

1995–1996

24 Episodes

201

'The One With Ross's New Girlfriend'

Writers: Jeff Astrof & Mike Sikowitz
Director: Michael Lembeck
First US transmission: 21.09.95
First UK transmission (C4): 28.06.96

Guest Cast: Cosimo Fusco (Paolo), Lauren Tom (Julie),
Buck Kartalian (Frankie the Tailor)

Summary: Rachel waits at the airport to meet Ross . . . and Julie! When Rachel returns home looking breathless and distressed, Monica, Phoebe, Chandler and Joey are perplexed until Ross arrives, introduces Julie and everything becomes clear. After the dust has settled, Monica tries to persuade Phoebe to give her a new look. Reluctantly, Phoebe agrees to give Monica a haircut just like Demi Moore. But Phoebe confuses Demi for Dudley, and Monica is left distraught.

Joey recommends his family's tailor to Chandler. Frankie has been making suits for the Tribbiani family for decades, but Joey had never realised that his tailor is 'a very bad man'. It seems that Frankie, while taking Chandler's measurements, interfered with more than just Chandler's stitching . . .

Freaky Monica: When she asks Phoebe if she'll cut her hair, Phoebe refuses, claiming to be 'incredibly anal, and an unbelievable control freak.' When a confused Monica disagrees, Phoebe replies, 'I know *I'm* not, but you *are* and I was trying to spare your feelings.'

Phoebisms: 'You know what I'm thinking?' Monica asks, as a prelude to pestering Phoebe to cut her hair. 'Oh, OK,' chirps

Phoebe, excited at the idea of this new game. She sits and thinks for a second, then answers with growing certainty, 'How . . . it's been so long since you had sex, you're wondering if they've changed it?' There's also her brilliant pep-talk to Monica's hair prior to cutting it: 'Now, some of you are going to get cut, and some of you aren't. But I promise none of you are going to feel a thing.'

Slow Joey: He has a really hard time trying to remember when Frankie made him his first suit. 'I was fifteen,' he says. 'No wait, sixteen. No, 'scuse me, fifteen.' Finally, he requests some clarification: 'All right – when was 1990?' (at which point, Chandler advises him to 'stop the Q-tip when there's resistance'). Later, when he is trying to console Rachel, he confesses that he can 'sense when women are depressed and vulnerable. It's one of my gifts.'

The Ballad of Ross & Rachel: After a season where we had Ross pining after Rachel, the tables are suddenly turned. We're left with Rachel realising she's lost what she never realised she'd always wanted. Her initial reaction to Ross's return and Julie's arrival is magnificently acted by Aniston, as are her breathless attempts to tell the rest of the gang about it while Ross and Julie are only a few steps behind her on the stairs.

It's painful to see how Ross has come to terms with the fact that he should move on from Rachel, and is now happy with Julie. Rachel's discontent with this is hilariously apparent, especially when Ross is on the phone with Julie and neither of them want to hang up first: 'No, you hang up. You, you, y–' To rightful cheers from the audience, Rachel does it for him.

Whatever happened in China, it's obvious that Ross still cares deeply about Rachel; his reaction to her little indiscretion with Paolo is proof of that. 'I hate him,' he tells her. 'I physically hate him.' But still it's not enough and, just as Rachel is about to tell him how she feels, he begins to tell her how happy he is to be with Julie. While, in season one, Ross listened patiently as Rachel talked about one date after another, Rachel resolves to be a bitch to Julie, making sure she gets the wrong haircut from Phoebe – Roddy, rather than *Andie* MacDowell.

Generation X: Chandler compares Phoebe to celebrated hair stylist, Vidal Sassoon. As Phoebe reminds us, Dudley Moore appeared in the films *Arthur* (Steve Gordon, 1981) and *10* (Blake Edwards, 1979), whereas Demi Moore, as Monica is at pains to point out, starred in *Disclosure* (Barry Levinson, 1994), *Indecent Proposal* (Adrian Lyne, 1993) and *Ghost* (Jerry Zucker, 1990). Monica notes woefully that even a haircut like Mary Tyler Moore would have been tolerable. Andie MacDowell *is* the girl from *Four Weddings and a Funeral* (Mike Newell, 1994), while Roddy McDowell is, of course, from the *Planet of the Apes* movies. For those that don't know, cotton buds are known as Q-Tips in the States.

The Story So Far: Phoebe gives us a brief recap of the previous episode. There are plenty of references to past events here, particularly those concerning Ross and Rachel (and Paolo who, we are reminded, once tried to seduce Phoebe – see 'TOW The Dozen Lasagnes'). Ross and Julie, it is revealed, went to grad school together.

The Last Word: 'It's like there's rock bottom, then 50 feet of crap, then me.' An assured start to the second series which surprisingly manages to not sideline anyone, despite the fact that it focuses on the relationship between Ross and Rachel. While Rachel struggles with her disappointment and her surprise that she should feel that way at all, we see the other friends slip into their normal roles. Phoebe and Joey seem a little more ditzy and stupid than before, but if that's the price to pay for the haircut jokes and the retroactive terror over years of sexual abuse from a tailor then so be it.

This episode and 'The One With The Breast Milk' were originally shown by Channel 4 as a double bill.

202
'The One With The Breast Milk'

Writers: Adam Chase & Ira Ungerleider
Director: Michael Lembeck
First US transmission: 28.09.95
First UK transmission (C4): 28.06.96

Guest Cast: Joel Beeson (Hombre Guy), Jane Sibbett (Carol Willick), Jessica Hecht (Susan Bunch), Lauren Tom (Julie), Emily Proctor (Annabel), Richard Lyons (Man), Stan Sellers (Manager), Lou Wills (Customer)

Summary: Carol and Susan are visiting Monica's with Ben, when the baby gets hungry. No worry, though: Carol just whips out a breast and starts to feed him. Chandler and Joey are instantly uncomfortable with this, but not as much as Ross is when he sees Phoebe test the temperature of some bottled breast milk a little later. She puts a few drops onto the skin of her arm, and then licks it clean off. The rest of the episode is spent with Ross trying to gather the strength to try Carol's milk for himself. After all, Susan's tried it.

Joey's latest job as a cologne sample guy at Saks is giving him problems. A mysterious cowboy has appeared at the edge of his territory, offering passers-by a new fragrance called 'Hombre'. Soon, he feels that he is being seriously threatened by this cowboy, especially when Joey is transferred to Hombre duty himself. It seems the only thing left is for him and the cowboy to settle their score the old-fashioned way: using perfume bottles, not pistols, at dawn.

Julie asks Monica to come shopping at Bloomingdales with her. Although it feels like betraying Rachel, she goes along, only to feel incredibly guilt-ridden. But these feelings are as nothing compared to Rachel's wrath when she finds out that her best friend has 'cheated' on her.

Poor Ross: Seeing Phoebe drinking the breast milk freaks him out, and Carol wonders why. 'Because it's gross!' he squeals. 'My breast milk is *gross*?' asks Carol. Susan sits back in the sofa, smiling, and says, 'This should be fun.' The final sequence of Ross sitting at a table gathering strength to try the milk is brilliant. After a long preparation period, he swipes the bottle up and sucks a huge mouthful, swallows it, and then stuffs his face with a pile of cookies to get rid of the taste.

Spoilt Rachel: Her attempts to get on with Julie are fantastic. She makes no secret of the fact that she doesn't like Julie. When Julie makes attempts to be her friend, Rachel initially makes some effort, but once Julie's gone, Rachel sneers: 'Manipulative bitch!'

Slow Joey: When Joey is grossed out by breast-feeding, Ross tells him that it's the most natural and beautiful thing in the world. Joey says, 'I know, but there's a baby sucking on it!' When he is asking questions about breast-feeding, he wonders,

'If he blows into one, does the other one get bigger?' It's perfectly clear, then, where his interest with breasts lies.

Phoebisms: Phoebe has to excuse herself at one point, saying, 'I have to take my grandmother to the vet.' No explanation is offered and we just have to accept that Phoebe is beyond comprehension.

The Last Word: All credit to Aniston and Cox: the confrontation between Rachel and Monica when Monica admits that she has been shopping with Julie is bizarre, being played out as if the two of them are lovers and Monica has cheated on Rachel with someone else. The scripting is impeccable, and the performances flawless.

203
'The One Where Heckles Dies'

Writers: Michael Curtis & Greg Malins
Director: Kevin S. Bright
First US transmission: 05.10.95
First UK transmission (C4): 05.07.96

Guest Cast: Maggie Wheeler (Janice), Larry Hankin (Mr Heckles),
Danny Dayton (Buddy Boyle)
and introducing: Michael G. Hagerty (Mr Treager – credited as Treeger)

Summary: Mr Heckles, the man who lives in the apartment below Monica's, complains once again that the girls are making too much noise. When he returns to his own apartment he begins to bang on his ceiling with a broom. In retaliation, the girls stomp on the floor until he gives in. Later, though, they discover that Heckles has died, seemingly in the middle of their thumping match. The next day, Heckles' attorney arrives to tell Monica and Rachel that he's left his entire worldly belongings to 'the noisy girls upstairs'. Although they're initially excited, they discover that Heckles had no money, and has left them an apartment full of garbage and tack in an act of final revenge.

Rachel decides to keep his hideous shell lamp as a memento, against her roommate's wishes. When Monica accidentally breaks it, Rachel jumps to the conclusion that she did it out of spite, and that Monica still thinks of the apartment as hers alone, meaning Rachel is just her lodger.

Chandler breaks up with another girlfriend because he feels her nostrils are too big. The girls feel that his selection process is a little extreme, rejecting girls for really insignificant things – though they allow him some slack over Janice. But after reading Heckles' old yearbook, he discovers that he and Heckles had many things in common, leaving Chandler to worry that he too might end up alone. In desperation he phones Janice only to find she's both married and heavily pregnant.

. . . And Ross tries to enlighten Phoebe on the theory of evolution, a fairytale she's just not willing to accept.

Freaky Monica: Yes, it is a horrible lamp, but Monica really hounds Rachel for bringing it into her home. 'Y'know what we haven't played in a while? . . ."Hide The Lamp".' The little war with Rachel over the lamp, and the 'ownership' of their apartment, is great. It makes perfect sense that she would be unwilling to let go of control over her home, despite the fact that she has been sharing it for over a year.

Spoilt Rachel: To be fair, apart from her asking about whether there's any money in Heckles' will, Rachel's not at all spoilt in this one. But it's fun to see her getting one over on Monica by insisting that they keep the lamp. When Monica claims she's allergic to shellfish, Rachel tells her: 'Well, you'll just have to eat the other lamps.'

Chandleresque: Chandler has a wonderfully pathetic list of reasons for dumping various women. Even after promising to be less selective, Chandler can't help himself. On his date with Alison he tries to think of five things he likes about her: 'Nice smile, good dresser . . . BIG HEAD BIG HEAD BIG HEAD!' When he discovers Heckles' similar list of women he's dumped for the lamest of reasons, he begins to fear that he will end up just like him. In fact, Chandler has already worked out exactly what he'd be like – he'd be Crazy Man with a Snake! 'I'll get more snakes, call them my babies; kids won't walk past my place, they will run. "Run away from Crazy Snake Man!" they'll shout.' Perry's increasingly terrified and manic performance throughout this is a wonder to behold.

Slow Joey: Joey tells the gang that when he first moved to

Manhattan, he dated a girl with an enormous Adam's apple. Ross feels compelled to tell him that women don't have Adam's apples but quickly backs down to spare him from an unpleasant realisation. When a visibly pregnant Janice turns up at Central Perk, Joey turns to Chandler and says: 'Jeez, look how fat she got!' And watch out for the way Joey tries to understand Chandler's problem with women who pronounce it 'supposably': 'Did they go to the zoo? . . . *supposably*'.

Dinosaurs ROCK!: Ross tries to prove his argument about evolution by using Heckles' finger puppets to illustrate 'opposable thumbs' (which Phoebe suggests might be because the 'Overlords' needed them to steer their space craft), and by pointing out that all across the world they've found fossils that prove that evolution is a scientific fact, to which Phoebe asks, 'Who put those fossils there, and why?' Eventually their bickering flares up into a full-scale war of attrition, 'Scary Scientist Man' versus Earth Mother. The way in which Ross is completely unwilling to let his friend keep to her own beliefs is very telling of his own obsessive faith in science. Phoebe, in seemingly angry retaliation, tries to persuade Ross to see that 'there's a teeny, tiny possibility [he] could be wrong' – citing the fact that at one time the smartest men in the world believed the Earth to be flat. Ross can do nothing but admit that, yes, there's a chance he might be wrong. An appalled Phoebe just gasps, 'I can't believe you caved,' as a demoralised Ross gathers up his 'briefcase of facts' and leaves. Thank goodness, for his sake, he didn't pursue her lack of faith in gravity!

Just Plain Weird: Mr Heckles complains that the girls' 'stomping' is disturbing his birds. When Rachel points out that he doesn't have any, he says defensively: 'I could have birds.' He then rejoins his imaginary dinner party. His indexed list of ex-girlfriends includes comments like 'too tall', 'big gums' and 'makes noise when she eats'.

The Story So Far: Chandler was voted 'Class Clown' and played clarinet in High School (and so did Mr Heckles). The gang play poker at one point (see 'TOW All The Poker'). Although the credits always list Treager's name as 'Treeger' we have a very good reason for disagreeing with them – see 'TOW Chandler Crosses The Line'.

Generation X: Phoebe believes Heckles' spirit is still around and prompts him to 'go into the light' in a tribute to *Poltergeist* (Tobe Hooper, 1982). Yanni is a Greek pianist-composer who claims his goal is to 'connect with people emotionally'. We think Chandler's hatred of him is entirely justified.

The Last Word: Laughing through the pain, this is an episode that encourages us to face up to the reality of an unknown future. Chandler's (and our own) fears come from not knowing if there's a pattern in life, in contrast with Ross and Phoebe's argument, which is basically a conflict of certainties. Ross takes comfort in his belief in science, while Phoebe thinks that 'facts' are just elements to be played with, allowing her to imagine many alternative (and generally ludicrous) possibilities. While most of us would tend to side with Ross initially, Phoebe's theories *are* much more fun.

204
'The One With Phoebe's Husband'

Writer: Alexa Junge
Director: Gail Mancuso
First US transmission: 12.10.95
First UK transmission (C4): 12.07.96

Guest Cast: Lauren Tom (Julie), Steve Zahn (Duncan),
Janice Davies (Woman on Bench)

Summary: A man calls at Monica's claiming to be Phoebe's husband! Apparently, Phoebe married Duncan, a gay Canadian, so that he could get a Green Card to work as an ice skater in the USA. While the others are simply shocked, Monica is appalled: Phoebe was always secretly in love with Duncan. Now, to complicate things, Duncan wants a divorce. After years of denial, he has realised that he's actually straight and he wants to divorce Phoebe so that he can get married to his girlfriend.

Ross confesses to Rachel that he and Julie have not yet had sex. Rachel is determined to make sure it never happens. She advises Ross to put it off even longer, which almost works, but

Joey suggests that he should just get right down to it, leaving Rachel to watch as Ross moves even further out of her grasp.

Chandleresque: The secret's out – Chandler's got a third nipple! When asked if it does anything special, he claims, in a voice dripping with sarcasm that it 'opens the delivery entrance to the magical land of Narnia'.

Joey's an ACTOR: The secret's out – Joey was in a porno movie! Joey explains that he was going to be one of the, shall we say, participants in the movie, but he lost his nerve at the last minute. Instead, he played the photocopier repair man who walks in when a couple are having sex on the copier. His only line in the film is, 'You know, that's bad for the paper tray.' Joey claims that Chandler told him his extra nipple was just a 'nubbin'. When the gang wonder why he believed him, he says, 'I don't know. You see something, you hear a word – I thought that's what it was.'

Phoebisms: The scene where Duncan tells Phoebs he's straight is very well observed, played as an exact reversal of a gay man 'coming out'. For example, Phoebe's summation of the situation: 'You're married to someone for six years, you think you know him, and then, one day, he says, "Oh, I'm not gay".' Her nervous behaviour around Duncan is brilliant, and Kudrow plays the unrequited love of her character very well – check out the way she laughs, embarrassed, at her own '*Olé*!' joke.

The Ballad of Ross & Rachel: Telling Ross that women think 'there is *nothing* sexier than a man who does not want to have sex' is incredibly cruel of Rachel, but brilliantly funny. Her triumphant sashay as she walks away from the conversation, casually throwing a tea towel over her shoulder, makes you want to cheer, despite the fact she's just done something spiteful. When Monica confronts her with the fact that she's just going to have to get over it, Rachel bitingly replies, 'Oh, I'm going to have to get over it. I didn't know *that*'s what I had to do!' The sequence where Rachel describes exactly what she'd like a man to do is toe-curlingly erotic, treading a fine line between seediness and romance. Once Rachel has finished her steamy descriptions, we all feel like Ross: flabbergasted, but incredibly horny.

Generation X: Chandler mentions Narnia, the magical kingdom from *The Lion, The Witch and The Wardrobe* by C.S. Lewis. Ross performs a version of the classic dance sequence from *Singin' In The Rain* (Stanley Donen/Gene Kelly, 1952).

The Story So Far: In an episode full of revelations and indiscretions, Phoebe blabs that there's an item of Monica's underwear on the telephone pole below her apartment which somehow got stuck there after she had sex with Fun Bobby (see 'TOW The Monkey', 'TOW Russ'). Chandler is revealed to have three nipples (see 'TOW Phoebe's Ex-Partner'). Julie is only the second woman Ross has slept with. Ross and Julie have been dating for about two months.

The Last Word: The way Duncan comes out about being straight is innovative, with Phoebe aghast, claiming that he always threw such great Oscar parties, him reassuring her that his parents already have one straight son, so they were OK about it. But good as it is, it'll never stick in the memory as well as some other things in this episode. Like a Machiavellian Rachel trying to ensure Ross and Julie don't sleep with each other; or the revelation of Chandler's nubbin; or the closing sequence of Ross skipping down the street, as an old woman observes, 'Someone got theirs last night.' 'Twice,' confirms Ross proudly.

205
'The One With Five Steaks And An Eggplant'

Writer: Chris Brown
Director: Ellen Gittelsohn
First US transmission: 19.10.95
First UK transmission (C4): 19.07.96

Guest Cast: Brittney Powell (Jade), Chris Young (Steven Fisher),
Spencer Cherashore (Waiter)

Summary: The fact that Joey, Phoebe and Rachel make less money than Chandler, Monica and Ross threatens to make Ross's birthday a troublesome time for the less well-off members of the gang, and this is compounded by Monica's sudden promotion to chief chef and head of purchasing. When they tell their friends how they feel, it instigates a huge row and while Chandler, Monica and Ross enjoy a live concert by Hootie And The Blowfish, the two other girls are forced to endure an evening guessing how many fingers Joey is holding up behind his back.

Chandler begins screening his calls through his answerphone and manages to intercept a call from Jade, a beautiful, drunken and naked girl who thinks she's calling Bob, the previous occupant of Chandler's apartment. Chandler pretends to be Bob and arranges a date with Jade, in the hope that when Bob doesn't turn up, he'll be able to sweep her off her feet as the caring and sensitive man on the next table. Chandler's plan goes perfectly and he ends up sleeping with Jade. Unfortunately, when Jade calls and Chandler pretends to be Bob again, she moans to him about the way he stood her up and that she found herself with a man who wasn't very good in bed, much to Chandler's disappointment.

The meat suppliers at Monica's restaurant give her a thank you gift of an eggplant and some steaks but when her boss hears about it he tells her that she's contravened corporate policy and that he has to fire her.

Spoilt Rachel: When Ross apologises for never thinking of money as an issue, Rachel rightly points out: 'That's because you have it!'

Chandleresque: Ross calls Chandler 'pure evil'. Chandler visibly weighs up pure evil in his left hand and 'horny and alone' in his right, offering the excuse that he's tried 'horny and alone' already. At the restaurant, the waiter asks Chandler if there'll be anything else, so Chandler asks for a verse of 'Killing Me Softly', then sees the waiter's tired facial expression and says: 'You're gonna sneeze in my fish, aren't you?' (These two lines, if used in conjunction, will always give you a good indication as to the quality of service you can expect in any restaurant.)

Slow Joey: Joey complains that the wealthier members of the gang are 'always saying "let's go here, let's go there". Like we can afford to go "here" and "there".' When Monica tells them she wants to celebrate her promotion, Joey asks Phoebe: 'How much d'you think I can get for my kidney?'

Chandler's appearance in *Caroline In The City*

First US transmission: 02.11.95
First UK transmission: 26.07.96
Writers: Fred Barron & Marco Pennette
Director: James Burrows

Shown on NBC in the slot immediately before *Friends*, *Caroline In The City* centres around the daily lives of a cartoonist (Caroline), her assistant and her man-mad best friend, Annie. Though it's not an actual episode of *Friends*, we include it here for completion's sake. In the episode 'Caroline And The Folks', we see Annie looking around a video store when 'Chandler' (played by Matthew Perry) sidles up to her with a copy of *The Piano* in an attempt to impress her with his sensitivity and complete lack of interest in 'gratuitous nudity in film'. However, when he spies the copy of *Sorority House Massacre II* that Annie's holding, he realises he could have just approached her as himself. Annie suggests: 'So be yourself.' Chandler smiles, fidgets a little, then walks straight out of the store in a panic!

Generation X: Jade lies in her first phone message to Bob when she says that her legs appear on the new Bond movie posters (*Goldeneye*'s posters didn't have that kind of design). The guys watch Dwarf Wrestling on WWF (The World Wrestling Federation). Chandler refers to 'Killing Me Softly With His Song', the 1973 hit for Roberta Flack that was recently covered by The Fugees. Chandler explains to Ross that he's given Jade Ross's telephone number so that she doesn't work out that he's been posing as Bob, which prompts Ross to ask: 'What do I do when Mr Roper calls?' in reference to the type of confusing situation that might occur in the sitcom *Three's Company*. We hear Hootie And The Blowfish's song 'I Go Blind'.

The Story So Far: Obviously, this is set on and around the date of Ross's birthday (see 'TOW Joey's New Girlfriend'). Chandler has been living in his apartment for less than three years – Jade's phone message reveals that Bob lived there three years ago. Chandler tells Ross, 'We don't know Bob,' suggesting that either his impression of Bob on the phone is spookily accurate, or else Jade is so into self-delusion that her love for this guy's made her forget how he used to talk. At the concert, Monica bumps into Stevie Fisher who she used to babysit when he was a kid.

The Last Word: We asked our American friends if they would ever spend $310 on a friend's birthday (which, split five ways is $62), and they said, 'Are you crazy?', which pretty much sums up Joey, Rachel and Phoebe's point. This episode paints itself into a corner on this issue, but as the sacking of Monica distracts the friends from their problem the issue's never really resolved satisfactorily. It's supposed to be a balanced argument but it does end up looking just a little one-sided.

206
'The One With The Baby On The Bus'

Writer: Betsy Borns
Director: Gail Mancuso
First US transmission: 02.11.95
First UK transmission (C4): 26.07.96

Guest Cast: Max Wright (Terry), Victor Raider-Wexler (Doctor),
Chrissie Hynde (The New Singer), Catherine Bell (Robin), Hugh Dane (Jim),
Jennifer Sommerfield (Becky),
Giovanni Ribisi (The 'Condom Boy' – uncredited)

Summary: When Ross takes a mouthful of what he thinks is Key Lime Pie, his tongue begins to swell. Monica explains that it's *Kiwi* Lime Pie, forgetting that one of Ross's many allergies is kiwi fruit, and she and Ross must rush to the hospital so he can get a shot. But who's going to look after Ben? The only available candidates are Joey and Chandler and, worryingly unsuitable as they are, this is an emergency, after all. Deciding to take Ben out with them, the guys meet two women on a bus. When the women say that they're about to get off, Joey and Chandler suggest they all go for a coffee. But on the pavement, Joey and Chandler suddenly realise they've left (oh, you guessed it) the baby on the bus.

While Chandler and Joey race around New York trying to

find Ben, Rachel has her own problems at Central Perk. Her boss, Terry, has asked her to break the news to Phoebe that she has been replaced as the cafe's musician-in-residence by Stephanie Schiffer, a professional singer with real talent. Even though Terry is prepared to let Phoebe play as well, he is unwilling to pay her the same rate as Stephanie, and so Phoebe storms out and sets up shop as a busker on the street outside.

Chandleresque: Chandler gets to deliver one of the simplest, and one of the very best, lines of the whole series. Finding that there are two babies at the lost property office, Joey and Chandler toss a coin to decide which they will choose. But which baby is heads, and which is tails? Well, one has ducks on his shirt and the other has clowns. Since ducks have heads, Joey suggests, heads on the coin should be for the baby with the ducks. 'What kind of scary-ass clowns did you have at your parties?' a frightened Chandler asks. When chasing after the bus that Ben is riding, Joey calls the baby's name. An exasperated Chandler says, 'Maybe he'll hear you, and pull the cord!'

Freaky Monica: Ben bursts into tears whenever Monica holds him, so she begins to worry: 'What if my own baby hates me?' Somewhat less than helpfully, Chandler tells her she's going to have to wait a long time before she has to worry about that – 'You haven't even got a boyfriend,' he reminds her. There's a short pause, in which Monica stares at Chandler, her face like thunder. Chandler quickly reacts to a comment that, curiously, no-one else heard: 'Joey, she does not look fat!'

Spoilt Rachel: She's still obviously not got the hang of that 'responsible attitude' thing. When she's trying to bargain with Terry to keep Phoebe on, she tells him that she'll 'even clean the cappuccino machine.' This shocks her boss, so Rachel quickly back-pedals and explains that she means that she'll '*cleeeean* it'.

Phoebisms: There's a slew of songs, including the first celebrity duet of 'Smelly Cat'. Phoebe sings her latest composition to Rachel: a song that reveals that 'tegrin' spelled backwards is 'nirget'. Later, when she's busking, she insists in a song that 'I don't need your charity', but chirps a friendly thanks to someone who gives her some money. Then we hear her sing of the strange 'double-double-double-jointed boy'. After all this, we begin to understand Terry's summation of her talent: 'It's not that your friend is bad,' he tells Rachel. 'It's that she's *so* bad, she makes me want to put my finger through my eye, into my brain, and swirl it around.'

Slow Joey: Ross worries that Joey doesn't have much experience of looking after children but he explains that, with his seven Catholic sisters, he's perfectly used to caring for kids. When Ross's tongue swells in reaction to the kiwi, only Joey understands him. He explains that his Uncle Sal has 'a really big tongue'. 'Is he the one with the beautiful wife?' asks Chandler.

Boys Will Be Boys: Joey sees the baby-sitting gig as simply a chance to pick up women, claiming that 'women love babies'. Of course this backfires first of all when the first woman they meet assumes Joey and Chandler are a gay couple with an adopted child. This leads Chandler to suggest that, the next time they want to find women, they should just 'go to the park and make out'.

Generation X: Chrissie Hynde was the lead singer of rock group The Pretenders. Her set contains a cover of P.P. Arnold's 1968 single 'Angel of the Morning', more recently sampled by The Fugees for their single 'Rumble In The Jungle'.

The Story So Far: Ross is allergic to lobster, peanuts and kiwi and is scared of needles. He once jammed a pencil in Monica's hand and forced a broom into the spokes of her bike. She once hit him in the face with a pumpkin. Joey now claims to have 'seven Catholic sisters' (see 'TOW Mrs Bing', 'TOW Chandler Can't Remember Which Sister'). Joey says he has an Uncle Sal who has a big tongue. Rachel's boss Terry (Max Wright) also appears in 'TOW Underdog Gets Away'. Giovanni Ribisi (series regular, Frank Jr – see 'TOW The Bullies') makes his first appearance, uncredited, in this episode as the boy who fishes out the condom from Phoebe's guitar case. For continuity, we're presuming that this is Frank Buffay Jr.

The Last Word: One of the best episodes of the season without a doubt, focusing on the brilliant Perry and Le Blanc double act. This is more than enough to shoulder the cavalcade of laughs in this episode. Simply the sight of them weighed down with all the brightly coloured baby gear is enough to raise a smile (as is Chandler questioning whether Joey remembered to 'pack the baby's anvil'). The two actors have such perfect synergy that the episode just breezes by, ending long before you want it to.

207
'The One Where Ross Finds Out'

Writer: Michael Borkow
Director: Peter Bonerz
First US transmission: 09.11.95
First UK transmission (C4): 02.08.96

Guest Cast: Lauren Tom (Julie), Arye Gross (Michael),
Barry Diamond (Phone Guy), Marcus D. Jacques (Waiter)

Summary: Phoebe convinces Chandler that he's putting on weight, so he agrees to start an exercise regime with Monica – who, after all, has nothing better to do with her time at the moment. Her relentless energy, though, soon begins to grind him down and, before long, he's had enough of their tiring keep-fit. Rachel, meanwhile, is trying to move on from Ross. She goes on a date with a guy called Michael, but proceeds to make a disaster out of it all. Ross and Julie had earlier announced that they were going to get a cat together, which is as good a sign of long-term commitment as any. All Rachel can talk about on the date with Michael is Ross, and Julie, and the cat. As the evening wears on, she gets more and more drunk and depressed about Ross. Michael, a divorcee who's been through a similar thing, suggests that all she needs is closure. Borrowing someone's mobile phone, Rachel leaves a message on Ross's answering machine, saying she's happy that things have worked out for him, and telling him, 'I am over you. And that, my friend, is what they call closure.'

The next day, a hung-over and faintly amnesiac Rachel lets Ross use her phone to check his messages. She, of course, has forgotten all about the message she left – and it isn't until Ross starts listening to it that she remembers what she said . . .

Chandleresque: During one of their exercise sessions, Monica challenges Chandler to do five sit-ups – if he does, she will flash her breasts at him. He only manages two and a half – 'Just show me one of them,' he says. Resenting this invasion of his private life, Chandler complains that Monica's got him doing butt clenches at work 'and now, they won't bring me my mail any more'. At the end of the episode, Chandler has finally had enough of the exercising, so he cleverly compliments Monica on her boundless positive energy, especially considering she has no job, no boyfriend, and she lives in constant fear of disappointing her parents. Deflated, Monica sinks to the sofa, drained of all her energy. As she falls asleep, a gleeful Chandler skips into his own bedroom to do the same. Although this is unspeakably cruel, it's also one of the funniest parts of this episode.

The Ballad of Ross & Rachel: Rachel insists that she's over Ross, and no longer concerned that he's with Julie. When she sees Ross kissing Julie, she claims not to mind that he's passionately pushing her on to the window of Central Perk: 'For all I care, he can throw her through the damn thing.' But, of course, she's not over him – despite her insistence that she is on the answering machine message. When Ross hears this, he and the audience lapse into a stunned silence. 'Over me?' he stammers. 'When were you under me?' The two try to talk it through, but Ross is too shocked to cope – and Julie's waiting downstairs so that they can go and collect their cat. The most nail-biting moment comes when Ross tries once more to get clarification: 'And now you're over me?' he asks. 'Are you over me?' Rachel says. Neither answers the other's question, and it's left until the end of the episode – featuring that beautifully passionate first kiss – before it's resolved.

Boys Will Be Boys: Throughout this episode, Phoebe is seeing a guy called Scott who seems nervous of getting physical with her. Although she likes him a lot, she wonders how much longer she's going to have to wait. Finally, he explains that he is worried that sex will complicate things between them, so Phoebe tells him that it's OK and he needn't feel obliged to her just because they'd slept together. Hearing this, Joey points out that Scott got Phoebe to sleep with him, got her to agree that she would happily never hear from him again, and convinced her that this was 'a good thing'. 'This man is my god,' he says.

Generation X: Arye Gross (Michael) played Adam in the first few seasons of the sitcom *Ellen*. Michael mentions the film *Diner* (Barry Levinson, 1982), claiming he's spent much of the date with Rachel running it through his head. As Chandler prances away from the sleeping Monica we hear an excerpt from 'The Dance of the Hours' by Ponchelli from *La Gioconda* (a.k.a. 'Hello Mother, Hello Father').

The Story So Far: Monica once had a cat called 'Fluffy Meowington'. Ross discovers that Chandler blabbed to Rachel about his feelings for her (see 'TOW Rachel Finds Out') and mentions Paolo and Barry.

The Last Word: So it took over a year, but finally Ross and Rachel tickle tonsils! That scene in Central Perk, where he comes to chastise Rachel for complicating his life, is brilliant, no matter how many times you watch it. Although it looks for a second as if nothing will happen – Ross storms off after telling Rachel that he's happy with Julie – Ross, of course, returns, and the pair of them kiss at last. Keep the tissues handy, this is one of Aniston's finest.

208
'The One With The List'

Writers: Marta Kauffman & David Crane
Director: Mary Kay Place
First US transmission: 16.11.95
First UK transmission (C4): 09.08.96

Guest Cast: Lauren Tom (Julie), Michael McKean (Mr Ratstatter)

Summary: Despite having wanted Rachel for the last ten years, Ross realises he can't just ditch Julie as he still loves her. He turns to the guys for help and Chandler suggests they compile a list of the plus and minus points of each girl. He completes the bad list first, but Ross doesn't even need to complete a list of Rachel's good points as Rachel's always been the girl for him. But then Rachel sees the list of things Ross claims not to have liked about her. Can it really be over before it's begun?

Picky Monica: When Ratstatter, the Mockolate promoter, asks her if she still wants to work with him she says with a hint of desperation, 'I have no morals and I need the cash.'

Slow Joey: Joey asks Monica if she's willing to cook naked. When she asks incredulously if there's an ad for a naked chef, he confesses, 'No, but if you're willing to cook naked, then you might be willing to dance naked, and then . . .'

Chandleresque: Chandler is typically unsympathetic with Ross's predicament: 'This must be so hard. "Oh no, two women love me, they're both gorgeous and sexy, my wallet's too small for my fifties and my diamond shoes are too tight".'

Phoebisms: She sings a not-quite fictional song called 'Two Of Them Kissed Last Night'. Phoebe takes exception to Chandler's use of the phrase 'karma crap' and says, 'Good luck in your next life as a dung beetle.' After tasting one of Monica's Mockolate concoctions, Phoebe spits, 'Oh sweet Lord! This is what evil must taste like!'

Boys Will Be Boys: While Rachel is telling the girls about how passionate and intense the kiss was, the guys simply ask Ross one question: 'Tongue?'

The Ballad of Ross & Rachel: Rachel worries that Ross will pick Julie: 'She's gonna be all "Hi, I'm Julie, Ross picked me and we're gonna get married, have lots of kids and dig up stuff together."' Meanwhile Ross's list describes Rachel as being 'too into her looks' and 'a little ditsy'. Despite all this, his main point for Julie is 'she's not Rachel'. Later, Rachel sums up just how hurt she is by Ross's selection process: 'Imagine the worst things you think about yourself. Now, how would you feel if the one person that you trusted the most in the world not only thinks them too, but actually uses them as reasons not to be with you.' Ross tries to get her to see his point of view, saying that there's nothing she could put in a list that would stop him wanting to be with her, but Rachel believes that must be the difference between him and her: 'See, I'd never make a list.'

Just Plain Weird: Mr Ratstatter, creator of Mockolate, a synthetic chocolate. His FDA approval is refused due to 'something about laboratory rats'. His next project is 'fish-tachios', pistachios with reconstituted fish bits. Mmmm, nice!

Generation X: Chandler asks the guys if they want a game of Doom, the ultra-violent 1st-person shoot-'em-up computer game that spawned its own genre. The people on the computer helpline that Chandler calls are watching an episode of *Star Trek* in which Spock and his father hug (this *never* happened, by the way, so they are lying). Michael McKean appeared in, and wrote the music for, the spoof documentary *This Is Spinal Tap* (Rob Reiner, 1984). The song that Ross requests the radio station to play is U2's song, 'With or Without You', which is Ross and Rachel's song. After Rachel phones the station to tell them what Ross did, they play 'In My Room' by The Beach Boys instead.

The Story So Far: Ross reminds us that he's loved Rachel from afar for ten years. Monica says she's allergic to cat hair.

The Last Word: 'That is funny. That is painfully funny. No, wait. Wait, yeah, that's just painful.' Ross and Rachel finally get together, but it lasts for mere seconds thanks to the damaging effect of the eponymous list. It's nice that the writers can still surprise us; when Ross gets the radio station to play U2's emotive ballad, we're all certain this will be enough to melt Rachel's heart and encourage her to forgive him, so it's great when she tells the DJ what it was he did and he takes her side.

209
'The One With Phoebe's Dad'

Writers: Jeffrey Astrof & Mike Sikowitz
Director: Kevin S. Bright
First US transmission: 14.12.95
First UK transmission (C4): 16.08.96

Guest Cast: Audra Lindley (Frances),
Michael G. Hagerty (Mr Treager, the Superintendent),
James Michael Tyler (Gunther)

Summary: Christmas is growing near, and the friends discuss the ethics of tipping. Monica and Rachel, strapped for cash, have been giving home-made cookies to everyone, but they don't seem to be appreciated. The paper delivery boy has mashed them into the sports section of their paper, while the postman has shattered a parcel of ornaments from Monica's mother. Later, the gang are gathered at Central Perk, where Ross shows them all the presents he has been buying for people. One of them is a picture frame, containing a sample picture of a model. Phoebe sees it and excitedly claims that it's her birth father. Monica breaks the news to her that that's unlikely, so Phoebe confronts her grandmother to find out the truth. As lie after lie about her father is shattered, Phoebe's grandmother reveals that not only does she know who he is, but she also knows where he lives. Enlisting the support of Chandler and Joey, she sets out to find him. But when she gets there, she finds she is too frightened by the prospect of finally meeting her real dad and chickens out.

Monica and Rachel prepare for their Christmas party, but disaster strikes when Ross breaks the knob on their radiator and their apartment begins to get unbearably hot. They call Mr Treager, but he claims that he can't do anything about it until after the weekend. Ross, suspecting that Treager was also less than impressed by Monica's cookies, sees a way of impressing Rachel by 'seizing the day' (something Rachel had told him he never did – see 'The Ballad of Ross & Rachel') and offering to 'tip' him $100 to fix it. But, once again, Ross makes a fool of himself: Treager was telling the truth and, to top it all, he loved the cookies – 'they were so personal, really showed you cared.'

Poor Ross: After trying so hard to impress Rachel with his attempt to 'seize the day' by offering Treager money to fix the radiator, we really feel his embarrassment when he realises that he's making a fool of himself. We can't help smiling at Rachel's smug closing comment, though: 'Nice seizing, gel boy.'

Phoebisms: 'A plate of brownies once told me a limerick . . .' she reveals. When asked if they were 'funny' brownies, a wonderfully blasé Phoebe comments, 'Not especially.'

Slow Joey: 'So I'm trying to get my boss's ex-wife to sleep with me,' Joey tells the gang, just after Phoebe's illusions of her father have been shattered. When the others just gasp at his lack of tact, he retorts, 'Oh, but when Phoebe has a problem, everyone's all ears.' Later, when Phoebe has resolved not to meet her father, a desperate Joey asks, 'Do you think it would be all right if I went in and used his bathroom?' Luckily, the plans for relieving himself change when he looks out of the car's window. 'Cool! Snow! Kinda like a blank canvas.'

Chandleresque: As Christmas looms, Monica is appalled at Chandler and Joey's lack of planning. She squeals, 'You guys haven't gotten your presents yet? Tomorrow's Christmas Eve, what're you gonna do?' Chandler, amazed, asks, 'Don't you have to be Claymation to say stuff like that?' Later, when he returns from the trip to find Phoebe's father, he strides into Monica's sweltering apartment and blurts a wonderfully twisted Christmas greeting. 'Ho! Ho! Ho- holy crap, is it hot in here!'

Boys Will Be Boys: Chandler and Joey end up buying presents from a 24-hour garage. They buy Rachel some windscreen wiper blades and an air freshener that guarantees a 'new car smell' (despite the fact she hasn't got a car). Phoebe is, bizarrely, grateful for her packet of toilet seat covers. Ross is given brand-less cola and lemon and lime drinks. ('This is too much,' he stutters. 'I feel like I should get you another sweater.') Monica is handed a mysteriously small packet, about which Joey comments, 'They're ribbed, for your pleasure.' Ross and Monica swap presents.

The Ballad of Ross & Rachel: The list of the pros and cons of seeing Rachel comes up again, as Ross tries to patch things up with her using an impromptu gift of a Slinky. (You remember them – those springs that used to, well, slink down stairs.) Ross suggests that Rachel make a list of her own about him, to try and make her feel better. With clearly apparent relish, she does so: 'You're whiny, you're obsessive, you're insecure, you're gutless . . . you don't just sort of seize the day, you know . . . and you wear too much of that gel in your hair.' This – not unreasonable – précis of his character sends Ross sliding into a bout of extreme paranoia; he spends most of the time at Monica and Rachel's party telling guests that he only uses as much gel as the bottle suggests.

Families – Who Needs 'Em?: We see Phoebe's grandmother updating the phone book, crossing out all the names she finds in the newspaper's obituaries. Chandler reminds us of his father's cross-dressing, recalling a time when he used to dress up in a red suit, with big black boots, and stumble around their house in a drunken state. When Rachel – thinking that Mr Bing was dressing as Santa – comments that it sounds like Christmas in his household must have been pretty horrible, Chandler just says, 'Who said anything about Christmas?'

Yo Gunther!: Gunther is finally listed on the end-credits for the first time!! When Ross's Slinky is turned down by Rachel, he turns to Gunther. When he finds out that Gunther has stairs in his apartment, he hands him the spring and tells him to 'go nuts!'

Ugly Naked Guy: Phoebe spies on him as he puts up his Christmas decorations. 'Oh my God!' she gasps. 'You should see the size of his Christmas balls.' Unsurprisingly, no-one rushes to see.

Just Plain Weird: Mr Treager fails to notice the sweltering heat in Monica's apartment. 'My body always stays cool,' he tells them, 'probably because I have so much skin.' Later, he corners Rachel under what looks like mistletoe. She lies, and tells him it's basil, 'If it was mistletoe,' he says, 'I was gonna kiss you.' Rachel firmly asserts that 'it's still basil'. Phoebe's grandmother gives her a picture of her real father – Einstein!

The Story So Far: We're reminded of Phoebe's tortured family history. Phoebe's father is not a tree surgeon in Burma as she's always believed, but a pharmacist whose last known address is 74 Laurel Drive in Middletown. When he left Phoebe's mother, she couldn't bear having to break the news to her daughters so she just lied to spare them the pain. Phoebe's grandmother still describes him as the 'irresponsible creep who knocked up your mom and stole her Gremlin'.

The Last Word: Sadly, for what should have been quite an emotional storyline, the parts of this episode dealing with Phoebe's father don't quite have the impact they should. The exception, of course, is the scene where she realises that she's not quite ready to face the possible disappointment of her father not living up to her expectations. The accompanying storyline of the party, and Ross's oafish attempts to impress Rachel, are funnier and stick in the memory more.

210
'The One With Russ'

Writer: Ira Ungerleider
Director: Tommy Schlamme
First US transmission: 04.01.96
First UK transmission (C4): 23.08.96

Guest Cast: Vincent Vintresca (Fun Bobby), Snaro (Russ),
Scott Stewart (Waiter)
and introducing: June Gable (Estelle Leonard, Joey's agent)

Summary: Rachel's moving on. Or so she says. She announces to everyone that she's got a date with a new guy, to help her get over Ross after the list incident. When he arrives at Central Perk, though, she seems to be the only one to not see what everyone else does. Her date, Russ, bears a striking similarity to a certain palaeontologist they're all familiar with. While everyone else is more than a little freaked out by the similarity, she just carries on as if there's nothing unusual about him. Ross himself also fails to see that he's practically looking into a mirror; he is more concerned with playing little, jealous games of one-upmanship.

Monica, meanwhile, has her own boyfriend problems. She's back together with Fun Bobby, and is only now beginning to realise exactly why he's so much fun. Bobby seems to have a drink problem, so she persuades him to go on the wagon. When he does, though, all the fun drains out of him and he becomes the most boring person on earth. The only way Monica can cope with going out with him is by getting completely drunk!

Joey's an Actor: The gang rush to the nearest newsstand to read the reviews of Joey's latest play. Chandler begins, and reads out a review that is quite damning of his performance. Pointing out that it's only one opinion, he asks anyone else to read their review. Phoebe obliges, and begins to read exactly the same one. Ross sheepishly refuses to read his, and just as

Joey's about to give up on his dream of being an actor, Monica pipes up that hers says that 'Joey Tribbiani reaches brilliant new levels of . . .' She tails off, as she leafs through the paper to find the continuation of the review. '. . . Sucking!' she completes. Things begin to take a turn for the better, though, when Joey gets an audition for *Days Of Our Lives*. When he goes to the call-back, he refuses to sleep with the casting woman – until the stakes are upped and he manages to secure the regular role of Dr Drake Ramoray, neurosurgeon. Joey refers to 'The Little General' – his name for . . . well, you can probably guess. Chandler is sure he used to call it 'The Little Major', and Joey explains that he had to promote it after his time with Denise De Marco.

Spoilt Rachel: As she's handed a cup of coffee, Monica asks if it's made with non-fat milk. Rachel says she isn't sure and that Monica should try it to find out: she does, and it isn't. Monica offers it back to Rachel, but she explains that she can't take it back as she's already had some. Now that's service.

Freaky Monica: When the gang decide to celebrate Joey's success in getting the *Days Of Our Lives* audition, Rachel tells them that she's already made plans. An incredulous Monica cries in horror, 'You have other friends??'

Dinosaurs ROCK!: Chandler uses a mug that only Ross could have bought. It is emblazoned with the legend 'I got boned at the Museum of Natural History'.

The Ballad of Ross & Rachel: Of course, it's clear to everyone (even Rachel, in the end) that she's still hung up on Ross. The scenes of Russ and Ross meeting, but completely failing to recognise their similarity, are great. When Ross the palaeontologist discovers that Russ is a periodontist, Monica, trying to look on the bright side, comments that 'they're as different as night and . . . later that night.' Rachel's grossed-out 'euw, *euw*' when she finally realises that she's dating a Ross-alike is a brilliant overreaction.

Just Plain Weird: Finally we meet Estelle Leonard, Joey's agent. This wonderful creation is one of the best recurring characters in the show, ranking right up there with Heckles for out-and-out strangeness. When Joey tells her that he's got a call back for the *Days Of Our Lives* job, she asks him, 'Have you ever seen me ecstatic?' She then breaks into a horrific grin – like a chain-smoking, snarling gerbil. She also has the creakiest little 'Uh-huuuh' when she's speaking on the phone. More please!

Generation X: Despite being fairly obvious, the actor who plays Russ, credited as Snaro, is in fact David Schwimmer under not-very-heavy make-up. Phoebe refers to Lorne Greene, veteran (now deceased) star of *Battlestar Galactica* and *Bonanza*. *Days Of Our Lives* is actually a real daytime soap opera that runs on the NBC Network in the States. Created by Betty and Ted Corday, it started on November 8, 1965 as a half-hour melodrama, expanding to an hour later on. It's set in the fictional town of Salem, in America's Midwest, and tells of the high drama and emotional crises in the lives of two families, the Hortons and the Bradys. Obviously its references on *Friends* are written as pastiche, but if you've ever seen the real thing you'll know that Joey's storyline isn't that far removed from the kind of plots they actually do.

The Story So Far: We first met 'Fun Bobby' in 'TOW The Monkey'. June Gable (Estelle Leonard) previously appeared in 'TOW The Birth' as a nurse.

The Last Word: A nice little episode, with much to recommend it. Schwimmer's turn as Russ is entertaining, and the difficult sequences of both Ross and Russ having conversations are pulled off very well indeed. Their childish bickering is great, made all the better by neither of them noticing their similarity to the other. The only criticism that can be levelled at this episode is the way the cop-out ending to the Julie plotline left us feeling somewhat cheated. It would have been better for her to fade into obscurity, rather than drag her back and have her unconvincingly fall for Russ.

211
'The One With The Lesbian Wedding'

Writer: Doty Abrams
Director: Tommy Schlamme
First US transmission: 18.01.96
First UK transmission (C4): 30.08.96

Guest Cast: Jane Sibbett (Carol Willick), Jessica Hecht (Susan Bunch),
Phil Leeds (Mr Adelman), Candice Gingrich (the Minister),
Symba Smith (Chrissy), Lea DeLaria (Woman)
and introducing: Marlo Thomas (Sandra Green)

Summary: Carol and Susan have news for Ross: they're going to get married, and they'd love him to come along. Ross, of course, is completely freaked out by this and refuses to be a part of it. But when Carol's parents bow out the night before the ceremony and she argues with Susan, it looks as if they're not going to go through with it. Ross, putting his own feelings aside, persuades Carol that she has to go ahead with it and he eventually walks her up the aisle to give her away.

Rachel's mum comes to visit to see how the younger side lives. She announces that she is planning to divorce Rachel's father. A shocked Rachel has to cope with the idea of her parents breaking up and has great difficulty understanding why her mother wants to do this, until Mrs Green says, 'You didn't marry *your* Barry, honey.' Mrs Green feels she has been trapped for too long in a marriage she was never sure she wanted, and now she's searching for a new life.

Rose Adelman, one of Phoebe's massage clients, dies on her massage table. Although she's quite shaken by this alone, she also has to cope with the spirit of Mrs Adelman, which has decided to take up residence in Phoebe's body. Phoebe meets with Mr Adelman to find out if his wife had any unfinished business in this world. All he can think of is that his wife once said she wanted to see everything before she died . . .

Poor Ross: Trying to come to terms with Carol and Susan's wedding isn't the easiest thing for Ross. Somewhat bitterly, he wonders why he shouldn't go along to the ceremony – after all, he had fun at her *first* wedding!

Freaky Monica: Asked to cater for the wedding, Monica goes into terrifying overdrive. She bullies everyone into helping, barking orders at them from every corner of the kitchen: 'I feel like you should have German subtitles,' says Chandler at one point. As her stress increases, her friends begin to wonder whether she should just calm down and take it easy – 'Do you want to see me cry? Is that what you want?' she asks, with a crack in her voice. When Carol arrives to say that the wedding might be off, the first thing Monica says is, 'You're still going to pay me, right?'

Slow Joey: At the lesbian wedding, Joey gets frightened and agitated by the women's total lack of interest in him: 'I feel like Superman without his powers,' he moans.

Chandleresque: In response to these comments from Joey, Chandler laments that 'the world is my lesbian wedding'. His final gambit to strike up conversation with a very stern-looking lesbian is sheer embarrassment: 'Look. Penis, schmenis – we're all people!' not surprisingly, she just walks away.

Joey's an Actor!: On his first day on *Days Of Our Lives*, Joey is taught about 'Smell the Fart' acting, a method daytime soap actors use when they have a long and complicated line to remember (which is most of the time, with Joey): they take a pause and give a serious, considered look, almost as if they're smelling a fart.

Parents – Who Needs 'Em?: Rachel's mum is just superb! She practically dances through all her scenes, filled with an obvious glee at the prospect of living a different life for a few days. She asks Rachel if she has any marijuana, then she enquires, 'What's new in sex?' Later, at the wedding reception, she seems to be flirting with lesbians. Her sheer *joie de vivre* is marvellous.

Just Plain Weird: Mr and Mrs Adelman seem to be quite a couple. She's obviously a smart woman who says exactly what's on her mind, even if she does use Phoebe's mouth. The final 'Now I've seen everything' joke is pretty obvious, but funny nonetheless. Mr Adelman is a charming character. When Phoebe asks if his wife still had something to do on earth, he suggests that she always said she wanted to sleep with him once more. Phoebe just stares at the wizened little man and smiles. 'I'm sorry,' she explains, 'there's laughing in my head.'

Ugly Naked Guy: Mrs Green spies 'an unattractive nude man' playing a cello. She's told to be thankful that it's not a smaller instrument.

Generation X: Candice Gingrich, who plays the minister at the wedding, is a celebrated author and gay activist. Phoebe's possession by Mrs Adelman is possibly inspired by either the

Steve Martin film *All of Me* (Carl Reiner, 1984) or by *Prelude to a Kiss* (Norman René, 1992). Lea DeLaria (the butch woman at the wedding) is a well-known lesbian stand-up comic.

The Last Word: For an episode that focuses around Carol and Susan, it's rather sad that they don't get more screen time than a handful of scenes. The wedding itself is very low-key, and almost unromantic. However, the appearance of Candice Gingrich as the minister was apparently a major coup for the production team, adding a 'seal of approval' on the proceedings as she proclaims that there's nothing that pleases God more than to see two people in love – regardless of their sexual orientation. This might not seem that far-reaching to a British audience, but, considering just how right-wing the American TV sponsors are, in reality it is an incredibly brave testament, pushing the boundaries of tolerance and love that bit further.

212
'The One After The Superbowl, Part 1'

Writer: Michael Borkow
Director: Michael Lembeck
First US transmission: 28.01.96
First UK transmission (C4): 06.09.96

Guest Cast: Brooke Shields (Erika Ford), Chris Isaak (Rob Donan),
Dan Castellaneta (the Zoo Keeper), Roark Critchlow (Doctor),
Fred Willard (Mr Lipson), Tahj Mowry (little boy),
Sean Masterson ('Monkeyshine' Guy),
Lawrence A. Mandley (Security Guard),
Elliot Woods (Waiter), Karman Kruschke (Coma Woman)

Summary: Phoebe gets a gig singing for children at the local library. The kids love her because she tells them the truth, but the parents are concerned that her songs are inappropriate and she's fired.

Joey gets his first fan mail, from a woman called Erika, who encloses fourteen of her own eyelashes with the letter as a sign of her love for him. But when Monica sees that the letter was hand-posted to their address rather than the show, Joey realises that he has his own stalker. Erika then comes to their apartment, and Joey is torn between dating a beautiful woman who is infatuated with him and running the risk of being axed to death should she ever realise that he isn't really Dr Drake Ramoray from *Days Of Our Lives*, he's just the man who plays him on TV. But this is a concept that Erika just doesn't get. When Erika confronts Joey about him kissing another woman in that day's episode, Ross is compelled to tell her the truth – he is in fact, Drake's evil twin!

A monkey appearing in a TV advert for Monkey Shines Beer reminds Ross of Marcel. Eager to see how his old pal is doing, Ross goes to visit him at the zoo in L.A., only to be informed by the zoo administrator that Marcel has died. However, one of the zoo janitors manages to let slip that Marcel is working in movies now – he IS the Monkey Shines monkey! Better still, he's currently filming a movie in New York where Ross is sure he'll be able to meet up with him again!

Phoebisms: Nervous about performing to a child audience, Phoebe suggests to Rob that she might just picture her audience naked, but Rob doesn't think that's such a good idea: 'That's kind of the reason why the last guy got fired.' Phoebe's songs include one about how grandparents die, a cheerful song about things you shouldn't do (such as sleep with people to get them to like you) and a song explaining the origins of hamburgers and one about sexual orientation. 'Not at all inappropriate,' chirps Rachel.

Slow Joey: When he and Chandler are trying to escape his 'stalker', Joey suggests just walking past her on the stairs, as they've never met, so she'll never recognise him (Chandler points out that that's how *radio* stars escape their stalkers). Trying to wriggle out of the fact that, despite Erika's misguided beliefs that he's a doctor, he didn't help a man in a restaurant who was choking, Joey explains that he's a neurosurgeon and that it had clearly been a case of 'foodal chokage'.

Chandleresque: When Joey asks him to guess what he got, Chandler answers: 'rhythm?' Later, Joey asks him what he'd like to do for dinner; his response, that they might stay in and cook for themselves, forces them to fall into hysterics. Ross complains that he hasn't seen his monkey in almost a year, prompting Chandler to joke, 'You never look down in the shower?' Ross glares at him, forcing him to ask, 'Oh please! I'm not allowed to make one joke in the "monkey-is-penis" genre?'

Monkey Business: Rachel jokes that thanks to Marcel she has a Malibu Barbie 'that will no longer be wearing white to the wedding'.

Just Plain Weird: Maybe it's something to do with animal people in general (see 'TOW The Fake Monica') but the way the zoo administrator breaks the news of Marcel's 'death' to Ross is either insensitive or just downright cruel. Equally unsettling is the clandestine zoo janitor, who tries to bribe Ross AFTER telling him everything he needs to know. And then there's Erika, who Chandler accurately describes as '. . . a total whack job'!

Generation X: Chandler describes Erika as being the exact opposite of Kathy Bates in *Misery* (Rob Reiner, 1990). Phoebe inadvertently compares herself to Barney, a big, banal purple dinosaur that passes for edutainment these days. Brooke Shields made a number of films when she was a teenager, including the infamous *Blue Lagoon* (Randal Kleiser, 1980). Chris Isaak starred in *Twin Peaks: Fire Walk With Me* (David Lynch, 1992) and *Little Buddha* (Bernardo Bertolucci, 1993), and played the leader of the swat team in *Silence of the Lambs* (Jonathan Demme, 1990) but is best known as a singer/songwriter whose biggest hit was 'Wicked Game', the theme from David Lynch's *Wild at Heart* (David Lynch, 1990). Dan Castellaneta is, among others, the voice of Homer Simpson. Tahj Mowry played Teddy in the sitcom 'Full House'. Fred Willard played Larry Crockett in the TV series *Salem's Lot* (Tobe Hooper, 1979). Ross gets Marcel's attention by singing 'The Lion Sleeps Tonight'(see 'TOW All The Poker'). Chandler refers to George Gershwin's 'I Got Rhythm'. Incidentally, the episode title refers to the fact that it was transmitted the evening of Superbowl XXX (Dallas Cowboys v Pittsburgh Steelers – final result: Dallas Cowboys 27, Pittsburgh Steelers 17).

The Last Word: There are some lovely moments of slapstick in this episode. Watch out for what Matthew Perry does with the washing-up liquid when he first sees Erika, and the glee with which the gang throw glasses of water into Joey's face for increasingly ludicrous reasons, finishing with Chandler's 'You left the toilet seat up – you bastard!' Chris Isaak is possibly a little too laid back to be paired with Phoebe (in fact he looks positively wooden) but Dan Castellaneta's creepy janitor is fun, if only to see how different Homer Simpson and the man who does his voice really are.

213
'The One After The Superbowl, Part 2'

Writers: Mike Sikowitz & Jeffrey Astrof
Director: Michael Lembeck
First US transmission: 28.01.96
First UK transmission (C4): 06.09.96

Guest Cast: Jean-Claude Van Damme (himself), Julia Roberts (Susie Moss),
Lisa Roberts (Cathy), Seth Isler (Monkey Trainer),
Steven M. Porter (Security Guard)

Summary: As Ross discovers how 'starry' Marcel has become, Joey tries anything to get a part in Marcel's movie. Chandler bumps into Susie Moss, a girl he once ridiculed back in school, and asks her out on a date. Before they leave his apartment, Susie persuades him to wear her knickers (as you do) and then at the restaurant she manoeuvres him into the bathroom and gets him to strip off. She then runs off with his clothes in retribution for him pulling her dress up when they were in the fourth grade. Revenge for Susie is certainly a dish best served cold.

Rachel tries to ask Jean-Claude Van Damme for a date on behalf of Monica, but the movie star seems only interested in Rachel. This causes friction between the girls and Phoebe is forced to mediate. Rachel agrees to cancel the date and arrange one for Monica instead – by telling Van Damme that Monica is prepared to have a 'threesome' with him and Drew Barrymore . . .

Spoilt Rachel: During their second fight, Rachel hits Monica where it will really hurt: 'You give me back my sweater or it's "Handbag Marinara"!'

Slow Joey: Joey complains about Ross blowing him out for a monkey. Ross offers to reschedule for later in the week, but Joey responds bitterly, 'Yeah, unless you hook up with a bunch of pigeons.' When he discovers Chandler in the cubicle of the Gents at the restaurant he sympathetically observes, 'Talk about your bad luck . . . The first time you try panties and someone walks off with your clothes!'

Chandleresque: Speaking to two extras from *Outbreak II*: 'Are you guys in the movie or are you just really paranoid?' To an extra in fatigues: 'Nice camouflage, man. For a minute there I almost didn't see you.' Chandler tells Susie Moss, 'Back then I used to use humour as a defence mechanism. Thank God I don't do that any more.'

Phoebisms: (After breaking up the fight between Monica and Rachel): 'Y'know what? If we were in prison you guys would be, like, my bitches.' And Phoebe provides a cracking punchline to the episode, where she says that one of the strings on her guitar is broken and asks Chandler if she can borrow his 'G-string'.

Joey's an ACTOR!: He tries to get the attention of the director as he tells Phoebe about a 'HORRIBLE FLESH-EATING VIRUS!!' When he finally gets a part in the film they have to kill him off instantly because of his dire overacting.

Generation X: As Ross and Marcel do a tour of the city, we hear Barry Manilow's 'Looks Like We Made It'. Joey and Chandler whistle 'Buffalo Gals won't you come out tonight?' in the Gents, and 'Habenera (L'Amour Est Un Oiseau Rebelle)' from Bizet's 'Carmen' is played as Chandler walks out of the restaurant, covered only by his dignity and a toilet cubicle door. The name of Marcel's cuddly elephant is a play on the name of singer Harry Belafonte (famous for, among others, 'The Banana Boat Song – Day-O!'). Jean-Claude Van Damme is world renowned for his action movies (all of them terrible). Julia Roberts was the star of, among other movies, *Pretty Woman* (Garry Marshall, 1990). She claimed she begged the producers for a part because she was such a big *Friends* fan (though this may have had a lot to do with her also being a bigger Matthew Perry fan). Susie describes one of the actresses from the set as having an upper lip so hairy she could be mistaken for Gabe Kaplan, the eponymous star of the 70s sitcom *Welcome Back, Kotter*. The film that Marcel and Jean-Claude are making is a sequel to *Outbreak* (Wolfgang Petersen, 1995), in which a monkey is the source of a lethal virus that threatens to wipe out America. And yes, Marcel played that monkey too. Susie's revenge on Chandler is inspired by the Italian soft-porn movie *Eleven Days, Eleven Nights* (Aristide Massacchesi – a.k.a. Joe D'Amato, 1986), in which a couple *both* strip in a toilet cubicle. She then puts on his clothes but leaves her own, forcing him to walk out in drag, rather than naked as with Chandler.

The Story So Far: Marcel had a toy elephant called Harry Elephanté. His favourite food is bananacake with mealworm. Susie Moss was in fourth grade with Chandler, when he used to wear a denim cap with mirrors all over it. They both knew a guy called Stephen Hurs who would eat anything for money and a guy called David Stein who had no elbows. Susie remembers someone who was caught masturbating at school, but Chandler defensively tells her that 'he' had just been looking for his bus money. Chandler also tells her that he went to an all-boys school [high school].

The Last Word: Well this might be little more than a mid-season ratings boost but the bickering between the girls makes up for it (and Phoebe's 'STOP THE MADNESS!' outburst is the icing on top). Julia Roberts makes a fine guest-star, but Jean-Claude Van Damme is just embarrassing, something that the writers apparently became aware of after they saw how bad his delivery of his lines was.

214
'The One With The Prom Video'

Writer: Alexa Junge
Director: James Burrows
First US transmission: 01.02.96
First UK transmission (C4): 13.09.96

Guest Cast: Elliott Gould (Jack Geller), Christina Pickles (Judy Geller), Patrick Kerr (the Manager), Michael Ray Bower (Roy Gublick), Lou Thornton (Gail), Tim Bohn (Jonathan)

Summary: Joey gets his first cheque for *Days Of Our Lives* and decides to pay Chandler back for all of the favours he's done for him over the years. In addition to an envelope of money, he decides to give Chandler an obscenely tacky, engraved bracelet, which he insists Chandler wears. Unfortunately, as Chandler discovers, it also doubles as a 'woman repellent'. As Chandler launches into a routine about how much he hates it, Joey walks in and Chandler realises too late how much his ingratitude has hurt his best friend. Chandler begs Joey to forgive him, pointing out that, considering he hated it that much, the fact that he wore it anyway should count for something – but then he loses the bracelet!!

After Ross gets in the way of her speaking to a new man, Rachel spells out once and for all that she will never go out with him. That evening, Monica puts on a video of her and Rachel's prom night. But for Rachel at least, the events are shown from a different point of view to how she remembered them . . .

Freaky Monica: After the interview from hell, Monica takes five showers just to get herself clean. When Phoebe asks her if she has any other possibilities, she replies, 'There's the possibility that I won't make rent.' Her father does a little trick in pretending to pull a quarter from behind her ear, prompting her to ask, 'Anything larger back there?'

Phoebisms: Phoebs is pleased with her mastery of the male language: 'Dude, 11 o'clock, totally hot babe checkin' you out.' She adds as an afterthought, 'That was really good. I think I'm ready for my penis now.'

Chandleresque: Joey gives Chandler $812 as a payback. 'I don't know what Big Leon told ya,' says Chandler, 'but it's an even thousand if you want me for the whole night.' After an overenthusiastic Joey asks him what he thinks the bracelet will do for his sex life, Chandler says that it'll probably slow it down at first, then acknowledges, 'but once I get used to the extra weight, I'll be back on track'. When Ross asks what someone called Casey would want with Rachel, culture-junky

Bing can't help himself: 'I'm guessing he wants to do a little dance, y'know, make a little love . . . well, pretty much get down tonight.'

Dinosaurs ROCK!: Ross has dinosaur cheques, so he can get his money and learn something at the same time. When he lends Monica some money, she affectionately calls him a 'cheaposaurus'.

The Ballad of Ross & Rachel: Ross 'saves' Rachel from a conversation with an interesting, attractive man because he thinks she's being pestered. But Rachel takes exception to his constant interference in her life: 'OK, Ross, listen to me, I am not yours to save!' Ross still believes she is, having spoken to Phoebe, 'Well, you're, um, you're my lobster'. But Rachel has run out of patience with Ross, explaining to him that when she fell for him she got 'clobbered', and then when he fell for her, she got clobbered again. 'I'm tired of being clobbered, y'know? It's, it's just not worth it.' But later on, she sees the prom video and discovers that Ross had prepared himself to stand in as her date when it had appeared she'd been stood up, and all her recriminations fall away as she rushes over to kiss the man who has loved her all these years. 'See', says a smug Phoebe, 'he's her lobster!'

Parents – Who Needs 'Em?: Ross suggests that Monica should borrow some money from their parents, 'You feel guilty and tense around them already. You might as well make some money off of them.' Later on, Mr Geller puts his foot in it with Rachel when he talks about her parents' separation, letting slip that Rachel's parents have been unhappy since 'that incident in Hawaii'. Fortunately for Rachel, he doesn't enlarge on that. Unfortunately for Monica, the prom video gives her an insight into parental love that she could well have done without.

Just Plain Weird: The interviewer who seems to get turned on by the thought of Monica making a salad: 'Is it dirty? . . . I like it dirty.' Euch!

Generation X: Chandler paraphrases from K.C. and The Sunshine Band's 1975 single 'Get Down Tonight', as well as mentioning Liberace (the late, camp, flamboyant pianist), Mr T (star of the action adventure series *The A-Team*) and celebrated mime artist Marcel Marceau (of whom Joey does a surprisingly good impression). Ross's mention of 'Casey at the Bat' is a reference to Ernest Thayer's poem of the same name, which was published in the *San Francisco Examiner* on June 3, 1888. It became popular at the turn of the century and is a story of missed opportunity that sank deep into the heart of American culture, so it's ironic that Ross quotes it here. Ross tries to reassure Chandler, saying that his bracelet isn't at all flashy 'for a Goodfella', in reference to *Goodfellas* (Martin Scorsese, 1990). Chandler chats up a girl by joking with her that he reminds people of Dave Thomas, founder of Wendy's, one of America's largest burger chains (there are *some* branches in the U.K. too). Thomas appears as himself in a series of adverts in the States. Jack Geller is apparently an admirer of German tennis ace, Steffi Graf. Seeing Ross with a moustache and afro hairdo, Joey is reminded of the 70s sitcom *Welcome Back, Kotter*. We hear Ross playing 'Axel F', Harold Faltermeyer's theme tune to the *Beverley Hills Cop* trilogy.

The Story So Far: The Gellers decide to convert Monica's room into a gym, as Ross's was full of science trophies, plaques and merit badges and they 'didn't want to disturb them' (see 'TOW The Cat'). We knew that Monica was once a little larger than she is today (see 'TOW The Sonogram At The End'), but nothing could have prepared us for quite how big she was. As the gang watches her old prom video, she claims that the camera adds ten pounds, and Chandler asks her just how many cameras were on her. We also learn that Rachel has had a nose job, allegedly because of a 'deviated septum'. Rachel's date for the prom was a guy named Chip (see 'TOW The Cat'), and Monica's was Roy Gublick, who saw *Star Wars* 317 times!

The Last Word: What starts as just another episode ends as a watershed in the history of the show. After a couple of false starts Ross and Rachel are (finally!) together and *Friends* fans across the world cry with tears of joy. It's the sign of a good show that they can switch so effortlessly from comedy to pathos to romance in one short scene. But then this is *Friends*, and would we seriously expect anything less?

215

'The One Where Ross and Rachel . . . You Know'

Writers: Michael Curtis & Gregory S. Malins
Director: Michael Lembeck
First US transmission: 08.02.96
First UK transmission (C4): 20.09.96

Guest Cast: Tom Selleck (Richard Burke)

Summary: *Days Of Our Lives* extends Joey's contract, so he treats himself and Chandler to an enormous TV and a pair of leather reclining chairs. But the chairs are so comfortable the boys can't bring themselves to leave them even for a second. Meanwhile, Monica and Phoebe cater a party for Richard Burke, a friend of Monica's father. Richard has recently split from his wife and is trying to get back into socialising, but he finds all of his friends dull and spends most of the party in the kitchen with Monica. Despite the age gap, Monica and Richard are slowly drawn together by their strong mutual attraction.

Ross and Rachel go on their first date and prepare to consummate their relationship, but Rachel gets a fit of the giggles and the moment is lost. They are about to go on a second date when Ross is called to the museum. He finishes work too late for them to get to the restaurant they'd booked, so Ross improvises with some sweet music and a planetarium.

Freaky Monica: Mon is hesitant about dating Richard because he's a 'grown-up'. As Richard points out, he's a 'whole person who can drink' older than her. She, on the other hand, is worried about dating a guy whose pool she once peed in.

Chandleresque: Joey gets Chandler to cover his eyes to surprise him and Chandler warns him that he'd 'better be wearing clothes when I open my eyes'. Ross asks him if a girl has ever started laughing while they were making out: 'Yeah, but it was 1982 and my Flock of Seagulls haircut was tickling her chin.'

Boys Will Be Boys: The guys order pizza and get it delivered to the girls' apartment so they don't have to get out of their chairs: 'Inside – good. Outside – baaad!' When the fire alarm goes off in their building, Chandler checks the floor to see if it's getting hot yet.

The Ballad of Ross & Rachel: Ross is worried by Rachel's spontaneous hysterics each time he touches her ass. He tells the guys that he's wanted this since he was in '9th grade typing' and that he just wants it to be 'perfect and right' (no pressure from high expectations there then). The new couple on the block go to see a subtitled movie on their first date and finally consummate their relationship under a rug at the museum on possibly the most romantic date of all time (see 'TOW Chandler In A Box').

Dinosaurs ROCK!: Ross gets called to the museum because one of the displays has been set out incorrectly (someone got their *australopithicus* confused with their *homo habilus*. Duh!).

Cruelty to Animals: After Phoebe complains about cows having made the ultimate sacrifice just for their chairs, Chandler reassures her by telling her that they were chair-shaped cows: 'They never would have survived in the wild.'

Generation X: The guys watch an episode of *The Dick Van Dyke Show*, *Beavis and Butthead*, an infomercial for Miracle Wax and about two days' worth of non-stop TV. Flock of Seagulls were a Liverpool band from the early 80s whose biggest hit was 'Wishing (If I Had A Photograph Of You)' in 1983. *Xanadu* (Robert Greenwald, 1980) is evidently one of Phoebe's favourite films, but pretty much any sane person would say it sucks. Ross and Rachel make out to 'Wicked Game' by Chris Isaak (see 'TO After The Superbowl', Part 1) from the album of the same name. Tom Selleck's most famous role is that of Thomas Magnum in the TV show *Magnum P.I.*

The Story So Far: Richard's ex-wife was called Barbara, he has a daughter called Michelle, a grandson called Henry (with another on the way) and he is 48 years old. Monica is 27. Rachel remembers getting a kiss from Dr Burke when she'd crashed her bike outside his house aged seven. Rachel wears glasses (she didn't want to wear them on her first date with Ross). Ross knows very little about astronomy.

The Last Word: The title says it all, but what really makes this episode stand out is the amount of on-the-edge innuendo –

notably Chandler's joke about *australopithicus* never being erect because 'maybe he was nervous' and the 'premature ejaculation' set-up when Rachel rolls over onto the juice carton and quickly reassures Ross. Possibly the bravest subject an American sitcom can cover. Commendable.

216
'The One Where Joey Moves Out'

Writer: Betsy Bornes
Director: Michael Lembeck
First US transmission: 15.02.96
First UK transmission (C4): 27.09.96

Guest Cast: Elliott Gould (Jack Geller),
Christina Pickles (Judy Geller),
Tom Selleck (Dr Richard Burke),
Audrie Neenan (Emily, Judy Geller's friend),
Warren Berliner (Bob), Josie Di Vincenzo (Tattoo Artist), Stephen Samuels
(Arik, Jack Geller's friend)

Summary: Phoebe and Rachel decide to get tattoos. Rachel hasn't told Ross as she wants to surprise him, but when Ross tries to talk Phoebe out of getting hers, she in turn is forced to talk Rachel into doing what she wants to do and to be her own boss. However, after her tattoo is finished, Rachel discovers that Phoebe chickened out. But she is surprised by Ross's reaction to the rose she's had done on her hip – he loves it! Ross and Monica go to their father's birthday party. Everyone is quizzing Richard about his new 'twinkie' girlfriend and eventually Monica feels compelled to tell her parents that she and Richard are dating.

Joey is offered a new apartment by one of his co-stars. He considers taking it, but an argument with Chandler makes his mind up for him, leaving them with one final decision to make – who gets to keep the foosball table?

Phoebisms: While she has decided on a lily, to represent her Mother's open, giving spirit, she's equally tempted by the thought of Foghorn Leghorn.

Slow Joey: Joey is surprised to realise that Captain Crunch's eyebrows are on his hat, yet he hasn't worked out that he's been captain of a cereal for the last 40 years. He sees nothing wrong with licking a spoon and putting it straight back in the drawer and he used Chandler's toothbrush to unclog the drain. He's not completely dumb though, as he points out to Chandler that there's little difference between sharing a toothbrush and sharing soap: 'Think about the last thing I wash and the first thing you wash.' Playing foosball to decide who gets to keep it, Chandler boasts that Joey's little men are going to 'get scored on more times than your sister'. Joey is understandably appalled: 'Which sister?' And a surprisingly perceptive Joey breaks his best friend's heart when he points out, 'It's not like we agreed to live together forever. We're not Bert and Ernie.'

Chandleresque: Grossed out about Joey's unsanitary habits, Chandler cries, 'Oh God! Can open – worms *everywhere*!' When Joey expresses concern about leaving Chandler 'high and dry', he says, 'I've never been lower or wetter.'

Parents – Who Needs 'Em?: Joey asks Monica if she's going to tell her parents about Richard, to which she sarcastically says that of course she is, as she's decided to give her father a *stroke* for his birthday (which would be original at least). Ross is only a little more supportive: 'Remember when you were nine and Richard was 30 how Dad used to say, "God, I hope they get together"?' After Richard tells Monica that both his parents are dead, Monica cries, 'God, you are *so* lucky!'

Generation X: Phoebe momentarily considers getting a tattoo of Foghorn Leghorn, the Looney Toons rooster. Jack Geller describes Richard's revitalisation (thanks to his 'twinkie in the city') as being like a scene from *Cocoon* (Ron Howard, 1985). Courteney Cox was a cast member of the sequel, *Cocoon: The Return* (Daniel Petrie, 1988).

The Story So Far: Jack Geller celebrated turning 50 by buying himself a Porsche. Phoebe's Mother's name was Lily. Joey is 28 years old. Monica reminds Ross about the video she once saw of her parents having sex, telling him, 'I just caught the live show' (see 'TOW The Prom Video'). Joey and Chandler once used one of Rachel's bras to fling water balloons down at some Junior High kids. According to Judy Geller, Richard has a son (see 'TOW Chandler In A Box').

The Last Word: It must be hard for Jack and Judy Geller to accept that their 'little Harmonica' is dating an older man who just happens to be their best friend, but Monica's heart-warming speech about how much he means to her must have helped in some way to make it easier for them. Courteney Cox is superb in this episode, enjoying a lot of physical comedy (the slapstick squirting of the can of cream and the shocked expression on her face after witnessing her parents make out), as are the two Matt(hew)s. To see Chandler's expression after Joey moves out is just heartbreaking, especially when Joey runs back to give him one last hug.

217

'The One Where Eddie Moves In'

Writer: Adam Chase
Director: Michael Lembeck
First US transmission: 22.02.96
First UK transmission (C4): 04.10.96

Guest Cast: Adam Goldburg (Eddie Minowick),
Dee Dee Rescher (The Record Producer),
Barry Heins ('Pie In The Sky' Man), Linda Lutz (Horrible Woman)

Summary: Joey's happily moved into his new apartment, and decked it out with the biggest and weirdest collection of tat anyone's ever seen. Chandler, meanwhile, has decided to get a new roommate, and so Eddie moves in. Joey is surprised and a little hurt that he has been so quickly replaced, but Chandler appears to be getting on very well without him.

Phoebe has good news for the gang: she's been 'discovered' by a record producer who wants to tape a demo of 'Smelly Cat', make a video of the song, and possibly go on to record an album of Phoebe's songs. When everyone eventually sits down to watch the video, though, they realise that Phoebe's voice has been replaced by that of another, better singer.

With Rachel and Ross in the glory days of their new relationship, he is spending most of his free time round at Monica and Rachel's apartment. This is getting on Monica's nerves, and she and her brother soon devolve into the same kind of antics that led Monica to hate Ross as a child. Can the two of them smooth over their differences and, more importantly, can Rachel put up with their squabbling for much longer?

Slow Joey: He proudly shows off his new apartment, and its tacky *objets d'art*. But, leaving aside the plastic parrot, the porcelain dog, the rain-soaked fake window and the 'Muppet-skin' cushions, Joey's proudest novelty in his new home is the phone right by the toilet. Everyone else is a little freaked by this, and Monica makes him promise never to use that phone to speak to her.

Chandleresque: Alone for the first time in his apartment, Chandler sits on a kitchen worktop, wearing a pair of cuddly wolf slippers. He asks them if he should give Joey a call, and then squeezes the right slipper's ear. It makes a tinny barking noise, to which Chandler replies, 'Ask your slippers a question . . . you're going crazy.' Later, Joey and Chandler watch *Baywatch* in their separate apartments, talking all the while on the phone. Seeing Yasmine Bleeth break into a brisk jog, an excited Chandler cries, 'Run, Yasmine! Run like the wind!'

Phoebisms: When she goes into the studio to record 'Smelly Cat', she isn't aware that she'll be singing with backing vocalists. She's not entirely happy about this, though, and has to explain the ethic behind the song to them. But she must do it quickly, as studio time is money: 'The cat stinks, but you love it,' just about sums it up. When she finally sees the video, she initially believes that it's her own voice. 'I'm sorry, but I am so talented,' she asserts.

Spoilt Rachel: Carefully making her way past a customer seated at the bar, she stumbles and drops a slice of apple pie into the hood of his coat. She later implores Ross to rescue the pie from the coat as the man is leaving: to do so, Ross has to put on an act as a complete lunatic, who also plans to fish some coffee out of another man's trousers.

Dinosaurs ROCK!: Ross argues with a work colleague about whether Dino on *The Flintstones* was a velociraptor or not.

Generation X: Joey and Chandler watch *Baywatch*, admiring both Yasmine Bleeth and the character Lt Stephanie Holden (played by Alexandra Paul). As Chandler and Joey start really missing each other, we hear 'All By Myself' by Neilsson.

The Story So Far: This is the first time we hear the full 'Smelly Cat' lyrics.

The Last Word: With no hint of his insanity to come, Eddie makes a perfectly level impression on his debut. A fair episode, the best parts are the childish arguments between Ross and Monica, and the full video of 'Smelly Cat', but on the whole it's not that memorable.

218
'The One Where Dr Ramoray Dies'

Writers: Alexa Junge (story), Michael Borkow (teleplay)
Director: Michael Lembeck
First US transmission: 21.3.96
First UK transmission (C4): 11.10.96

Guest Cast: Tom Selleck (Dr Richard Burke),
Adam Goldburg (Eddie Minowick),
Roark Critchlow (Dr Horton), Mary Gallagher (Tilly),
Vanessa Sandin (Amber, Dr Drake's half-sister),
Brian Posehn (Messenger), Jim Reilly (Writer)

Summary: Joey foolishly claims in an interview that he has an influence over the scripts for *Days Of Our Lives*. When one of the script writers reads this, he writes a little surprise into the script. Suddenly, and unexpectedly, Dr Ramoray is to leave the series in a definitely final way – he falls down an elevator shaft to his death.

Meanwhile, Chandler is beginning to have problems with his new roommate. For one thing, Eddie just isn't into the same things as Chandler – he doesn't like sports, and won't watch *Baywatch*. When Phoebe forces him to try to get to know Eddie better, Chandler begins to discover that his roommate has a very big screw loose. The break-up from his girlfriend has left him in an unstable mental state, and when the girlfriend shows up again, he leaps to the wrong conclusion that Chandler has slept with her . . . *and* killed his fish!

Phoebisms: Chandler tries to get Phoebe to play a game of foosball with him, but she vehemently declines, describing the game as a 'human rights violation'. She is disgusted by the fact that all the little people are forced to do nothing but play football for the whole of their lives. When she suggests to Eddie that she, he and Chandler hang out and get to know each other, she slips away with the excuse that she has to go to her *Green Eggs and Ham* discussion group. 'Tonight, it's "Why He Would Not Eat Them on a Train".' We also hear the closing refrain of a new song about a crusty old man and maraca-playing rats.

Freaky Monica: After Joey has got the push from *Days Of Our Lives*, the gang gather at his apartment to cheer him up. The only nice thing Monica can think of to say is, 'I straightened out your shower curtain so you won't get mildew . . . to me, that's nice.' We also *don't* discover how many people she's had sex with, although it's 'definitely less than a ballpark'.

The Ballad of Ross & Rachel: Rachel makes the fatal error of saying that sex with Paolo was 'meaningless, animal sex'. Ross immediately wonders what's so bad about his technique that means they can't even have 'chipmunk sex'. Rachel desperately tries to claw back the situation, claiming that sex with Ross is different because they 'connect', and saying that it's a great deal better than Paolo sex because of that. Once he's convinced that she's telling the truth, Ross takes the plunge and promises Rachel some animal sex in his own style (complete with hilarious growls and snorts).

Just Plain Weird: The cracks in Eddie's veneer of normality are starting to show. After he becomes convinced that Chandler has slept with Tilly, his ex, Chandler suspects that 'he's stolen all the insoles from my shoes'. He also buys himself a goldfish – although it's only a goldfish-shaped biscuit – and he names it Chandler. Can anyone else hear that violin strain from *Psycho*?

Generation X: Phoebe mentions Dr Seuss's book *Green Eggs and Ham*. Sean Penn is one of Hollywood's maverick actors, having appeared in, among other movies, *Casualties of War* (Brian De Palma, 1989) and *Shanghai Surprise* (Jim Goddard, 1986) in which he starred alongside his then wife, Madonna.

The Story So Far: According to Eddie's ex-girlfriend, his surname is 'Minowick'. Richard tells Monica that his ex-wife

Barbara was his high-school sweetheart, and that they were married for 30 years. Rachel tells Ross that the only guys she's ever slept with apart from himself, are Billy Dreskin, Pete (the weeper) Carney (see 'TOW The Candy Hearts'), Barry and Paolo. Richard and Ross argue over which 'nam movie starred John Savage with no legs (it was *The Deer Hunter* – Michael Cimino, 1978) and which starred Jon Voight where he couldn't feel his legs (*Coming Home* – Hal Ashby, 1978) – Richard was right. Dr Drake Ramoray has a half-sister called Amber and a half-brother called Ramon.

The Last Word: The sex farce that takes place in Monica and Rachel's apartment, as they argue over the condom, while Ross and Richard discuss moustaches and the Vietnam War, is excellent; as are Chandler's growing fear of Eddie, and Rachel's desperate attempts to placate a hurt Ross. And poor old Joey. We're sad to see the back of Drake Ramoray, but he more than makes up for it with his final on-screen line. Realising he can't improvise his way out of falling down the lift shaft, he ignores a character's pledge of love for him, saying merely, 'Yeah, whatever . . .' before stepping into the black abyss.

219
'The One Where Eddie Won't Go'

Writers: Michael Curtis & Greg Malins
Director: Michael Lembeck
First US transmission: 28.03.96
First UK transmission (C4): 18.10.96

Guest Cast: Adam Goldberg (Eddie Minowick),
June Gable (Estelle Leonard), James Michael Tyler (Gunther)

Summary: The girls are all fired up by a book called 'Be Your Own Windkeeper' that shows them how men steal their 'wind', preventing them from becoming Goddesses. But instead of empowering them, the book just makes the girls bicker and fall out. Despite having *Days Of Our Lives* on his résumé, Joey is finding it hard to get work. After he gets a Visa bill so big it comes in two envelopes, Joey is forced to audition for the small role of a cab driver in another soap opera. Unfortunately he doesn't get the part and is forced to stand by and watch as all of his stuff is reclaimed by the companies. Back at Joey's old home, Eddie's behaviour is getting worse and Chandler decides he's had enough – he wants him out! But every time he tells him to leave he seems to forget. In the end he resorts to using Eddie's memory problems against him, convincing him that he's never lived there and that Joey never moved out. When a confused Eddie finally leaves, Chandler turns to Joey: 'Welcome home, man.'

Phoebisms: Having introduced the girls to the life-changing book, Phoebs accuses Joey of foisting upon them 'phallic-shaped man cakes'.

Slow Joey: Joey becomes uncharacteristically verbose after Chandler buys him Word-of-the-Day toilet paper. After Ross complains about Rachel's infatuation with the book, Joey notes: 'See this is why I don't date women who read'.

Joey's an Actor!: Estelle, his agent, puts him up for cab driver number two in *Another World*, but Joey thinks this is too much of a step backwards: 'How can I go from being a neurosurgeon to driving a cab?' He eventually goes for the interview and tells the casting director that he has a background in medical acting. Estelle ends up giving him the same advice she gave to Al Minser and his Pyramid of dogs: 'Take any job you can get, and don't make on the floor.'

Spoilt Rachel: Having read the book, Rachel turns on Ross, demanding why they always have to follow his timetable (Ross points out that it's the movie theatre that has the timetable). She later buys the girls some cakes as an apology for arguing with them, then when they accept that she's sorry she takes them away because otherwise they'd come out of her pay cheque.

Gunther's an Actor?!: He once appeared on *All My Children* as Bryce until they killed him off in an avalanche.

Just Plain Weird: And Eddie comes in for the third episode on the run. He's started dehydrating fruit and watching Chandler while he sleeps, and later on he turns up with a show dummy's head that he stole from Macy's department store. He also has selective memory loss and cannot seem to grasp that Chandler has thrown him out three times.

Generation X: Chandler tells Eddie that he'd prefer Hannibal Lector from *Silence of the Lambs* (Jonathan Demme, 1990) as a roommate. Later on he sings 'Ding Dong The Psycho's Gone', in reference to 'Ding Dong The Witch Is Dead' from *The Wizard of Oz* (Victor Fleming, 1939). Rachel compares the book they're all reading to J.R.R. Tolkien's *The Hobbit*. *Another World* is another of NBC's daytime soaps, which tells the ongoing story of four families living in the fictional Bay City in Illinois.

The Story So Far: The girls reassess their past relationships: Monica reminds Phoebe about how she let 'The Puppet Guy' 'wash his feet in the pool of [her] inner power' (see 'TOW The Boobies'), and Phoebe points out that Monica allowed Paul into her 'forest of righteous truth' on the first date (see 'Pilot'). Monica also accuses Rachel of cheating her out of a chance with Danny Arshak in 9th Grade after a 'Spin the Bottle' game, as Monica was convinced the bottle had been pointing at her, 'Only 'cause you took up half the circle,' counters Rachel. Rachel reveals that Phoebe slept with Jason Hurley one hour after he broke up with Monica. Chandler has lost the foosball and replaced it with a dried cantaloupe.

The Last Word: 'How do you expect me to grow if you won't let me blow?' If the girls have learned one thing from that book it's that they don't need a book to tell them how to run their lives, even one with such interesting metaphors. But thank God Eddie finally goes ('Goodbye, you fruit-drying psychopath') and Joey comes home where he belongs. The scene where he and Chandler move the porcelain dog into the living room is a treat, finished perfectly by Chandler's reactions to it: 'Is he housetrained or is he gonna leave little bathroom tiles all over the place? . . . Stay! Good fake dog.'

220
'The One Where Old Yeller Dies'

Writers: Michael Curtis & Greg Malins (story), Adam Chase (teleplay)
Director: Michael Lembeck
First US transmission: 04.04.96
First UK transmission (C4): 25.10.96

Guest Cast: Tom Selleck (Dr Richard Burke),
Jane Sibbett (Carol Willick), Jessica Hecht (Susan Bunch)

Summary: Phoebe discovers just how protective her mother was when she finds a whole load of films with sad endings that her mother had never allowed her to watch. Acquiring copies of some well-known emotional wrenchers, Phoebe gets a rude awakening as she realises that the world might not be the nice place she's always believed it is.

Monica convinces Joey and Chandler to take Richard along to the Knicks game with them, despite their aversion to spending time with someone that, erm, mature. But she's surprised by the effect her boyfriend has on the guys when Joey starts holding a cigar between his lips and Chandler grows a moustache. They eventually blow it when they accidentally compare Richard to their own 'Dads' and Richard realises that maybe they still have a problem with the age gap.

Ross is excited by his son, Ben, managing to pull himself up to stand, but his excitement wanes when he finds out that Carol and Susan saw him do the same thing the previous week. Ross feels that he's missing out on too many 'first time' things and asks to look after him for a whole weekend. When he sees how badly Rachel handles Ben, he tries to reassure her that she'll be better when it's their own children. This freaks Rachel out a little, especially when she discovers that Ross has got their whole future mapped out in his mind. But after they discuss their thoughts on the future, and after Rachel has been shown how to change Ben's nappy, they both seem just a little bit happier, especially Rachel, who is the first person to hear Ben's first word!

Freaky Monica: Even though she is hopelessly in love with Richard, she still makes him smoke on the balcony, just like she did with Chandler.

Phoebisms: Her new-found pessimism is just as extremist as her previously rose-tinted optimism: 'You're ultimately just gonna die or get divorced or have to blow your pet's head off.'

Chandleresque: Monica tries to divide up the food, saying she has a leg, three breasts and a wing, and Chandler can't resist asking, 'How d'you find clothes that fit?' He then tries to explain why he and Joey don't want to invite Richard to the game, only to dig himself further into a hole: 'He's, y'know, old . . . er than some people,' adding as an afterthought, 'but, um, younger than some buildings.' When Chandler makes a joke about Richard's age, he retaliates by mocking Chandler's moustache, 'When puberty hits that thing's really gonna kick in.'

Slow Joey: The guys phone Monica to ask what she's wearing. When she claims to have nothing on but rubber gloves, the guys are through her door in a second, only to be disappointed by the sight of a fully clothed Mon: 'One of these times you're gonna really be naked and we're not gonna come over,' Joey warns. Monica is evidently tiring of Joey asking if she sees other women naked at the gym, and of confirming that no, she doesn't ever look.

Poor Ross: Trying to get Ben to say 'Dada' he gets only 'Seh!', which he erroneously hopes will grow into 'Seh-condary care giver'. He later misses out on Ben's first word, but gets to hear his second – which kind of makes up for everything else.

The Ballad of Ross & Rachel: Ross asks her to hold Ben for a moment and she grasps him gingerly. When Ross tells her she should hold him like she might hold a football, she snaps: 'This *is* how I would hold a football' (see 'TOW The Football). She apologises, saying she's not very good with babies, 'I haven't been around them, I mean, you know, since I *was* one.' After Ross's pre-planning her life makes her run in terror from Central Perk, Rachel tells him that she doesn't want to think that far ahead, and jokes that he's probably already named their children – only to discover that he's been thinking of the name 'Emily', thanks to 'The Big Book Of Children's Names' (see 'TOW Joey's Dirty Day'). Rachel explains to him that this was one of the reasons she left Barry – that her whole life had been decided for her. Ross agrees that he'll try to understand that, so long as Rachel accepts that he's the kind of person who does think ahead to their future, simply because he's certain that they'll end up together. In among all this bickering, they suddenly realise that they've both just told each other that they love each other for the first time . . .

Cruelty to Animals: Phoebe's pertinent outcry after the end of 'Old Yeller': 'What kind of a sick doggy snuff-film is this?'

Generation X: Poor Phoebe. *Old Yeller* (Robert Stevenson, 1957) is supposed to be a family movie, yet it's famous for emotionally scarring more people for life than any single other childhood experience. Other famous weepies that Phoebe tries are: *Love Story* (Arthur Hiller, 1970), in which Ryan O'Neal falls in love with Ali MacGraw, and then she dies; *Brian's Song* (Buzz Kulik, 1971), in which James Caan plays an American football player dying of lung cancer; *Terms of Endearment* (James L. Brookes, 1983), in which Debra Winger's character dies; *Alive* (Frank Marshall, 1993), in which a football team's plane crashes and they're forced to eat the flesh of the victims; *E.T. – the Extra-Terrestrial* (Steven Spielberg, 1982): boy meets alien, alien dies, alien comes back to life and leaves; *Rocky II* (Sylvester Stallone, 1979), where Rocky loses; *Charlotte's Web* (Charles Nichols, 1973), based on the children's book by E.B. White, in which a spider changes everyone's lives, and a pig gives birth and dies; *Pride of the Yankees* (Sam Wood, 1942), in which, Phoebe is shocked to discover, a guy named Lou Gehrig dies of Lou Gehrig's disease (otherwise known as amythropic lateral sclerosis – by doctors); and the classic Christmas flick, *It's a Wonderful Life* (Frank Capra, 1946). Unable to cope with all this emotion, Phoebe ends up watching tapes of *Sesame Street* with Ben, though even this is a little too emotional for her. Ross refers to Joey's roommate as 'The Artist Formerly Known As Chandler', in reference to how the rock 'genius' Prince renamed himself. Phoebe's phrase 'snuff movie' came from the notoriously gory *Snuff* (Michael Findlay, 1974) – the movie that shocked America after allegations that actors in it were killed for real on screen.

The Story So Far: Chandler has a friend called Eric Prower who has bad breath, and one called Dan who incessantly pokes people with his finger as he talks. Monica and Ross think that, with the moustache, Chandler looks like their Aunt Sylvia (see 'TOW The Dozen Lasagnes'). Ross and Rachel have been dating for six weeks. Ben's first word is 'Hi!'

The Last Word: We're with Rachel on this one – saying

'poopy diaper' doesn't make the thought of changing a baby's nappy any less unpleasant, but then again, if it's a kid as cute as Ben we'd probably . . . still ask someone else to do it. Tom Selleck continues to solidify his position in the cast, verbally sparring with Chandler and coming off the better for it, but as you've probably guessed, Phoebe is the show-stealer this episode, especially when she and Ben are left alone to watch *Sesame Street*. It's rare for a grown-up to get just how scary some supposedly 'family' entertainment actually is (we know one person who finds *Tom and Jerry* absolutely terrifying) and it's just so reassuring to think that Ben will have Phoebe as an 'auntie' when he's growing up, just to keep his mind open and warn him when TV gets just that little bit too unsettling. Charming.

221
'The One With The Bullies'

Writers: Sebastian Jones & Brian Buckner
Director: Michael Lembeck
First US transmission: 25.04.96
First UK transmission (C4): 01.11.96

Guest Cast: Peter DeLuise (Carl, the Big Bully),
Nicky Katt (Arthur, the Little Bully),
Laraine Newman (Mrs Buffay), James Michael Tyler (Gunther)
and introducing: Giovanni Ribisi (Frank Jr)

Summary: After a series of typically tenuous 'coincidences', Phoebe becomes convinced that the world is sending her signs telling her to try to find her father. When she tries to go up to her father's house again, she's attacked by the family's overenthusiastic dog. She takes this as a bad sign and tries to leave, only to accidentally drive over the dog. Having taken the dog to the vets, she returns it to its owners only to discover that her father has left his second family too. A despondent Phoebe gives up on ever meeting her father again, but consoles herself with meeting the half-brother she never knew she had.

Monica has become hooked on stock trading after spending too much time watching the Business Channel. To avoid taking a job in a 50s-themed restaurant, she puts every penny into stock using a highly dubious selection process. But when she ends up losing it all in bad investments, she's forced to take the 50s restaurant job after all.

At Central Perk, Ross and Chandler come into conflict with a pair of bullies after one of them steals Chandler's hat. When the guys are forced to ask Gunther to help, the bullies warn them away from ever setting foot in the coffee house again. Eventually, Ross decides that enough is enough and the pair head down to Central Perk to sort out the situation. Removing their jewellery, watches and keys, the four men prepare for a rumble . . .

Freaky Monica: She gets hooked on stock trading because she sees some stock with her initials: 'Sometimes I have to watch for two or three hours before it comes up again but when it does it's pretty exciting.' According to Joey, she threatens one of the stock traders on the phone by warning him not to make her 'come down there and kick your Wall Street butt!' She ends up buying stock in CHP because she used to fancy Eric Estrada, and ZXY because she thought it sounded 'zexy'. All this because she doesn't want to wear 'flame-retardant boobs'.

Slow Joey: We get a better idea of why the guys are always round at Monica's for food as Joey makes himself an olive loaf and ham spread sandwich (no mayo). Rachel comments, 'The dog will lick himself but he will not touch your sandwich – what does that tell you?' When Monica claims her new motto to be 'Get out before they go down', Joey boasts: 'That is *so* not my motto.' He later phones the owners of the dog for Phoebe. When Rachel asks him why he put on a strange voice for the call, Joey just shrugs: 'Hard to say.' Seems he just can't help but act.

Chandleresque: Joey volunteers to go down to Central Perk and get Chandler's cap back: 'Nah, forget it,' says a defeated Chandler. 'It's probably stripped and sold for parts by now.' When the bullies lay a claim to the couch in Central Perk, Chandler unadvisedly suggests: 'I'll tell you what – you call the couch and then . . . and then we'll call the couch, and we'll see who it comes to'. In preference to confronting the bullies, he suggests to Ross that they might just try to lose their virginities again, 'because I think actually mine's growing back'. Before the rumble can begin, a robber runs off with the cap containing all their valuables. As the four men chase him, Chandler trips on a little girl's skipping rope.

Gunther's a Hero!: Gunther briefly intervenes in the War of the Couch.

Cruelty to Animals: Schnoodle, the Buffay's dog, immediately attacks Phoebe: 'Alright, get the Hell off my leg, you yippity piece of crap!' After waiting till nightfall for the dog to go away, Phoebe accidentally knocks over the dog, which was hiding in front of her cab. The doctor tells her that he'll need stitches and that 'only once in a blue moon does a dog's ear grow back'.

Just Plain Weird: Phoebe's idea of a sign is just out there! OK, so the buffet and franks references are understandable, but the rotisseries with spinning chicken, which is not, as Monica suggests, his Indian name, remind her of how she 'chickened out' from seeing her father last time, and somehow Phoebe gets from hamburger to pharmacist with less degrees of separation than Kevin Bacon. Later on, we see that she carries round a small box of Kibbles dog food just in case . . . she finds a dog or something. But now at least we can see it does run in the family, as Frank Buffay sounds weird (he liked stilts), and Frank Jr's definitely weird (see 'TOW Frank Jr').

Generation X: One of the dishes at the diner is the Laverne and Curly Fries in tribute to the criminally under-appreciated 70s sitcom, *Laverne and Shirley*, which was a spin-off from *Happy Days*. Monica's first 'performance' there is the 1978 anthem 'Y.M.C.A.' by The Village People. Eric Estrada was the co-star of the long-running highway patrol series *CHiPS*. After Ross insists they go down to the coffee house to sort out the bullies, Chandler calls him 'Custer' in reference to the General famous for his 'last stand'. Peter DeLuise is the son of actor Dom DeLuise (the little guy in all those 70s Burt Reynolds movies). Giovanni Ribisi appeared in *The X Files* as Darren Peter Oswald in the episode 'D.P.O.'.

The Story So Far: Monica now works at a 50s-themed diner where the staff are forced to dress in 50s costumes and sing.

Although this episode introduces Giovanni Ribisi as Frank Jr, Ribisi first appeared back in 'TOW The Baby On The Bus'. For the purposes of continuity, we're presuming that the character he played then was also Frank Buffay.

The Last Word: This is possibly the most disappointing episode of the season. It's OK, but it does kind of feel like everyone else has been given storylines just to give them something to do while Phoebe goes in search of her father again. Rachel and Joey are pretty much sidelined while the Gellers and Chandler deal with their problems, which aren't really that interesting, and while the climax to the episode is hilarious, Monica's ensemble dance routine to Y.M.C.A., it's maybe just a little too late to save this episode from veering towards the quality threshold of 'Who's the Boss'.

222
'The One With Two Parties'

Writer: Alexa Junge
Director: Michael Lembeck
First US transmission: 02.05.96
First UK transmission (C4): 08.11.96

Guest Cast: Marlo Thomas (Sandra Green),
James Michael Tyler (Gunther), Nancy Rubin (Guest), Lewis Dix (Man)
and introducing: Rob Leibman (Dr Leonard Green)

Summary: The gang are planning a surprise birthday party for Rachel. After much deliberation, it is decided not to invite her parents; their impending divorce is getting Rachel down, and her mother and father are incapable of being in the same room without arguing. But Monica admits that she has already invited Mrs Green, and then Dr Green turns up out of the blue to wish his daughter a happy birthday.

In an effort to make sure the parents don't meet, a second party is set up in Chandler and Joey's apartment. Here, Dr Green is kept in the dark, while Mrs Green is entertained in Monica's apartment. As the evening goes on, people desperately try and slip away to Joey and Chandler's party, since Monica's consists of no-fun party games, which she rules with an obsessive iron fist. With the night drawing to a close, Rachel is once again depressed, as she has had to listen to her mother and father independently moan about the other's foibles. Could this be the worst birthday she's ever had?

Freaky Monica: While planning the party, she outlines exactly how things are going to work. The others ask why they can't just get a gang of people round, to have some drinks and some fun: 'Why do we always have parties with committees?' they ask her. At her party later on, she is getting people to write their most embarrassing memories down on pieces of paper. She gives everyone a marker pen, and then makes a little speech about making sure that they put the caps back on – firmly, so they click. It's no wonder that Phoebe has to run a secret railroad of escapee party people, helping them across the hallway to freedom at Joey and Chandler's. At one point, Phoebe makes a distraction so that some people can get away: she looks at one of Monica's tables and gasps, 'Did someone forget to use a coaster?'

Slow Joey: When the gang are trying to decide who to invite, Joey vetoes Shannon Cooper, saying 'she steals stuff'. This is shorthand for the real reason – that he slept with her, then never called her again. When Stacy Roth is suggested, he says, 'She also steals.' It's quite clear, though, that he's fooling no-one.

Spoilt Rachel: She tells Ross that she loves the earrings he bought her. When he says that she can exchange them if she wants, she says, 'Now I love you even more' (see 'TOW The Embryos').

Chandleresque: When he sees Rachel is upset by her bickering parents, he calls her 'Tiger', explaining, 'When my parents were getting divorced, I got a lot of "Tigers" . . .' Rachel asks him how he coped when his mother and father split up, and he confesses that he relied on a 'carefully regimented program of denial and bedwetting'.

Poor Ross: Throughout the episode, to cover for the fact that he's running errands for her husband, Ross has to pretend to Mrs Green that he drinks the same drinks as Dr Green, wears the same glasses, and smokes the same cigarettes. This leads Mrs Green to suggest to Rachel that she see a therapist – she's obviously hooked up with Ross just because he reminds her of her father.

Yo Gunther!: He lives in mortal terror of Monica's obsessive-ness, and is grateful to Phoebe when she says that she can get him out of her dull party. The guilty look on his face when he is eventually discovered by Monica at Joey and Chandler's party is unique.

Generation X: As the party begins to get farcical, Chandler ponders what 'Jack and Chrissy' would do – another reference to the sitcom *Three's Company* (see his comments in 'Pilot'). Ross mentions Neil Sedaka, the pianist/singer with the perma-nently upbeat persona. According to Dr Green, one of Rachel's mother's favourite films is *The Bridges of Madison County* (Clint Eastwood, 1995).

The Story So Far: We learn that the place where Monica works is called 'The Moondance Diner'.

The Last Word: This is a fantastic episode, a good, confident attempt at a farce. Throughout the whole thing, the tension rises as we wonder exactly when Mrs and Dr Green are going to see each other. It seems such an inevitability, that the fact that they never do comes as a surprise. When the two of them are in the hallway outside the apartments at the same time, the lengths to which the gang go to ensure they don't meet are phenomenal. Firstly, Joey, Chandler and Ross dance Dr Green across the hallway, then Joey has to passionately kiss Mrs Green to hide her from her husband. Terrific stuff.

223

'The One With The Chicken Pox'

Writer: Brown Mandell
Director: Michael Lembeck
First US transmission: 09.05.96
First UK transmission (C4): 15.11.96

Guest Cast: Tom Selleck (Dr Richard Burke), Charlie Sheen (Ryan), Dorien Wilson (Mr Kogen), Mary-Pat Green (Jeannie), Steve Park (Scott)

Summary: Phoebe's excited as Ryan, her on-off boyfriend in the Navy, is coming into dock. He spends months at a time in a submarine, visiting Phoebe on those few days he has free. This time, he's coming for two weeks, and Phoebe's delighted to be able to spend so much time with him. But her plans run aground when she discovers that she's got chicken pox, and that Ryan has never had it: in theory, he should stay well clear of her. Romance and sheer physical attraction take over, though, and soon they both have 'The Pox'.

Monica is beginning to have trouble with Richard, because he doesn't 'have a thing'. While she is crazily obsessive about almost everything, Richard is quite easygoing. He frantically tries to think of something, anything, kooky about him, to make Monica feel like less of a freak.

Joey, now out of work, accepts a job as a temporary processor at Chandler's company. He treats this work as an acting job, slipping into the role of 'Joseph the Processing Guy', making up a wife and children to fill out his character's background. While Chandler thinks this is bad enough, things take a turn for the worse when Joey starts to point the finger at Chandler over lax working practices. Eventually, Chandler realises he has to get rid of 'Joseph the Processing Guy', or his job could be in danger.

Chandleresque: The episode opens with Chandler and Monica arguing over ownership of a muffin. He solves the problem by licking right down one side of it. As he begins to eat it, Phoebe arrives to tell everyone about Ryan. 'This guy goes down for, like, two years at a time?' asks Rachel. Chandler, desperate to make the obvious joke, can only give a muffled scream, as his mouth is gummed up with cake. 'That'll teach you to lick my muffin,' says Monica. More muffled protests ensue.

Freaky Monica: She enters her bedroom to see that Richard has made the bed, but he's got it all wrong: the duvet tag should be at the bottom right corner, and the flowers in the pattern should point towards the headboard, 'because . . . the head of the bed is where the sun would be.' Monica then sets about trying to organise Richard's life by her own mad rules. First of all, she makes sure everything on his desk is perpendicular ('If it's not a right angle, it's a wrong angle,' Richard intones), then she says she's going to set all his clocks 'to my time' (which differs, depending on which room of the house you're in). All this adds up to make this one of the definitive Freaky Monica episodes.

Phoebisms: She finds the fact that she has chicken pox 'so ironic', considering she's a vegetarian. When she's bidding a final goodbye to Ryan as they stand outside the gang's favourite haunt, she says that she is sorry they couldn't do everything she'd planned, 'like a picnic in Central Park, a coffee at Central Perk – Oh! I just got that!' There's also a mention of a song of hers called 'Salt-Water Taffy Man', which the gang mistakenly presume she wrote about Ryan.

The Ballad of Ross & Rachel: Rachel is a very big fan of the naval uniform, it turns out, and Ross stops at nothing to hire his own for the night. When he appears to collect her from work, he swoops her into his arms and begins to carry her out of Central Perk. Rachel ruins the spontaneity of the moment, though. First, she realises that she's left the cappuccino machine on, then she forgets her purse . . . Eventually, Ross just dumps her on the sofa, and says he'll meet her upstairs.

Generation X: Charlie Sheen is the star of such films as *Platoon* (Oliver Stone, 1986), *Wall Street* (Stone again, 1987) and the *Hot Shots* comedies (Jim Abrahams, 1991, 1993) as well as being the brother of Emilio Estevez and son of Martin Sheen. When Ross walks into Central Perk dressed as a sailor we hear a rendition of 'Up Where We Belong', a nod to the ending of *An Officer And A Gentleman* (Taylor Hackford, 1982).

The Story So Far: All of the gang have had chicken pox, apart from Phoebe – until now. Richard mentions Jim Croce's song 'Bad, Bad, Leroy Brown', who was the baddest, not the fattest, man in town. As Ross leaves Rachel in Central Perk, telling her he'll see her 'upstairs', we can presume that the coffee house is on the same block as the friends' apartments (but round the corner from the views we usually see when they track up from the street to a window).

The Last Word: Not one of the best episodes, but it has a few things to recommend it. Phoebe and Ryan's lost battle to avoid scratching is hugely entertaining, as is Monica's fussiness overdrive. The big let-down, though, is the Chandler and Joey plotline: Joey seems a little bit too clever here, being devious

in the way he gets people to like him. It's frankly wrong that
Joey should get one over Chandler in anything other than
chasing women.

224
'The One With Barry And Mindy's Wedding'

Writers: Ira Ungerleider (story), Brown Mandell (teleplay)
Director: Michael Lembeck
First US transmission: 16.05.96
First UK transmission (C4): 22.11.96

Guest Cast: Tom Selleck (Dr Richard Burke),
Mitchell Whitfield (Barry Farber),
Marie Hupp (Mindy Hunter-Farber), Peter Spears (Joel),
Jackie Bright (Mr Weinberg), Fritzi Burr (Mrs Weinberg),
Mindy Sterling (Wedding Planner), Maggie Wheeler (Janice)

Summary: Joey auditions for Warren Beatty for a part that
demands he convincingly kisses another man and, apparently,
Mr Beatty feels that he's a good actor but a lousy kisser.
Phoebe agrees to let him practice on her (having already kissed
him once), but Monica suggests that maybe Joey's problem is
that he's just not used to kissing men. Unfortunately for Joey,
none of his male friends are willing to go that far to help him in
his career – despite many attempts on Joey's part to convince
them otherwise. Eventually Ross kisses Joey – only to hear
that he'd already been turned down for the part.

Asked to be Mindy's matron of honour, Rachel prepares
herself to face all of the guests who'd turned up for her
non-wedding to Barry. Her lack of confidence isn't helped by
having to wear a dress that makes her look like the pink
fondant version of Little Bo Peep. It's made worse when she
ends up walking down the aisle with her dress tucked into her
knickers, and worse still when she finds out that all of the
wedding guests had been told that she ran out on Barry
because she'd gone mad with syphilis.

Monica and Richard are prompted by the wedding to assess
their own future together. Monica is desperate to have children, so she's understandably disappointed to discover that

Richard is not that keen on going through the parent thing again so late in life. Such a problem is too great for the relationship to withstand and the couple realise that it'd be for the best if they separated.

... and Chandler begins a relationship via the internet with a married woman. Realising he's falling for her, he agrees to meet up with her. She finally arrives at Central Perk – it's Janice, and the couple fall instantly into a passionate kiss.

Slow Joey: He complains that saying he's not a good kisser is like someone accusing Mother Theresa of not being a good mother.

Chandleresque: He admits to sometimes getting a little 'defended and quippy'. He visits the website for the Guggenheim Museum because his cyber-chick likes museums and he likes funny words. He asks Joey: 'How come you don't fall down more?' after he makes a daft suggestion.

Phoebisms: She tries to convince Chandler to give his cyber-girlfriend a chance, despite the fact she's married: 'If you don't meet her now, you're gonna be kicking yourself when you're 80 – which is hard to do and that's how you break a hip!' Yeah, Phoebs, we just about understand you there.

Cruelty to Animals: Monica reads an article that advises against throwing rice at weddings because rice can kill pigeons. Richard observes that this is why so few pigeons eat at sushi bars.

Generation X: Warren Beatty is a respected actor/director, having starred in films such as *Bonnie and Clyde* (Arthur Penn, 1967) and directed *Heaven Can Wait* (1978), *Reds* (1981) and *Dick Tracy* (1990). He's also managed to acquire a reputation as a bit of a Lothario, hence the comedy in Phoebe's question, 'What does Warren Beatty know about kissing?' When Monica tries to reassure Richard over her desires for children, she says that she's thinking way into the future, a time when 'apes [are] taking over the planet', in a reference (unsurprisingly) to *Planet of the Apes* (Franklin J. Schaffner, 1968). 'Copa Cobana' has become a bit of an anthem for its writer/singer, the legendary Barry Manilow. The website for the Guggenheim Museum can be found at www.guggenheim.org and is really informative. Honest!

The Story So Far: In 8th grade, Rachel was forced to sing 'Copa Cobana' in front of the whole school but she 'freaked out' and ran off stage. Mindy takes Barry's surname to create a new hyphened name for herself – Mindy Hunter-Farber.

The Last Word: Ross really is the perfect partner here, standing by his girlfriend and making her confront her fears – and being there for her afterwards. His speech at the wedding is really sweet, acknowledging just how much courage it took for Rachel to turn up, though he might have wanted to leave out the reference to syphilis. Rachel's impromptu performance of 'Copa Cobana' is just painful, yet she manages to finish with at least the dignity she had been striving for. It's sad, though, to see a couple as good as Richard and Monica splitting up, especially as Tom Selleck has been such a welcome addition to the regular cast. And, of course, Chandler's one chance of love comes round again, and the cast's reaction to Janice's appearance is spectacular (all together now, 'OH – MY – GAHHHDDD!!'). On reflection, maybe the episode should have ended here, as the payoff with Ross finally agreeing to kiss Joey isn't really as good. But Joey is, for once, absolutely right: 'Rachel is a very lucky girl.'

Third Season

1996–1997

25 Episodes

301

'The One With The Princess Leia Fantasy'

Writers: Michael Curtis & Gregory S. Malins
Director: Gail Mancuso
First US transmission: 16.09.96
First UK transmission (C4): 04.07.97

Guest Cast: Maggie Wheeler (Janice),
Christina Pickles (Judy Geller), Elliott Gould (Jack Geller)

Summary: Since Monica broke off the relationship with Richard, she's done nothing but mooch around the house and everyone soon realises that she hasn't slept for days. Every little thing reminds her of Richard – even a clump of hair she finds in the bathroom drain. Phoebe decides to step in with some meditative techniques designed to take her to a 'Happy Place', but even these won't work.

Chandler and Janice run into problems when Joey makes it clear that he still can't stand the woman. Chandler, a little hurt by this, tells Janice about Joey's feelings – she then sets about arranging 'Joey and Janice's Day of Fun'. ('Does it have to be a whole day?' Joey asks. 'Yes,' Janice replies, 'because that's how long it takes to love me.') The whole thing is to little avail, though, as Joey returns hating Janice just as much.

Rachel, a little peeved at Ross spending so much time in bed working on dinosaurs instead of working on her, tries to find out how she can spice up their love-life. With a little cajoling, Ross admits to having a fantasy about Princess Leia's gold bikini outfit in *Return of the Jedi*. When Rachel, a little shocked by this, shares this information with Phoebe, she tells

Rachel that it's not that surprising a fantasy at all. So, she kits up and plays the part for Ross – but Ross has the moment shattered for him by the memory of Chandler's frightening confession . . .

Chandleresque: When Ross tells Chandler that the women share everything, he suggests that they should do the same. Ross admits to his Princess Leia fantasy, while Chandler confesses that during sex he sometimes pictures his mother. Ross, deeply appalled, cries, 'I said "share" not "scare"!' Later, when he tells Joey how much he loves Janice, he declares, 'I think this could be the "Real Thing". Capital "R"! Capital "T"!' adding for Joey's benefit, 'Don't worry, those *are* the right letters.'

Slow Joey: After Ross tells him about Chandler's sick admission, Joey tries to reassure his flatmate by confessing that he suffers from exactly the same affliction: 'I always picture your mom when I'm having sex.' Earlier in the episode, he is watching the game-show *Wheel of Fortune*. The legend _OUN_ _USHMORE is on the screen, to which he screams, 'It's Count Rushmore!' Chandler later points out that there was no such person as Count Rushmore; Joey responds, 'Yeah? Then who's the guy that painted the faces on the mountain?'

Poor Ross: Learning that the women tell each other 'pretty much' everything, Ross proudly asks Rachel if she tells people about The Night Of Five Times only to be reminded that was with Carol. Both Phoebe and Monica take their opportunities to have a dig at his Leia fantasy. Early on, Phoebe holds two Danish pastries to the side of her head and wonders where her brave 'Ross Skywalker' is – before noticing that he's right in front of her. Later, Rachel asks a distraught Monica if she wants to be taken home. 'Uh-huh,' she replies, 'or maybe to a galaxy far, far away.'

Freaky Monica: Monica is desperately hoping that Richard is feeling as bad as she is and refuses to rest easy until she knows that this is the case. When she plaintively cries, 'Why hasn't he called?', Phoebe suggests it's 'because you told him not to'. 'What are you?' she snaps, 'The Memory Woman?'

Phoebisms: Phoebe, having received a phone call at two in the morning, when all she could hear was a 'high squeaky sound', discovers it was Monica weeping. She'd presumed it had been a mouse or a possum, but soon dismissed that, because 'where would a mouse or a possum get the money to make the phone call?' Phoebe tells Rachel that she has also dated a man with a Princess Leia fantasy. When Rachel asks if it was fun, Phoebe replies, 'Oh, yeah. Mmm-mmm. Oh!' Rachel begins to think this Leia thing is a good idea, but Phoebe points out that the response had more to do with her new pager – she had it in her pocket, set to vibrate. When Monica accidentally drops the wad of 'drain-hair' into Ross's breakfast, Phoebs claims it looks like a tiny little person drowning in his cereal.

Just Plain Weird: It's not that weird, but it goes to show how familiar the producers expect their audience to be with the show. In the opening scene, we see the gang walk into Central Perk, see strangers sitting at the couch, and dejectedly walk straight out again.

Parents – Who Needs 'Em?: It's a visit from her father, seeking 'a little Monicuddle', that finally enables Monica to sleep soundly and relax about the break-up. Ross, meanwhile, has problems with his mother. Thanks to Chandler's confession, an image of his mother in the gold bikini replaces the beautiful sight of Rachel in the same outfit and we see 'Mrs Geller' say to Ross, 'Come on, sweetie, you're, like, freaking me out here.'

Boys Will Be Boys: There's one thing they won't discuss when Ross and Chandler embark upon their failed attempt at sharing. Ross says that the girls talk about everything: 'stuff you like, stuff she likes, technique, stamina, girth . . .' Panicked, Chandler checks: 'We're not going to talk about girth, are we?'

Generation X: The 'Most Romantic Song Ever' debate includes votes for 'Tupelo Honey' by Van Morrison (Ross) and 'The Way We Were' by Barbra Streisand (Rachel). Phoebe votes for 'that one that Elton John wrote for, um, that guy on *Who's The Boss?*', which turns out to be 'Hold me close, young Tony Dan-za' (she means 'Tiny Dancer', a huge hit for Elton in the States). Oh, and a little-known trilogy called *Star Wars* (notably *Return of the Jedi*) is referenced . . . a lot.

The Story So Far: Ross mentions the naval uniform he hired in 'TOW The Chicken Pox'. It's also revealed that

Joey once dated a prostitute, and had sex on the Staten Island Ferry.

The Last Word: A pretty low-key beginning to the season, especially when compared to the frenetic, harrowing events of season two's opener, but entertaining nevertheless and including the unforgettable sight of Rachel as Princess Leia. If anything, everything's a little too normal: all's fine between Ross and Rachel (for now); and Chandler and Joey (excepting the Janice thing); Chandler's happy (for the moment); Monica's down (which is about the only interesting thing on a dramatic level); and Phoebes . . . well, Phoebe's Phoebe. It only serves to highlight the rest of the season's descent into soap-opera.

302
'The One Where No-one's Ready'

Writer: Ira Ungerleider
Director: Gail Mancuso
First US transmission: 26.09.96
First UK transmission (C4): 11.07.97

Guest Cast: Peter Dennis (Sherman Whitfield),
Tom Selleck (the voice of Dr Richard Burke)

Summary: Ross has an important speech to make at a museum dinner, and he wants everyone to come with him. The only problem is, it starts in half an hour and, well, no-one's ready. Ross has to contend with all sorts of things before they can leave: Joey and Chandler fighting over sovereignty of an armchair, Phoebe getting hummus down her dress, and Monica obsessing over a message she's heard on Richard's answering machine. Worst of all, he loses his temper with Rachel and she then refuses to go. Will he be able to save his relationship *and* get to dinner on time?

Freaky Monica: Playing back her messages, Monica hears one from Richard and panics when she can't work out whether it's old or new. Eventually she phones him, leaving what she describes as a 'breezy' message on his machine. When she plays it back to everyone (of course, she still knows the code to 'break into' his machine), she realises that it's not as breezy as she'd hoped. This leads to a riotous series of calls, her neurosis increasing with every one. The final indignity comes when she leaves a message to Richard excusing her behaviour, saying that her period may be to blame – what she's actually done is left it as his *outgoing* message, letting anyone who calls him hear it. This brilliant sequence of events is the best thing about this otherwise tired and tiring episode, and Monica's trademark '*No!*' (used here twice, with little pause) possibly explains why Cox ended up in those *Scream* films.

Slow Joey: Joey explains that he wants to wear underwear when he puts on the hired tuxedo: 'I'm not going to go commando in another man's fatigues.' When he puts on all of Chandler's clothes in revenge for his flatmate hiding his underwear ('Look at me! I'm Chandler!' he mocks. 'Could I *be* wearing any more clothes?'), Joey is still going commando. Chandler's horror is perfectly justified when Joey starts to lunge.

Chandleresque: Having completed the Cosmopolitan quiz while in the bathroom, Chandler concludes, 'It turns out, I *do* put career before men.' His verbal sparring with Joey over ownership of the chair is good, with Chandler claiming he wrote a song today called 'GET UP!', and finally resorting to quote 'the words of A.A. Milne: "Get out of my chair, dillhole!"' It's also revealed that he once borrowed some inflatable sheep that went with Rachel's Little Bo Peep outfit, although he claims, 'We used them as pillows when we went camping.' When Chandler tells his roommate to taste what he thinks is cider, Joey discovers the 'cider' is actually fat. Chandler calmly tells him, 'Yeah, I know, I did that two minutes ago.'

Phoebisms: During a fight between Joey and Chandler, some hummus is spilled on her dress. After calling them 'rotten boys', the only thing she can do – given the time constraints, and the fact that Ross is getting freaky – is to cover the stain with a Christmas decoration. She explains that she thought, 'All right, fine. I'll be political.' When Chandler asks, 'What are you supporting?', she just replies, 'Duh, *Christmas*!'

Poor Ross: Of course, the whole episode is about 'Poor Ross', but one particularly good put-down comes when Monica sees him all dressed up in his bow tie and suit, and asks if he's going to 'do magic'.

The Ballad of Ross & Rachel: Having seriously upset Rachel by shouting at her when she takes too long to get ready, Ross has to find a way to paper over the cracks so that he can persuade her to come to the dinner. Joey suggests that he drink a glass of fat that Monica has been keeping in the refrigerator, to prove just how sorry he is. Rachel supports the suggestion, and he's about to do it when she stops him, amazed that he might have drunk something so gross out of love for her. In return for this weird display of love, Rachel quickly gets dressed in a stunning gown, revealing to Ross as they leave that she's going 'commando' too.

Dinosaurs ROCK!: When Rachel asks whether one of her many outfits looks like 'something the girlfriend of a palaeontologist would wear', Phoebe says, 'I don't know. You might be the first one.' Ross also has a dinosaur watch.

Generation X: Chandler refers to A.A. Milne, the author of the 'Winnie The Pooh' stories.

The Story So Far: We're reminded that Joey often wears no underwear (see 'TOW The Boobies').

The Last Word: Well, if the last episode was a bit lame, this one is trying to walk without any legs at all. While the set-up seems promising – the six of them spend the entire episode in Monica and Rachel's apartment – the execution is frankly poor. The script is dull and the performers seem to know it, with none of them trying particularly hard to make it work. The scenes focusing on Monica's answering machine exploits are by far the best, and Cox does a great job with them. But it's not enough to save this episode from being forgettable.

303
'The One With The Jam'

Writer: Wil Calhoun
Director: Kevin S. Bright
First US transmission: 03.10.96
First UK transmission (C4): 18.07.97

Guest Cast: David Arquette (Malcolm), Maggie Wheeler (Janice),
James Michael Tyler (Gunther), Lisa Kudrow (Ursula Buffay)

Summary: Monica, trying to fill the hole in her life left by Richard, has become a one-woman jam factory, churning out jar after jar of the stuff. While Joey is in heaven – he loves the stuff – she soon realises that it's something she can't do forever. Instead, she decides to make a visit to the nearest sperm bank and get herself pregnant!

Phoebe notices that she's beginning to get unwanted attention: she is being stalked by a man called Malcolm who, she learns, mistook her for her twin, Ursula, who has a restraining order on him. Somewhat taken by Malcolm, Phoebe suggests that they go for a coffee and she begins to fall for him, unaware that he's still stalking Ursula . . .

Freaky Monica: Monica gets the best line of the episode, and one to remember when an over-helpful friend is trying to talk over you. When Ross tries to interrupt her explanation of wanting to become pregnant, Monica snaps, 'Lips moving! Still talking!' It is also revealed that Monica signs little notes to Rachel using her *full* name.

Slow Joey: As Chandler sits alone in the living room of their apartment, a rhythmic bed-spring squeak starts up from Joey's room. A yelp follows, and Chandler bursts in on him to point out that this is why his parents warned him not to jump on the bed. His love of jam is revealed in this episode: he explains to Rachel how, when he was younger, his mother would drop him off at the cinema, leaving him a pot of jam and a little spoon. Rachel, smiling, looks at him and says, 'You're so pretty.' Later, Chandler holds out a hand, representing, 'The girl from the Xerox place, buck naked.' He then holds out his other hand and adds, 'Or a big tub of jam.' Joey just grins and says, seedily, 'Put your hands together.' Joey considers claiming that his arm just 'fell out of its socket' until Chandler warns him that the doctor is unlikely to believe him.

Chandleresque: Resentful over the amount of space Janice takes up in his bed, Chandler eyes the other side of the bed: 'You could fit a giant penguin over there!' he thinks to himself. 'That'd be weird, though.' After Monica tells everyone she's ditched the jam-making for baby-making, Chandler advises that she's 'gonna need much bigger jars'.

Phoebisms: Her efforts to 'de-Ursula-ize' Malcolm fail

miserably when she discovers that he is still stalking her sister. She suggests instead that he stalk her for a while: 'I'll be like an Ursula patch.' It is revealed that Phoebe, when she was in school, thought she was a witch. She tells of how her guidance counsellor gave her these words of wisdom: 'OK, you're not a witch, you're just an average student.' She apparently took all their hidden meanings to heart, summarising the advice as, 'Get over it.'

Spoilt Rachel: Although she has lived in New York for over two years, there's still a couple of things Rachel doesn't know. When Monica explains that she bought all her jam-bound fruit at the docks and boasts, 'Bet you didn't know you could get it wholesale', Rachel says, 'I didn't know there were docks.' Later, when Monica says she knows where she can get some sperm, Rachel suggests, 'Down at the docks again?'

The Ballad of Ross & Rachel: The lovers give Chandler advice on how to handle a girlfriend asking if she looks fat. Immediate response is the key, and Rachel adequately demonstrates how that works both ways. As an example, Ross asks, 'Does size matter?', to which she snappily responds, 'No!' But, when Chandler tells them of the cuddling-in-bed problem, Rachel says, 'I'm sorry, we can't help you there, because we're cuddly sleepers.' Ross playfully agrees, but the minute she leaves, he begins to explain his Hug-Roll technique ('Hug for her, roll for you'), which is apparently the key to their successful relationship.

Generation X: Malcolm is played by David Arquette (brother of actor Alexis and actresses Patricia and Rosanna) who starred in the *Scream* movies alongside his future wife, Courteney Cox. Monica's ideal sperm donor describes himself as a male Geena Davis, star of among other films, *Thelma and Louise* (Ridley Scott, 1991).

The Story So Far: Shortly after his fertility experiment for the NYU, Joey made a 'donation' to a sperm bank (see 'TOW Rachel Finds Out'). Monica finds his details in her list of prospective donors. When Joey checks with the bank, he discovers that no-one has taken any of his donations and considers adding his work on *Days Of Our Lives* (see 'TOW Russ') to attract more potential buyers. This episode is the first time we hear of 'The girl from the Xerox place' (see 'TOW Ross And Rachel Take A Break'). In Joey's sperm donor description we learn that Joey was born in Queens.

The Last Word: Once again, Monica's moving plotline is keeping this series afloat. It seems that whenever Phoebe is given a sizeable piece of the action, her dizziness has to take second place, making her less interesting and far less funny. While there are enough laughs to keep you entertained, this is a fairly run-of-the-mill outing. We're just grateful that everyone is too polite to see the irony in Matthew Perry asking Ross and Rachel if he looks fat.

304
'The One With The Metaphorical Tunnel'

Writer: Alexa Junge
Director: Steve Zuckerman
First US transmission: 10.10.96
First UK transmission (C4): 25.07.97

Guest Cast: Jane Sibbett (Carol Willick), Jessica Hecht (Susan Bunch),
Maggie Wheeler (Janice), Charlie & Jack Allen (Ben),
Edo Azran (Young Ross), Sierra Dawn Hill (Young Monica)

Summary: Chandler is reaching crisis point in his relationship with Janice. Now that he's fearing that they're becoming 'a couple', all sorts of alarm bells are ringing and he's beginning to want to run a mile. When Monica and Rachel persuade him that commitment is no bad thing, he over-compensates and, over dinner with his girlfriend, makes the mistake of saying that he might be ready for them to live together. To Chandler's surprise, she freaks out and he must embark on some serious damage limitation if he is to save his relationship.

Phoebe gets herself in trouble with Joey when she forgets to remind him about an audition, so to apologise, she offers to pretend to be his agent, phone the casting director and get the audition rescheduled. Joey immediately starts to ask Phoebe to arrange more auditions for him. But, although it's fun to begin with, Phoebe soon has a problem finding ways to tell Joey that people think he sucks without breaking his heart.

Phoebisms: Her wonderful methods of fooling people into thinking she's an agent, while she calls from the phone in Central Perk, are breathtaking. Putting on two voices (the agent, and her secretary), she's soon arranged a multitude of auditions for Joey. But trouble starts when she has to tell him he's being rejected by all of them. When she breaks the first bit of bad news to him, she says, 'Oh God, I don't want to be the person who makes your face look like that.' Joey, though, relies on her honesty, and bravely sticks it out when Phoebe reports that people have said that he has a terrible Italian accent (although it *is* terrible), that he isn't 'believable as a human being', and that he's 'pretty but dumb' – sorry, that's 'pretty dumb'!

Poor Ross: Carol and Susan bring Ben round to visit his dad, and Ben brings with him his new favourite toy – a Barbie doll. Ross spends the rest of the episode trying to persuade Ben to part with the Barbie in favour of something more manly, like Monster Trucks, Dinosoldiers, and GI Joe. His efforts are finally successful, but Monica still doesn't see what the big deal is. She recalls a time when, as a child, Ross used to dress up in his mother's clothes, including 'the big hat, the pearls, the little pink handbag'. Ross called himself Bea, and he sang a song: 'I am Bea, I like tea, Won't you dance around with me?' Susan's glee at this is barely disguised: 'I've literally never been this happy.' Over the closing titles, we see film of a younger Ross at a table in the garden, dressed as Bea and singing his song.

Freaky Monica: She explains that she always keeps notepads around, so that notes can be taken in any emergency – like when you're panicked and in the middle of a game of hide-and-seek, as Phoebe was. She suggests that, if Phoebe had done the same, she wouldn't have had to write the message from the casting director on her hand – Phoebe confesses that this was why they didn't invite her to play.

Chandleresque: Joey suggests he should confront his fears and enter the metaphorical tunnel: 'Jump off the high dive, stare down the barrel of the gun, pee into the wind!' Chandler replies, 'I assure you, if I'm staring down the barrel of a gun, I'm pretty much peeing every which way.' When Janice finally calls him back after he freaked her out, Monica and Rachel suggest he should act sleepy and grumpy: 'Stop naming dwarves!' he cries.

Joey's an ACTOR!: Joey appears in an infomercial for the Milk Master 2000, a device designed to stop you covering yourself in milk when you try to open the carton. When he finally convinces Phoebe to tell him exactly what the casting directors thought of him, she's forced to tell him they claimed to have never met an Italian with a worse Italian accent (and they're right, too!).

Girl Power: We learn the secrets of ice cream usage in emotional emergencies. Monica and Rachel use the 'low-cal, non-dairy, soy milk junk' for everyday crises, because 'when you start to get screwed over all the time, you gotta switch to low-fat'. They bring out the full-fat ice cream for Chandler when his obsessive need to express his feelings for Janice has seemingly driven her away.

Generation X: When Monica asks if anyone has seen her left boob, Joey confuses it with the movie *My Left Foot* (Jim Sheridan, 1989).

The Story So Far: Joey's arm is still in a sling from the previous episode. We are reminded that Joey's real agent is Estelle (see 'TOW The Butt').

The Last Word: The troubles between Chandler and Janice give Matthew Perry the perfect chance to play Chandler with a sadness and desperation that's truly touching. The scene in the supermarket, when he is faux-casually trying to coax Janice back, is side-splittingly funny yet almost tear-jerking. Meanwhile, Ross and Phoebe get a couple of decent scenes. While there are duds in season three, this episode is pretty much standard – and it's a good standard too.

. . . And are any of you beginning to actually *like* Janice yet? 'I gotta buy a vowel, because . . . oh – my – Gahhhd!!'

305
'The One With Frank Jr'

Writers: Scott Silveri & Shana Goldberg-Meehan
Director: Steve Zuckerman

First US transmission: 17.10.96
First UK transmission (C4): 01.08.97

Guest Cast: Isabella Rossellini (herself), Giovanni Ribisi (Frank Jr)
and introducing: Cynthia Mann (Jasmine)

Summary: Phoebe's spending the weekend in the city with her half-brother Frank Jr but is worried that their lack of mutual interests is preventing them from connecting. She tries to engage him in all sorts of conversations, but he seems far more interested in melting things. When she takes him with her to work and offers him a free massage, his ideas of the seedy city land him in trouble: he thinks this is a different kind of 'massage parlour' and tries it on with one of the other workers.

Chaos reigns at Chandler and Joey's: Joey is building an 'entertainment unit', and their apartment is full of pieces of wood and power tools. Rachel and Ross, meanwhile, work out their 'Freebie Lists': the lists of those five celebrities they are allowed to have sex with, should they meet them. Neither of them ever expects to ever have the opportunity . . . and then one of the women on Ross's list walks into Central Perk. What will Ross do? More to the point, what will *Rachel* do?

Chandleresque: Originally intending to build a mail-box, Joey gets carried away with himself, prompting Chandler to ask: 'You're building a post office?' When Frank Jr says that his friend Larry wants him to bring a photo of a prostitute back from Manhattan, Chandler muses, 'You know, we don't really take advantage of living in the city.' His Freebie List, by the way, comprises Kim Basinger, Cindy Crawford, Halle Berry, Yasmine Bleeth, and Jessica Rabbit (Roger Rabbit's wife who, Rachel feels compelled to mention, is a cartoon, and therefore way out of his league).

Phoebisms: Waiting outside Central Perk for Frank Jr to arrive, she tells Rachel that he's always late. When Rachel gets Phoebe to confirm that she's only met her half-brother once, Phoebe says, 'I think it sounds big-sistery, you know? "Frank's always late".' Exhibiting unusually quick wits, Phoebe manages to win the shadow game with Monica. After Monica starts to copy everything Phoebs says, she eventually tells her that she doesn't have the time to waste. 'No, that is what the game is,' Monica explains. 'Which you gave up really quickly!' Phoebe explains, victoriously. When the entertainment unit is finally finished and erected, it blocks half of Chandler's bedroom door and half of Joey's. Joey wonders whether his ruler is wrong. 'Maybe,' ponders Phoebe, '*all* the rulers are wrong.'

Spoilt Rachel: When asked who might appear on her Freebie List, Rachel *instantly* lists Chris O'Donnell, John F. Kennedy Jr, Daniel Day Lewis, Sting, and Parker Stevenson (the Hardy Boy). At Central Perk, she brings a customer his order: 'Let's see if I got this right. So, this is a half-caf, double tall, easy hazelnut, non-fat, no foam, with whip, extra-hot latte, right?' Amazingly, she *has* got it right, but as she walks away, she whispers to herself: 'Freak!'

Freaky Monica: Joey tells her that her bathroom floor is 'old and dingy', but Monica won't believe him until he moves her laundry basket to show her the original colour of the floor underneath. Seeing it, she gasps, 'I can't live like this! What are we going to do? What are we going to do?'

Poor Ross: While considering his Freebie List, he names Isabella Rossellini as a possible candidate. Chandler points out that she's too 'international' and is never around. 'Yeah,' laughs Rachel. '. . . that's why you won't get Isabella Rossellini – geography.' When he reveals his final decisions, he pulls a little credit-card sized list from his pocket – typeset and laminated! The final list includes Uma Thurman, Winona Ryder, Elizabeth Hurley, Michelle Pfeiffer, and Dorothy Hammell (the ice-skater). When, ironically, he gets the chance to meet Isabella Rossellini, Rachel decides to let him have her as 'an alternate'. Making an embarrassing botch of it, as everyone else looks on, he is eventually forced into showing her the list. 'That's not the final draft,' he explains. 'It's laminated!' she says. Once he has explained that she was 'bumped' in favour of Winona Ryder, Isabella claims that she has a list of five 'goofy coffee-house guys' and that (pointing to another customer) 'yesterday I bumped *you* for that guy over there.' She leaves, and Ross tells the others, 'We're just going to be friends.'

Just Plain Weird: On meeting Rachel and Monica, Frank Jr asks the boys, 'How do you guys get anything done?' (To which Chandler replies, 'We don't, really.') Trying to get to know him a little better, Phoebe asks, 'What kind of things do you like to do at home?' 'Melt stuff,' Frank replies, blankly. Later, Phoebe watches while Frank melts a plastic spoon. She asks him if his hobby is art, and Frank says, 'Yeah, you can melt art.' Saying that she's going to bed (the fumes are giving her a headache), she leaves him a fire extinguisher – 'Just in case.' 'Cool!' says Frank, trying to melt its nozzle. After clearing up the misunderstanding with Phoebe's co-worker, Frank starts to list all the things he enjoyed about the weekend. 'I almost got my arm broken by a hooker,' he says. 'She wasn't a hooker,' Phoebe corrects him, once again. 'Well,' explains Frank, 'when I tell my friends about her, she will be.'

The Story So Far: Phoebe's birthday is 16 February (she *is* a typical Aquarian), and Frank Jr's is 25 October (Scorpio). Frank can fold his tongue in half (!) though Phoebe can't. Although this episode introduces Cynthia Mann as Phoebe's co-worker, Jasmine, she did make an appearance as a waitress in the very first episode.

The Last Word: Giovanni Ribisi (Frank Jr) is the star turn of this episode, and we're ecstatic that he's become a series regular. It's quite sweet to see Phoebe trying so hard to get on with Frank, wanting to build herself a family. This must be the first time that a serious Phoebe subplot doesn't become the most boring thing in the episode. The appearance of Rossellini, while so obviously gratuitous, is brilliantly funny; although she sticks out like a sore thumb at Central Perk, that only serves to highlight the fact that Ross doesn't have a snowball's chance in hell.

306
'The One With The Flashback'

Writers: Marta Kauffman & David Crane
Director: Peter Bonerz
First US transmission: 31.10.96
First UK transmission (C4): 08.08.97

Guest Cast: Maggie Wheeler (Janice), John Lehr (Eric, the photographer), Larry Hankin (Mr Heckles), Michele Maika (Kiki), Marissa Ribisi (Betsy), Christy L. Medrano (Waitress)

Summary: It all starts when Janice innocuously asks whether any of the friends have ever slept with each other. When an emphatic 'no' comes back, she asks if they've ever come close. What follows is a tale of the gang exactly a year before Rachel moved to the city, before anyone had met Joey, before Ross and Carol broke up, and before Phoebe moved out of Monica's. At least, before Monica *found out* she'd moved. We discover that Joey nearly didn't move in – but Mr Heckles' intervention saw that he did. Rachel was doubtful about marrying Barry well before the wedding itself – and she used to have a horrible perm.

As this slice of history draws to a close, Janice has her question answered. Phoebe and Ross were very close to making out shortly after Carol told him she was a lesbian; Monica had the hots for Joey the minute they met, and Joey mistook her offer of a lemonade for an offer of sex; Chandler and Monica shared a tender moment in each other's arms; and Rachel fantasised about having a fling with some weird bloke she met in a bar – who is later introduced to her as Chandler!

Phoebisms: When Janice asks, 'Who, of the six of you, has slept with the six of you?' Phoebe, dazed, replies, 'Wow, it's like a dirty math problem.' During the flashback, we see how Phoebe tries to hide that she's moved out of Monica's. Ross and Chandler know, but Monica has no idea. When Monica notices that Phoebe's bed is missing, she asks her where it's gone. 'It's not in the apartment?' Phoebs asks lamely. After the gang almost catch Ross and Phoebe making out on the pool table, Phoebe diffuses the situation by stroking the green felt on the table and declaring that Ross was right. 'I don't know why I always thought this was real grass!'

Slow Joey: Joey alludes to one time when Monica and Rachel got together. When they strongly protest that there was no such event, Joey smiles and says, 'OK, but let's say there was. How might that go?' (See 'TOW All The Haste' to find out.) During the flashback, we see Joey moving his stuff into Chandler's. Monica invites him in for a lemonade. As she pours, she tells him to make himself comfortable, which Joey does by stripping naked. Monica, shocked, asks, 'When someone asks you in for lemonade, to you that means they want to have sex?' Joey, putting his clothes back on, replies, 'Well, usually, yeah! Well, not just lemonade: iced tea, sometimes juice . . .' At the close of the episode, Ross tells the gang that, 'My wife's a lesbian,' Joey – who hasn't even been introduced to Ross, let alone his marriage problems – grins. 'Cool!'

Freaky Monica: When Phoebe finally admits that she has moved out of the apartment, she confesses that Monica's tidiness drove her away: 'I need to live in a land where people can spill!' 'You can spill,' Monica asserts, '. . . in the sink.' Answering a question most of us have pondered, we discover that Monica's apartment actually belongs to her grandmother, who let her have it when she moved to Florida, 'otherwise I could never afford a place like this,' she explains to Joey.

Poor Ross: Ross is over the moon when Carol meets another woman at the gym, called Susan. 'I think it's going to make a difference,' he smiles naively, pleased she finally has a friend of her own. In the bar later, he explains to Phoebe that he suspects his marriage might be over, because his wife's a lesbian and he's not, '. . . and apparently it's not a mix-and-match situation.' Commenting on it later, he criticises himself, saying, 'Maybe this wouldn't have happened if I'd been more nurturing, or I'd paid more attention, or I . . . had a uterus.'

Chandleresque: Joey, being shown around Chandler's flat, tells his prospective new flatmate that he's 'totally OK with the gay thing.' Chandler blankly stares at him, asking, 'What gay thing?' Monica is practically begging Chandler to let Joey move in, as she fancies him. Chandler replies, sarcastically, that he's always wanted a roommate that enables him to be referred to as 'the *funny* one'.

Spoilt Rachel: Meeting Monica in the bar that will become Central Perk, Rachel shows off her engagement ring ('You can't even see where the Titanic hit it,' gasps Monica), explaining that her husband-to-be is 'a doctor, thank you very much.' 'Just like you always wanted,' coos Monica. Rach admonishes the waitress for getting her order wrong. As the waitress walks away, she turns to her friends. 'I mean, how hard is it to get a couple of drinks right, huh?'

Just Plain Weird: 'You're disturbing my oboe practice,' Mr Heckles (resurrected thanks to the flashback) tells Phoebe. In an inspired moment of quick-thinking, Phoebe replies, 'Then I'm going to have to ask you to keep it down.' Later, Heckles scares off Eric, the photographer with the porn star sister who's due to move into Chandler's by introducing himself as Chandler's new roommate.

Ugly Naked Guy: 'Oh, that is so unfortunate,' says Phoebe at the start of the flashback, staring out of the window. 'Cute naked guy is really starting to put on weight.'

Generation X: As Rachel fantasises about Chandler, we heard The Zombies' 'Time of the Season' from 1968. Chandler didn't start watching *Baywatch* until 1993 (the year Joey moved in), meaning he missed the first four seasons (it kind of went downhill after then).

The Story So Far: On top of everything else, we learn that Central Perk used to be a bar. It has been noted that there's a major continuity problem with this episode as it seems to contradict the events in 'The Pilot'. We suggest that while Carol tells Ross she's having an affair with Susan in the flashback, she doesn't actually move all of her stuff from their apartment until a year later. As Ross doesn't discover that Carol's pregnant until a year after they split up, we again suggest that they briefly got back together or had a one-night stand. This may go some way to explaining why Susan hates Ross even more than one might expect.

The Last Word: A blessed relief from the plot-heavy episodes that surround it, 'TOW The Flashback' is a welcome burst of pure *Friends*, something both new and wonderfully familiar. We get to see how the gang got together, and what life was like before Rachel and Joey came along. On the flip side, there's dramatic irony-a-gogo, particularly in the way we're just waiting for Ross's marriage to fall apart. The most surprising moment is also the most funny: having seen a couple of years of Ross not thinking much of Phoebe, to see that the two of them came so close to making mad, passionate love is a complete shock. The sequence itself ('I can't get it out.' 'That's not something a girl wants to hear.') is blinding – a masterpiece!

307

'The One With The Race Car Bed'

Writer: Seth Kurland
Director: Gail Mancuso
First US transmission: 07.11.96
First UK transmission (C4): 15.08.97

Guest Cast: Ron Leibman (Dr Green), Khalil Kain (Cal),
Maggie Wheeler (Janice), Mark Cohen (The Mattress King),
Rosey Brown (Delivery Man), James Michael Tyler (Gunther),
Simon Harvey (Jester), Shashi Bhatia (Acting Student #1),
Steven Harad (Acting Student #2)

Summary: The gang are at Monica and Rachel's watching television, when they see Janice's estranged husband, The Mattress King, advertising his latest sale. He uses his depression over his upcoming divorce as the reason for slashing his prices, which Janice finds abhorrent: Monica, though, points out, 'At $499 for a pillow-top queen set, who cares about the divorce? Those babies will sell themselves!' She adds to Janice, after an uncomfortable pause, 'And I'm appalled for you by the way.' Appalled or not, she's still taken enough by the idea of the sale to head down to the showroom and pick up a bed for herself. It's due to be delivered while Monica is out, so Phoebe signs for it on her behalf and, as she is distracted by Joey's nosebleed, fails to notice that the delivery men are dragging in a child's race car bed instead of the one Monica ordered. When she and Joey return to the showroom to complain, Joey catches a glimpse of the Mattress King kissing a woman in his office – it's Janice!!

Ross is not looking forward to a night out with Rachel and her father; Dr Green appears to take pleasure out of being as rude as possible to him. During dinner, Dr Green is his usual self and Ross feels resigned to the fact that they will never get along. However, when they begin to discuss Rachel's lifestyle (seeing a two-bit chiropractor and failing to get renters' insurance), the two men finally find some common ground.

Joey finally has some work, teaching a class on soap opera acting. He seems to have found a niche, and things get even better when he receives a call to an audition for *For All Our Children*. The only problem is, one of his students is up for the role too – and Joey knows he's better than him . . .

Phoebisms: Just how psychic and mad is she? When everyone else is thinking of other things, as Ross tells his dinosaur story, Joey's thoughts are taken up entirely with him (or, more accurately, his brain) singing. Phoebe, distracted, silently wonders, 'Who's singing?' When she is accompanying Monica to the Mattress King's showroom, she comes across a young boy driving the race car bed that will later cause her so much trouble. 'You know,' she confides in him, 'in England, this car would be on the other side of the store.' The kid, though, doesn't find her joke funny at all: Phoebe, brilliantly, just supposes that it has gone over his head. When she is signing for Monica's bed – pretending to actually be Monica – she asks Joey, 'Do I have a middle name?' before making one up: 'Falula!'

Joey's a Teacher!: His acting classes are a delight. At the start of the first one, he writes his name on the blackboard, turning to face his students *as he does so*. The resultant 'Tribbiani'-slide (brilliantly highlighted by a line that should pass under his name, but instead passes *through* it) is one of the funniest moments in the episode. His first lesson to the class is teaching them how to react. This does not, he tells them, mean 'acting again', perhaps remembering a mistake he himself once made. The insight into Joey's acting methods afforded by these classes is terrific: pulling out pubic hair with tweezers to illicit tears, pretending to have a fish-hook through your eyebrow to evoke nastiness, and attempting long division to simulate shock and confusion. As far as studying Joey's bizarre choice of career goes, this episode is a big hit.

Spoilt Rachel: She admits to Ross that if she received a tip as low as the kind her father normally gives out, she'd be giving that customer 'sneezers'.

Freaky Monica: When the bed is delivered, Phoebe tells the men to carry it into 'the compulsively neat [room] by the window'.

Chandleresque: The image of him playing on the race car bed, making car noises and pretending to shout at and chat up

other drivers, is brilliantly child-like. This innocence, of
course, is all the more poignant when you consider that the
audience has just seen Janice and her husband kissing – the
poor kid doesn't know what's going to hit him.

The Ballad of Ross & Rachel: 'I just want him to love you
like I do,' Rachel tells Ross of her father's impending visit.
'All right, well not exactly like I do . . . but if you do come to
dinner, I'll love you like I do in the black thing that you like.'
Ross mulls over the quandary. 'I'll go,' offers an over-eager
Chandler. Rachel's desperate attempts to make Ross and her
father get on are quite touching, especially when she explains
that it's bad enough that her parents can't stand being in the
same room as each other. 'I don't want to have to have a separate room for you too.'

Dinosaurs ROCK!: Ross is talking about work, but we soon
hear the sound of his voice fade away to be replaced by the
thoughts of the other gathered friends. 'I love how he cares so
much about stuff,' Rachel thinks. 'If I squint, I can pretend
he's Alan Alda.' Monica, though, is less impressed. 'Oh good,'
she thinks, 'another dinosaur story. When are *those* going to
become extinct?'

Gunther's There For You, Rachel: We finally get an affirmation of what we've always suspected as we hear Gunther
longing for Rachel: 'I wish she was my wife,' he laments.
Later on, as Rachel asks Ross to join her and her father for
dinner we can see Gunther glaring at Ross. As Ross says hello,
Gunther warns him, 'We'll see . . .'

Generation X: As we hear everybody's thoughts, Joey hums
'Baby Elephant Walk'.

The Story So Far: Ross tells Dr Green that he doesn't like
lobster (see 'TOW The Baby On The Bus'). Phoebe learned to
box when she spent some time at the YMCA. 'Some of the
young men weren't acting Christian enough,' she explains.

The Last Word: A nice little episode which, like all the best,
has plenty going on. The only casualty, really, is Chandler who
doesn't get the chance to do much at all; but, since he's the
hook for the whole of the next episode, we'll let it pass. A typically funny script, with a couple of blisteringly smart
moments, this makes for some good viewing.

308
'The One With The Giant Poking Device'

Writer: Adam Chase
Director: Gail Mancuso
First US transmission: 14.11.96
First UK transmission (C4): 22.08.97

Guest Cast: James Michael Tyler (Gunther),
Maggie Wheeler (Janice), Charlie & Jack Allen (Ben)

Summary: Wracked with guilt and driven by loyalty, Joey tells Chandler that Janice is cheating on him. Chandler confronts Janice with this only to realise that he should stand aside and let her go back to her husband and child, however hard he finds it to let go. Ross is called into the museum at short notice, so Rachel looks after Ben. During the afternoon, though, Monica knocks Ben's head against a wooden beam and panic ensues. Will he be all right, and how on earth are they going to tell Ross? Of course, they decide not to. And they would have got away with it, too, had Ross not noticed the bump on Ben's head, and Rachel hadn't cracked and grassed on Monica.

Phoebe is suffering from agonising toothache, but refuses to seek help because every time she goes to the dentist someone dies. Eventually, she realises she has no other choice and is relieved to find her weird curse broken. Until, that is, Joey notices that Ugly Naked Guy is 'awfully still'. Together, the gang fashion a 'Giant Poking Device' from old chopsticks and feed it over through his apartment window to see if he's still alive . . .

Freaky Monica: Her panic over Ben's bump is superb: 'Push it in! Push it in!' she screams at Rachel, as if the child is a cartoon character. When Ben starts to repeat 'Monica bang!' over and over, she says, 'We all do it all the time. See, watch this . . .' She then proceeds to hit her head repeatedly against the wooden beam, before entreating Rachel to join her. When they decide to hide the bump using the hat from Rachel's Rainy Day Bear, Rachel is dismayed to find that the hat is sown on to the soft toy's head. Monica snatches it from her and tugs hard at the hat, pulling the bear's head off in the process, sending stuffing everywhere. 'Oh,' moans a distraught Rachel, 'it's just like a bloodbath in here today!'

Spoilt Rachel: When she offers to baby-sit Ben, Ross is obviously wary of leaving him alone with her. But behind Rachel's back, Monica clearly mouths, 'I'll be here the whole time,' so Ross feels safer about the whole thing. Later, Rachel is holding Ben and showing him a spoon: 'Look, Benny. Spoon! Spoon! . . . I think he's bored.' Meaning, of course, that *she* is.

Phoebisms: Her fear of killing someone by visiting the dentist is pure Phoebe: 'Be on the lookout for anything that you can fall *into*, or that can fall *on* you, or . . . All right, just look out!' It all becomes too much for her, though, so she bursts into tears and runs out. After the visit to the dentist, she frantically phones everyone she knows to check that they're still alive. When she tries Chandler, she doesn't realise that he's in the middle of a deeply serious conversation with Janice. She runs across the hallway, bursts in on them and yells, 'If you're alive, you *answer* your phone!'

Slow Joey: He has some difficulty coming to terms with the idea of Homo Sapiens. He asks Ross if the reason Homo Sapiens became extinct was because they '*were* "Homo" Sapiens'. Ross corrects him, telling him, 'Homo Sapiens are *people*.' 'Hey,' says Joey, 'I'm not judging!' Later, Rachel is listing a number of reasons why Monica can't bribe Ben into not telling Ross about the 'bonking incident'. 'Number one, I don't think Ben understands the concept of bribery, and number two –' She is interrupted by a snigger from Joey: 'You said "number two".' Rachel points out that she also said 'number one', to which Joey just laughs again, saying, 'I know!'

Chandleresque: Chandler's desperation at the thought of losing Janice is played out wonderfully by Perry. Their final scene together, in Central Perk, where Chandler is telling Janice that she must go back to her husband, that it's for the best, is heart-rending. When Janice says that their love is like 'movie love', that he is her 'soulmate', and that she 'can't believe we're not going to be spending the rest of our lives together', Chandler just responds with a hysterical, 'Then don't leave me!' But, of course, it has to end, and watching

Perry give Chandler the same kind of desolate terror of loneliness we saw in 'TOW Heckles Dies' is a bitter pleasure.

Gunther's There For You, Rachel: More Rachel obsessing. Ross asks him for a napkin, and he just snaps, 'Like you don't already have everything.' When Chandler stands in front of him holding Janice's shoe – the only thing of her he was able to cling on to – Gunther stares at it and sighs that Rachel has similar shoes in burgundy. Ahh, bless.

Ugly Naked Guy: Joey watches him sleep in a new hammock, remarking that it looks like a 'Play-Doh Fat Factory'. When Phoebe thinks that her dental curse has killed Ugly Naked Guy, she laments that the curse is getting stronger too, to bring down something that big! When they've poked him and got him riled, he comes to his window, prompting Rachel to say, 'Now he's showing us *his* poking device.' Joey takes one look and shouts, 'That's never gonna make it all the way over here, buddy!'

Generation X: Phoebe and Chandler sing Lionel Ritchie's classic ballad, 'Endless Love'.

The Last Word: Fabulous Phoebe and cracking Chandler make this a must-see episode for them alone, especially their final scene where they try (and fail) to harmonise on 'Endless Love'. Unfortunately, the poking device plot is a little dull, and proves why Ugly Naked Guy is funny: because he's never normally responsible for more than just a throwaway line in an episode.

309
'The One With The Football'

Writer: Ira Ungerleider
Director: Kevin S. Bright
First US transmission: 21.11.96
First UK transmission (C4): 29.08.97

Guest Cast: Susanna Voltaire (Margha)

Summary: The gang prepares for another Thanksgiving dinner. Well, the girls are preparing while the boys lounge on the sofa watching a football match. Having never played the game before an intrigued Phoebe suggests that they should all play a quick game of football before dinner is ready. Joey and Rachel agree, but there is dissent from the others. Chandler is still depressed about breaking up with Janice, and Monica and Ross reveal that their mother won't let them play football any more as they get too competitive. They explain to the gang that they always used to play football, holding an annual tournament called the Gellerbowl. But the final Gellerbowl ended in tragedy, when Monica broke Ross's nose and their family forbade them from playing ever again, lest any more injuries be sustained. It's obvious that they're still unsure about letting themselves play again, but the gang eventually manage to bring them round. Little do they know how deeply Monica and Ross's competitiveness runs.

As the game goes on, the rivalry between the brother and sister reaches ridiculous heights, while Joey and Chandler develop a rivalry of their own. A beautiful young Dutch woman, Margha, appears at the side of the pitch, and they invite her to watch. The game soon develops into a Ross vs. Monica / Joey vs. Chandler match, with poor Phoebe and Rachel being pushed (literally, in Rachel's case) to the sidelines. Eventually, Monica offers to make the game Girls vs. Boys, and then the fun really begins . . .

Freaky Monica: As Rachel prepares the dessert for the meal, Monica complains that she should be putting 'the marshmallows in concentric circles'. Rachel just responds by stuffing a marshmallow up Monica's nose – which she promptly 'sniffs' out into the bowl.

Chandleresque: Smarting over the break-up with Janice, Chandler is accused of not wanting to do anything any more. He snaps that he does – he wants to loaf around the house, and he's even started to want to drink in the mornings. 'Don't say that I don't have goals!' he cries. When he takes the ball for the first time at the beginning of the game, he mutters a little mantra to himself: 'The ball is Janice. The ball is Janice.' And when he 'beats' Joey by being the chosen beau of Margha, he gleefully tells his friend that 'From now on *I* get the dates, and *you* have to stay home on Saturday nights watching "Ready, Steady, Cook"!'

Spoilt Rachel: The poor woman doesn't get much of a look-in on the game, as everyone is convinced that she's going to be no good. First, neither Monica nor Ross pick her for their teams: when she is the last choice, Ross invites her on to his team, saying, 'Sweetie, now I pick you.' She just grumbles, 'You don't pick me – you're *stuck* with me.' During the game, she is always told to 'go long' (at one point, Ross tells her to go so long that 'we start to look very small'). Eventually, she turns up in the middle of the field eating a pretzel. When Ross asks where she got it from, she explains that she 'went really long'. When she is switched to Monica's team, she finally gets to have a go at running with the ball, only to end up panicking, screaming 'Catch!' and thwacking Monica in the face with it. Of course, it is Rachel who scores the final, winning touchdown . . . or at least she thinks she's won. As Chandler explains, she was about five yards short of the line. Later, when she and Phoebe are seriously considering joining some sort of league so they can play more football, she is told of the National Football League, who, Chandler claims, play on Sundays and Mondays. 'Oh, shoot!' she says. 'I work Monday nights.'

Phoebisms: When Monica, discussing their football tactics, complains that she thought Phoebe knew what she was doing, a confused Phoebs says, 'I thought you meant in *life*.' When she catches the ball for the first time, she takes it full on the chest, squealing, 'Ooh! Broken boobs!' And, of course, it's her boobs that are responsible for the funniest moment in the episode. When the game becomes Girls vs. Boys, as Chandler tries to run for a touchdown, Phoebe lifts up her top and flashes her boobs at him. Mesmerised, Chandler is unable to resist when Phoebe snatches the ball from him and makes a run for it. The second time she uses this tactic Chandler is ready for it, covering his eyes to protect himself. Of course, this means he doesn't notice the big shrub he is about to stumble into.

Slow Joey: A quick lesson in 'Geography for the Insane', as Joey fumbles with his ignorance of the world when meeting Margha. 'You're like from a whole other country!' he states, amazed, when he hears her accent for the first time. Later, when Chandler is trying to impress the Dutch Margha, he asks Joey – in front of the woman – where Dutch people come from. He is stumped, so Chandler gives him a clue. He says they come from 'somewhere near the Netherlands'. Joey's not going to be fooled, though, because he *knows* that the Netherlands is where Peter Pan lives.

Generation X: During the ballgame we hear 2Unlimited's 'Get Ready For This' and 'Misirlou' by Dirk Dale & His Del-Tones, a.k.a. the theme from Quentin Tarantino's *Pulp Fiction* (1994).

The Story So Far: Phoebe once dated a guy with a glass eye. Ross, rather cruelly, invokes what seems to be a childhood chant when, in the middle of the game, he accuses Monica of being a 'cheater, cheater, compulsive eater!' Ross's nose was broken by Monica at the last 'Gellerbowl', twelve years ago. We always knew that Ross and Monica had a pretty competitive, spiteful relationship as children, but this episode really shows the depths it went to. As punishment for the violence of Gellerbowl VI, along with being banned from playing the game ever again, Monica's father took the prized Geller Cup and threw it into the middle of a lake (Chandler, terrified by the story so far, asks, 'Was the curse lifted?'). Even the story of the loss of the Geller Cup is nearly enough to bring Ross to tears, which is why it's even more amazing when the Cup is revealed to still be in Monica's possession. She explains that while Ross was at the hospital, she swam into the middle of the lake to save the prized trophy. The Cup itself, the source of so much anguish, is revealed to be just a plastic troll (the sort with the ugly face and wild hair) nailed to a bit of wood.

The Last Word: The jewel in season three's crown. 'The One With The Football' brings Monica and Ross to centre stage once more, with their twisted childhood rivalry back with a vengeance. We're used to Monica's extreme competitiveness by now, so it seems more like Ross is being the petty one. The love rivals, Joey and Chandler, counterbalance this well, though it's distressing to note how Perry's clothes are now literally hanging off him, and how the physical comedy at which he's usually so adept seems to be draining him. Regardless, the pace and direction of this episode make it one of the best episodes of the season.

310
'The One Where Rachel Quits'

Writers: Michael Curtis & Gregory S. Malins
Director: Terry Hughes
First US transmission: 12.12.96
First UK transmission (C4): 05.09.97

Guest Cast: Mae Whitman (Sarah Tuttle), Shelley Berman (Mr Kaplan, Jr),
James Michael Tyler (Gunther), Kyla Pratta (Charla Nichols, 'Scrud'),
Romy Rosemont (Troop Leader), Sandra Gould (Old Woman),
Gene Crane (Christmas Tree Customer)

Summary: Rachel learns that her boss wants her retrained. Grudgingly, she enters a training programme designed for first-timers, and it soon begins to drag her down. Joey and Chandler suggest that maybe she should leave and search for a job she really wants. As the demeaning retraining continues, she does what they suggest, but The Fear sets in when she realises that she has no job to go to.

Ross, while demonstrating the fine art of racketball, knocks Sarah, a little 'Brown Bird' down a flight of stairs, breaking her leg. Overcome with guilt, he goes to visit her and discovers that she can no longer sell cookies for the Brown Birds. Sarah wanted to sell the most, so she could win her dream trip to Space Camp and stand aboard a real space shuttle. Out of remorse, Ross takes her box of cookies and sets out to sell them himself.

Joey has a seasonal job selling Christmas trees, which Phoebe finds reprehensible. When she is told, though, that the poor, hacked-down trees are actually fulfilling their 'Christmas Destiny', she is somewhat appeased. Trouble strikes when she visits Joey at work only to discover what they do to the aged and dying trees . . .

Phoebisms: This is an exceptional episode for Phoebe as she tries to accept Joey's claim that Christmas trees are actually happy to die in the name of the holiday they celebrate. Once she has got over this, with a fair degree of discomfort, she is then confronted with the horrible truth about the trees that aren't (excuse the pun) spruce enough to be sold. When she discovers that old, unwanted trees get thrown in 'the chipper', she asks

Joey, 'Why do I have a feeling that's not as happy as it sounds?' Her screams of terror (accompanied by well-chosen horror-movie music) as a tree is fed into the chipper are superb.

Chandleresque: Walking into the girls' apartment and seeing all the trees they rescued for Phoebe, Chandler claims it looks like 'Night of the Living Dead Christmas Trees'.

Slow Joey: Joey arrives with 'great news'. He then tells Rachel that he's heard about an opening in a fashion house, and his father might be able to get Rachel an interview. Then he says, 'And now for the great news . . .' He rummages around in his pocket, pulling out an aerosol: 'Snow-in-a-can!'

Freaky Monica: The roots of her compulsive eating as a teenager are probed here as we learn that she used to be a Brown Bird, but that she used to eat all her own cookies, forcing her father to pay for them all. When Ross's cookie sales rekindle Monica's passion for the demon biscuit, she ends up becoming hooked again, finding it difficult to go 'cold turkey' when they finally run out: 'Just a couple more boxes,' she pleads. 'It's no big deal, all right . . . you gotta help me out with a couple more boxes!'

Spoilt Rachel: Rachel's retraining is made all the better by Gunther having to help her with it. With every line, you can see his discomfort at having to demean the object of his affections. Highlights include: Rachel being told about the Tray Spot, which she'd heard other waiting staff talk about but had just assumed it was a club they went to; Gunther promising to tell Rachel why she shouldn't just trap spiders under coffee mugs and leave them there; and Rachel's distress at the talents of her replacement. 'Last night,' she tells her friends, 'she was teaching everybody how to make napkin . . .' And that's as far as she gets before emotion takes over and she begins to whine and shed tears. 'That word was "swans",' Ross completes on her behalf. When she finally quits, she tells a shocked Gunther that she just doesn't care which is decaf and which is regular. Once again, she's dropped everything and stepped out on her own, without any promise of something to go to. As much as we know Rachel's done the right thing, the scene where she serves her final coffee (and still gets it wrong) is almost enough to bring a tear to the eye. Great stuff.

Poor Ross: After the Sarah incident, Ross's friends enjoy making a joke out of his growing reputation as a batterer of small, helpless beings. Chandler, reading from a paper, tells him, 'Says here that a Muppet got whacked on *Sesame Street* last night . . . Where exactly were you around ten-ish?'

Chandleresque: Seconds after Rachel quits, on his advice, he wonders whether this means they'll now have to pay for their coffee. Helping Ross count up his box sales, Chandler sniggers to himself, having just worked out how to spell 'BOOBIES' on the calculator.

Gunther's Still There For You, Rachel: As Rachel walks away disconsolate, he tells her, 'It's all right.' Once she's out of earshot, he adds, 'Sweetheart.' His barely restrained tears at her departure is a wonderful touch.

Generation X: Phoebe's exclamation, 'God bless us, every-one!' evokes the spirit of Christmas as laid out by Tiny Tim in Dickens's *A Christmas Carol*. Brown Birds are, of course, the American equivalent of the British 'Brownies'. The gang hum 'Land of Hope and Glory' as Rachel serves her last ever coffee.

The Story So Far: Rachel leaves Central Perk to work at Fortunata Fashions.

The Last Word: Another excellent episode puts paid to the myth that season three isn't much cop. Everyone is on top form and there are tons of great lines. Highlights, without a doubt, include Phoebe's campaign to save the older Christmas trees (particularly the well-directed chipper scene) and Rachel biting the bullet and leaving her job.

311

'The One Where Chandler Can't Remember Which Sister'

Writer: Alexa Junge
Director: Terry Hughes
First US transmission: 09.01.97
First UK transmission (C4): 12.09.97

Guest Cast: Mimi Lieber (Mary Theresa), Alex Meneses (Cookie),
Penny Santon (Nonna), K. J. Steinberg (Gina), Lisa Melilli (Dina),

James Michael Tyler (Gunther), Shelley Berman (Mr Kaplan, Jr)
and introducing: Steven Eckholdt (Mark)

Summary: Fortunata Fashions turns out to be a big disappointment for Rachel; ironically for someone who was sick of making coffee, her biggest responsibility at this new job seems to be just that. When Mark, a handsome customer at the Moondance Diner, overhears her moaning to Monica about her crappy new job, he pipes up and tells her that he works as an assistant buyer at Bloomingdales and that there's a job vacancy. When Rachel tells Ross the exciting news, he is immediately concerned that Mark's intentions are less-than-altruistic, suggesting to Rachel that all he wants is sex. Rachel won't listen though and is eventually proven right when she gets an interview and is hired. Through it all, Ross's jealousy of Mark steadily increases.

Phoebe takes on Monica and Rachel's noisy neighbour upstairs, but only ends up having the socks (and a lot more) charmed off her. Just as she begins to fall for him, the gang overhear him having sex with another woman. But when the guys head upstairs to sort him out, they too are charmed to meet him.

Chandler, depressed at losing Janice, gets hammered on vodka jelly and, during Joey's birthday party, gets amorous with one of Joey's sisters in a storage cupboard. The next day, he remembers that he fooled around with 'a sister', but he can't remember which one – after all, all seven of them are very similar. Mary Angela – for it is she – phones Joey to tell him what happened, and he confronts Chandler. Was he just taking advantage of Mary Angela, or is he serious about her? Chandler, faced with the wrath of his friend, claims he was serious – much to Joey's delight. Chandler knows he must come clean, but when he calls round at the sisters' house, he is met by Joey and his entire family. He still can't remember which sister is Mary Angela and desperately hopes to extricate himself from the relationship without causing himself pain, embarrassment, humiliation or serious bodily harm from the Tribbiani family . . .
Slow Joey: The episode opens with Joey's brilliantly bad demonstration of how his hand is quicker than his eye. He shows

off his new card trick, asking Monica to pick a card and look at it. As he puts it back in the pack, he quite clearly takes a look at it. He thinks he's got everyone fooled, and they humour him. Later, he talks about his bad feelings after breaking up with a woman called Katherine: he claims to remember how cut up he felt when he saw her walking down the street with her friend Donna. 'Yes,' says Chandler, 'but you ended up having sex with both of them that afternoon.' Joey smiles: 'Any excuse to tell that story.'

Chandleresque: Chandler drunk is a wonder to behold. He lollops around Joey's party, desperately trying to be sensible. Erasing Janice's number from his speed-dial list, he ponders, 'Why must we dial so speedily?' just before he tells one of Joey's sisters that she has 'huge breasts'. For an episode focused around what is usually Perry's forte – a mixture of angst, desperation and excitement – it's when he's incapable of feeling any of these that he's at his best. The morning after, he tells everyone that 'when I've been drinking, sometimes I tend to get overly friendly, and I'm sorry', in reference to the fact that he kissed Monica. 'That's OK,' she replies. As does Rachel. And Ross.

Parents – Who Needs 'Em?: When Chandler is told that the jelly he's just wolfed down is composed of pure vodka, he says that it's 'just like Mom used to make'.

Just Plain Weird: Joey's sisters have among them a fair crop of nutters. Cookie, in particular, seems slightly deranged. When Phoebe tells her that she's drinking vodka and cranberry juice, Cookie replies that it's 'the exact same drink I made myself right after I shot my husband'. Joey's grandma, too, is a force to be reckoned with. According to Joey she was 'the sixth person to spit on Mussolini's hanging body'.

Generation X: The Moonlight Diner's corny film-related menu includes a 'Yentl soup' (presumably a lentil soup named after Barbra Streisand's 1983 movie *Yentl*), a 'James Beans' inspired by, we guess, James Dean and a 'Howdy hold the Dowdy', named after a clown.

The Story So Far: Rachel's interview for the Bloomingdales job is conducted by an unnamed woman, but it's a safe bet to assume this was Joanna (see 'TOW The Dollhouse').

The Last Word: Unfortunately, this episode really shows how off-form Matthew Perry was at this time. Although it's a good script, with plenty of typical Chandler hilarity, there are times when it doesn't quite work. At this stage, the Ross and Rachel aggravation is merely refreshing, although it gets annoying as this plotline unfolds: all it achieves is drawing our sympathies away from Ross. As he's one of the central characters, that's not necessarily a wise thing to do.

312
'The One With All The Jealousy'

Writer: Doty Abrams
Director: Robby Benson
First US transmission: 16.01.97
First UK transmission (C4): 19.09.97

Guest Cast: Steven Eckholdt (Mark), Obba Babatunde (the Director), Carlos Gomez (Julio), James Michael Tyler (Gunther), Wendy Schall (Jeannine), Hillary Matthews (Nancy)

Summary: Monica, whose love life has been less than busy since Richard, gets to date Julio, a cute waiter from the Moondance Diner. As well as being handsome, he turns out to be creative too: he has aspirations to be a poet, and writes a poem just for Monica called 'The Empty Vase'. Her excitement at this romantic gesture wanes when Phoebe explains the meaning of the poem to her: he seems to be suggesting that Monica is something of an airhead.

Joey is auditioning for a role in a musical version of *A Tale of Two Cities*. The liberal untruths on his CV, though, backfire. He claims to be an accomplished and well-practised dancer, and is horrified to learn that the role requires a *lot* of dancing. When he turns up for the call-back dance audition, the casting director announces that the person who was originally going to go through the routines with everyone at the audition can't make it. He asks Joey to step in, since he is so experienced, but poor Joey hasn't a clue about anything except his own 'special' style of dancing.

Rachel is blissfully happy learning the ropes at her new job at Bloomingdales. Mark is teaching her everything, which is giving Ross deep, jealous concerns. He begins to shower Rachel with gifts at work, the final one being an embarrassing barbershop quartet who ram the point home about her having a boyfriend. All this over-zealous attention begins to get on Rachel's nerves . . .

Chandleresque: When Ross is desperately seeking advice on how to cope with his jealousy over Mark, Chandler – equally desperate, and displaying his typically twisted emotions – tells him, 'Don't do anything. Keep it inside. Learn how to hide your feelings!' He realises his gaff, though, and follows it up with a sheepish, 'Don't cry out loud.' At the bachelor party, he's given a pen which shows a picture of a woman whose clothes all fall off when the button is pressed.

Slow Joey: Chandler tries to patiently explain what Joey's letting himself in for in his *A Tale of Two Cities* audition, but Joey is completely unfamiliar with Charles Dickens, Cliff Notes, and the concept of abridgement. This is a brilliant little exchange – especially Joey's clear belief that 'Mr Dickens' is still alive today. When Monica tells him that she and Julio stopped during sex, so he could write a poem, Joey brags that he couldn't stop if a meteor hit him. When told that the bachelor party stripper is called Crystal Chandelier, he says, 'You name a kid that, what do you expect them to grow up to be?'

Dinosaurs ROCK!: Ross is invited to the bachelor party of one of Chandler's friends. He doesn't even know the guy and wonders why he's been asked along. Chandler explains that the groom doesn't have many friends – he's a botanist. Understanding, Ross says that 'botanists are such geeks', right before showing off his dinosaur tie (complete with roaring noises).

Gunther's There For You, Rachel: Ross laments that he is worried that he could lose Rachel to another man. 'Let it be me, let it be me,' mutters Gunther to himself.

The Ballad of Ross & Rachel: And so, as the title suggests, Ross's jealousy increases. His tirade of flowers and gifts to Rachel's workplace is desperately obsessive, and makes for worrying viewing. The final barbershop quartet gambit is a strange sight: it's as embarrassing as it's meant to be, in context, but is without doubt the creepiest, most stalker-level thing Ross has ever done. Finally, Rachel tries to convince Ross that he has nothing to worry about, giving him a huge romantic kiss. All fired up, Ross then heads out to a 'play date' with the stripper from the bachelor party and her kid. Although she's proud of how she handled Ross's feelings, Chandler points out to Rachel that she may have 'just turned him on and sent him to a stripper'.

Generation X: Considering what songs to sing at his *A Tale of Two Cities* audition, Joey decides to plump for 'New York, New York' and 'I Left My Heart in San Francisco'. Though 'New York, New York' became something of an anthem for Frank Sinatra, it was actually written for Liza Minelli for the film of the same name (Martin Scorsese, 1977).

The Story So Far: Phoebe's unique purse leads us to discover that Rachel is scared of turtles.

The Last Word: Joey is the stand-out turn in this episode, demonstrating his amazing stupidity in almost every scene. Of all the Ross/Rachel/Mark episodes, this one remains the best, if only because there seems to be some sort of resolution to it – Rachel convincing Ross, by kissing him, that he has nothing to worry about. But as we know, this plot carries on, and will become more irritating before it is finished.

313
'The One Where Monica And Richard Are Just Friends'

Writer: Michael Borkow
Director: Robby Benson
First US transmission: 30.01.97
First UK transmission (C4): 26.09.97

Guest Cast: Tom Selleck (Dr Richard Burke),
James Michael Tyler (Gunther), Markus Flanagan (Robert),
Gina Hecht (Richard's Date), Steven Harad (Clerk)

Summary: Monica bumps into Richard at the video store (noticing that his 'lips went bald') and they begin chatting. It's obvious to both of them that they still get on like a house on fire and, although Monica suspects that it might be a bad idea, they decide to spend a little time together again – as friends. One thing leads to another, though, and while they are both wrist-deep in squished tomatoes, their hands meet and they realise that they're still attracted to each other. Only one course of action is left, so they stay friends. Friends that sleep together. When Richard announces that he's going on a blind date, though, Monica's jealousy becomes apparent and they have to decide once again whether to stay together or break up.

Phoebe has her own relationship problems when she meets Robert, a Californian sports fanatic who has a penchant for wearing shorts, even in the dead of winter. Not only that but, as Chandler is first to discover to his wide-eyed shock, he doesn't like to wear anything under them. When Phoebe herself finally finds out about his love of the open air, she decides she has to find a way to tell him about it.

Rachel and Joey, throughout all this, have decided to swap their favourite novels with each other. Rachel has to read *The Shining*, while Joey tackles *Little Women*.

Freaky Monica: The poor honey has to cope with all her feelings over Richard coming back to the surface. Her slightly weird obsessive streak is on display again, as she begins to plan a future for Richard and herself based around them being friends: 'Maybe some day,' she suggests, they could be 'friends who stood up in front of their other friends and vowed to be friends forever.' We love her put-down of the annoying video-store clerk: 'Y'know, in a weird way, you have too much power.'

Chandleresque: On meeting Robert for the first time, Chandler asks him why he's wearing shorts when it's so cold. He simply answers that he's from California, to which Chandler nods and says, 'Right, right. Sometimes you guys just burst into flames.' Later, when Phoebe gives Robert something new to wear instead of the revealing baggy shorts he always wears, Chandler's excitement at the idea of Robert's modesty being covered is palpable: 'Stretchy pants! Why, those are the greatest things in the world! If I were you, I would wear them every day, *every day*.' And of course, Chandler gives us all a new euphemism – 'showing *brain*'.

Phoebisms: On being told that Monica and Richard just went for an innocent burger, Phoebe comments, 'There's no such thing as an innocent burger', in reference to her refusal to eat anything with a face.

Slow Joey: He's read *The Shining* many, many times, but still gets frightened by it – so frightened, in fact, that he regularly has to hide the book in the freezer. (That's Joey logic for you.) When he is finally nearing the end of *Little Women* and bad things are starting to happen to the characters, he turns up at Rachel's, close to tears. She offers to put the book in their freezer, and he accepts. The funniest moment in the episode comes when Joey and Rachel start to ruin the plots of each book to each other, after Joey accidentally lets slip the ending of *The Shining* (Joey revealing the scene 'when Jack almost kills them all with that "blank", but then at the last second they get away'). In a particularly bitchy swipe, Rachel blurts out that Beth dies and Joey's world nearly falls to pieces.

Gunther: Warns Robert about his revealing shorts, pointing out that Central Perk is a family place: 'Put the mouse back in the house.'

Generation X: Monica and Richard joke that one of the customers in the video store is likely to go rummaging in the porn section any minute, speculating that he'll probably rent *Citizen Kane* (Orson Welles, 1941), *Vertigo* (Alfred Hitchcock, 1958), and *Clockwork Orgy*, another of the *Friends* writers' attempts to pun-out for porn (see 'TOW The Free Porn'), inspired by *A Clockwork Orange* (Stanley Kubrick, 1971). Joey and Rachel read *The Shining*, the horror novel by Stephen King, and *Little Women* by Louisa May Alcott. For anyone who hasn't read these books, they *do* spoil the endings in this episode.

The Story So Far: Obviously there are some references to 'TOW Barry And Mindy's Wedding'. Ross reminds us that he's 29. According to Chandler, Monica and Richard split up six months ago.

The Last Word: One of the finer examples of this season's habit of the ongoing story overshadowing the comedy. Hey, viewers! Remember Richard? Remember how mad Monica was about him, and him for her? Remember why they broke up, and how distraught Monica was afterwards? Yeah? Yeah? Oh, hey! We forgot the jokes! Grrr. As affecting as this is, it leaves little room for anything actually funny. The plot about Robert's shorts is funny, but a one-joke thing (which is erm, milked *four* times). So that just leaves us with the read-off between Rachel and Joey. At least *that's* good.

314
'The One With Phoebe's Ex-Partner'

Writer: Wil Calhoun
Director: Robby Benson
First US transmission: 06.02.97
First UK transmission (C4): 03.10.97

Guest Cast: Sherilyn Fenn (Ginger), E. G. Daily (Lesley),
James Michael Tyler (Gunther), Steven Eckholdt (Mark)

Summary: Lesley, a new singer at Central Perk, impresses everyone – except for Phoebe. She reveals that Lesley used to be her singing partner, but she walked out on Phoebe to make money writing advertising jingles. Leslie has returned to patch things up with Phoebe and, although she feels reluctant at first, Phoebe soon remembers that her times with Lesley were the happiest in her life. The pair reunite briefly, but things go sour when Lesley tells Phoebe that she should sell 'Smelly Cat' to a kitty litter advertiser.

Chandler meets a beautiful girl called Ginger and they start to date. But Joey reveals to the others that *he* once dated Ginger, and he has a terrible secret shame about their time together. Ginger has an artificial leg, and one night Joey accidentally threw it on to the fire. When Chandler himself finds out about the leg, he has to confront his own feelings over it. And Ginger has to face up to the facts of Chandler's own physical abnormality.

Rachel is deliriously happy to have finally found a job that she both cares about and is good at. But Ross is concerned that the job is pulling her away from him, so he begs Rachel to let him accompany her to a fashion lecture instead of Mark. She agrees, but Ross falls asleep there, later telling her that it was boring. When Ross says that he is worried that Rachel has a whole new part of her life that he doesn't belong to, Rachel tells him that she loves her new job, and he's just going to have to live with it.

Phoebisms: Before we learn of her history with Lesley, it's great to see Phoebe's disparaging comments about the obviously talented singer. When everyone says they like one of her songs, she snaps, 'A song with rhyming words. Ooh, I never thought of that before.' To everyone's surprise, Lesley announces the title of her next song: 'Phoebe Buffay, What Can I Say? I Really Loved When We Were Singing Partners, And I Shouldn't Have Left You That Way'. Phoebe, trying to cover, mutters that it's 'one of those "look for the hidden meaning" songs.' Explaining her out-of-hand dismissal of Lesley's attempts to get back together, Phoebe says, 'Once you betray me, I become like the ice woman . . . very cold, hard, unyielding . . . Nothing can penetrate this icy exterior.' For a minute she seems convincing, until she asks Monica for a tissue. A veritable album-full of songs appear in this episode, including (of course) 'Smelly Cat', 'Sticky Shoe' and the apparently 'sad' song 'Magician Box Mix-up', which she must turn her guitar upside-down to play. Although she claims to have no hard feelings over Lesley using 'Smelly Cat' in the cat litter advert, when she debuts her new song it's obvious that she's lying. 'Jingle Bitch screwed me over,' she sings. 'Go to hell, Jingle Whore!'

Slow Joey: The highlight of the episode comes when Joey is explaining what happened between him and Ginger. He tells the story of the fateful leg-burning incident, and Monica and Phoebe are truly appalled at how terrible his actions were – they are even worse, it seems, than throwing Ginger's dog on to the fire (which they briefly think he did – Joey's only reaction to this is 'I wish!').

Chandleresque: Just when he seems to have got over the fact that Ginger's leg freaks him out, their burgeoning relationship hits a major bump when she finds his third nipple. Driven then to have it removed (by a procedure he calls a 'nubbinectomy'), Chandler later finds a further problem when a very obvious joke is made, but not by him. Immediately, he suspects that the third nipple was the source of all his 'powers', and now he worries that his power might have gone. 'Oh dear God, what have I done!'

The Ballad of Ross & Rachel: Their argument after the fashion lecture is sharp. When Rachel complains that she was polite enough not to fall asleep when she went to a boring palaeontology lecture given by 'Professor Pitstains' ('Pittain,' corrects Ross), Ross counters with the factoid that 'a hundred million people went to see a movie about what I do', saying that there'd be no such interest in a film called *Jurassic Parka*.

The Story So Far: Joey hasn't seen Ginger since 'that night', four years ago. And of course, from this episode on, Chandler no longer has his 'nubbin'. Phoebe has known Lesley ever since their mothers lived together on a barge.

The Last Word: Chandler on form, Phoebe having some great lines, and a funny argument-with-a-point between Ross and Rachel makes for not a bad episode. The lion's share of comedy belongs to Phoebe, though, whose bitterness over the break-up from Lesley is beautifully vicious.

315

'The One Where Ross And Rachel Take A Break'

Writer: Michael Borkow
Director: James Burrows
First US transmission: 13.02.97
First UK transmission (C4): 10.10.97

Guest Cast: Steven Eckholdt (Mark), Stephen Kearney (Mischa), Jim Pirri (Sergei), Angela Featherstone (Chloë), Maury Ginsberg (Isaac)
and introducing: Laura Dean (Sophie)

Summary: Phoebe's new enterprise of giving free massages outside the UN has paid off in an unexpected way: she's dating Sergei, a foreign diplomat who doesn't speak a word of English. On their dates, Mischa, his translator, keeps getting in the way and spoiling the moment, so Phoebe suggests to Monica that she come along to meet Mischa to give her and Sergei a little quality time alone. Unfortunately, Phoebe gets a little too much quality time: Monica hits it off with Mischa so much that Phoebe can't drag him away to chat on her behalf with Sergei.

Chandler and Joey, meanwhile, are obsessing about Chloë, the girl from the Xerox place. When she has figured out that they fancy her, she invites them both to a party at a nightclub. Ross, meanwhile, is still behaving jealously about Rachel's new job. On their one-year anniversary, Rachel can't get away from work to celebrate so Ross decides to take a picnic to her office instead. But this gesture is met with anger, and eventually Ross storms off upset. When Rachel arrives home, Ross forgives her for their earlier argument. Rachel, who was going to give *him* the chance to apologise, suggests that maybe they should take a break from the relationship. Ross leaves the apartment to join Joey and Chandler at the nightclub, where he meets Chloë again – he once had some work done at the Xerox place, and Chloë is obviously slightly smitten with him. When Ross phones Rachel to try to apologise, he hears Mark's voice in the background (he has come round simply to chat to Rachel) and overreacts. Slamming the phone down, he returns to the dancefloor where he kisses Chloë and decides to take her home . . .

Phoebisms: Her attempts to woo, and be wooed by, Sergei – with Mischa interrupting, necessarily, all the while – are terrific. Once Mischa is out of the picture, thanks to Monica, the awkwardness of her conversation with Sergei is brilliant: 'Plate,' he says, picking up a plate. 'See, we don't need them!' Phoebe asserts. Sergei then picks up a cup, saying, 'Plate' again. Phoebe is unimpressed.

Slow Joey: Joey and Chandler, fantasising about a threesome with Chloë, have a bizarre conversation. Initially, they feel they should keep their eyes closed. But what if they fondled the wrong person? Then Joey wonders how they would work out where each of them would be during the act itself. Chandler suggests they toss a coin, but Joey wants clarification on what heads and tails would be. 'If you don't know that,' says Chandler, worried, 'then I don't want to do this with you.'

The Ballad of Ross & Rachel: It's all-out Ross-and-Rachel-Rama in this episode. Ross's unreasonable jealousy finally comes to a head, and Rachel is clearly painted as the innocent party. Quite why the producers decided to make Ross so unequivocally the bad guy is beyond us, but it does at least mean that, forever after, the phrase 'We were on a break!' becomes one of the most successful catchphrases in the show.

Generation X: As Ross's infidelity begins, we hear Ross and Rachel's song, U2's 'With or Without You'. Sergei sings a version of Don McLean's 'American Pie' in his own language.

The Story So Far: Chloë is the Xerox girl mentioned by Chandler in 'TOW The Jam'. There's a reference to one of Phoebe's friends, a 'Spackle Back Harry', whom Monica thinks is unattractive – Phoebe seems terribly protective of him, though.

The Last Word: Phoebe's fling with Sergei is not quite as funny as it should be, but the whole thing is redeemed by her and Monica's bitchiness as Sergei and Mischa separate. So, if that's not funny, it leaves us with the break-up of Ross and Rachel. The scene where Rachel suggests they take 'a break from us' is heart-shattering; Aniston gives her all, investing Rachel once again with a great little-girl-lost fear, combined with the strength to make a decision (it has, after all, almost always been her who made the actual moves in their relationship). Oh, wait – that's not funny either. Well, there's always the fantastic scene where Joey and Chandler work out what they'd do if they had a threesome with Chloë. Now, *that* is funny. Just not very nice.

316
'The One The Morning After'

Writers: Marta Kauffman & David Crane
Director: James Burrows
First US transmission: 20.02.97
First UK transmission (C4): 17.10.97

Guest Cast: Angela Featherstone (Chloë),
James Michael Tyler (Gunther), Maury Ginsberg (Isaac), Cynthia Mann
(Jasmine)

Summary: It's the next day (like you hadn't guessed), and Ross has to come to terms with two things. First, he's slept with Chloë. Second, there's a message on his answering machine from Rachel, telling him how much she loves him and how she wants them to work things out. She tells him that she'll call at his apartment in the morning to talk about it. It's now morning, and Chloë's still there. Rachel arrives, and it's only by luck that she doesn't see the living proof of Ross's infidelity. Following the advice of Chandler and Joey, Ross resolves to make sure Rachel never finds out about what happened with Chloë. He chases around New York, begging everyone who knows not to tell Rachel – until he reaches Gunther and discovers that she already knows.

Later at Rachel and Monica's, Ross and Rachel argue, discuss and pore over the situation. In Monica's room, the rest of the gang – gathered there by several unfortunate incidents involving waxing – listen in, trapped behind the door, unable and unwilling to interrupt the discussions outside. Finally, in the small hours of the morning, they can breathe again when Rachel makes her decision.

Freaky Monica: Monica is feeding fruit into a blender as she talks to Rachel when she suddenly leaps to the wrong conclusion, that her friend and Mark have slept together – the resultant shock makes her accidentally switch the blender on and spray her kitchen with banana. Momentarily anxious about the mess, she brings herself back to Rachel's problems, almost begrudgingly admitting that 'this is more important than fruit . . . on my ceiling.' When she is telling Phoebe about the new miracle pain-free hair-removal wax that she bought from an offer on the television, she explains that she has never fallen for such infomercial tactics before – except when she bought a mop (see 'TOW The Fake Monica').

Chandleresque: On the matter of when Ross should confess his fling to Rachel, Chandler comments that there is a right time for doing it: 'That's what death beds are for.' When Phoebe and Monica are screaming with anguish as they rip the strips of supposedly pain-free wax off their legs, Joey and Chandler rush in (ever the gentlemen), thinking that the girls are being attacked. While Joey is sensibly armed with a heavy brass pan, Chandler bizarrely wields a kettle. While they're all trapped in Monica's room, a screaming row progressing between their friends outside, Monica wonders whether they should do something. 'Yeah,' says Chandler. 'Never cheat on Rachel.'

Phoebisms: When told that Monica has banana on her ceiling, Phoebe instantly takes an interest: 'Wow,' she says. 'I have the spirit of an old Indian woman living in mine.' When Monica tells her about her new wax, Phoebe gets all excited at its organic ingredients, particularly the pain-free formula developed using substances found in the rainforests – 'They have the best stuff in there!' Hearing about the argument between Ross and Rachel, she says, 'I knew something had to be wrong, because my fingernails did not grow at all yesterday.'

Slow Joey: He knows all about covering tracks after cheating on people. You've got to find 'The Trail', the list of people who link the cheated-upon with the cheated-with. In the depths of everyone else's concern for Ross and Rachel, all Joey can wonder is whether he should develop a 'new walk', the kind that gets you noticed the minute you enter a room. Later, as he sneaks past an exhausted Rachel asleep on the couch, Chandler asks him if that is his new walk. 'No,' he whispers so as not to disturb Rachel, 'I really have to pee.'

The Ballad of Ross & Rachel: And that's just about the only thing that this episode is about. The scenes of them arguing are sometimes quite harrowing, but marvellously broken up by the comments of the listening friends in Monica's room. Rachel, quite rightly, has the script on her side, and Aniston seems to have a whale of a time delivering some of the episode's finest lines. When Ross says that it was just a mistake, she snaps, 'What were you trying to put it in? Her purse?' Later, when Ross tries to excuse himself by saying that he thought the relationship was dead, she says, 'Well, you sure had a hell of a time at the wake.' Crisply scripted and finely acted, the scenes of the end of their relationship are the highlight of this episode. It's just a shame that the bitching and sniping, and this distinctly unfunny plotline, had to dominate the rest of the season.

Gunther's a BASTARD!: Our fine apron-clad friend is the one link in The Trail that Ross didn't get to in time. Yes, folks, we have him to thank for Rachel discovering Ross's infidelity.

The Story So Far: (Take a big breath) Chloë works with a guy called Isaac. Isaac's sister is called Jasmine, and she works with Phoebe at the Healing Hands Massage Parlour. Obviously

Phoebe is friends with Rachel – but Jasmine's roommate is Gunther, whose undying love for Rachel is what forced him to tell her. We saw Jasmine in 'TOW Frank Jr' and, way back, in 'The Pilot'.

The Last Word: This is the big event of the season, and it's not a happy one (echoing the tone of the season as a whole). A fine script manages to deliver some terrible news, while also managing to be seriously funny in places. We defy the hardened viewer not to blub, even a little – at the final lines between Ross and Rachel.

'This can't be it,' says a confused and devastated Ross.

Rachel stares back, finally realizing that it's over. 'Then how come it is?'

317

'The One Without The Ski Trip'

Writers: Scott Silveri & Shana Goldberg-Meehan
Director: Sam Simon
First US transmission: 06.03.97
First UK transmission (C4): 24.10.97

Guest Cast: Jane Sibbett (Carol Willick)

Summary: Rachel invites her friends (except Ross, of course) to her sister's ski cabin for the weekend, just before Ross suggests they have a laser-disc-*cum*-darts marathon that same weekend at his flat. Since Rachel asked first, they all awkwardly admit that they should go on the ski trip. The tension of his friends' break-up reminds Chandler of his parents' divorce, and his anxiety leads him back to smoking. As they journey up to the ski cabin in Phoebe's grandmother's cab, Chandler engineers a stop-off so that he can have another cigarette. They all get out into the cold night air, slamming the car door behind them and locking the car keys inside. When Joey manages to break back into the car (ingeniously using the under-wire from Phoebe's bra), they prepare to set off. But the car splutters to a standstill as Phoebe tries to drive away. 'This has happened before,' she says, so Monica figures she must know how to fix it. 'Yep,' Phoebe replies, 'put more gas in.'

Cold, alone and lost in the middle of nowhere, their only salvation is Ross. If they call him, he can come and look for them and help them out. But Rachel is insistent that they don't ask for his help . . .

Chandleresque: 'You're smoking again?' gasps Joey early in the episode. 'Well, actually, yesterday I was smoking again,' Chandler replies. 'Today, I'm smoking still.' Seeing as he first started smoking after his parents' divorce, when Rachel chides him for taking up the habit again, he cries: 'Hey, shut up! You're not my real mom!' He also explains that it was the divorce that set off his habit of using humour as an emotional shield: 'So,' says Monica, 'if your parents hadn't got divorced, you'd be able to answer a question like a normal person?' One brilliant example of this is when he hears a knock at the door and worries that 'with my luck, that's going to be him.' 'Him?' says Phoebe. 'Him, Ross?' 'No,' replies Chandler acidly, 'Hymn 253: "His Eyes are on the *Sparrow*".'

Slow Joey: He sees Chandler reading a newspaper and asks, 'Can I see the comics?' Chandler, a little snobby and affronted, tells him that it's the *New York Times*, to which Joey replies, 'All right. *May* I see the comics?' Later, he marvels at the length of time it's taking Rachel and Ross to come to terms with things – it's been a week now: 'It's never taken me more than a week to get over a relationship.' 'It's never taken you more than a *shower* to get over a relationship,' says Monica. Some wonderfully twisted lateral thinking from Joey: trapped at the restrooms on an unknown road, Joey spells out a big 'HELP' using twigs. But he's spelled it 'PLEH': 'that's "help" spelled backwards, so that the helicopters can read it from the air.'

Phoebisms: Phoebe likens the dilemma over taking sides to something she saw on *60 Minutes*: 'At first you're really mad at that pharmaceutical company for making the drug and then, y'know, you just feel bad for the people because they need it to make their hair grow.' In Central Perk a while later, she cunningly tries to defuse the situation by trying to trick Ross and Rachel into getting back together: in a quiet ventriloquist's mutter, she says, '[in a Ross-like voice] Um, Rachel I'm really sorry. [in a Rachel-like voice] That's OK, do you want to get back together? [back to Ross] Yeah, OK . . . Did anyone else hear that?'

Freaky Monica: Her idea of fun, when she offers to stay home and spend the weekend with Ross: 'We can make fudge!' which Ross understandably sees as pity for him on her part.

Spoilt Rachel: Rachel has a little rule explaining why she never uses public toilets: 'No tissue, no tushie.' When it is suggested that Ross comes to pick them up, she says, 'I am not getting in a car with Ross. We'll just have to . . . live here.'

Poor Ross: Or should that be 'Poor Carol'? He calls round unannounced at her flat, to find he is interrupting preparations for an anniversary dinner between her and Susan. He moans his excuse: 'Candles, champagne. Yeah, anniversaries are great. 'Cause you know love lasts forever, y'know? Nothing like it in this lifetime, money in the bank, so Rachel and I broke up.' When Carol challenges him about sleeping with another woman, Ross retorts: 'You're the one to talk!'

The Ballad of Ross & Rachel: It's that nasty period when the friends get dragged into the break-up, but Rachel and Ross do try their hardest not to involve people too much. Their resolution to be civil at the end of the episode is sweet, and a relief. It's surprising to see Rachel, particularly, thank Ross for letting them continue with their ski trip. It's not surprising, though, to see how Ross ensures Carol is on his side: he obviously paints himself as the innocent victim, making Carol believe that Rachel fell in love with Mark. But Phoebe sets the record straight for Carol, and she is rightly appalled.

Girl Power: After Joey asks for the wire from a bra to open the cab door with, the girls argue about who has the biggest breasts – all of them insisting theirs are smallest! Monica claims hers are 'non-breasts' compared to Rachel's. As the friends are trapped miles from anywhere, Monica discovers that the tampons in the rest-room are only a penny each, suggesting they stock up.

Parents – Who Needs 'Em?: 'This is like when my parents got divorced,' Chandler explains. 'Man, I hope Ross doesn't try to kidnap me after Cub Scouts.'

Just Plain Weird: There's a sign in Phoebe's grandmother's cab that reads 'Beam Me Up, Jesus'.

Generation X: Although we can't see how it *could* be, Chandler's freaking out is supposed to represent Shelley Winters from *The Poseidon Adventure* (Ronald Neame, 1972), in which we see Ms Winters swim underwater to save her friends, but die in the process. Yeah, *you* work it out!

The Story So Far: Chandler reveals that he was nine years old when his parents got divorced and he started smoking. The cabin the gang goes to belongs to Rachel's sister (see 'TOW The Dozen Lasagnes'). Ross remembers that Carol and Susan got married in January (see 'TOW The Lesbian Wedding').

The Last Word: A great episode, where everyone gets a fair crack at the whip. Perry and Kudrow are on good form, and have most of the best lines. Although this is an episode about the break-up, it's refreshingly low on bitchiness, choosing to concentrate more on the plight of the people caught in the middle. Fine stuff.

318
'The One With The Hypnosis Tape'

Writer: Seth Kurland
Director: Robby Benson
First US transmission: 13.03.97
First UK transmission (C4): 31.10.97

Guest Cast: Giovanni Ribisi (Frank Jr), James Michael Tyler (Gunther), Jeffrey D. Brooks (Trent)
and introducing: Jon Favreau (Pete Becker), Debra Jo Rupp (Alice)

Summary: Frank Jr, Phoebe's weird half-brother, stops by Central Perk to give her some good news: he's going to get married. Although she is initially very excited about this, when she meets Frank's fiancée, she is secretly outraged and wants the wedding to be called off. Frank is going to marry Alice (or 'Mrs Knight', as he keeps calling her), his Home Economics teacher – a woman almost twice his age. Although they are obviously passionately in love, Phoebe sets about trying to persuade Frank against the idea. Or at least, she sets Ross and Joey the task, but things go awry and they end up agreeing to become ring bearer and best man respectively. Phoebe decides to confront Alice but, although it seems she has managed to convince them of their haste, the minute they see each other again they fall into a loving clinch and Phoebe has no choice but to give them her blessing.

Monica, while working at the Moondance Diner, tells Rachel that she is getting frustrated that she hasn't had a date in months. Pete, sitting nearby, once again offers to go out with her. Although she refuses, when she and Rachel later discover that he is a multi-millionaire, Rachel manages to cajole her into going for dinner with him – in Rome. But even after that, she's still not attracted to him.

Chandler, meanwhile, tries self-hypnosis to quit smoking. It's surprisingly successful – but it does have one very strange side effect . . .

Spoilt Rachel: When Monica is bemoaning her lack of dates, she asks Rachel if she could set her up with someone at work. Rachel then points out something about her industry that has obviously escaped Monica's notice. 'Well, that shouldn't be a problem,' she replies. 'I mean, I work in fashion and all I meet are eligible *straight* men.' When she finds out that Pete is rich beyond her wildest dreams, she realizes that the $20,000 dollar tip he left Monica is genuine: 'I can't believe this is a real $20,000 cheque, oh this is just so exciting.' 'Or incredibly offensive,' Monica points out. Grasping the cheque, Rachel just says, 'Oh yeah, sure, that too.'

Freaky Monica: She really has no life. When trying to persuade her to go out with Pete, Rachel asks her what happened on last Saturday's *Walker: Texas Ranger*. Monica, laughing warmly at the memories, says, 'Well, Walker was looking for this big bus load of kids . . . All right, I get your point.'

Slow Joey: When Frank asks him, 'Isn't sex better when it's with one person that you really, really care about?' Joey, incredulous, replies, 'Yeah, in a poem, maybe.' In the final scene we see how Joey, with the power of hypnotism at his fingertips, tries to get Chandler to make him a cheese sandwich every night (see 'TOW The Embryos').

Chandleresque: At Central Perk, he sits in front of Rachel and puts a cigarette in his mouth, preparing to light it. Rachel just pulls it out and throws it on the floor. He takes another one and puts it to his lips; again, Rachel grabs it and throws it away. 'OK,' he says, 'that's like the least fun game ever.' When Rachel gives him the hypnosis tape, he places it to his arm and watches it fall to the ground: 'Nope, that patch is no good,' he observes. He consents to try the tape, however, and plays it while sleeping: 'Cigarettes don't control you,' it proclaims. 'You are a strong, confident woman, who does not need to smoke. A strong, confident *woman* . . .' Chandler then starts to act very strangely, and Matthew Perry does a marvellous job with this new Chandler, totally at ease with his feminine side. When he shares Rachel's excitement at Monica's date with a rich guy, the look on everyone's faces says it all.

Phoebisms: Phoebe's surprising summation of her brother's relationship: 'I don't want to be all judgmental, y'know, but this is sick. It's sick and wrong!' 'Is it the age thing?' Ross asks her. 'I'm fine with the age thing, until it starts sticking its tongue down my little brother's throat!'

Joey's an Actor?: At the opening of the episode, he is practising his fake laugh. Soon, Monica is practising with him – and they both get the perfect opportunity when Chandler makes his first crack of the episode.

Gunther, can you spare a match?: Gunther is an ex-smoker. When he sees Chandler walking in, smoking, he walks over to him and tells him to put it out. Chandler agrees, but only if he can finish it first. Gunther's prepared to let him, if he'll give him a drag. The waiter takes a deep breath, and lets out the smoke with a sigh. 'Oh, dark mother,' he says. 'Once again I suckle at your smoky teat.' When he offers the cigarette back to the disturbed Chandler, he just waves it away. 'Why don't you hang on to that one?'

Parents – Who Needs 'Em: Phoebe gives her own suggestion for how to stop smoking: 'You have to dance naked in a field of heather, and then bathe in the sweat of six healthy young men.' 'Or what my father calls "Thursday night",' deadpans Chandler.

Just Plain Weird: Welcome back Frank, whose grasp of the real world seems even more tenuous than his sister's. Joey, trying to persuade him to think again about the marriage, points out that 'you're eighteen, OK, she's forty-four. When you're thirty-six, she's gonna be eighty-eight.' Frank just says, 'You don't think I know that?' Frank gets some of the best lines in this episode, and it's great to see Giovanni Ribisi not going to waste. Alice is a scream too – literally, as her trademark startling (but infectious) giggle makes its debut.

The Ballad of Ross & Rachel: Ross, when confronted by Frank's love for Alice, realising that he's really messed up something special with Rachel, is wonderfully done. Here, for once, they play the break-up for laughs not bitterness. Earlier in the episode, Ross appears to deride hypnosis simply because Rachel supports it; he claims it 'is beyond crap'. Rachel reminds him of the time he appeared in a stage hypnotist's act, but he claims he wasn't actually hypnotised. 'Oh, right,' splutters Rachel, 'you *always* pull your pants down at the count of three and play "Wipeout" on your butt cheeks.'

Generation X: Jon Favreau starred in the critically acclaimed film *Swingers* (Doug Liman, 1997) and the blockbuster *Deep Impact* (Mimi Leder, 1998). 'Wipeout' was originally a hit for the Surfaris in 1963, though the Fat Boys and The Beach Boys teamed up to cover it in 1987. Monica has become hooked on the CBS action series *Walker: Texas Ranger*, which stars Chuck Norris. Pete Becker is a thinly-veiled take on Bill Gates, the Microsoft king.

The Story So Far: Monica reminds Rachel that she's only dated two men this year, Richard (see 'TOW Barry And Mindy's Wedding') and Julio ('TOW All The Jealousy').

The Last Word: A good episode, featuring a fine turn from Kudrow as Phoebe tries to come to terms with something she thinks is wrong. Perry as the empowered Chandler is frighteningly brilliant, and it's a bit of a shame that more couldn't be made of this little plot. Still, there's a good balance between the heart-warming and the rib-tickling here.

319

'The One With The Tiny T-Shirt'
(a.k.a. 'The One With The Lousy T-Shirt')

Writer: Adam Chase
Director: Terry Hughes

First US transmission: 27.03.97
First UK transmission (C4): 07.11.97

Guest Cast: Steven Eckholdt (Mark), Jon Favreau (Pete Becker),
James Michael Tyler (Gunther), Ethel Ayler (Hospital Administrator)
and introducing: Dina Meyer (Kate Miller),
Reg Rogers (Marshall Talmant, the Director)

Summary: Rachel asks Ross round to her apartment. He is
convinced that this is the first step on the road to reconciliation, so he's upset when he discovers that all she wants to do is
return a box full of his things. Unreasonably irate, he starts to
demand that he takes everything back, including a 'FRANKIE
SAY RELAX' T-shirt that Ross used to wear when he was
fifteen. Although it's ridiculously small and Rachel uses it as
nightwear, Ross storms off wearing the shirt.

Later, Mark admits to Rachel that he has had a crush on her
for a while and – now that she's no longer with Ross – asks her
out on a date. Ross gets wind of this, and spends that evening
at Chandler's, ceaselessly staring through his peephole,
waiting for Rachel's return. When she and Mark finally do get
back, he watches them go inside together and Chandler has to
physically restrain him from following them in. Telling him
that he must finally let go, Chandler manages to convince Ross
that Rachel is moving on. Meanwhile, Rachel tells Mark that,
nice as he is, she just can't use him to get back at Ross. A little
disappointed, Mark leaves.

Joey is having trouble with a fellow cast member in his new
play. The beautiful, fiery Kate meets all his efforts to get along
with arrogant, snide comments. Joey can't stop talking about
the woman, and Chandler points out that this might be because
he has a crush on her. Pete and Monica are still dating, but he
is beginning to get a little impatient. He asks Monica whether
their relationship is going anywhere, and she admits to him
that she still doesn't find him attractive. Will Pete's patience
run out . . .?
Joey's an Actor!: Kate recognises Joey from the Milk Master
2000 infomercial (seen in 'TOW The Metaphorical Tunnel'),
claiming, 'You're the guy who doesn't know how to pour
milk!' Joey explains that this shows what a good actor he is,
because of course he can pour milk. Then, Kate remembers

that he 'choked on a cookie' during the commercial. Embarrassed, Joey admits, 'That was real.'

Freaky Monica: It's revealed in this episode that Monica paints numbers on all her mugs, so that they can be easily tracked down. At one point, Monica is lamenting the fact that she can't get into a decent relationship – here's Pete, who's handsome, clever, funny, but she just feels nothing for him. 'Does it sound like there's something wrong with me?' she asks Phoebe. 'Yeah,' her friend replies. 'Kind of.'

Phoebisms: Apropos of nothing, Phoebe wonders at one point, 'Why isn't it Spiderm'n? You know, like Goldman, Silverman . . .?' This wonderfully twisted little conversation continues, with Chandler explaining that it's not his surname – 'it's not, like, Phil Spiderm'n' – and then Phoebe insisting there should be a superhero called Gold Man. Although it has nothing to do with anything, this little exchange is a nice distraction.

Chandleresque: Chandler's own wonder at the fact that he's in his late twenties, but still so childish, comes to the fore when he meets Pete for the first time. 'You're *our* age,' he keeps repeating, stunned by Pete's financial success. This little Peter Pan aspect of Chandler's character isn't touched on very often, but it goes a long way towards explaining his behaviour. Like when he does a High Chaparral show-down, using the footrest on a leather armchair instead of a six-shooter. 'Draw!' he yells at the empty chair, and whips his own chair into its reclining position. Joey then walks in, and Chandler suddenly turns round and says cagily, 'I wasn't doing anything.'

The Ballad of Ross & Rachel: So, what Ross suspected all along is true: Mark did want to go out with Rachel and, furthermore, she is at least partly open to the idea. But, as she explains to Phoebe later, she just couldn't do it. 'I mean,' she says, 'I'm standing there with this charming, cute guy, who's asking me to go out with him – which I'm allowed to do – and I felt guilty.' Phoebe thinks that she's obviously still not over Ross, and that she has issues with her father. When Rachel says she has no such issues, Phoebe – as if she had just performed some great feat of psychoanalysis –

announces, 'It's probably just the Ross thing, then.' Ross, meanwhile, is quite clearly not over Rachel. His vigil at Chandler's peephole is wonderful: first he wants to see what happens, then he doesn't. Eventually, Chandler has to physically restrain him from going over to spoil Rachel's date. He throws one arm around Ross's neck, clambers onto his back, and takes hold of the foosball table with the other hand. Even with all this luggage, Ross still soldiers on towards the door. Finally, Chandler has a heart-to-heart with Ross, convincing him to let go of Rachel. (That this conversation is carried out while Chandler is resting on Ross's back, his legs braced half-way up his front door, brings a brilliant note of crazy comedy to the moment.)

Gunther's There For You, Rachel: At the opening of the episode, Gunther is thinking to himself how he might approach Rachel for a date now that Ross is out of the picture. As he silently contemplates asking Rachel to come to dinner ('as my lover'), he watches Mark swoop in, admit his crush, ask her for a date, and get a pleasantly stunned 'Wow' in reply. A hurt look on his face, he disappears into the bowels of Central Perk. We hear an almighty crash, like ten Welsh dressers have just collapsed, and then he reappears. 'I dropped a cup.' When Monica claims that Pete has everything, Chandler challenges her by asking if he has a life-sized Imperial Stormtrooper from *Star Wars* (Monica claims he has two!).

Generation X: Dina Meyer co-starred in the sci-fi movie *Starship Troopers* (Paul Verhoeven, 1998). The craze that was 'Frankie Say . . .' was the product of Paul Morley's superb PR promotion of the band Frankie Goes To Hollywood. The T-Shirts, like the group, were everywhere in the summer of 1984.

The Last Word: The Ross and Rachel stuff is getting boring by this point, which lets the episode down somewhat. Monica's problems with Pete are also too serious to be very funny, as are Joey's feelings over Kate. Altogether, this episode is a little too soapy: the only laughs are provided by Chandler and Phoebe, and their little random moments of comedy.

320
'The One With The Dollhouse'

Writer: Wil Calhoun
Director: Terry Hughes
First US transmission: 10.04.97
First UK transmission (C4): 14.11.97

Guest Cast: Dina Meyer (Kate Miller),
Reg Rogers (Marshall Talmant, the Director),
Jennifer Milmore (Lauren), Laura Dean (Sophie)
and introducing: Alison LaPlaca (Joanna)

Summary: Women trouble for Joey and Chandler: Joey wants one who doesn't want him, and Chandler doesn't want one who wants him. Of course, there are complications. Joey's fallen for Kate, one of his fellow-actors in his current play, in a big way. But she's seeing the director, Marshall, and Joey's being torn apart – he can't understand why she doesn't want him. When their performances in rehearsal begin to suffer, Marshall storms out in over-dramatic disgust and Kate and Joey wonder how they can spice up their acting. But they get a little too spicy, and end up in bed together. Joey is on top of the world, until he discovers that Kate is doing what he has done to a thousand women. It looks like she is now going to just cast him aside.

Chandler, meanwhile, meets Rachel's boss, Joanna. She falls for him instantly, and Rachel sets them up on a date. While Chandler is completely unimpressed by her, she is totally smitten – so much so that she fails to spot that Chandler is trying to give her the brush-off. When he tells her he'll call, she thinks he means it. When she learns the truth, things get nasty for Rachel.

Ross and Monica's Aunt Sylvia has passed away ('Yes!' yelps Monica. 'She was a cruel, cranky, old bitch!') and left her dollhouse to Monica. She's delighted, because she was never allowed to play with it. She suggests to Phoebe that she should bring her dolls round so they can finally use the dollhouse for what it's for – playing. But Phoebe's choice of dolls (a dinosaur, a handkerchief ghost and a three-storey dog) doesn't go down well with Monica, so Phoebe decides to build a dollhouse of her own . . .

Chandleresque: As Joey laments the fact that Kate is the first woman he wants who isn't interested in him, he turns to Chandler and asks, 'Is this what it's like to be you?' Monica is explaining that Aunt Sylvia would always say that the dollhouse was a thing to be looked at but not played with, to which Chandler says, 'My grandmother used to say that exact same thing to me.' When he is introduced to Joanna, she just repeats his surname like it's a timer going off: 'Bing!' Chandler explains that his name is 'Gaelic for "thy turkey's done".' After he has had the date with Joanna, he tells Rachel that he *never* wants her to set him up with anyone; from now on he makes his own dates. Then he adds, 'That's just a lot of big talk, you know?'

Phoebisms: Her games with Monica's dollhouse involve it being built on both an Indian burial ground and a nuclear waste dump. When Ross suggests that seems pretty unlikely, she comments that 'obviously you don't know much about the US government.' So, the giant dog has to protect the inhabitants from an attack by a Tyrannosaurus Rex, with a handkerchief haunting the attic all the while. When Monica freaks and says that Phoebe can't play with her house any more, she dubs Monica's house 'the House of No Imagination'. Phoebe builds her own house (complete with slide, edible furniture, bubble-blowing chimney, fairy lights and an aroma room). When a spark from the aroma room causes her house to be burned to the ground, she immediately tries to find out who survived the blaze. While nearly all her toys are OK, there's something lying under a handkerchief (probably the ghost) on the table. She lifts the hankie and screams as she sees the charred remains of the Foster puppets.

Slow Joey: Kate sneers at his choice of dates, by calling her understudy, Lauren, 'the sweater'. Joey retorts, 'It's what's under the sweater that counts.' When Kate suggests there needs to be something more between their characters when they kiss, Joey suggests, 'Maybe he could slip her the tongue.' Subtle and charming as ever. At the end of the episode, when he now knows how it feels to be tossed aside by someone you like, Joey sets about phoning all his ex-girlfriends to apologise.

Joey's an ACTOR: Lauren, Kate's understudy, comes up to him and announces that she's a big fan of his, to which Joey gasps, 'What?'

The Ballad of Ross & Rachel: When Rachel arrives home to tell Chandler that she wants to set him up on a date, she walks through the door and says, 'I need to talk to you.' Ross turns round and asks, 'What's up?' She tells him that she meant Chandler and there's an embarrassed exchange which ends with Ross saying, 'Well, if something comes up . . .' Chandler, breaking the tension, says, 'I'm glad you guys are past that little awkward phase.'

Dinosaurs ROCK!: After the dinosaur attack on Monica's dollhouse is over, Ross politely points out to Phoebe that 'dinosaurs don't go "ruff!"' Phoebe, with equal authority, states that 'the little ones do'.

Just Plain Weird: Marshall, the manic director whom Joey likens to a cartoon character, starts rehearsals with the affirming, 'All right, it's time to act, my talking props!'

Boys Will Be Boys: Chandler escorts Rachel to her desk so she can fetch him a copy of her 'summer catalogue'. Think about it.

Shut Up, Sophie!: With Joanna's debut, we see the start of the I-suck-up-to-you/I-see-through-you relationship between her and her other assistant, Sophie. When Sophie suggests that Chandler might be 'intimidated by really smart, strong, successful women', Joanna says, 'Sophie, will you please climb out of my butt?'

Parents – Who Needs 'Em?: When Chandler walks in to see Phoebe's dollhouse all lit up with fairy lights and blowing bubbles, he comments, 'Hey, my father's house does that!'

The Story So Far: Monica's Aunt Sylvia has previously been mentioned in 'TOW The Dozen Lasagnes' and 'TOW Old Yeller Dies'. Phoebe's jealousy for Monica's dollhouse is because when she was a child, all she had was a barrel – not to play with dolls in, just a barrel. Lauren refers to the time Joey played Dr Drake Ramoray on *Days Of Our Lives* and they dropped him down an elevator shaft (see 'TOW Dr Ramoray Dies').

The Last Word: A great episode for Phoebe, as Kudrow brings bucketfuls of relish to her games with the dollhouses. Phoebe's own dollhouse knocks spots off Monica's, and it's a great tragedy to see it go up in flames. (Ross's final solution of putting the fire out – by shoving it under the shower while Monica is in there – is brilliant. And, yes Monica, we believe you when you say you were 'just checking the shower massager'.)

321

'The One With A Chick. And A Duck'

Writer: Chris Brown
Director: Michael Lembeck
First US transmission: 17.04.97
First UK transmission (C4): 21.11.97

Guest Cast: Jon Favreau (Pete Becker), James Michael Tyler (Gunther)

Summary: Working at the Moondance Diner has reached a new low for Monica. The management are now insisting that all the waiting staff wear roller-skates. Monica is practising her skating outside Central Perk when an interruption from Gunther causes her to crash into Rachel, sending them both tumbling to the floor. By the time she gets to work, she's still no better at skating and keeps falling over as she welcomes back Pete from his trip to Japan. It seems that her humiliation might come to an end, though, when Pete tells her that he's bought a restaurant and he wants her to be head chef. Once he's convinced her that he's not doing it just to win her over, Monica agrees and immediately leaves her job at the diner. But later, she realises that Pete has been lying, and very nearly calls the whole thing off, until a kiss changes her mind about everything.

Ross is excited because he's been asked to join a panel of palaeontologists on a television programme but, when he briefly calls in at Monica and Rachel's before the recording of the show, his plans are derailed when he sees the state that Rachel's in. It seems she took quite a beating when Monica skated into her; she needs to go to the hospital and obviously needs someone to go with her.

There's happiness on the other side of the hallway though, as Chandler and Joey greet a couple of new arrivals to their apartment. Joey decides to buy Chandler a fluffy little chick as an Easter present. They soon decide, however, that she is too much responsibility for them and Chandler tries to take her back to the store. They won't take her back though, and when he tries the animal shelter, he discovers that they are likely to have her destroyed. So, back he comes with the chick, and another rescued animal – a duck!

Chandleresque: It's the first regular appearance of the short-lived goatee (after its brief appearance back in 'TOW The Flashback'). Maybe it's just that Matthew Perry was so thin at this point that it didn't work, but we definitely prefer him without it. We agree with Joey when he says that 'with that goatee, you kinda look like Satan'.

Slow Joey: A smile of delight crosses Joey's face when he exits Central Perk just after the shaking accident to find Monica writhing on top of Rachel. When he sees a news report about the plight of abandoned and ill-cared for chicks on television, he takes it as an advertisement for a great gift idea.

Phoebisms: She manages to work out that Pete is lying to Monica when he says he has met another woman. When Pete implores her not to tell Monica, Phoebe says, 'Absolutely, I promise. Tell her what?' Thinking that she's pretending to have forgotten their whole conversation, Pete thanks her. 'No, I'm serious,' she replies. 'I mean, I'm intuitive, but my memory sucks.' At Central Perk, Phoebe announces to Monica, 'I have to tell you something' but 'I can't tell you'. She proceeds to have Monica try and guess what she can't tell her. As her methods of communication get increasingly strange, Monica gives up, saying, 'I feel like I'm talking to Lassie.' And of course, it was her suggestion to the manager of the Moondance Diner that leads to Monica being forced to wear skates!

Poor Ross: He turns up at Monica and Rachel's wearing an extremely cheesy white suit and red bow tie. When Rachel criticises his outfit, he points out that they're not going out any more, so he can wear whatever he likes. Rachel agrees, saying he's 'free to look as stupid as you like'.

Freaky Monica: She reveals that she always used to dream of being a head chef: 'I mean, this has been my dream since I got my first Easy Bake Oven and opened Easy Monica's Bakery.' She doesn't, however, seem to notice how inappropriate her bakery's name was.

Gunther: He may be the one who unwittingly started to bring Rachel and Ross back together. If Gunther hadn't offered Rachel that coffee when she should have been catching the skating Monica, then she wouldn't have been distracted and Monica wouldn't have crashed into her, breaking her rib. The resultant care and attention she needed could only be given, of course, by Ross.

Dinosaurs ROCK!: When Ross announces that he's going to appear in a programme about 'these fossils they just found in Peru', Chandler seems excited. 'Oh my God!' he says, before adding, 'Who's going to watch that?'

Magna Doodle: Introduced in this episode is the Magna Doodle message board, which is pinned to the wall by the door in Joey and Chandler's apartment. In later episodes it becomes the source of many hidden gags, but for its debut, someone's merely drawn a big happy face.

The Chick and the Duck: When he and Joey get their first new pet, Phoebe asks if they know anything about chicks. 'Fowl? No,' says Chandler. '*Women* (in a now-we're-talking tone) . . . 'No.' Later, he is alone with the chick as they both watch *Baywatch*. 'I know,' he says as the little bird chirps at the picture on the screen. 'That's Yasmine Bleeth. She's a completely different kind of chick. I love you both. But in very different ways.' This is the moment of inspiration where the chick is given its name: Yasmine. Chandler hauls the unnamed duck out of the apartment into the hallway as Ross and Rachel are passing by. 'You stay out here,' he yells at it, 'and you think about what you did . . . that chick is not a toy!'

Cruelty To Animals: Chandler asks the gang if they know how to get a chick out of a VCR. Over the closing credits, Joey arrives home to see Chandler giving the duck a bath, while Yasmine watches on from dry land. Joey wonders whether chicks can swim too, so they give it a try – only to discover that they can't. As Chandler cradles and comforts poor, drenched Yasmine, a look of horror crosses his face when he hears Joey turn on the hairdryer.

The Ballad of Ross & Rachel: This is the one where they nearly get back together. With Rachel injured and in pain, Ross has to help her with her make-up (putting it on very badly) and then she asks him to help her get dressed. Rachel doesn't want him to see her naked, though, and Ross finds this ridiculous – after all, he has seen her this way many times before. He begins to gently freak Rachel out by closing his eyes and imagining her naked, until her pain finally drives him to take her seriously and suggest that she really should get to the hospital. He agrees to go with her, even though it means missing his television appearance. When Rachel finds out what he's given up for her, there's a second – just a second – where it looks like they are about to kiss.

Generation X: Joey watches *Quincy, ME*, the medical detective series. Monica compares Ross's white suit to something Colonel Sanders, founder of Kentucky Fried Chicken, might wear. When Joey cuddles the chick, Chandler warns: 'Easy, Lenny' – a reference to the character from John Steinbeck's *Of Mice and Men*. Chandler gives us an impromptu performance of 'Old MacDonald' ('Here a chick, there a chick . . .'). Something Joey and Chandler obviously don't know is that even male chicks don't have external sex organs (see 'TOW The Embryos').

The Story So Far: A guy called Stu Vincent offered Monica a necklace when she was in seventh grade (she turned him down as he was her health teacher). According to Monica, Chandler keeps a sock by his bed – and we really don't want to know why.

The Last Word: Yay for the chick and the duck! This is a brilliantly scripted episode, especially the sequences where Joey and Chandler, like a married couple coping with a new child, begin to argue and worry that the chick is driving a wedge between them. Matthew Perry, though still not back on top form, gives one of his best performances of the season, as he gradually falls in love with Yasmine (chick, not Bleeth). The scenes between Rachel and Ross are genuinely sweet, and the script shows a marvellous warmth and understanding between them. One of the best episodes ever.

322

'The One With The Screamer'

Writers: Scott Silveri & Shana Goldberg-Meehan
Director: Peter Bonerz
First US transmission: 24.04.97
First UK transmission (C4): 28.11.97

Guest Cast: Jon Favreau (Pete Becker), Dina Meyer (Kate Miller)
Reg Rogers (Marshall Talmant, the Director), June Gable (Estelle),
Jennifer Milmore (Lauren), James Michael Tyler (Gunther),
Ben Stiller (Tommy), Laura Cayouette (Cailin),
Jeffery D. Brooks (Stage Manager)

Summary: Joey invites everyone to the premiere of his new play. When Ross announces that he's bringing along a date, Rachel quickly gets herself a date too, a guy named Tommy. When Rachel leaves Tommy with Ross to find their seats, Ross is terrified when he alone witnesses him shouting hysterically at another audience member who has mistakenly sat in his seat. Ross tries to convince Rachel that her new man is psychotic, but of course, she thinks he's just acting out of jealousy and it isn't until she herself sees Tommy shouting at the duck that she discovers the truth.

Meanwhile, Joey's feelings for Kate are even stronger after they spend a night together, just talking and learning everything about each other. But the next day, Joey is devastated when Kate tells him that she has a part on *General Hospital* and is leaving that night, her part taken by her understudy.

Slow Joey: In preparation for meeting Kate again, Joey borrows some of Chandler's cologne. Chandler explains, though, that he has no cologne – Joey's actually used the duck's worm medicine.

Phoebisms: Phoebe spends the entire episode at Monica's, on hold to the manufacturer's support line to get help for her own broken telephone. She misses Joey's opening night because the recorded voice has told her that she is the next caller in the queuing system . . . which keeps her on the line *all night*. This little diversion makes for some wonderful moments, especially when Phoebe puts the phone down and tries to put on a jumper in a panic: she ends up trying to squeeze her head through the

sleeve, while shouting, 'I'm right here! . . .Wait one second!'
Caught in the jumper, she has to cry for Monica's help, claiming, 'I'm scared!' While she is on the phone, she takes another
call for Monica from her father, telling her that 'he said call
him as soon as you get a chance, he's at Flimby's.' When
Monica says she doesn't know where Flimby's is, Phoebe
explains that that's the word she uses when she can't remember the real thing.

Joey's an Actor!: Joey's agent, Estelle (one of our favourite
guest stars), makes an appearance after the play, telling
Monica and Rachel that she was really impressed with them.
When they explain that, not only were they not in the play,
they're not even actors, Estelle moans, 'What a shame!
Because [she points at Monica] with her face [then at Rachel]
and her chest I could really put something together.' When
Marshall, the director, reads the review, he sees that his direction is criticised. True to form for a stage-director stereotype,
he blames everybody else for ruining his life. The after-show
party for the first night of the play drags on till the early hours
when the reviews are printed. Marshall runs in with the first
one and reads, 'Mr Tribbiani is not the worst thing in this production.' Delighted, Joey shouts, 'Yes!' and punches the air.
Later, he keeps the newspaper for himself – obviously as a
memento of his best review yet.

Freaky Monica: Still high on finally getting together properly
with Pete, when Joey asks how many tickets she wants for his
play, she excitedly says, 'I need two. I'm bringing Pete. My
boyfriend. I have a boyfriend now!' Her little burst of glee is
really sweet.

The Ballad of Ross & Rachel: Rachel, not unreasonably,
assumes that Ross's aversion to Tommy is just jealousy. When
he suggests she stops seeing him, Rachel nods and says that,
instead, 'Maybe I should stay away from *all* men.' Ross then
says, deflating his argument somewhat, 'It's not just because
I'm jealous.' For once, the viewer can sympathise with Ross,
but the bitter memories of his behaviour over most of this
season are still too fresh to be able to root for him totally.

The Chick and the Duck: Chandler brings Yasmine and The
Duck through to Monica's and asks if they can go to see Joey's

play. When she says no, a vindicated Chandler looks at them and says, 'I just wanted them to hear it from somebody else.' Later, when Tommy is screaming at the innocent pair, we see that Chandler and Joey have left a little something in Yasmine's basket in case she gets bored – a GameBoy.

Gunther Plays Cupid: In a totally unconnected scene, Gunther brings a cup of coffee to Chandler, explaining that it's been bought by a woman at the bar. He looks over at her, and the woman whispers something to Gunther: 'Sorry,' he says, taking the coffee away, 'she thought you were someone else.'

Generation X: Ben Stiller appeared in, and directed Jim Carrey's mega-hit *Cable Guy* (1996).

The Last Word: Quite good fun, particularly Phoebe's telephone traumas and Tommy's insanity – the point where he's screaming at Ross outside Central Perk, with him tapping on the window to try to catch Rachel's attention is priceless. The best part, though, is Joey's fond farewell to Kate as he boards his space-ship. Bizarre, but great nonetheless.

323
'The One With Ross's Thing'

Writers: Andrew Reich & Ted Cohen
Director: Shelley Jensen
First US transmission: 01.05.97
First UK transmission (C4): 05.12.97

Guest Cast: Jon Favreau (Pete Becker), Kevin McDonald (Guru Saj),
Matt Battaglia (Vince), Robert Gant (Jason), Richard Gant (Dr Rhodes),
Carole Goldman (Pete's Mum, billed as 'Woman'), Doug Looper (Fireman)

Summary: Having discovered what can only be described as a 'thing' on his butt, Ross seeks advice from Joey and Chandler. When they fail to identify it, he decides to bite the bullet and see a doctor. But the doctor is as clueless as his friends, so he calls in a colleague. Then he calls another. And another. Before long, the whole hospital is staring at Ross's backside, but to no avail – they just can't work out what it is. Eventually, he agrees to see Phoebe's herbalist, Guru Saj, whose first attempts to cure it seem only to 'anger' it. Then Saj decides to treat it with love, waving his hands above the thing: the method works, but only because Saj catches the thing on his watch and rips it right off.

Pete is away, and Monica heads round to his house to talk to him over the videophone – it turns out he has something important to tell her. The gang go with her, just to check out his pad. Joey happens across a cheque made out to 'Hugo Lindgren Ring Design', and Rachel is immediately convinced that Pete is going to propose to Monica. Mulling over it for a while, Monica decides that her answer would be 'yes', but when Pete returns he tells her that he is planning to become the world's Ultimate Fighting Champion, and that he's even had his own ring designed.

Phoebe, meanwhile, is high on the fact that she's dating two men at once. She can't decide between the two: Vince, a fireman, has an incredible body, while Jason, a teacher, is sensitive, kind and intelligent. And when she discovers that Vince writes about his feelings in a journal, and that Jason has a stunning physique, she's even more confused – and Heaven forbid the two men should ever find out about each other . . .

Spoilt Rachel: Her excitement at the idea that Monica might be marrying Pete is classic rich-girl material. 'Monica's going to marry a millionaire!' she yells, with open glee. She suggests that they should have a themed wedding, her idea for the theme being 'Look How Much Money We've Got!' At one point in the middle of an unconnected conversation, she flings her arms into the air and screams with joy. 'Sorry,' she says, 'I was just imagining what it'd be like to catch the money bouquet.' Rachel even goes to the lengths of picking out a dress that Monica could wear: Phoebe is so taken with the frock that she suggests to Monica that she buy it whatever, 'for clubbing'.

Phoebisms: Phoebe's not quite being herself here, as she plays the man's game of 'two-timing'. She describes herself, with not a small amount of pride, as an 'oat-sowing, field-playing juggler'. Later, she is performing a song at Central Perk which is probably best titled as 'Crazy Underwear (Creeping Up My Butt)'.

Slow Joey: When Pete announces to Monica that he has

something serious to talk about, she immediately thinks that their relationship is over. Joey, showing just how amoral he can be, says that maybe it's not that bad – 'Maybe he just cheated on you.' Chandler offers to go over to Pete's apartment to 'water' the plants in retaliation for this supposed dumping; Joey – characteristically – misses the point and says, 'Or, we could go over there and pee on them!'

The Chick and the Duck: The duck, here named Dick, is taken to see Guru Saj as he has a 'bad cough'. When Saj asks if the duck would be prepared to eat a whole bat, a marvellous synchronicity occurs: the duck starts to flap its wings in a mad panic, while Le Blanc holds him down. The look on Perry's face here is brilliant – just like it was when Joey was about to blow-dry the chick in 'TOW A Chick. And A Duck'.

Gunther's a Sharp-Dressed Man!: Check out his tie in the background scenes!

Just Plain Weird: Guru Saj is simply not funny. On seeing *Friends* for the first time, it's quite easy to see Phoebe as a kook and nothing more. Repeated exposure to our favourite weirdo, though, brings her closer to your heart – Kudrow is funny, warm, and has the exceptional ability to deliver her lines *just so*. Kevin McDonald, who plays Saj, though, has none of these charms. Get him off our screens! Oh, and Joey's pondering about what to call the offspring of a chick and a duck is quite weird too.

The Story So Far: When Ross tries to warn Monica against rushing into marriage, Rachel spitefully reminds him that he married a lesbian. Because, of course, we've forgotten that, haven't we viewers.

The Last Word: Joking about Ross's 'Thing' offended many viewers who thought it in very poor taste. But this is supposed to be a comedy and we dislike it simply because it's a very dull plot, that Schwimmer clearly approaches half-heartedly. Phoebe's flings with Jason and Vince are entertaining, but the most laughs come from Monica's thoughts about marrying Pete and, more specifically, Rachel's reaction to the whole thing.

324

'The One With The Ultimate Fighting Champion'

Writers: Mark J. Kunerth & Pang-ni Landrum (story),
Scott Silveri & Shanan Goldberg-Meehan (teleplay)
Director: Robby Benson
First US transmission: 08.05.97
First UK transmission (C4): 12.12.97

Guest Cast: Robin Williams (Thomas), Billy Crystal (Tim),
Jon Favreau (Pete Becker), James Hong (Hoshi), Steve Dark (Phil),
Joe O'Connor (Stevens), John McCarthy (Referee),
Bruce Buffer (Announcer)
and introducing: Christine Taylor (Bonnie), Sam McMurray (Doug)

Summary: Monica begins to think Pete is going insane: he's still determined to become the Ultimate Fighting Champion. She goes with him to his first fight and watches him get soundly pulverised. Despite the fact that he has been beaten to a bloody pulp, Pete obstinately carries on in his dream. Monica finally realises she can't watch someone she cares about so much go through it all, so they agree to go their separate ways.

Chandler has a new boss at work, who insists on patting him on the behind after every meeting. Though Joey insists that it's just a male bonding gesture, Chandler is uncomfortable with it. Chandler eventually decides to tell his boss that the other men in the office are getting jealous of all the attention lavished on Chandler, only for the behind-slapping to spread throughout the department.

Phoebe asks Rachel if she can set Ross up with Bonnie, a friend of hers. Rachel checks that Bonnie is the girl with the shaved head, which Phoebe confirms; knowing that, Rachel's more than happy for the two of them to go out on a date. When Bonnie turns up, though, her hair has grown back – into long, beautiful blonde locks. She and Ross hit it off, and Rachel can do nothing but watch helplessly from the sidelines.

Phoebisms: Phoebe is much more excited by the prospect of Pete becoming a wrestler than Monica is, until she learns that in this kind of professional fighting, they don't have costumes like those on WWF. Is this some hitherto unknown kink of Phoebe's, or does she simply like the bright colours? We think it's the latter.

Cruelty To Animals: Phoebs tries to distract Rachel from staring at Ross and Bonnie by pointing to the pavement at a line of ants. It's a weak distraction, and it doesn't work. When Rachel is finally dragged away, they sit on the kerb and Phoebe realises with brilliant sorrow that, when they sat down, they killed all the ants.

Freaky Monica: On the balcony of her apartment, Ross prepares the barbecue for everyone to eat as they watch Pete's second fight on television. In a reference to her past obsessive eating habits, Monica asks for four hot dogs. 'I'm really nervous,' she explains.

Chandleresque: After Chandler tells the gang about the way his boss keeps slapping him, Rachel supports him, saying that if Monica made a great stew she wouldn't congratulate her by, say, grabbing her boob. Chandler agrees: 'For a really great stew you just, y'know, stick your head in between 'em.' Good one, Chandler.

Slow Joey: He suggests to Chandler that, to avoid the butt-slapping of his boss, he could cover his behind with something that smells bad, so that the boss would end up with bad-smelling hands. 'Now,' wonders Joey, 'what could you rub on your butt that would smell bad?'

Just Plain Weird: As Monica tries to talk to her friends at Central Perk about Pete's crazy plan, she is interrupted when a couple of noisy guys muscle in on their sofa. One of them thinks that his wife is having an affair with her gynaecologist. The other then reveals that it is in fact he who is sleeping with his wife. Despite the fact that these men are played by Billy Crystal and Robin Williams (who puts on a ridiculous accent), this just isn't funny and smacks of opportunistic guest-star wrangling. Hoshi, Pete's fighting trainer, apparently used to be an assassin-for-hire. When Pete tells Monica this, Hoshi loudly complains that his secret is out and Pete corrects it to 'house painter'.

The Ballad of Ross & Rachel: This time, it's Rachel who's the all-out loser. Her feelings about Ross and Bonnie getting together quietly pave the way for the wonderful events of the episode that follows. Even so, like Ross's whining when it goes on too long, there are elements to her jealousy that are neither entertaining nor interesting. It's at times like these you wonder what the producers were thinking when they broke these two up in the first place, inflicting them on unsuspecting others.

Generation X: Comedians Robin Williams and Billy Crystal both started out their careers on *Saturday Night Live*, but shot to fame on sitcoms; Williams in a bit-part in *Happy Days* as Mork, an alien from Ork (which led to the series *Mork and Mindy*); Crystal in the classic spoof series, *Soap*. It was, of course, for this reason that they appeared in this episode, and not because they wanted to plug their latest movie, *Father's Day* (Ivan Reitman, 1997). Rachel claims to have been served a pretzel by one of the kids from *Fame*, the musical drama based around New York's School for the Performing Arts.

The Story So Far: Phoebe reminds Rachel that she met Bonnie at Phoebs's birthday party two years ago (presumably the one shown in 'TOW Two Parts – Part 2'). We see Chandler's boss, Doug, for the first time here (see 'TOW Chandler's Work Laugh').

The Last Word: Focusing mainly on Monica having to choose between staying with Pete and saving herself the pain of watching him being regularly beaten to a pulp, this episode is really quite touching in places. Her final speech to him ('I've got to do this,' he says. 'Then I've got to go,' Monica replies), considering how long it took for her to realise how much she liked him, is very moving. Perry is beginning to get back on form as Chandler, and his facial expressions that accompany each butt-smack are a wonder to behold.

325
'The One At The Beach'

Writers: Pang-ni Landrum & Mark J. Kunerth (story), Adam Chase (teleplay)
Director: Pamela Fryman
First US transmission: 15.05.97
First UK transmission (C4): 19.12.97

Guest Cast: Christine Taylor (Bonnie), James Michael Tyler (Gunther),
Teri Garr (Phoebe Abbott)

Summary: One of Phoebe's clients invites her and her friends
to use his beach house for a weekend. The gang, with Bonnie,
all pile down for a few days of sun and sand. All they get is
sand, though, as there's been a flood which has pushed a pile
of sand inside the beach house. While she is there, Phoebe
intends to look up Phoebe Abbott, a woman who appears in a
photograph of her dead mother. After their first meeting, they
agree to go for dinner the next day, so Phoebe Jr can learn
more about her mother and father. But Phoebe Abbott pulls
out. Phoebe Jr is very disappointed and decides to break into
the other Phoebe's house and snoop about for more information on her parents. When Phoebe Sr catches her creeping
about she eventually admits that she is in fact her biological
mother.

Rachel manages to convince Bonnie that the shaved-head
look really suited her, and that she should do it again. When
she does, proudly showing the results to a disgusted Ross,
Ross accuses Rachel of engineering the whole thing. Rachel
claims she did it because she thinks she still has feelings for
him. They kiss, but are interrupted by Chandler and Joey.
Rachel goes to her room and, later, Ross is faced with a choice
of doors – Rachel's on one side of the hall, Bonnie's on the
other . . .

Freaky Monica: Post-Pete, Monica is worried that she'll end
up alone and 'die an old maid', but Chandler tries to reassure
her that won't happen – although she might die 'an old spinster
cook'. He suggests that maybe he might be suitable 'boyfriend
material', getting only a laugh from Monica as a response. He
finds the laugh somewhat annoying, and spends the rest of the
episode trying to convince her that he could be her boyfriend.

Slow Joey: His suggestion to lift the boredom at the beach
house is a characteristic one: why don't they play strip poker?
When they find out that they have no cards, they change it to a
game of strip Happy Days. Of course, it backfires on him terribly and he ends up completely naked while everyone else is
fully dressed. When he falls asleep after the game, drunk on

margaritas, the gang cover him in sand and mould it so that it looks like he's got the body of a mermaid. When he wakes, he looks down at his new breasts and smiles in appreciation. Later, he tries to suggest to Chandler that they practise one-on-one strip poker, but Chandler point-blank refuses.

Phoebisms: Phoebe throws a brilliantly ineffectual tantrum when Phoebe Sr tells her that she's not going out to dinner with her: she simply pushes a stool gently, and watches it thud quietly on the sand-covered floor.

Chandleresque: He tries to give Ross advice on how to handle the developing situation with Rachel, but he seems to realise the futility of his involvement. As he talks on, he says feebly of his own experience in such things, 'Take it from a guy who's never had a long-term relationship.'

Dinosaurs ROCK!: Playing the Happy Days game, Ross shakes the dice in his cupped hand and mutters, 'Daddy needs a new pair of electromagnetic microscopes for the Prehistoric Forensics Department.' When everyone looks at him like the sad man he is, he shuts up and plays the game.

The Ballad of Ross & Rachel: Well, this is it. After nearly a year of bitchiness, Ross and Rachel finally realise what everyone else has known from the minute they broke up – they're still crazy about each other. The scene where Rachel chases Ross around the room, intending to paint his toenails, closes with a wonderfully surprising moment. Ross collapses on the sofa, and Rachel tumbles on top of him. They hold a look for a second before Phoebe arrives to interrupt them. In that second, although we've known all along it could happen, Aniston and Schwimmer manage to remind us why we ever thought the idea of Ross and Rachel was a good one, and it's enough of a reminder to make us forget the months of tiring nastiness we've gone through to get here.

Just Plain Weird: Teri Garr as Phoebe Abbott is an example of intelligent, perfect casting – she's obviously carefully studied Kudrow's role, and successfully emulates her unique take on wackiness. Particularly impressive is when she leaps to her feet and suggests making sangria as a tactic to avoid talking about Phoebe Jr's heritage. This line alone brilliantly shows how she's got a handle on Phoebe's habit of trying –

and often failing – to avoid a topic by desperately going off on a tangent (just check out last episode's line of ants).

Generation X: Teri Garr starred in, among other movies, *Tootsie* (Sydney Pollack, 1982) which is sadly not the story of Chandler's father.

The Last Word: With this episode, it's like the memories of all the bad things about this year are erased. Phoebe finding her real mother, and Ross and Rachel so nearly getting back together, are the dramatic highlights of the entire season. And, like all the best *Friends*, all this serious stuff is handled with style, wit, panache and a bellyful of laughs. The cliff-hanger itself (we see Ross go into one of the girls' rooms, and say, 'Hi' – but we don't know who to) is a brilliant moment, guaranteed to make you hold your breath until the conclusion.

Fourth Season

1997–1998

24 Episodes

401

'The One With The Jellyfish'

Writer: Wil Calhoun
Director: Shelly Jensen
First US transmission: 25.09.97
First UK transmission (Sky One): 08.01.98

Guest Cast: Christine Taylor (Bonnie), Teri Garr (Phoebe Abbott)

Summary: Ross chooses Rachel's door, but is surprised to find Bonnie there too – Rachel's massaging lotion into Bonnie's burned scalp. After Bonnie leaves, Ross tells Rachel that he wants her back and that he's going to finish with Bonnie. Ross goes to do the dirty deed and when he returns, he discovers that Rachel has written a huge letter detailing her feelings over their relationship. She insists that she won't consider getting back with Ross unless he agrees with the letter's main point. As he begins to read it, Ross falls asleep, waking the next morning. Realising he can't tell Rachel that he hasn't read it yet, Ross claims to agree with everything she has written. But later, when he finally gets a chance to read the letter, Ross learns that Rachel expects him to accept total responsibility for their break-up, something he realises he cannot accept. Unable to reconcile their differences, Ross and Rachel split up again.

Phoebe confronts her newly discovered 'birth-mother'. Apparently, Phoebe senior, Lily and Frank senior were 'a couple' and when she discovered she was pregnant, Phoebe senior panicked and handed her twins over to Frank and Lily. Phoebe senior is keen to try and make it up with her daughter, but Phoebe junior is unforgiving and leaves, having told her mum that she never wants to see her again. When Phoebe senior follows Phoebe to New York though, she manages to convince her daughter that maybe they have a lot of things in common after all and that maybe they could begin again from scratch.

Back at the girls' apartment, Chandler, Monica and Joey are acting very strangely. Evidently, something happened at the beach, but no-one will say exactly *what* . . .

Freaky Monica: Having been stung by a jellyfish, Monica's wrath gets the better of her: 'Damn the jellyfish – damn *all* the jellyfish!' Trying to rebut Chandler's advances one final time, Monica reassures him by saying that she thinks he's sweet and smart, and that she does love him, 'but you will always be the guy who peed on me'.

Slow Joey: Joey tries to explain to us what happened at the end of the last series, only to give up and go looking for Chandler to help out. Later, we see how his excitement over the hole he's dug prevents him from being any help to the distressed Monica. When the trio try to explain what happened to the other three, Joey justifies himself: 'She's my friend and she needed help! And if I had to, I'd pee on any one of you!'

Chandleresque: Still asking Monica if she'd consider going out with him, he poses the question in the context of him being the last man left after a nuclear holocaust: 'I've got canned goods', he adds persuasively.

Poor Ross: After Ross reminds everyone that he and Rachel were 'on a break', Chandler warns: 'If you say that one more time, *I'm* gonna break up with you!'

Phoebisms: Phoebs sings a song about the 66 colours of her bedroom – two of which are fuchsia and mauve.

The Ballad of Ross & Rachel: In Rachel's eighteen-page epic, she asks Ross to accept full responsibility for their break-up: 'Does that seem like something you can do? Does it?' Chandler convinces Ross that it's something he *must* do, if he wants to avoid losing the best thing that's ever happened to him. But when Rachel labours the point about how much it means to her, Ross screams 'WE WERE ON A BREAK!!' and the relationship ends once again. Rachel, of course, gets the last word when she tells Ross (and anyone else who's listening) that 'it's not that common, it doesn't happen to every guy and it *is* a big deal!!'

Just Plain Weird: Joey has seen a documentary on The Discovery Channel about jellyfish. Weirder – he remembers the facts from it!

The Story So Far: Phoebe gives her birth-mum a potted history of what it was like when she was eighteen: 'My mom had killed herself, and my dad had run off, and I was living in a Gremlin with a guy called Sidney who talked to his hand'. Phoebe is now 29. We see Phoebe's older twin, Ursula, again (see 'TOW Two Parts', 'TOW The Jam'). Ursula already knew about Phoebe senior, but she lies to Phoebe when she claims to have Lily's suicide note. Both Phoebs claim to like The Beatles and pizza, and they both think puppies are '*so* cute!' (see 'TOW Phoebe's Uterus'). Rachel reminds Ross that he cheated on her with the girl from the photocopy place (see 'TOW Ross and Rachel Take a Break'). In drawing Rachel's attention to the difference between 'your' and 'you're', Ross reminds us that Rachel's spelling is pretty poor (see 'TOW Mrs Bing').

The Last Word: So it's off, and on, and off again in rapid succession, though it's doubtful that we really care any more. As later episodes will show, they're far funnier at each other's throats with anger than with love. The playful sexual tension between Monica and Chandler resurfaces once more at the end, but it's probably best left alone for the moment. Strangely, no-one notices that Chandler's hair is now sunbleached and that he's gained about a stone in weight (thank God!) overnight. But picky continuity problems aside, it's reassuring that in one episode many of series three's detractors are silenced. Best scene has to be the moment where Monica et al reveal just what happened at the beach; the way they pace the floor and build upon the melodrama, punctuated by the other three's cries of 'Euuuwww!'

402

'The One With The Cat'

Dedicated to the memory of Dorothy Kauffman

Writers: Jill Condon & Amy Toomin
Director: Shelley Jensen
First US transmission: 02.10.97
First UK transmission (Sky One): 15.01.98

Guest Cast: Dan Gauthier (Chip Matthews), James Michael Tyler (Gunther), Mathew Kaminsky (Tony), Ken Weiler (Peter), Marc Unger (the Thief)

Summary: Chandler decides it's time to get rid of Joey's entertainment centre, which takes up too much space and keeps snagging on Chandler's jacket. Joey is adamant that they mustn't throw it out, but he agrees to sell it. While making a sale he shows a prospective buyer that the unit is big enough for a grown man to fit into – and is promptly locked in by the buyer who proceeds to steal everything of value from the place, including the reclining chairs.

Monica bumps into Chip Matthews, Rachel's prom date in High School, and agrees to go out on a date with him. Rachel is furious, remembering how badly that prom went for her and Chip, but reluctantly consents to letting Monica go anyway. However, Chip hasn't changed much since High School; he still thinks wedgies are funny and still works at the local multiplex because he gets free posters for his room. Monica returns home to tell Rachel the joyous news – she got to go out with Chip from High School – and got to dump him!

Phoebe, meanwhile, becomes drawn to a cat that she swears has a smile just like her dead mother, Lily. Strangely enough, it also looks a lot like Julio, the lost cat of a little girl from SoHo, but no-one can bear to tell Phoebe . . .

Freaky Monica: Monica tells Rachel that she feels she owes a good time to the fat girl inside of her as she never lets her eat.

Spoilt Rachel: Not thinking of Monica's feelings for a second, she asks her if she could help her get some kind of revenge on Chip Matthews by leaving him somewhere to have sex with someone else, just like he did to Rachel at the prom.

Phoebisms: She sings a song ending in the words '. . . DUMB

DRUNKEN BITCH!' Lovely! She later feels certain that the
cat is the reincarnated spirit of her dead mother, based on some
pretty dodgy thinking involving an orange felt-lined guitar
case and the fact that cats like fish (!). To spare the feelings of
the cat, Phoebe tells her friends she's going to call her mum at
the B-E-A-C-H, before realising that she should have spelled
out the word 'mom'. Reasserting her belief that the cat is her
dead mother, Phoebe also forces Ross to accept that he's not
always right about everything, and spells out some simple
rules about being a friend. 'Even if I'm wrong, who cares? Just
be a friend, OK? Be supportive.'

Chander's Job?: Joey believes Chandler has undervalued the
entertainment centre: 'And you call yourself an accountant,' he
mocks. 'Noooo!' replies Chandler, but apparently no-one else
knows what he does either – although Rachel knows it's
'something to do with numbers'.

Slow Joey: Joey can't help but point out that the cat that
Phoebe believes is her 'mom' has got a 'huge peni–' 'Let it
go,' warns a tactful Chandler. Joey's selection process for the
new owner of the entertainment centre is a little strict. Chandler
notes: 'Apparently, not everyone is qualified to own wood and
nails.' Joey not only falls for the 'trapped inside the unit' trick
twice, he actually tells the thief how to do it! Joey is understandably upset when all their stuff is robbed: 'If I ever run
into that guy again, do you know what I'm gonna do?' 'BEND
OVER!??' cries Chandler, having finally lost his patience.

Chandleresque: After the robbery, Monica asks Chandler
what happened: 'Um, Joey was born, and 28 years later, I
was robbed!' Ross asked him what his insurance company
said about it all: 'They said, uh, "You don't have insurance
here, so stop calling us."' When Phoebe tells her 'mom' that
she's welcome back any time, Chandler tells her they'd
really appreciate it if her mum could come back as a couch
next time.

The Ballad of Ross & Rachel: Rachel sarcastically complains
to Ross that she has an eight-page report to read and doesn't
want to fall asleep (in reference to her eighteen-page letter in
the previous episode). Ross rebuts with: 'Why, did *you* write
it?' Rachel gets her own back later, as she tries to prove Ross's

obsession with always having to be right by tempting him with a sadistic: '*Jurassic Park* could happen.'

The Chick and the Duck: Are housed inside the entertainment centre, with their own disco ball and fairy lights.

Magna Doodle: The thief leaves the boys a rather cruel message: 'Thanks for all your stuff!'

Generation X: Chandler refers to Geppetto, 'father' of Pinocchio (see 'Pilot').

The Story So Far: We saw a young Chip briefly in 'TOW The Prom Video', where he was Rachel's prom date (played by a different, non-credited actor). Chip apparently went missing on Prom Night, leaving Rachel alone. She eventually discovered he'd been having sex with a girl called Amy Welch. Monica's band uniform in school had to be specially made as she was so fat, and Rachel was in the Home Economics class that had to make it. Chip reminds Monica of his old schoolmates: Simmons, Zana, Spindler, Devane, Kelly, Goldie, Steve Brown, Zuchoff, McGuire, J.T., Breadsley and Richard Dorfman (who is now an architect). Rachel and Ross allude to the letter, again (see 'TOW The Jellyfish'). Phoebe's mother died 17 years ago. Joey tells the thief about the time Chandler trapped him inside the entertainment centre (see 'TOW Frank Jr'). According to Chandler, Joey is now 28. As a result of the robbery, the guys acquire a canoe to replace their chairs.

The Last Word: Oh, will Ross ever learn? Surely he realises by now that Phoebe can never be dissuaded from believing anything she wants to (see, for example, 'TOW Heckles Dies'). He is actually a little cruel in the force he uses to shatter Phoebe's illusions. One good thing about the break-up of Ross and Rachel is the way their bickering can result in some of the funniest scenes in an episode; in this instance, the glee with which Rachel informs Ross that *Jurassic Park* could happen – that's really underhand, but he was really asking for it! The main thread of this plotline, the cat, is a little silly even for Phoebe, but the joy it gives her far outweighs any need for logic.

403
'The One With The 'Cuffs'

Writer: Seth Kurland
Director: Peter Bonerz
First US transmission: 09.10.97
First UK transmission (Sky One): 22.01.98

Guest Cast: Alison LaPlaca (Joanna), Penn Jillette (The Salesman),
Laura Dean (Sophie), Christina Pickles (Judy Geller)

Summary: Desperate for money, Monica agrees to cater a party for her ever-critical mother. To avoid getting hassle about biting her nails, she wears false ones, but one of them goes missing and it can only be in one of the quiches that she's just made for the party. Monica's mother then makes the situation worse by revealing that she had frozen lasagnes on standby, just in case her daughter 'pulled a Monica'.

Chandler starts dating Rachel's boss Joanna again, despite having previously called her a 'big, dull dud'. Rachel is really annoyed about this as last time she nearly lost her job over the way Chandler led Joanna on. But Chandler is drawn to Joanna's bossy ways and ends up fooling around with her in her office, and when she's called away to a meeting she hand-cuffs Chandler to a chair and leaves the keys out of arms' reach.

An encyclopædia salesman calls at number nineteen – but only Joey's at home. The salesman asks him if he ever feels left out of conversations because he doesn't know what his friends are talking about. If only he knew . . .

Slow Joey: As a replacement for all of their stolen furniture, Joey procures some rusty patio furniture and some bubble wrap: '. . . and some of it is not even popped!' he cheers. When the salesman asks him if he ever feels people are talking above his head, Joey has a flashback to a few incidents that illustrate the problem. After the flashback we realise that Joey's been reminiscing in real-time, leaving the salesman waiting for two and a half minutes. Joey thought Van Gogh cut off his ear because his paintings must have sucked. In response to the question 'Where does the Pope live?' Joey answers: 'In the woods . . . no, wait, that's the joke answer.' And of course 'Vulcanised rubber' is 'Spock's birth control'. When the salesman tells Joey that the full set of encyclopædias will cost $1,200, Joey is not impressed: 'I'm home in the middle of the day and I got patio furniture in my living room. I guess there's a few things you don't get from book learning!' But even after Joey has swotted up on volcanoes, vivisection and the Vietnam War, he still finds he's left out of the conversation when Monica asks if anyone saw the documentary on the Korean War.

Chandleresque: An unsympathetic Rachel tells Chandler he'll have to get himself out of the 'cuffs: 'You must have me confused with "The Amazing Chandler"!' Despite being in such discomfort, he still takes time out to look up the skirt of a small statue near Joanna's desk.

Spoilt Rachel: Monica cries 'How desperate am I?' to which Rachel says that it's a good thing Chandler's not there as 'he always wins at this game'. Worried that she might get fired, she demands that Chandler dump Joanna, oblivious to the fact that presumably, this would put her job in greater danger than if he kept on seeing her. Having phoned Phoebe and Monica to tell them about Chandler's predicament, Rachel manages to get him back in the 'cuffs through blackmail: 'When they ask me what I saw, I can be very generous . . . or very *stingy*.'

Shut it, Sophie!: Joanna's other assistant, Sophie, tries to be nice to her intolerable boss. When she brings Joanna a macaroon, she's told: 'Great! I'll keep it in my butt with your nose!'

Parents – Who Needs 'Em?: Monica agrees to cater for her mother because she needs the money and 'thought it'd be a great way to get rid of that last little smidgen of self-respect'. Judy Geller's tactlessness strikes again; she tells Monica that she'd just assumed the fact that Richard raved over her catering was because he was sleeping with her, but that she paid attention when she heard about the catering at the lesbian wedding [from Sandra Green, Rachel's mother] as she assumes she wasn't sleeping with anyone there. 'Though at least that would be something,' she adds.

Magna Doodle: Someone has drawn a big smiley face again (see 'TOW A Chick. And A Duck').

The Chick and the Duck: Dick the Duck comes to see what

Joey's up to. Joey, without looking, waves him back into the bathroom and he waddles back in despondently.

Generation X: Chandler's quip about the 'Algonquin kids' table' in Joey's flashback is a reference to the literary intelligentsia of the 1920s, which included notorious wits Dorothy Parker and Robert Benchley (father of *Jaws* author, Peter). They used to meet at the Algonquin Hotel and became known as 'The Vicious Circle'. The salesman is played by Penn Jillette, one half of the blackly comical magicians Penn & Teller. Milton Berle is otherwise known as 'Mr Television', having been one of TV's first great stars. He's also renowned for his 'romantic' links to a number of Hollywood's biggest names (including Marilyn Monroe and Lucille Ball).

The Story So Far: Judy Geller tells her daughter that her blue nails look just like her grandmother's when they found her (see 'TOW Nana Dies Twice'), and recalls Richard's party and Carol and Susan's wedding (see 'TOW Ross and Rachel . . . You Know' & 'TOW The Lesbian Wedding'). Chandler and Joanna first dated in 'TOW The Dollhouse'. Monica has, at one time, been in therapy with a Dr Weinberg. When Mark left (see 'TOW Phoebe's Ex-Partner'), he gave Rachel the keys to Joanna's office, though Joanna doesn't know Rachel has got them. Chandler still doesn't know Joanna's last name by this point. We see how Monica's room back at her parents' house has been converted into a gym (see 'TOW The Prom Video).

The Last Word: Joey's imitation of the creaking noises from Chandler's room are superb – especially the one for the sounds Chandler makes on his own. Matthew Perry reminds us how great he is with physical comedy – how many other actors could be so animated while handcuffed to a chair?

404
'The One With The Ballroom Dancing'

Writers: Andrew Reich & Ted Cohen
Director: Gail Mancuso
First US transmission: 16.10.97
First UK transmission (Sky One): 29.01.98

Guest Cast: Jason Brooks (Rick),
Michael G. Hagerty (Mr Treager – billed as 'Treeger'),
Rhoda Gemignani (Mrs Potter), E. J. Callahan (Mr Simon),
Brien Perry (Gym Employee), Christopher Carroll (Bank Officer),
Amber Smith (Maria), Hope Allen (Karen Lambert),
Cheryl Francis Harrington (Interviewer)

Summary: Mr Treager, the superintendent of the apartment block, roars at Rachel after she blocks a garbage shoot he's spent half-an-hour unblocking. When Rachel returns to her apartment crying, Joey becomes her night in shining armour – only to worsen the situation and risk getting the girls evicted. Joey offers to do anything for Mr Treager to keep the girls in their home – but isn't expecting 'anything' to mean becoming Treager's dance-practice partner.

Chandler is a member of a gym that he never goes to but still pays $50 a month for. With Ross in tow for moral support, Chandler tries to quit the gym, only for Ross to be enlisted too. Their attempts to cut the gym off at source by closing their bank accounts are similarly unsuccessful – they end up opening a joint account together.

Phoebe is distracted by one of her clients at the massage parlour as she finds him very attractive and he provokes her to want to do things to him she's 'not allowed to charge for'. But then she finds herself biting his backside mid-massage and she has to tell him how she feels . . .

Spoilt Rachel: She has never, in the three years she's been living there, taken out the trash, as she presumed Monica liked doing it. Treager mocks how pampered she is: 'Daddy buy me a pizza, Daddy buy me a candy factory. Daddy, make the cast of *Cats* sing Happy Birthday to me!' Rachel is driven to tears, and later complains to her friends that his comments were only 'partly true'. Joey defends Rachel because Treager made her cry, but Monica is wonderfully unsympathetic, pointing out that Rachel *always* cries!

Phoebisms: Phoebe has made herself swear a 'Masseuse Oath': No fooling around with clients and always be prepared' (she stole the last one from the Boy Scouts). Trying to excuse the fact that she's paid extra-special attention to her feet (because that's the only part of her the client sees), Phoebe claims that it's Arabian Princess day at work. After spending half an afternoon on him, Phoebe tells her client that it had been only an hour: '. . . in Really Long Hour World'. Finally, she tells a prospective employer that she left her previous job because her boss thought she was a whore. Good going, Phoebs!

Chandleresque: He describes Maria at the gym as being a 'lycra spandex gym treat'. Standing up to Ross's temptation of the thought of having a 'washboard stomach and rock-hard pecs' Chandler cries weakly that he just wants 'a flabby gut and saggy man-breasts'.

Slow Joey: Trying to explain away letting slip about the chick and the duck to Treager, he tells him that they're nicknames – he's the chick and Chandler's the duck. Treager is surprised – he thought it would have been the other way round! When Treager asks Joey to be his dancing partner, Joey asks if that's 'prison lingo'. When Joey's trying to avoid getting too over-excited during sex, he thinks of sandwiches, baseball and Chandler to calm himself down.

Generation X: The sexy client of Phoebe's is a supporter of the environmental campaigners 'Greenpeace'. The superintendent's annual dance is called the 'Super Ball' (hahaha). Treager and Joey practise their dancing to Cole Porter's 'Night and Day'.

The Story So Far: Treager knows that Monica is subletting her grandmother's apartment [her father's mother] (see 'TOW The Flashback'). Joey, Chandler and Ross all use the same bank (according to Joey, they're 'bank buddies'). Prior to this episode, Phoebe has never been sacked from a job before.

The Last Word: Joey clearly enjoys learning how to dance, despite not knowing how to lead. We love the bit where Treager swings Joey around and he gives out a little 'Wheheyy!!' We also love Chandler's mantra of 'I wanna quit the gym!' which should be put onto T-shirts and bumper stickers NOW! As for Rachel, well maybe it's about time she was mocked for crying at the drop of a hat. Good call, Monica.

405
'The One With Joey's New Girlfriend'

Writers: Michael Curtis & Gregory S. Malins
Director: Gail Mancuso
First US transmission: 30.10.98
First UK transmission (Sky One): 05.02.98

Guest Cast: Laura Stepp (Amanda), James Michael Tyler (Gunther),
Brian 'Fish' Smith (Josh),
Charles Thomas Allen & John Christopher Allen (Ben)
and introducing: Paget Brewster (Kathy)

Summary: Chandler tries to chat up a beautiful woman at Central Perk only to discover she's Joey's new girlfriend, Kathy, who he met in acting class. But secretly, Chandler is falling in love with Kathy and, realising how this could jeopardise his friendship with Joey, tries to avoid her. When Chandler finally confesses just how he feels for her, Joey thinks that he's just making too much of an effort to be nice to her, much to Chandler's frustration.

Rachel starts dating a guy who is still in college and might be stealing from her, while Ross meets a really sexy woman . . . who uses him as a babysitter. Phoebe catches a cold which, she discovers, makes her voice all husky and sexy. So when her cold clears she tries everything to catch another one!

Chandleresque: When Rachel reveals that Chandler told her that Ross and Amanda didn't even kiss on their 'date', Chandler explains that he tells people secrets: 'It makes them like me.' He tells Kathy that whenever he sees women in fishnet stockings it reminds him of his father.

Phoebisms: She starts to make shoes by getting old ones and tarting them up with really tacky decorations. She sings 'Smelly Cat' (the sexy bronchial remix) and has new songs too – 'Sticky Shoes', 'Plaiting Goats' and 'Pepper People' in which she sneezes as part of the last verse. At the end she sings a song about a 'Papier-Mâché Man' à la Brigitte Bardot. She feels that with her new sexy voice she should write about something sad but claims that nothing sad has ever happened to her – forgetting, of course, her mother's suicide and the time she spent living rough.

The Ballad of Ross & Rachel: Ross tries to get Rachel jealous by showing off a piece of paper with the phone number of a 'really hot girl' on it. Ross waves it annoyingly in her face, so when Phoebe starts to sneeze, Rachel snatches the paper out of Ross's hand for Phoebe to wipe her nose on.

Gunther Sneezes!: . . . and Phoebe snogs him senseless in the hope of catching his cold. Torn up with guilt, Gunther tells Rachel about it to just check that she's 'cool' about it. Rachel, of course, has no idea why she shouldn't be.

The Chick and the Duck: Chandler lifts the Chick into the canoe. When Kathy asks 'What about the duck?', he explains that the duck can swim. Later on he plays an unsuccessful game of 'Hide and Seek' with the pets.

Cruelty to Animals: Kathy goes off to buy hamsters – she works for a medical researcher part-time, which Phoebe thinks is nice: 'It's great that the medical community is finally trying to help sick hamsters,' she says, missing the point somewhat.

Generation X: As Chandler runs towards Kathy we hear the theme tune from *The Mod Squad*, a crime drama series that ran in the States from 1968 to 1973 in which young offenders were given a second chance by joining an underground counter-culture that fought crime. Chandler sits watching the classic 'B' movie, *Attack of the 50-Foot Woman* (Nathan Hertz, 1958).

The Story So Far: Rachel's birthday is 5 May, and Ross's is sometime in December (but see 'TOW George Stephanopolos'). Ross introduces to Rachel the gesture he used to do as a kid, where he'd bang the sides of his fists together so that he could give 'the finger' to his parents without them knowing. Monica claims she cried the night he made that up, as she finally realised she was cooler than him. This sign is used regularly throughout the rest of the season. Joey tells Kathy about the time Chandler got drunk and fell asleep with his head down the toilet. Monica recalls that Phoebe was living rough when she was fourteen. When Ross was in High School he organised the football team's schedules on his Commodore 64 computer.

The Last Word: It's a little unfair to keep harping on about Chandler's show-stealing abilities, but if one episode justifies it, it's this one, just for the scene where he runs after Kathy, colliding with a car, a hot-dog vendor, the leads of a pack of dogs and a big pile of garbage *just* to say 'Hi!' to her. But by the end of it, the laughter has stopped for Chandler as he finds it harder and harder to hide his feelings for her.

406
'The One With The Dirty Girl'

Writers: Scott Silveri & Shana Goldberg-Meehan
Director: Shelley Jensen
First US transmission: 06.11.97
First UK transmission (Sky One): 12.02.98

Guest Cast: Paget Brewster (Kathy), Rebecca Romijn (Cheryl), Gretchen Wyler (Mrs Burkart), James Michael Tyler (Gunther)

Summary: Ross starts dating a beautiful, yet incredibly unhygienic and untidy woman. Meanwhile, Monica is forced to turn down a catering job because she can't afford the equipment she'd need, so Phoebe offers to lend her some money. Accompanying her to a wake, Phoebe helps out when Monica has difficulty getting paid by a merry widow. Realising how great a team they make together, they decide to form a partnership.

Chandler buys Kathy a first edition copy of her favourite childhood book for her birthday, but when Joey only buys her a tacky watch/pen, Chandler realises that his present might make his feelings towards her too obvious, so he allows Joey to give her the book. But Kathy guesses who got her what and thanks Chandler. It's slowly becoming obvious to both of them that they are very much attracted to each other, but Joey's in their way.

Rachel spends her time completing a crossword puzzle without help from any of the others . . . even if they do actually end up giving her most of the answers.

Slow Joey: He offers girlfriends coupons for an hour of 'Joey Love' in lieu of a real present. When Chandler tells him that the first edition book he got Kathy cost 'an even twenty [dollars]', Joey can't believe it: 'That's almost as much as a *new* book!' When he finally gives Kathy the book, he says it's because he knows she likes both rabbits *and* cheese, missing the point that it was her favourite book as a little girl.

Phoebisms: When Rachel tells her she wants to complete the crossword without help, Phoebe huffily tells her that she won't let her help create her new universal language (and you just *know* she means a language that can be spoken anywhere in the universe). When Monica suggests that she cooks in their partnership while Phoebe looks after the money, Phoebe notes how it'll be like she has a wife in the 50s.

Poor Ross: His description of Cheryl's apartment is enough to make you itchy, so she really has a cheek saying his apartment has a weird smell [it still smells of Marcel?]. When Cheryl creeps up behind him and asks 'Guess Who?' his only response is a hopeful 'Department of Sanitation?' After Chandler tells Rachel not to touch the book, because she's got 'destructive oils' on her fingers, Rachel tells him not to get it near Ross's hair.

Freaky Monica: After Ross and Cheryl split up, Monica calls round and practically begs to clean up for her – she's been having sleepless nights just at the thought of it!

Gunther's There For You, Rachel: When Rachel finally finishes her crossword, she audibly bemoans the fact that there's no-one there for her to hug – cue Gunther, who pushes customers out of the way to get to her, slips and disappears down the back of the couch. As the rest of the gang walk in and congratulate her, we just see Gunther slope back to work.

Dinosaurs ROCK!: Ross's date Cheryl is a palaeontologist, specialising in the Cenozoic era (which Chandler jokes is the easier era to study). They do a variation on the 'Is the Pope Catholic/Do bears . . . etc' joke with 'Did homo erectus hunt with wooden tools?'

The Ballad of Ross & Rachel: Rachel guesses that maybe Cheryl had a bet with her friends as to which of them could bring home the biggest geek, which is fine by Ross as he hopes she wins.

Cruelty to Animals: Ross pulverises a rat hiding underneath the rubbish in Cheryl's flat.

Generation X: Chandler buys Kathy an early edition of *The Velveteen Rabbit (or How Toys Become Real)* by Margery

Williams. The 1996 Tony Award Winner was, of course, *Rent*, which won four awards that year, including Best Musical. The Tonys are the Oscar equivalent for theatre productions. The grieving widow is heard singing the patriotic standard 'You're a Grand Ole Flag' and the sprightly 'Jeepers, Creepers' (Murrell-Sheller-Canfield-Peu-Archer).

The Story So Far: Chandler still owes Phoebe a present for her last birthday. Joey claims his ex-girlfriend Angela Delvecchio never had a birthday while they were dating – for three years! (see 'TOW The East German Laundry Detergent', 'TOW The Dozen Lasagnes').

The Last Word: Chandler's (lack of) love-life still dominates the plot (and it's great to see on-going storylines that don't just focus on Ross and Rachel). But there is one part of this episode it would have been nice to follow up on at some point – we'd really like to see Monica and Phoebe fighting crime as 'Hard Ass and Wuss'.

407
'The One Where Chandler Crosses The Line'

Writer: Adam Chase
Director: Kevin S. Bright
First US transmission: 13.11.97
First UK transmission (Sky One): 19.02.98

Guest Cast: Paget Brewster (Kathy), James Michael Tyler (Gunther)

Summary: Ross reveals to the gang how he created his 'sound' – basically a cacophony of crappy sound effects which mean far more to Ross than anyone else with hearing. But Phoebe thinks his noise is the mark of a genius, causing her to lose confidence and refuse to play at Central Perk. Realising how unhappy she is, Ross 'deliberately' plays badly and asks Phoebe if she'll continue his set. Meanwhile, Joey has arranged a date with another woman, explaining to Chandler that he and Kathy are not exclusive. When Joey is delayed, leaving Kathy alone with Chandler, the two begin to reveal their feelings for each other and end up kissing. Feeling guilty, Chandler buys a new entertainment centre, stereo and TV to replace the one that was stolen. But when Kathy dumps Joey for 'another guy', Chandler feels that he must confess what happened.

Phoebisms: After Chandler sits on the worktop in Monica's kitchen, moaning about accidentally seeing Kathy in the shower, Phoebe waits until he leaves before asking everybody else if they could see up his bathrobe. Phoebs sings a song about a tiny Tarzan swinging on a nose-hair. Euch! Being the only person who thinks Ross's music is any good, Phoebe complains that she can't follow his act, comparing it to the bicycle-riding chimps that followed The Beatles. She later bemoans the fact that Ross is evidently unappreciated in his own time: 'I would give anything not to be appreciated in my own time!' The girls tell her honestly that she sucks too, but the ever-certain Phoebe thinks they're just trying to make her feel better.

Freaky Monica: Listening to Ross talk about his 'sound' makes Monica laugh while drinking: 'Orange juice just came out of my nose, but it was totally worth it!' she gurgles.

Slow Joey: Chandler tells Joey he must 'make a choice, pick a lane' to which Joey asks: 'Who's Elaine?' When Kathy finished with Joey he thought she was acting a scene so he let her break up with him in front of everyone else.

Poor Ross: Warns his friends that his 'sound' is about 'communicating very private emotions', and that they should be thought of as 'wordless sound poems'.

Chandleresque: When Phoebe says that Ross's stuff is so different from what you usually hear, Chandler quips 'like *music*?' He tells Kathy that he only watches *Baywatch* for the articles. She offers to cut his hair for him, but jokes that she trained at her aunt's dog-grooming salon: 'OK,' says Chandler, 'but don't make my tail too poofy.' She tells him he has great hair: 'Thanks, I grow it myself.' (He just can't stop himself!). After the kiss, Kathy starts to tell Chandler how she feels, but he stops her mid-sentence, saying that she's confusing him: 'I'm starting to yearn!' he protests.

The Ballad of Ross & Rachel: Hearing Ross's 'sound' for the first time, she suggests he should play in public – what a bitch! Later, she says that she can't believe she ever let him touch her with his fingers and claims that rats in the basement are hanging themselves because of his music.

The Chick and the Duck: The Duck starts quacking during *Baywatch*, prompting Chandler to reassure him that his breasts are just as firm and juicy as Yasmin Bleeth's.

Magna Doodle: There's a message from 'Treager' telling the guys to 'clean up duck feathers in hallway!' [Up until now his name has been spelled 'Treeger' on the credits, but we suspect he knows better than a credit writer.] Chandler later replaces this with a cartoon of his own face with the words 'I love you, man!' next to it.

Generation X: 'Play That Funky Music, White Boy', mentioned by Phoebe, was a 1976 American No. 1 hit for Wild Cherry, which was covered by Vanilla Ice in 1990. Ross's 'sound' is inspired in part by German synth masters Kraftwerk and by the late 70s/early 80s King of the Vocoder, Peter Frampton. Joey watches Lynda Carter in the 80s superhero series *Wonder Woman*.

The Story So Far: Ross began 'playing' keyboards in high school. His father soundproofed the basement for him to practice in (and now Monica is really grateful to her dad for that!). Chandler is now 29 years old.

The Last Word: The Eternal Triangle storyline continues with Chandler and Kathy finally kissing. We can entirely understand Joey's reaction – despite the fact he was with another woman when it happened, Joey *does* have a basic code of honour, which Chandler broke. The tragedy is that every other friend of Joey seems to have known that Chandler could have told Joey how he felt for Kathy and he would have stepped aside.

408
'The One With Chandler In A Box'

Writer: Michael Borkow
Director: Peter Bonerz
First US transmission: 20.11.97
First UK transmission (Sky One): 26.02.98

Guest Cast: Michael Vartan (Dr Tim Burke), Paget Brewster (Kathy), James Michael Tyler (Gunther), Marcy Goldman (Nurse)

Summary: As Phoebe and Monica have very little money this Christmas, Phoebe suggests they play 'Secret Santa', meaning they each buy one present, but they won't know who they're getting a gift from. Phoebe is desperate to swap with anyone for Rachel, claiming that she always exchanges anything she's bought for something else. When Ross discovers that she exchanged a gold necklace he bought her, he's in a bad mood throughout dinner – until Rachel shows him all the mementoes she *did* keep from their relationship.

Monica gets a chip of ice in her eye, forcing her to go to the eye doctor. Having checked that Richard is away, she's surprised to discover that the on-call doctor is actually Richard's son, Tim. Against the advice of her friends, she invites Tim to their Thanksgiving dinner, but after kissing him she is reminded of his father and suddenly gets all grossed out.

Joey has been refusing to talk to Chandler, even by phone. Chandler tries every way he can think of to get Joey to forgive him, and as a last attempt suggests he pays his penance by sitting inside a wooden box for the duration of Thanksgiving, *in silence*, to help him concentrate on his great betrayal of his best friend. But while he's in there, Kathy comes to tell him that she doesn't want to come between such good friends and tells him she can no longer see him . . .

Chandleresque: Phoebe goes to answer a knock at the door only to find it's Chandler knocking the inside of his box. Later on, Chandler tries to break the tension by claiming to be mooning everyone from inside the box.

Slow Joey: Our Italian friend exclaims 'Va fa Napoli', which is *similar* to a very bad Italian swear-word. He later teaches Rachel the same phrase. Ross discovers that Joey has sentenced Chandler to five years: 'Don't do the crime if you can't do the time!' he preaches.

Spoilt Rachel: She claims that just watching Monica work hard makes her sleepy. We discover that she exchanges every gift she ever received. She asks Ross: 'Isn't it better that I exchanged it for something that I enjoy, and that I can get a lot of use out of?' When Ross asks what, she replies 'credit'.

Freaky Monica: In one of the series' all-time best lines, Monica compares her decision to date the son of her ex-lover with the mistakes of her friends: 'Judge all you want to but, [to Ross] married a lesbian, [to Rachel] left a man at the altar, [to Phoebe] fell in love with a gay ice dancer, [to Joey] threw a girl's wooden leg in a fire, [to Chandler] living in a box!!' Priceless!

Phoebisms: Due to the accident, Monica hands over the Thanksgiving duties to Phoebe. Phoebe claims she has to call her mum to ask her a 'left-handed cooking question'.

The Ballad of Ross & Rachel: Rachel offers to get Chandler a hands-free headset for his phone, prompting Ross to ask if they can all expect Christmas gifts that she can steal from her office: '*You* shouldn't't', Rachel replies, bitchily. Later on, she shows Ross her keepsake box with little treasures from their relationship: 'Maybe I exchange gifts sometimes, but I keep the things that matter!' Ross apologises, but can't help adding that the piece she kept from their first time together was from the museum and strictly speaking, she shouldn't have taken it.

Gunther's Confused: He always thought Joey was Chandler.

The Chick and the Duck: The feathered fowl, clearly distressed, walk in on Chandler and Joey's row. Chandler begs Joey to stay for their sake: 'They have had a very difficult year, what with the robbery and all.' It's probably a good job they didn't wander next-door – the sight of the Thanksgiving dinner might have emotionally scarred them for life!

Magna Doodle: Chandler has written 'I'M SORRY I'M SORRY I'M SORRY' over and over again on the Magna Doodle board.

The Story So Far: Chandler still has a downer on Thanksgiving (see 'TOW Underdog Gets Away', 'TOW The Thanksgiving Flashbacks'). Rachel claimed that a backpack that Chandler got her was stolen by a dog, and she exchanged a gold necklace that Ross got her for store credit. However, she also kept the movie stub from her first date with Ross and an artefact from the museum from the first time they slept together (see 'TOW Ross and Rachel ... You Know'). Richard's son was previously mentioned in 'TOW Joey Moves

Out'. Monica reminds her friends about their past mistakes (see 'Pilot', 'TOW Phoebe's Husband', 'TOW Phoebe's Ex-Partner', and every episode with Carol and Susan). Chandler claims that Joey's knowledge of Italian extends only to swearing.

The Last Word: Proving that Matthew Perry can make any situation funny, the writers must have been wetting themselves when they came up with the idea of putting him inside a box for half an episode. As we'd probably expect, even this doesn't stop him. Star of the show, though, is Courteney Cox, who captures with a beautifully fragile and childlike performance how vulnerable we all feel when confronted by the all-powerful Doctor. For a control freak like Monica, such a transfer of power must be terrifying. Yet, back home, she is the bossy, frenetic woman we all know and love, and her verbal attack on each of her friends is one of the all-time best speeches the show has offered us.

409
'The One Where They're Gonna PARTY!'

Writers: Andrew Reich & Ted Cohen
Director: Peter Bonerz
First US transmission: 11.12.97
First UK transmission (Sky One): 05.03.98

Guest Cast: Alison LaPlaca (Joanna), Taylor Negron (Allesandro),
Richard Fancy (Mr Posner – Man On Hiring Committee),
Jennifer Rhodes (Mrs Lynch – Woman On Hiring Committee),
Laura Dean (Sophie), James Michael Tyler (Gunther)

Summary: Gandalf, 'the Party Wizard' is coming to town and Chandler and Ross are very excited. It seems that when Gandalf is around, literally anything can happen. The guys decide to book the day off work and prepare for the ultimate night of recklessness and debauchery. When Gandalf phones to cancel, Joey tries to arrange a wild night out instead. The boys soon tire of this excitement however, and eventually they are forced to admit that maybe they're not as young as they once were.

Rachel is up for a job as purchaser for Junior Miss at Bloomingdales, but her boss Joanna, totally undermines her during the interview. Upset, Rachel confronts Joanna, only to find that she's a lot more valued than she'd thought. As an apology, Joanna offers to create a post for Rachel that would still allow her to work for her, but before she can set the wheels in motion, Joanna is knocked down by a cab and killed.

Monica offers to fill in for a restaurant critic friend and do a few reviews. When she slates an Italian restaurant, the owner comes to demand a retraction. But when Monica shows him how to cook proper Italian food, he ends up offering her the job of head chef. But how will she break the news to Phoebe?

Slow Joey: When Ross asks him if he read *Lord of the Rings* in high school, he brags, 'No, I had sex in high school.' Chandler once paid Joey $50 to eat a book.

Freaky Monica: In her scathing restaurant review, she says that if she ever returns to Allesandro's, she'd need to order two meals, one for her and one for the guy pointing a gun at her head. Marvellous!

Chandleresque: In anticipation of Gandalf's arrival, Chandler tells Joey: 'I am *so* excited – I may vomit!' Trying to fill out his day after Gandalf stood him up, he claims he spent his time giving first names to all the foosball players.

Phoebisms: Monica claims that Phoebe doesn't need her for the business, but Phoebe rightly points out that she's the cook – 'Without you,' she explains, 'it's just me driving up to people's houses with empty trays and asking for money'. But eventually, Phoebe realises that Monica really wants the Head Chef job: 'I don't wanna be the reason you're unhappy. That would make *me* unhappy and I *really* don't wanna be the reason I'm unhappy!' Phoebe reconciles herself with the thought of forming the new A-Team.

Shut Up Sophie!: During the interview, Rachel says she loves working with designers. Joanna corrects her: 'With them, under them, what's the difference, eh, Rach?' After she's left the room, Joanna claims that Rachel enjoys 'the occasional drink . . . ing binge'. As Rachel complains about her boss's behaviour in the interview, Joanna calls Sophie into her office and then claims Rachel is making Sophie uncomfortable.

When Sophie denies this, Joanna snaps: 'Congratulations – you've just crossed the line into "completely useless"!'

After Joanna dies, though, Sophie gets the last laugh – and laugh she does.

Just Plain Weird: Allesandro, owner of an Italian restaurant, is actually Lebanese.

Generation X: Gandalf was the wizard in J.R. Tolkein's epic *Lord of the Rings*. Kenny G. is a rather bland saxophonist. *The A-Team* was an action-adventure series from the mid 80s starring George Peppard, Mr T, Dirk Benedict and Dwight Schultz as mercenaries on the run in a customised van, wanted 'for a crime they didn't commit'. It was a major smash in the UK for a while, until complaints about the levels of violence got it taken off. It's unlikely Phoebe would have fitted in anyway. Taylor Negron (Allesandro) is well-known on the American comedy circuit and appeared in the movie *Punchline* (David Seltzer, 1988).

The Last Word: 'I'm getting too old for this . . .' was the catchphrase of Murtaugh in the *Lethal Weapon* films. It could easily become the catchphrase for the boys here, as they realise that they had much more energy when they were younger. If the show tells us one thing it's that in our twenties there are so many opportunities open to us, but that they slowly disappear as we get older. It's a sobering thought, but one which the guys take quite easily. We feel so sorry for Rachel as her dreams pass her by thanks to the intervention of fate, but once again, Monica gets some excellent scenes, notably at the end of the episode when she begins to suspect that her dream job might not be as dreamy as she first thought. 'Are you going to kill me?' she asks nervously.

410
'The One With The Girl From Poughkeepsie'

Writer: Scott Silveri
Director: Gary Halvorson
First US transmission: 18.12.97
First UK transmission (Sky One): 12.03.98

Guest Cast: Fred Stoller (the Waiter), James Michael Tyler (Gunther),
Jamie Kaler (Mike), Micheal DiMaggio (Drew),
Shannon Maureen Brown (the Woman On The Train),
Amy Smallman (the Kitchen Worker),
Yasemin Baytok (the Poughkeepsie Woman), Vic Helford (the Conductor)

Summary: Ross has started dating a girl from Poughkeepsie, and another from upstate, but due to the amount of time he spends travelling to see them both, he keeps falling asleep. Having decided to finish with both of them, he misses his stop and ends up in Nova Scotia – where he meets another girl!

Monica is still suffering harassment at work, so Joey suggests she hires him just so she can fire him and assert her authority over the staff. They come up with a plot, but when Joey gets his first tips he shrinks away from Monica and backs out of the deal. Eventually, after the staff have played one too many tricks on her, Joey lets Monica fire him in full view of the rest of the staff, which seems to do the trick.

Rachel asks Chandler to set her up on a date, so he lines up more than a few willing volunteers.

Slow Joey: He beats his previous 'personal best' by stuffing fifteen Oreos into his mouth at once. When he starts work at the restaurant, he tells the staff that his name is 'Dragon' because he fancies the idea of having a cool nickname.

Spoilt Rachel: When Chandler says that he'd always thought girls didn't just want a fling, Rachel complains: 'Believe me, it's a long time since I've been flung.'

Freaky Monica: Upset about the victimisation she's suffering at work, she sobs that she hasn't been picked on this much since kindergarten when they had to bring someone from Junior High to do the see-saw with her.

Chandleresque: Asking one of his work colleagues if he's dating anyone, Chandler reassures him that he's not gay. 'I didn't think you *were* gay,' he replies, 'I do now.' He describes ice hockey to Rachel as: 'angry Canadians with no teeth'. Later, he asks Rachel if she's ever been with a woman. She's shocked: 'So there is no good time to ask that question,' he notes.

Chandler's Job: His company has a 'Fine Foods' division. Thanks to a mix-up, Phoebe is convinced they have robots there who work for them.

Phoebisms: She is writing a seasonal song featuring all her friends, but she moans to Rachel that 'nothing rhymes with your stupid name!' She asks her if maybe she ever had a nickname, like for instance 'Budolph'. Monica shows her what her staff wrote on her chef's hat. Phoebe fails to make her feel better by suggesting they were trying to write 'Qui*et*, Bitch!'

Dinosaurs ROCK!: When Rachel says she doesn't want to date anyone with a boring job, Chandler reminds her, 'Ross was, like, what? A *lion-tamer*?'

Gunther's There For You, Rachel: When Rachel declares that she wants 'somebody', Gunther hovers behind her. But when she says, emphatically that she wants 'a *man*!' we see him slope away, depressed.

Generation X: Oreos, for those that haven't had the pleasure, are two layers of circular chocolate biscuit with a layer of cream in between. Orson Welles was the acclaimed director of such masterpieces as *Citizen Kane* (1941) and *The Magnificent Ambersons* (1942).

The Story So Far: Phoebe casually mentions that she once lived in Prague and, on noting Chandler's reaction to this, notes playfully: 'There's so much you don't know.' Apparently, Chandler took Rachel to his company's last Christmas party. Chandler points out to Phoebe that he's not Jewish (which kind of ruins one of her rhymes).

The Last Word: Our hearts go out to Monica, who suffers the cruelty of bullies in the work-place with ever-decreasing grace. Strangely, Rachel's sub-plot is not nearly as involving because of the way she rounds on Chandler, who, after all, is just doing exactly what she asked him to (he's a guy – of *course* he'd think the fact she just wants a fling would be a plus-point). In spite of this (and the fact that Chandler has taken to answering Phoebe and Joey's dumb questions with a terse 'yes'), Chandler's touchy-feeliness with her just makes him all the more perfect a friend. In fact the selflessness from both Chandler and Joey makes this episode what it is. Ross, on the other hand, actually surpasses Rachel in being just so self-obsessed that it borders on annoying. Is that why they were so perfect for each other, we ask ourselves? We just find

it unlikely that it'd be Rachel who can't get a date and Ross
having three on the go. As if!

411
'The One With Phoebe's Uterus'

Writer: Seth Kurland
Director: David Steinberg
First US transmission: 08.01.98
First UK transmission (Sky One): 19.03.98

Guest Cast: Teri Garr (Phoebe, Sr), Giovanni Ribisi (Frank Jr),
Debra Jo Rupp (Alice), Paget Brewster (Kathy),
Sherri Shepherd (Rhonda, the Tour Guide), Miles Marisco (the Smart Kid),
Jack Ong (the Older Scientist, with the pear),
Jim Bentley (Another Tour Guide), Chip Chinery (Another Scientist)

Summary: Phoebe's half-brother Frank tells her that he and
his girlfriend, Alice, have just got married. He also asks her if
she'll consider being a surrogate mother for them, as they've
already been trying for a year and a half and they are unable to
conceive. Phoebe tells her friends about it, but they're a little
worried for her and suggest she gets some advice from her
birth mother. Phoebe Senior tries to show how difficult it was
for her to give Phoebe up by lending Phoebe a puppy, thinking
that if she can't return the puppy then no way will she be able
to give up her child.

Ross gets Joey a part-time job as a tour guide at the museum.
Joey is shocked to find that the scientists and researchers don't
sit with tour guides during break periods. He's certain that this
won't apply to him and Ross, but when Ross chooses to sit
with the other 'white coats', Joey is offended. Explaining the
situation to his friend, he encourages Ross to try to break down
the barriers between the workers at the museum, with mixed
results.

Chandler still hasn't had sex with Kathy yet, as he's intimidated by the fact that she dated Joey. Monica teaches Chandler
the real facts of life, and ends up all sixes and sevens. Well,
mainly sevens . . .

Phoebisms: When her friends are less than enthusiastic about her becoming pregnant, Phoebe is disappointed: 'You guys were a lot more supportive when I wanted to make denim furniture.'

Chandleresque: Phoebe tells the gang that she wants to give her brother and sister-in-law the greatest gift she can; Chandler asks if she's getting them a baby *and* a PlayStation. Chandler speculates that either Joey's great in bed, 'or she just likes to agree with him a lot', whereas when he's with Kathy he claims she was more like, 'I see your point, I'm alright with it.' Ahhhh.

Freaky Monica: Seizing the moment, when Chandler uncharacteristically fluffs his joke, Monica crows: 'You're stoopid!' Ross tries to explain his point to Joey by asking Monica if the waiters ever sit with the chefs in her restaurant: 'I eat by myself in the alley,' she confesses, 'because everybody hates me.'

Slow Joey: When Joey hears his friend referred to as 'Dr Geller' he presumes it's a nickname. Rachel reminds them all that when they're in the audience, Joey doesn't talk to them . . . but he does sometimes wave.

Dinosaurs ROCK!: Practising for his new job, he claims that the Tyrannosaurus Rex came from the Jurassic period. When Ross corrects him (it was from the Cretaceous era), Joey explains that he can pronounce 'Jurassic'. Taking a party round the museum, a bratty kid points out that Joey has confused the (fictional) semi-late Jurassic period with the Pleistocene Epoch. Finally, in the cafeteria, Joey is encouraged by Ross to proclaim that he knows 'squat' about dinosaurs.

Just Plain Weird: One of the scientists, in Ross's 'Oprah' moment, confesses his compulsion to flip the light switch on and off seventeen times to prevent his whole family from dying.

Generation X: Rachel compares Phoebe's dilemma to *Sophie's Choice* (Alan J. Pakula, 1982), a movie in which Meryl Streep plays a refugee who's forced by the Nazis to choose which one of her children she must leave behind. Chandler compares the squidgy-faced puppy to Karl Malden, the actor who appeared in the TV series *The Streets of San Francisco*.

The Story So Far: Phoebe's mum makes erotic pottery. Frank Jr used to have a dog called 'Tumour' (see 'TOW The Bullies').

No-One Told Us Life Was Gonna Be This Way: Chandler learns to try a little variety in lovemaking rather than just sticking to 'seven' all the time. Phoebe learns it's better to give than receive (though this is apparently the opposite to what Kathy learns).

The Last Word: Just a couple of things to note here – that puppy is just adorable and he and Phoebe playing together make the thought of her giving him up even more painful. But Frank and Alice seem to love him just as much, so that's OK. Monica's explanation of the seven erogenous zones is, erm, educational, though there must be *so* many guys who never get a woman to pant 'seven' like she does.

412

'The One With The Embryos'

Writers: Jill Condon & Amy Toomin
Director: Kevin S. Bright
First US transmission: 15.01.98
First UK transmission (Sky One): 26.03.98

Guest Cast: Giovanni Ribisi (Frank Jr),
Debra Jo Rupp (Alice), Cindy Katz (Dr Zane)

Summary: Having been woken up in the early hours of the morning by Yasmine the Chick's crowing, everyone's just a little crabby with each other. After a silly argument blows into a debate about who knows who the best, the guys win a $10 bet, but Monica wants a rematch – and wants the stakes upped to $100! Ross designs a gameshow-style quiz in which each team has to pick a question from a set of categories. The game goes extremely well, with the guys and the girls locked at nine points each, so when Ross reveals his tie-breaker round, Monica and Chandler begin to play one-upmanship with the stake – if the girls win, the boys' birds have to go; if the boys win, they get Monica's apartment!

Meanwhile, as her friends bicker, Phoebe awaits the results of her pregnancy test . . . and gets much more than she had expected . . .

Spoilt Rachel: Woken up by the sound of crowing, Rachel

goes on the war-path. When Monica comments on Rach not being a 'morning person' she roars 'BACK OFF!', kind of proving Monica's point. When Phoebe warns the guys that their feathered pets shouldn't be living in an apartment, Rachel snaps: 'Especially not with all of these knives and cookbooks around!' After losing the bet, Rachel delivers her most damning assessment of her former friends: 'You are mean boys who are just being mean!'

Freaky Monica: According to Chandler, Monica will only eat tictacs in even numbers. When Alice and Frank buy Phoebe a lollipop and a home pregnancy test kit, Monica warns them not to get the two mixed up or they'll really ruin the lollipop.

Phoebisms: Phoebe gives a pep-talk to the embryos, and warns them not to worry if she's screaming the next time she sees them: 'That's supposed to happen.' She later explains the risks to the gang, saying that Frank and Alice 'are literally putting all their eggs in my basket!' She also claims that her body is a little faster than 'Western medicine'.

Boys Will Be Boys: The guys stayed up late the night before making scary faces with the aid of Scotch tape. Frank junior suggests that Phoebe should get drunk to help her get pregnant: 'That worked for a lot of girls in my High School.' When the girls unwillingly move into the boys' old apartment they find 'something' locked away. Rachel doesn't know what it is, 'but maybe if we keep that drawer shut it'll die,' she says, less-than-hopefully.

The Chick and the Duck: Yasmine the Chick is going through some changes. 'She' turns out to be a rooster. Considering he's called Yasmine, that chick's going to have a rough time when he starts school!

Generation X: *Dangerous Liaisons* (Stephen Frears, 1988) which starred Glenn Close, John Malkovich and Uma Thurman, was based on the French classic *Les Liaisons Dangereuses* by Pierre Choderlos de Laclos and was a high-brow tale of scandal in the upper classes. *Weekend at Bernie's* (Ted Kotcheff, 1989) wasn't.

The Story So Far: Before the competition even begins, Chandler correctly guesses that Rachel carries a half-eaten box of cookies in her handbag. He and Joey then go on to name every remaining item (a bag of apples, tortilla chips, yoghurt, diet soda and Scotch tape). Ross sets up the competition with categories 'Fears and Pet Peeves', 'Ancient History', 'Literature' and 'It's All Relative'. The info run-down goes as follows: Monica's pet peeve is animals dressed as humans, whereas Chandler's is Michael Flatley, Lord of the Dance ('His legs flail about as if independent to his body'). Monica and Ross's Nana who died was called Althea (see 'TOW Nana Dies Twice'). The literature question refers to the *TV Guide*, which gets delivered to the boys' apartment each week, addressed to 'Miss Chanandelor Bong'. Chandler's father owns an all-male burlesque in Las Vegas called 'Viva Las Gaygas'.

Monica's nickname on the hockey team was 'big fat goalie'. Rachel claims her favourite movie is *Dangerous Liaisons*. Her actual favourite movie is *Weekend at Bernie's*. Monica once got a pencil stuck in her ear. Monica has eleven categories of towel (including 'everyday', 'fancy', 'guest' and 'fancy guest').

Joey's favourite food is sandwiches (see 'TOW The Ballroom Dancing'); Chandler was nineteen when he first touched a girl's breast; Joey had an imaginary childhood friend called Maurice who was a Space Cowboy and Chandler's job is . . . well it's not a 'transpondster' as Rachel claims, thereby losing the tournament for the girls.

As the guys move into the girls' apartment we see Joey's porcelain greyhound again (see 'TOW Eddie Won't Go'). Everyone now knows Ross's fist-smash gesture (see 'TOW Joey's new Girlfriend').

The Last Word: Phoebe's storyline would be a major feature in most other episodes, but of course this is no normal episode as the Battle of the Sexes dominates the story. This is a sure-fire contender for best episode of all time with each question revealing a shocking or just plain bizarre fact about the people we claim to know so well. Not one to be missed under any circumstances, this is like a seven-horse accumulator coming in on the day you win the lottery on a roll-over week. Except without the money.

413

'The One With Rachel's Crush'

Writers: Shana Goldberg-Meehan
Director: Dana deVally
First US transmission: 29.01.98
First UK transmission (Sky One): 02.04.98

Guest Cast: Paget Brewster (Kathy), Paxton Whitehead (Mr Waltham)
and introducing: Tate Donovan (Joshua Bergen)

Summary: Rachel's department is closed down [after the death of Joanna], and she's forced to accept a position as a 'personal shopper' for all the snooty rich people who need advice on what to buy. But then she gets allocated to her dream man, a recent divorcee called Joshua who needs to buy a whole new wardrobe. Rachel is really excited by this, but he's showing no signs of asking her for a date and she feels nervous about asking him out. On Joey's suggestion, she gets two tickets for the next Knicks game and offers them to him, but he misunderstands the offer and takes the second ticket for his nephew.

Chandler is distressed when he sees Kathy in a sex scene in a play and begins to feel insecure about their relationship. Asking Joey for advice (!) he learns that everything will be OK as long as there's chemistry onstage – if actors are doing it off-stage, they lose the sexual tension onstage. But in the next performance, Chandler is sure Kathy and her co-star are acting really cool towards each other, which can mean only one thing . . .

Phoebisms: Phoebe tactlessly asks if she can have some of Monica's old clothes from High School because maternity dresses are so expensive.

Chandleresque: Having just seen Kathy simulate sex in a play: 'It's like someone literally wrote down my worst nightmare and then charged me $32 to see it!' An offended Kathy tells Chandler to call her when he grows up: 'Well don't expect *that* to happen any time soon!' shouts Chandler, missing her point somewhat.

Freaky Monica: She uses a fan to blow the freshly-baked-cookie aroma across the hall, buys the latest Playboy magazine, works for almost two days straight to completely redecorate the guys' old apartment and polish their floor, just to tempt the guys back over to their old apartment.

Spoilt Rachel: Rach threatens to quit because she had to help an 81-year-old woman into a thong that she didn't even end up buying. When she sees Monica hauling a floor-polishing machine towards their apartment, Rachel makes for the boys' place, then adds as an afterthought: 'Ohh, I just feel bad, I never vacuum.'

Slow Joey: In defence of his 'heat on stage' theory, Joey claims that there are plenty of theories that don't work: 'The Lone Gunman, Communism, Geometry . . .'

Magna-Doodle: Newly ensconced in Monica's old apartment, the boys have waggishly scrawled: 'Have you seen our VIEW?'

Generation X: Ross and Joey come up with a list of actors and actresses who met on a film and got together afterwards: Susan Sarandon and Tim Robbins met on the set of *Bull Durham* (Ron Shelton, 1988), Alec Baldwin and Kim Basinger's relationship became public knowledge after alleged sex-romps on the set of *Too Hot To Handle* – a.k.a. *The Marrying Man* (Jerry Rees, 1991). Tom Cruise and Nicole Kidman were already married by the time they made *Far and Away* (Ron Howard, 1992). At the time this aired, Jennifer Aniston was dating Tate Donovan (Joshua). Chandler calls Kathy a 'Devil Woman', possibly in reference to the song by Cliff Richard. Tate Donovan was the star voice in Disney's *Hercules* (Ron Clements, John Musker, 1997).

The Story So Far: The guys have been to every play Joey's ever appeared in. Rachel claims she's never asked a guy out before, but Phoebe has, 'thousands of times'.

The Last Word: Typical Chandler, he gets the best relationship of his life so far and he ruins it by being unnecessarily jealous, and then giving her cause to go off with someone else (and if Ross says the words 'on a break' once more we'll break *him*!). Rachel's new position will have quite an effect on her love life and, by association, that of one of her friends too (clue – her new boss Mr Waltham is a significant factor).

414

'The One With Joey's Dirty Day'

Writer: Wil Calhoun
Director: Peter Bonerz
First US transmission: 05.02.98
First UK transmission (Sky One): 09.04.98

Guest Cast: Charlton Heston (himself), Tate Donovan (Joshua Bergen),
Paxton Whitehead (Mr Waltham), Carlos LaCamera (the Assistant Director),
Rocky McMurray (Cigarette Guy)
and introducing: Helen Baxendale (Emily Waltham)

Summary: Chandler is depressed after breaking up with Kathy and is stuck in what Joey calls 'Phase One', where he won't change out of his sweatpants for days on end. Joey decides to go fishing, promising to be back in time for 'Phase Two' – going to strip clubs and getting drunk. But Joey comes back from the trip late, stinking of fish and worms. He then oversleeps and has to go to a film-shoot still reeking from his trip. Discovering that the star of the picture (Charlton Heston) has his own shower, Joey sneaks in to use it. Heston returns to his dressing room and catches Joey half-naked and Joey is forced to do some quick thinking.

None of this helps Chandler, who is now ready for 'Phase Two'. Distraught that his best buddy isn't available, Chandler is left to go to the strip clubs with the girls – who have a better time there than he does! As the girls discuss how much fun they had, Chandler suddenly finds himself jumping from Phase Two to an unprecedented 'Phase Four'!

Rachel seems to be making headway with Joshua – he invites her to the opening of a nightclub, promising to leave her name at the door. But she's also promised her boss that she'll escort his niece, Emily, who's visiting from England, to the opera. In desperation she asks Ross if he'll step in and go with Emily. Reluctantly, Ross agrees, unaware that his life is likely to change forever . . .

Slow Joey: We're not fishermen, so we don't know if Joey is being serious or if he just made up names for fishing equipment, but we agree with Phoebe, 'guggly worm' and 'glow-pop giggly jammer' are hilarious.

Phoebisms: She gets her morning sickness in the evening! She thinks that at one point she feels her baby kicking for the first time, only to realise that the elastic on her underwear had just snapped. She discovers that Phoebs is short for Phoebe: 'I thought that was just what we called each other!'

Chandleresque: Joey is disappointed at missing the chance to go to a strip club with Chandler, but his friend reassures him: 'You're gonna have plenty of chances – there are literally thousands of women out there just waiting to screw me over.'

Spoilt Rachel: Hearing that Ross and Emily have flitted off to Vermont the day after they first met, Rachel is shocked. But when Monica reminds her that she 'flitted off' to Vail with Barry when they first met, a tired Rachel snaps back: 'Would you just for *once* not remember every . . . little . . . *thing*?'

Cool Britannia Rachel's boss, Mr Waltham, tells Rachel that Emily is from London. 'Well Shropshire, really,' he corrects himself. Surely, being English, he'd know that geographically speaking there's quite a difference between the two places (and we're not just talking pottery-versus-smog here). Emily turns up at Rachel's looking like a drowned rat having been strip-searched at JFK Airport: 'Apparently, to you people, I look like someone who's got a balloon of cocaine stuffed up their bum!' she rants.

Boys Will Be . . . erm, Girls?: Monica and Phoebe offer to be one of the guys to cheer Chandler up: 'You don't wanna be guys, you'd be all hairy and wouldn't live as long.'

The Chick and the Duck: They follow Chandler into the bathroom: 'Will you give me one minute!!?' says an irritable Chandler.

Generation X: Of the three tenors, Luciano Pavarotti, Jose Carreras and Placido Domingo, the two who performed Strauss's *Die Fledermaus* (meaning 'The Bat') are most likely to have been Domingo and Pavarotti. In an epic career, Charlton Heston has played Moses in *The Ten Commandments* (Cecil B. DeMille, 1956), the eponymous hero in *Ben-Hur* (William Wyler, 1959 – winner of more Oscars than any other film to date) and, in the first two *Planet of the Apes* movies, he played the first astronaut ever to get a snog off a chimpanzee. Joey claims to be veteran actor Kirk Douglas, in a flawed attempt to excuse his presence in Charlton Heston's shower. Helen Baxendale shot to fame in the UK as the acerbic Dr Maitland in the medical drama *Cardiac Arrest*, and later starred in *The Investigator*, *An Unsuitable Job For A Woman* and *Cold Feet*.

The Story So Far: Rachel and Barry went to Vail when they first met, just like Ross and Emily went to Vermont. Rachel doesn't like people calling Joshua just 'Josh' (see 'TOW Joey's New Girlfriend').

The Last Word: There'll be some people out there who find the whole idea of spending a whole episode talking about strippers a little tacky. If so, you're watching the wrong show! The dream sequence at the end is choice, with Chandler directing his fantasy, having his female friends while cavorting with strippers who shout 'Chandler is the King!' (though typically, he can't help torturing himself by receiving unwarranted advances from the smoking man as part of the fantasy). We're sorry for all the female *Friends* fans out there, but this is what blokes are really like!

415
'The One With All The Rugby'

Writers: Andrew Reich & Ted Cohen (story),
Wil Calhoun (teleplay)
Director: James Burrows
First US transmission: 26.02.98
First UK transmission (Sky One): 16.04.98

Guest Cast: Maggie Wheeler (Janice), Helen Baxendale (Emily Waltham),
Mark Thomas (Liam), Adamo Palladino (Devon),
Robin McDonald (Ticket Counter Attendant)

Summary: Rachel persuades Chandler to accompany her to a beauty parlour, where he bumps into Janice. But to avoid getting back with her, he tells her his company is sending him to Yemen. This seems like a pretty good excuse to Chandler – until Janice decides she's going to see him off at the airport.

Ross finds himself volunteering to play rugby just to impress Emily. As everyone expected, he gets beaten to a pulp, but when Emily encourages him to play dirty and gives him a few sly tips, Ross manages to survive the experience . . . just!

And Monica discovers a mysterious switch in the boys' old apartment and is driven to tearing down the walls just to find out what it's for . . .

Spoilt Rachel: At the manicure parlour, Rachel finds that she's sitting on a huge fingernail: 'I hate to think what this woman was scratching when this broke off!' Rach asks Joey what the silver knob on the toilet is for. When he tells her it flushes the toilet, she asks him: 'When you come over, would you mind actually using it?'

Freaky Monica: She plugs things in around the house to see what gets switched on or off by the switch, then she goes down to City Hall, waits for three hours and pays for a copy of the electrical plans to their apartment. When Rachel comes home, she finds pictures hanging on the walls to cover the massive holes Monica made trying to find where the cables lead! After hiring a $200-an-hour electrician, asking Treager's advice and suffering several electric shocks, Monica finally gives up.

Phoebisms: As Monica absently flicks the switch on and off, we see the TV in the boys' apartment switching on and off (the switch controls the plug in that apartment!). Phoebe is watching the TV and repeatedly blinking in the belief that her eyes now control the TV.

Slow Joey: When Ross claims that the other rugby players don't look bigger than himself, Joey explains: 'Maybe that's because you're closer to you, so you look bigger to you from where you are.'

Poor Ross: Having reassured Emily that New York is safe, he panics when two large guys run towards them – only to discover they're friends of Emily. Ross later boasts that he's man enough to play rugby, but Joey says: 'Dude, you're not even man enough to order the channel that carries the sport!'

Cool Britannia: Ross jokes that although they don't have rugby in the USA, they didn't have freedom until 1776 (The War of Independence).

Magna Doodle: Someone has scrawled a rather cruel 'Nice nails Chandler!'

Generation X: Janice sang 'Old Man River', a song tradition-ally identified with a deep bass singer such as Paul Robeson. Ross recalls the gang all going to see *Dances with Wolves* (Kevin Costner, 1990).

The Story So Far: Janice is now divorced (see 'TOW The Race Car Bed'). Rachel reminds Ross that he once hurt himself playing badminton with her dad (though Ross claims it was because her mother's dog was psyching him out). Joey and Chandler's . . . er, Monica and Rachel's apartment is above that of a Mrs Chatracus, who presumably lived opposite Mr Heckles all those years. Ross claims he washed his father's Porsche with rocks when he was four [his father managed to get a replacement Porsche years later – see 'TOW Ross and Rachel . . . You Know'].

The Last Word: Ross is a fool, but you've gotta admire his eagerness to please Emily. Chandler's desperation to rid himself of Janice reaches ludicrous proportions and Monica's obsessions reach fever pitch. It's pretty worrying when Joey is the most normal member of the gang. It must be a warning for the end of civilisation as we know it . . . or just a fairly average episode.

416
'The One With The Fake Party'

Writers: Alicia Sky Varinaitis (story), Shana Goldberg-Meehan & Scott Silveri (teleplay)
Director: Michael Lembeck
First US transmission: 19.03.98
First UK transmission (Sky One): 23.04.98

Guest Cast: Helen Baxendale (Emily Waltham),
Tate Donovan (Joshua Bergen), James Michael Tyler (Gunther)

Summary: Phoebe discovers her baby doesn't like vegetarian food and is forced to eat meat. Joey helps her out with a few sandwich recipes, but she's still upset about the ethics of eating. Joey volunteers to become a vegetarian for as long as Phoebe is pregnant to even out the numbers.

It's Emily's last few days in the country and Ross wants to

spend as much time with her as possible. Unfortunately, in a last-ditch attempt to seduce Joshua, Rachel arranges a surprise leaving party for Emily to give her the excuse she's needed to invite Joshua to meet her away from work. Emily is bowled over by what she believes to be Ross's generosity and really enjoys herself, to the extent where the evening draws on and there's no time left for any of the things Ross had planned. Rachel tries every trick she can think of (and at least three different dresses) to seduce Joshua, but all of them go horribly wrong. Eventually she comes clean and confesses her less-than-honourable intentions towards him. Joshua is relieved – he's been coming back to her department and buying suits just so he could see her. But he also explains that his marriage has just ended and that he doesn't feel ready for a relationship yet.

Chandleresque: Rachel changes into her lucky dress. When Monica asks if 'lucky' means more cleavage, Chandler quips 'Does for me!'

Slow Joey: Joey eats a bologna and pickle sandwich in the shower. When Ross explains that he and Emily knew they only had two weeks together, Joey boasts: 'That's what all my relationships are like.' Chandler has to remind him that in Ross's case, they *both* know it's just for two weeks. Having agreed to become a vegetarian for Phoebe's sake, he checks one last detail: 'There's no meat in beer, right?' He later asks Phoebe: 'If a cow should die of natural causes, I can have one of those, right?' 'Not if I get there first,' challenges the ex-vegetarian.

Phoebisms: Joey tries to cheer her up by telling her she has 'that cool, pregnant lady glow', to which Phoebe says: 'That's *sweat*. You throw up all morning, you'll have that glow too.'

Gunther's There For You, Rachel: At the party, Rachel begins to illustrate the rules of Spin The Bottle by going to kiss Gunther, but sees the look of expectation on his face and decides against it. When she performs a less-than-successful cartwheel, Gunther's the only one that claps. He also tells Emily that Rachel is his girlfriend.

Cool Britannia: Emily's ever-so-English uncle drags her and Ross to a museum of Victorian doorknobs.

Magna-Doodle: During the 'leaving do', we can see the words: 'Emily . . . Bon Voy See ya!'

Generation X: Joey confuses *Footloose* (Herbert Ross, 1984) starring Kevin Bacon with *Flashdance* (Adrian Lyne, 1983), which starred Jennifer Beals. At Rachel's party, we hear Cornershop's 'Brimful of Asha'.

The Story So Far: Encouraged by Emily, Ross signed himself up for helicopter classes. Monica tells Emily that Ross used to dress up like an old lady and throw tea-parties when he was a boy (see 'TOW The Metaphorical Tunnel'). Rachel still uses her high-school cheerleader's outfit to seduce men. She is 28 by this episode.

The Last Word: Despite the fact that this episode shows just how far Rachel will go to get her own way, it's good to see her having to work for a relationship instead of just having one appear in front of her. But the best scene is probably where we see Ross and Rachel as friends for the first time since they took a break. About time, too.

417

'The One With The Free Porn'

Writers: Mark J. Kunerth (story), Richard Goodman (teleplay)
Director: Michael Lembeck
First US transmission: 26.03.98
First UK transmission (Sky One): 30.04.98

Guest Cast: Helen Baxendale (Emily Waltham),
Giovanni Ribisi (Frank Jr), Debra Jo Rupp (Alice),
Michael G. Hagerty (Mr Treager – billed as 'Treeger'),
Shirley Jordan (the Doctor)

Summary: Joey and Chandler suddenly find their lives grinding to a halt when they acquire a pornography channel for free. Terrified that they'll lose it if the TV set is switched off, they mount an all-night vigil. Meanwhile, Phoebe discovers that the baby she's carrying for her brother and his wife is actually triplets. Frank and Alice are thrilled, until they realise that three babies means three times the expense.

Monica convinces Ross to catch Emily before she leaves for England. At the gate, Ross tells her he loves her, but she seems really underwhelmed. Later he speaks to her on the phone and only then does she tell him there's 'someone else'. Bullied further by Monica, he goes to London, only to find that Emily has dumped her English boyfriend, having realised that she loves Ross, and is in New York!

Phoebisms: When her obstetrician discusses with her the possibility of multiple births, Phoebe at first misses his point: 'Why don't we just take care of this one, and should I get pregnant again I'll hold on to your card, OK?' Our favourite scene is where Phoebe tries to tell the gang her new money-making idea, while trying to stop Rachel from blowing the surprise. When Rachel claims it was her idea to call it 'Relaxi-Taxi' Phoebe nearly rips her head off when she shrieks: 'You did NOT!! Oh No! You came up with "Relaxi Cab"!' When Rachel explains that she meant 'Relaxicab, like "taxicab",' Phoebe visibly backs down.

Freaky Monica: Monica wants Ross to live out her fantasy for her and tells him he must get to the airport before Emily leaves. Describing what she imagines might happen when the two lovers are reunited, Monica suddenly balks at the style of her narrative, confessing, 'I've been watching way too much porn.'

Poor Ross: After discovering Emily has a boyfriend back in London, Ross tells Monica he won't listen to her advice any more, blaming her for him putting his fist through the wall. Chandler asks: 'You put your fist through the wall?' 'No,' confesses Ross, 'I missed and hit the door, but it opened really hard!'

Boys Will Be Boys: Treager explains that he once got a free porn channel too and describes it as being like finding money: 'Like finding money with naked people on it!' suggests Chandler. Treager tells them he lost the channel after he turned the TV off, prompting a baffled Joey to ask: 'Why would he turn off the TV?' Eventually the effect of the porn starts to addle what minds the boys still have. Chandler is dismayed to discover that the really sexy teller at the bank doesn't invite him to 'do it with her in the vault' and Joey is shocked when the 'woman pizza delivery guy' delivers the pizza and leaves without asking to inspect his bedroom.

Just Plain Weird: Frank Jr's response on hearing they're expecting triplets: 'I finally got my band!' He tells Phoebe he's enrolled in college – refrigerator college. It's quite weird that we can hear Emily's phone with amazing clarity from outside her apartment.

Magna Doodle: 'Knock knock. Who's there? . . . PORN' plus, strangely, 'Clean Bathroom'.

Generation X: The writing team had been keen to use a fake porn film title for the one Joey appeared in (see 'TOW Phoebe's Husband'), but we get a much better selection here. *Good Will Humping* is inspired by *Good Will Hunting* (Gus Van Sant, 1997), while *In & Out & In Again* is an obvious nod to *In & Out* (Frank Oz, 1997) which starred Kevin Kline. As Monica explains her fantasy to Ross it echoes the movie *Only You* (Norman Jewison, 1994), which starred Robert Downey Jr and Marisa Tomei.

The Story So Far: Emily had a British boyfriend called Colin.

The Last Word: OK, so this goes one step further than the strippers in 'TOW Joey's Dirty Day', but it is funny, especially the bogus film names that pop up here and there. Certainly the crudity is more fun than Ross and Emily's love story. However, Baxendale tries her best, and though the writers think they've written her terribly, terribly English, it does come across as slightly twee when they give her expletives like 'bugger off'. Something that might not be evident on first viewing, especially when taking into account what follows, is that before this episode, Ross and Emily were content to consider their relationship as a brief holiday affair. What follows is ENTIRELY Monica's fault, which is ironic, considering it works out well for her, at least.

418

'The One With Rachel's New Dress'

Writers: Andrew Reich & Ted Cohen (story),
Jill Condon & Amy Toomin (teleplay)
Director: Gail Mancuso
First US transmission: 07.04.98
First UK transmission (Sky One): 07.05.98

Guest Cast: Tate Donovan (Joshua Bergen), Jane Sibbett (Carol),
Helen Baxendale (Emily Waltham), Jessica Hecht (Susan),
Debra Jo Rupp (Alice), John Bennett Perry (Mr Burgin),
Pat Crowley (Mrs Burgin), Charlie Allen & Jack Allen (Ben)

Summary: Alice and Frank have chosen names for two of their triplets, but they want Phoebe to name the third. Asking Joey and Chandler for advice, she unwittingly provokes a fight over who she should name the child after. When Joey ridicules Chandler's name he suddenly becomes defensive and vows to change his name by deed poll. To stop him making such a rash decision, Phoebe tells him that she likes his name so much she's decided to name the third child after him. The second she leaves, Chandler breaks into a big smile – it has all been a ruse to get his own way.

Ross is concerned when Emily meets Susan for the first time and she offers to show his ex-wife's wife around London. Ross convinces himself that Emily, like Carol before her, has fallen for Susan. Expressing his fears to the gang, they all think he's paranoid; the only person who believes it's possible, ironically, is Carol.

Rachel plans a major seduction of Joshua for their first night together, but when he tells her about his morbid fear of fowl, he suggests they both go over to his parents' house, as they're out of town. But just as Rachel undresses down to her undergarments, Joshua's parents come home and she's forced to pretend she's wearing a fashionable dress – to dinner!

Phoebisms: Phoebe takes to playing a drum as she's too pregnant to play the guitar any more. This brings a whole new interpretation to 'Smelly Cat'. Phoebe's suggestions for the baby's name include 'Cougar', 'Exxon' and 'Chanoey', a combination of Joey and Chandler. When Joey suggests 'The Hulk', Phoebs says that she likes the idea of a name starting with 'The'.

Freaky Monica: When Rachel asks her advice on which night-gown she should wear for her 'first time' with Joshua, Monica says that she feels creeped out by the thought of choosing other people's 'sex clothes'.

Spoilt Rachel: Rachel boasts that she's had her hair coloured, bought new sheets and that she's cooking him a fancy meal –

only to turn to Monica to ask her what 'she' is cooking. It turns out that she's persuaded Monica to prepare an entire menu on her behalf, and Monica warns her that if she bitches about it, then she'll find herself making her 'famous baked potato and Diet Coke' instead. 'Wow, I really get crabby when I cook,' notes Rachel.

Slow Joey: Joey asks Chandler to name one famous person with his name. When he names Raymond Chandler, Joey demands it should be someone he 'didn't make up'!

Poor Ross: Emily worries about Ben getting the wrong idea if he sees her bra on Ross's shower rail. A pragmatic Ross says: 'If mommy can have a wife, daddy can have a bra.' Susan tells Emily that Ross doesn't like her: 'Oh come on! That's-that's . . . true.'

The Chick and the Duck: Yasmine and Dick still 'migrate' over to their old apartment every now and again, which really freaks Joshua out – he's afraid of farm birds!

Just Plain Weird: Alice tells Phoebe that they've chosen the name Leslie for one of the babies, and that Frank wants to name one of the boy babies 'Frank Jr Jr'. When Chandler asks her if that would make him 'Frank III', Alice sighs: 'Don't get me started.'

Girl Power!: Rachel tells the girls that when she went to dinner with the Bergens, the waiter spilled cold water down her back and one of her boobs popped out. Her friends try to console her, but she's OK: 'I got nice boobs,' she tells them confidently – and the girls have to agree with her.

Parents – Who Needs 'Em?: The Bergens seem massively dissatisfied with Europe. Asked how he enjoyed France and Italy, Mr Bergen's response is, 'It sucks!'

Generation X: In reference to Emily and Susan, Ross mentions *Personal Best* (Robert Towne, 1982) in which Mariel Hemingway hops in between the beds of her male coach and her female competitor. When Phoebe claims that Ross and The Hulk have very little in common, Ross refers to 'Issue 72' before everyone looks at him as if he's a geek (There never was an issue 72 of *The Incredible Hulk*. *The Incredible Hulk vol. 1* lasted a mere 6 issues, though the character returned as a strip-only character in *Tales To Astonish*. As he was by far the most popular character in it, *Tales to Astonish* was renamed *The Incredible Hulk* as of issue 102, so Ross isn't always right!). Raymond Chandler was a celebrated crime author, whereas Joey Buttafucco, who sounds made-up, most definitely isn't. He was a mechanic who alleged that after a young girl called Amy Fisher developed a crush on him, she murdered his wife in a jealous rage. She alleged that he'd seduced her, driven her to prostitution and bullied her into the murder. He became the butt of many jokes in the States, while Amy found her life-story transformed into three lurid TV movies. Joshua's father is played by John Bennett Perry, famous as the 'Old Spice guy' in a series of adverts. He also appeared in the film *Fools Rush In* (Andy Tennant, 1997) opposite his real-life son, Matthew Perry.

The Story So Far: Ross reminds Chandler and Phoebe that for six months before they split up, all he heard about from Carol was how great Susan was (see 'TOW The Flashback'). Rachel reminds Ross of how he got jealous of Mark even though nothing happened between them (see 'TOW All The Jealousy') and Monica reminds him that back in high school all of his girlfriends were cheating on him and he never got jealous once.

The Last Word: Rachel's quick-thinking in this episode is very impressive, telling Joshua's parents that her undergarment is a new dress from Milan, and that she's just product testing it: 'Obviously in this case, I am going to report back, "USA not ready".' The effort she goes to (OK the effort she and *Monica* go to) is nice to see, considering that she's never really had to work this hard for a relationship. Ross, meanwhile, seems not to have grown at all. Hearing that Susan and Emily have gone to a poetry reading together, he cries: 'Poetry? Susan's gay! They're being gay together!' His irrational jealousy is getting tired by now, and Rachel's spiteful response to his behaviour ('I hope Emily IS a lesbian!') is, for once, spot on.

419
'The One With All The Haste'

Writers: Wil Calhoun & Scott Silveri
Director: Kevin S. Bright
First US transmission: 09.04.98
First UK transmission (Sky One): 14.05.98

Guest Cast: Helen Baxendale (Emily Waltham),
James Michael Tyler (Gunther), Michael Connor (Singing Man)

Summary: The girls are really getting tired of living in the boys' old apartment and try anything to get their old home back. Having tried bribing them with Knicks tickets, they eventually find themselves caught in another 'Winner Takes All' bet. The boys win again and get both the apartment *and* the tickets! But while they're at the game, the girls plan a little house-swapping and get both apartments as they used to be, in record time!

Ross, meanwhile, is beginning to find seeing Emily for only a couple of days at a time emotionally draining. He considers asking her to move to America, but after discussing it with her they agree to go the distance and get married! What will Rachel's reaction be when she finds out?

Spoilt Rachel: Boy does she go overboard this episode! She roars at a man who's singing joyfully early in the morning, then rants at Joey: 'I hate this apartment! I hate the colour of these walls! I hate the fact that this place still smells like bird! I hate that singing guy!' Then she threatens to kill Joey. She is *so* not a morning person.

Phoebisms: She buys a pile of maternity clothes from a used clothes store, only to find that the maternity pants she bought (complete with a list of names, both naughty and nice) are the bottom half of a Santa costume. Her idea of a suitable question to decide who gets the nice apartment is to ask each pair in turn what their favourite thing about trees is. When Joey offers 'They're tall,' Phoebs marks him down because she was going for 'leafy'.

Chandleresque: Monica asks him what she should wear to a Knicks game: 'A T-shirt that says "I don't belong here",' he suggests. After Ross tells the guys about his intention to ask Emily to live with him, Chandler claims that he has a carton of milk he's had a longer relationship with. When Joey begs Chandler to risk the bet with the girls, on account of him being his best friend, Chandler relents: 'All right, but you can't use that [excuse] again for a whole year.'

Poor Ross: When Joey sees Ross's earring for the first time he asks him: 'We don't make enough fun of you already?' while Chandler asks him if he was aware that Wham! broke up.

Freaky Monica: They sure know how easy it is to get men to do what they want. As a last-ditch attempt to keep their apartment, Monica and Rachel agree to kiss in front of the guys for one minute! Phoebe speculates that if they'd just done that right after the last contest, they could have kept their apartment. Monica looks at her murderously and asks her to pretend that 'that's not true'.

Magna-Doodle: A chirpy 'What's up? Bro?'

Generation X: Wham! was the name of George Michael's early 80s double-act with his childhood friend, Andrew Ridgeley. One of their biggest hits was 'Wake Me Up Before You Go-Go'. *Flowers for Algernon* was a novel by Daniel Keyes about a mentally disabled man who is used in an experiment to increase his intelligence. The fact that Joey has not read this book *is* relevant.

The Story So Far: Ross has an earring from this episode on (having evidently overcome his fear of needles – see 'TOW The Baby On The Bus'). Rachel claims that her mother got her father's Knicks season ticket in the divorce (though she's possibly lying). Joey bemoans the fact that when he was a kid, his father's work used to award the best salesman with a season ticket, and that his father never won. Of course, his father didn't actually work in the sales division anyway. By this point, Ross and Emily have known each other for six weeks.

The Last Word: Phoebe's reaction to Ross and Emily's news is what we're sure most of us would say to a friend who's decided to get married after only six weeks: 'Are you pregnant too?' But of course, it's Rachel's response that everyone is waiting for, and the relief of the whole gang when Rachel wishes them both well is almost tangible. Obviously, that's not what everyone remembers this episode for, is it? MONICA AND RACHEL SNOG!! Admittedly, we don't get to see it, but the thought of it is enough for many viewers.

420
'The One With All The Wedding Dresses'

Writers: Adam Chase (story),
Michael Curtis & Gregory S. Malins (teleplay)
Director: Gail Mancuso
First US transmission: 16.04.98
First UK transmission (Sky One): 21.05.98

Guest Cast: Tate Donovan (Joshua Bergen), James Michael Tyler (Gunther),
Christina Moore (Marjorie), Anne Betancourt (The Saleslady),
Thea Mann (Sleep-Clinic Worker)

Summary: Joey's snoring is getting so bad that Chandler is having trouble sleeping, so he forces Joey to go to a sleep clinic. In preparation for the clinic, Joey mustn't sleep – something he's having trouble with. Chandler takes his friend to the clinic, and there, he meets an attractive woman; because Joey can't help falling asleep, he manages to arrange a date with her. Chandler's happy with himself, not least because the woman talks in her sleep, which keeps Joey awake!

Ross asks Monica to pick up Emily's wedding dress – being the groom, he's not supposed to see it until his wedding day. Monica is only too happy to help him out, especially when the shop assistant thinks it's for her and allows her to try it on. Soon, both Monica and Phoebe are wearing wedding dresses.

Trying to prove how 'OK' she is about Ross's impending marriage, Rachel speaks to Joshua about their future, pressurising him just a little into thinking about getting married. As he's only recently got divorced this almost frightens him away, but Rachel luckily manages to convince him that she wasn't that serious after all. But after she joins in with the girls and puts on a wedding dress, Joshua calls round, sees what she's wearing and runs off in a panic.

Freaky Monica: Monica tries to get Rachel to do the dishes, just once: 'I don't care if those dishes sit in the sink until they're all covered with [realises what she's saying] . . . I'll do them when I get home!' We see Monica wearing Emily's wedding dress and admiring herself in the mirror – until eventually the shop assistant tells her that the store is closing. 'I wish there was a job where I could wear this all the time,' she tells her friends. 'Maybe one day, there will be.'

Slow Joey: When Ross tells the gang the date of his wedding, Joey notes that it'll be the day after he stops menstruating – before realising that he's reading someone else's diary.

Chandleresque: (After Marjorie tells him she talks in her sleep): 'What a coincidence, I *listen* in my sleep.'

The Ballad of Ross & Rachel: Rachel surprises her friends by stating that she doesn't believe that Ross and Emily will even *get* married. 'You're gonna be dancing at my wedding before you're dancing at theirs,' she boasts. Later, she tells Monica that she'd kind of expected her and Ross to get back together again. Monica reassures her friend: 'I think we all did.'

Just Plain Weird: Phoebe rents a wedding dress just for the fun of it from a shop called 'It's Not Too Late'. Joey and Chandler have a disagreement about the noise a whip makes (!). Chandler goes for 'Whapahhh!', whereas Joey favours a more traditional 'Whitushhh!' – madness!

Gunther's There For You, Rachel: Overhearing Joshua reject Rachel's marriage proposal, Gunther shrieks: 'You IDIOT!!'

Magna Doodle: In a magic moment, the Magna Doodle is blank when Ross enters the guys' apartment, but in the shot where he's told his friends he and Emily have set a date, the board reads 'GET OUT!!' in surprise.

The Story So Far: Monica reveals that she sometimes snores in her sleep. Joey sleeps naked (see 'TOW The Boobies'). Rachel unpacks her own wedding dress (see 'Pilot').

The Last Word: The self-destructive side of Rachel strikes again as she frightens away a perfectly good boyfriend just to compete with Ross. The seed is sown for a dramatic finish to the season at Ross's wedding! An episode that is supported by loads of superb visual gags, notably where Monica and Phoebe throw bouquets to each other in a mock end-of-wedding celebration.

421

'The One With The Invitation'

Writer: Seth Kurland
Director: Peter Bonerz
First US transmission: 23.04.98
First UK transmission (Sky One): 28.05.98

Guest Cast: Helen Baxendale (Emily Waltham)

Summary: Ross and Emily are sending out their wedding invitations and discuss whether inviting Rachel is such a good idea. Trying to decide, Ross remembers some of the most prominent moments from his relationship with Rachel. Rachel, meanwhile, is deciding whether she's actually going to go to the ceremony. As she realises how much she still feels for Ross, she tells the rest of her friends that she's decided to stay with Phoebe to look after her.

Chandleresque: Chandler feels dissatisfied that the only thing he's achieved in his life is leaving his 'ass-print' on a chair. After Joey suggests they might climb Everest, Chandler feels enthused enough to say: 'It would be nice to leave an ass-print on Everest!'

Phoebisms: Phoebs dampens the boys' spirits by pointing out that climbing Everest costs over $60,000 and that it's possible they might die: 'And you *would* die!' she says, not at all reassuringly.

Slow Joey: Phoebe tells them that expectant mothers are not allowed to fly once their pregnancy reaches the third trimester, and Chandler confesses he didn't know that. Joey claims that he did, much to everyone's surprise, only to blurt: 'I *so* didn't know that, but you should see your faces!' Good one, Joe.

The Ballad of Ross & Rachel: Rachel tells the gang that she won't be going to the wedding: 'I mean, it's Ross. How can I *watch* him get *married* . . .?'

Cool Britannia: Emily offers Ross some tea: 'Earl Grey?' 'Yeah, fine. Invite whoever you want.'

The Story So Far: The Gellers have an Uncle Nathan who nobody likes. Ross remembers events from 'Pilot', 'TOW The Blackout', 'TOW The East German Laundry Detergent', 'TOW Ross Finds Out', 'TOW Ross and Rachel Take A Break', 'TO The Morning After', 'TOW The Jellyfish' and finally 'TOW The Fake Party'. Rachel's memories begin with 'TOW Rachel Finds Out', then go through 'TOW Ross's New Girlfriend', 'TOW Ross Finds Out', 'TOW The List', 'TOW Ross and Rachel . . . You Know', 'TO The Morning After', 'TO At The Beach', 'TOW The Jellyfish' and finally 'TOW The Prom Video'.

The Last Word: This episode was largely a series of clips, which some fans felt cheated by, but it serves as a nice reminder of Ross and Rachel's past. If nothing else, they must have saved enough money to afford the London episodes.

422

'The One With The Worst Best Man Ever'

Writers: Seth Kurland (story),
Michael Curtis & Gregory S. Malins (teleplay)
Director: Peter Bonerz
First US transmission: 30.04.98
First UK Transmission (Sky One): 28.05.98

Guest Cast: James Michael Tyler (Gunther), Lisa Rotondi (The Stripper),
Robert Koch (The Doctor),
Helen Baxendale (Emily Waltham – credited but does not appear)

Summary: Ross asks the guys to organise a bachelor party. Joey reminds him that he needs to pick a best man first, but Ross has already picked Chandler. After Joey complains, Ross agrees to let him be the best man *and* mind the wedding ring. Joey quickly starts arranging the party, and when the girls discover they're not invited they decide to throw a baby shower for Phoebe and get her gifts that she can use after the births. Unfortunately, Phoebe is suffering from mood swings and just gets upset at the thought of not being able to use any of her presents for two months.

The bachelor party goes well, but after Joey sleeps with the stripper he discovers that the wedding ring is missing and concludes that the stripper must have stolen it. However, when they finally trace her, she claims to know nothing about it. In all of this, one suspect remains unchallenged – no matter how loudly he quacks his confession . . .

Phoebisms: Her mood swings (which she actually denies having) are hilarious. At one point, Monica and Rachel shrink away from her, suspecting that she'll actually attack them. After the disastrous baby shower, the girls cheer Phoebe up by pointing out that as she's only a surrogate mother; she's free of all the worries about saving for their education or disciplining them, while she'll always be the one they turn to for advice about sex. She'll be their 'cool Aunt Phoebe'. 'I am pretty cool,' notes Phoebs.

Slow Joey: Joey, discussing the party, tells Chandler that Ross 'didn't say anything about no strippers'. When Chandler points out that 'no strippers' was exactly what Ross *did* say, Joey says that he 'chose not to hear that'. He gets T-shirts printed that say 'Ross Geller, Bachelor Bash 1998' which have a huge picture of Joey's face on the back under the heading 'Best Man'. The morning after the party, Chandler asks Joey the most naive question ever: 'You slept with the stripper?' to which Joey replies 'Of course!' Discovering that the ring is missing, Joey phones the emergency services, only to be laughed at: 'They said they're gonna look for it right after they solved all the murders,' he explains to Ross.

Chandleresque: When the stripper tells the guys that she makes $1,600 a week, Chandler begs her to marry him.

Spoilt Rachel: Rachel tells Phoebe that she's not going to Ross's wedding, and she initially says that it's just like when she was living rough and a man offered to buy her food if she slept with him. When Rachel asks her how that's the same as her problem, Phoebe has to agree that it isn't, '. . . Because, you see *that* was an actual problem and yours is just like, y'know, a bunch of high school *crap*.'

The Chick and the Duck: They hide in Joey's room while the party is on. Joey tells the stripper that he has them totally trained, and proves it by getting Dick the Duck to stare at the wall, hardly move and 'be white'.

Gunther . . . erm: Trying to choose a best man for a wedding he's not having, Chandler picks his 'best friend', Gunther. When Gunther asks him if he knows what his second name is, Chandler replies 'Central Perk?' He later thanks Ross for not marrying Rachel.

Magna Doodle: At Ross's bachelor party, the words 'Another one bites the dust' can just be made out.

Generation X: As the guys reminisce about the duck, we hear Barry Manilow's 'Weekend in New England'. Ahhh.

The Story So Far: Chandler was also Ross's best man at his first wedding. As the guys worry about Dick's health we see clips from 'TOW A Chick. And A Duck', 'TOW The Cat' and 'TOW Joey's New Girlfriend'. The wedding ring that Ross is going to give to Emily was originally his grandmother's. Ross's previous bachelor party was held at a Pizza Hut restaurant, courtesy of his best man, Chandler.

The Last Word: A nice introduction to the madness that will become Ross's wedding, with Dick the Duck giving his best performance so far. When we wait with baited breath to see if he'll survive the ring-removal, the flashback sequence is both emotional and somewhat distressing. Also distressing is the effect pregnancy is having on Phoebe. It's comical here, but none of us would want to be in the same building as someone whose moods could switch so suddenly.

423
'The One With Ross's Wedding, Part 1'

Writers: Michael Borkow
Director: Kevin S. Bright
First US transmission: 07.05.98
First UK transmission (Sky One): 31.05.98

Guest Cast: Sarah Ferguson (The Duchess of York),
Richard Branson (Vendor)

Summary: The gang prepare for their London trip while Phoebe and Rachel stay behind. Ross tries to talk Rachel into coming with them all, but she fobs him off with an excuse about having to work. Joey is visibly excited by the prospect of going to London, but his enthusiasm is already grating on Chandler's nerves before they even leave their apartment.

Joey and Chandler explore London. Joey insists on recording everything with his new video camera, much to Chandler's annoyance, and when Joey spies a hideous Union Jack hat, Chandler has had enough, warning him that he doesn't want to be seen with Joey if he buys it. Joey petulantly tells him that if it's a choice between him or the hat, the hat wins, so the two end up spending the rest of the day apart. When Joey finally returns to the hotel room, Chandler is apologetic, saying that he'd had a terrible day. But if he expected Joey to say the same he's sorely mistaken – Joey's too excited about meeting Fergie, as his video recording of the moment shows.

Emily is distraught to discover that the church they've booked is being demolished and suggests putting the wedding off. Ross tells her that this isn't an option, which upsets her even more. It takes Monica to explain to her brother that, for women, it's essential that their wedding day is perfect, as most of them have been practising it since they were five years old. Ever-resourceful Ross finds a solution. Convincing the demolition company to put off their work till the day after, Ross arranges for fairy lights to be placed strategically around the shell of the church, a romantic gesture which convinces Emily to go ahead with the wedding.

Back in New York, Phoebe tries to help Rachel overcome her feelings of love for Ross. Rachel denies having any such feelings and when she discovers that, actually, she does, she's shocked. Rather than quell Rachel's remaining feelings, Phoebe's aversion therapy only provokes Rachel to rush to the airport intent on stopping the wedding . . .

Freaky Monica: Monica tries to get the guys to rush their packing: 'The flight leaves in four hours! It could take time to get a taxi! There could be traffic! The plane could leave early! When we get to London, there could be a line at customs!' Chandler notes that a six-hour flight is 'a lot of Monica' to put up with. When Phoebe tries to explain to Rachel how obvious her love for Ross was to everyone, Phoebs compares it to telling Monica, 'Hey, you like things clean.'

Phoebisms: Monica remarks on the way her mother always

got her to pack her bags, realising that it's quite weird. Phoebe claims that her mother used to stick her head in the oven. 'Well, actually,' she corrects herself, 'she only did it the one time. But it was pretty weird.' She gives up trying to stop Rachel spoiling the wedding and sighs: 'Like I can really chase you. I'm carrying a *litter*.'

Spoilt Rachel: Monica leaves Phoebe by telling her where she keeps the vacuum cleaner and bin-bags. When Phoebe asks why she can't just ask Rachel where they are, Monica laughs: 'Yeah, OK, give *that* a try.' Rachel tries some retail therapy to clear her head of Ross, and when Phoebe asks her if it worked, she moans that 'Manhattan does not have enough stores.'

Slow Joey: When Chandler asks Joey if he's got his passport, Joey tells him that it's in the third drawer of his dresser. Chandler glares at him and it takes him a painfully long time to realise that he should have his passport *with him* for the journey. Phoebe tells Joey that she phoned out for pizza and ordered 'The Joey Special'. 'Two pizzas?' cries Joey.

Chandleresque: Joey tries to record Chandler with his video camera and tells him to 'do something': 'I am,' says Chandler, 'I'm ignoring you.' By the time they reach Westminster Abbey, Chandler's patience is wearing thin – he tells Joey that they're thinking of renaming the Abbey. Joey falls for his bait and asks 'To what?' and Chandler roars 'To "Put the Camera *Away*"!!' As Joey contemplates the horrible hat, Chandler murmurs, 'Well, I don't have to buy that "I'm with stupid" T-shirt any more.'

Cool Britannia: When Ross gives Emily the 'time out' signal, she misunderstands and cries, 'Well, up yours too!'

The Ballad of Ross & Rachel: You'd have thought that Ross's impending marriage would have put an end to this category – but no! Phoebe's attempts to distract Rachel from her feelings for Ross are superb, trying to get her to remember what it was like running her fingers through his hair. 'Euw-oh gross, it's some kind of grease!' Phoebe spits helpfully, but Rachel defends him, claiming that Ross's hair was 'always more crunchy than it was greasy'. Phoebe notes that this will be harder than she first thought.

Generation X: Sarah Ferguson is also known in the States as a

TV presenter. Sir Richard Branson (playing the hat vendor) is the 'Virgin' tycoon. Joey watches an episode of *Cheers*, famous for being the place 'where everybody knows your name'. As the gang reach London we hear The Clash's anthem 'London Calling'.

The Story So Far: We can infer that Phoebe's mother gassed herself (this has never actually been stated before this episode).

The Last Word: Although this was shown on first broadcasts as an hour-long special, it was actually made as two separate productions, hence the separate entries here. All the signs were pointing towards a traditional 'Brits drive on the wrong side of the road'-style show, but thankfully they (largely) veered away from that. We still have to endure the obligatory tourist scenes though – Sarah Ferguson's great, playing it down naturally, but Branson's part is pretty embarrassing. Matthew Perry's Chandler is evidently not having a good time stuck with the over-enthusiastic Joey, but his declaration that he refuses to be embarrassed any more (promptly falling backwards into a flower-stall) more than makes up for his glum face in this episode. But there are too many 'best moments' to list in detail; Monica's explanation to Ross about how important the perfect wedding is to girls; and Phoebe's attempt at aversion therapy, where she holds up a picture of Ross and then smacks Rachel around the head. 'How do you feel now?' Phoebe asks optimistically. 'Well, I like *you* less!' snaps Rachel. Thankfully, the best is yet to come.

424

'The One With Ross's Wedding, Part 2'

Writers: Jill Condon & Amy Toomin (story),
Shana Goldberg-Meehan & Scott Silveri (teleplay)
Director: Kevin S. Bright
First US transmission: 07.05.98
First UK transmission (Sky One): 31.05.98

Guest Cast: Helen Baxendale (Emily Waltham), Elliott Gould (Jack Geller),
Christine Pickles (Judy Geller), Tom Conti (Steven Waltham),
Jennifer Saunders (Andrea Waltham),
June Whitfield (the Walthams' Housekeeper),

Hugh Laurie (Gentleman on the Plane), Olivia Williams (Felicity),
Jane Carr (Ticket Agent), Daniel Caltagirone (the Waiter),
Heathcote Williams (Older Guest), Peter Eyre (Registrar)

Summary: As Phoebe tries to phone London to warn them
about Rachel, Joey begins to get homesick until he meets a
'hot bridesmaid' at the pre-wedding dinner. Ross and Emily's
parents have decided to split the costs of the wedding, but
when the Gellers find charges for new carpets, lawn ornaments
and a wine cellar, Jack Geller is outraged. Ross manages to
peace-broker an agreement between the two families, though
his father is (justifiably) adamant about the wine cellar.

Rachel finally arrives, sees Ross and Emily together and can
only wish her ex-boyfriend an emotional 'congratulations'. To
everyone's relief, the wedding takes place and the happy
couple read their vows to each other. Surely nothing can go
wrong now?

Phoebisms: After trying to warn the Walthams' housekeeper
about Rachel, Phoebe is given a lesson in telephone etiquette.
Losing patience, Phoebe roars that she's going to come over
there and kick her 'snooty ass all the way to New Glocken . . .
shire.' When the housekeeper hangs up, Phoebe realises that
'She knew I could kick her ass.'

Spoilt Rachel: Having sat through Rachel's self-pitying story
during a seven-hour flight to London, the passenger next to her
(guest-star Hugh Laurie in a show-stealing performance) feels
compelled to tell her, 'You are a horrible, horrible person!'

Slow Joey: Joey takes home-sickness to extremes: 'I miss my
family,' he tells Chandler. 'I miss the coffee house. I can't
even remember what Phoebe looks like.' Chandler points out
to him that it's only been three days.

Chandleresque: His best man speech is a joy, especially as it
falls flat on the humourless crowd. Telling them he remembers
Ross's first girlfriend, he jokes that he thought things were
going to work out, 'until the day he over-inflated her.'

Parents – Who Needs 'Em?: The Gellers arrive late, with
Judy apologising. 'I insisted on riding the tube,' she explains,
only for Jack Geller to misunderstand. 'Judy, the kids!' he
warns, before she explains that she was referring to what New
Yorkers would call 'the subway'. Judy can't help but

undermine Monica's confidence at every opportunity, telling the Walthams that Ross's wedding 'may be the only wedding we get to throw'.

Cool Britannia: After becoming exasperated by the Waltham's bill for half the wedding costs, Jack Geller fortunately manages to avoid any xenophobic slurs against the British couple. *Kind of*: 'You thieving would-be-speaking-German-if-it-weren't-for-us, cheap little man!'

Just Plain Weird: Understandably, Andrea Waltham is a little confused when Phoebe tells her that she's carrying her brother's babies. 'Am I on the radio?' she asks cautiously.

Generation X: Tom Conti played Costas in the film *Shirley Valentine* (Lewis Gilbert, 1989). Jennifer Saunders is known in the States solely for playing Edina Monsoon in the comedy series *Absolutely Fabulous* alongside June Whitfield, who played her mother. Hugh Laurie, one half of the comedy partnership Fry and Laurie, appeared in the remake of *101 Dalmations* (Stephen Herek, 1996) and was also a regular member of the *Blackadder* cast. Jane Carr (the ticket agent) played Louise, the sexually obsessed organiser of the lonely hearts club in the American version of the sitcom *Dear John* and, as a teenager, she played Mary MacGregor in the film *The Prime of Miss Jean Brodie* (Ronald Neame, 1969). Monty Hall is another name for the 'Three Doors' problem, where a con man places a good prize and two bad ones behind each of three doors, and invites the punter to guess which door is hiding the good prize (we didn't get Chandler's joke either). One of the guests mistakes Chandler for Leonardo Di Caprio, congratulating him on his performance in *Titanic* (James Cameron, 1997). When Felicity asks Joey to talk in a New York accent for her, he quotes Al Pacino's 'Forget about it' line from *Donnie Brasco* (Mike Newell, 1997).

The Story So Far: Rachel bores the passengers on the plane with her story about her and Ross, referring to when she proposed to Joshua ('TOW All The Wedding Dresses'). In a scene that the studio audience obviously adored, the passenger next to Rachel tells her that in his opinion it was quite obvious that they were 'on a break' (see 'TOW Ross And Rachel Take A Break').

The Last Word: So the last episode of the season ends on another cliffhanger, and in an action-packed special episode, more than just Ross and Rachel have an emotional tangle to sort out. Most viewers we've spoken to said that they didn't know what was more shocking – Ross's faux pas at the altar or Chandler and Monica ending up in bed together.

Many people have already complained that the show is called 'Friends', not 'Lovers', and that maybe the gang shouldn't enter into relationships with each other, but we disagree. It's inevitable that a small group of people like the Central Perk gang will, at one time or another, pair off. While everyone has focussed on Ross and Rachel since day one, there has always been a possibility of Chandler and Monica getting together, notably in a scene in 'TOW The Birth' in which we see them discuss getting married when they're forty. Personally, we think they always made a much better match than Ross and Rachel. Time will tell.

Fifth Season

1999–2000

23 Episodes

501

'The One After Ross Says "Rachel"'

Writer: Seth Kurland
Director: Kevin S. Bright
First US transmission: 24.09.98
First UK transmission (Sky One): 07.01.99

Guest Cast: Elliott Gould (Jack Geller), Tom Conti (Stephen Waltham),
Jennifer Saunders (Andrea Waltham),
Helen Baxendale (Emily), Christina Pickles (Judy Geller),
Peter Eyre (Registrar)

Summary: It's seconds after Ross said 'Rachel' instead of 'Emily' during his wedding vows. The ceremony continues and Ross thinks he might have got away with his little slip – until Emily punches him in the stomach, locks herself in a bathroom and escapes. Ross searches fruitlessly for his wife and remains hopeful that she will appear and join him on their honeymoon to Greece. Rachel is also at the airport, waiting on standby for a flight home. After waiting until the last minute, Ross realises that he'll be going alone and decides to throw caution to the wind and take Rachel on holiday instead. As they are about to board the plane, Emily finally turns up, sees Ross with Rachel and makes another quick exit. Ross chases after her, leaving Rachel alone on her way to Greece.

Chandler and Monica are worried that their 'holiday romance' might ruin their friendship. That doesn't stop them trying to make the most of it before they return home, though. Unfortunately, every attempt to be alone together is thwarted. They return home frustrated and resigned to the fact that their affair must end, only to discover that some feelings can't be ignored.

Chandleresque: With typical sensitivity, Chandler sums up Ross's performance during his wedding to Emily: 'It could have been worse . . . he could have shot her.' Later, while searching for a place for him and Monica to have sex, they creep into the bedroom booked for Ross and Emily. Monica is more than a little disturbed by the idea of making love in her brother's honeymoon suite, but a desperate Chandler points out that, as it is the honeymoon suite, 'The room *expects* sex.' When Ross walks in on them they try to slip away, Chandler explaining that they have to be up early to catch the plane back to New York; apparently, he thinks his excuse that 'it's a very big plane' is a good one. Chandler's sheer exuberance over the fact that he's about to have sex with Monica is summed up in his wonderful warning to her: 'In the middle of everything, if I scream "Yippee!" just ignore me.'

Slow Joey: 'No matter what happens with Ross and Emily, we still get cake, right?' asks a worried Joey as he arrives at the reception. When Mr Geller wonders how he's meant to eat a whole steak without the aid of a knife and fork, the answer is given to him when Joey wanders up, holding a steak in one hand and chomping merrily upon it. On the plane on the way home, Joey faces a crisis of confidence after his viewing of the film *My Giant* (Michael Lehmann, 1998). He's worried that he'll never measure up as an actor against the titular giant, clearly thinking he's just *acting* tall: 'What if I die an unsuccessful, regular-sized man?' He also seems to think that the science of the future may hold the key to making people taller on demand.

Phoebisms: Although she's still sidelined in America while the rest of the gang deal with the trauma in London, Phoebe still manages to get the lion's share of the funnier lines. In an effort to extricate Ross from the nasty situation he's got himself in, she phones Mrs Waltham pretending to be Ross's psychiatrist, 'Dr Philangi'. She explains that he forgot to take his 'brain medicine' with him to England, and that without it he is liable to mix up different women's names in his head. A suspicious Mrs Waltham tells her that she's sure she's talking to Phoebe, and Phoebs comes back with an amazingly quick-witted response: 'No, not Phoebe. *Dr Philangi* . . . oh no, you have it too!' When Monica, Chandler and Joey finally get back to New York, they find Phoebe at Monica's. The minute they walk in, she gasps at Joey, 'You ate meat!' Then she turns to Monica and Chandler and cries, 'You had sex!' Chandler, pan-icked, says that he didn't, to which Phoebe replies, 'I know *you* didn't, I was talking about Monica.' When she too denies having sex, Phoebe blames her pregnancy for her failing powers.

Poor Ross: Well, where to begin? The whole of this episode is a Poor Ross extravaganza, but it's undeniable that he has brought it on himself. It's a painful delight to watch first his mania and then his depression as Emily fails to reappear after the wedding. The only words exchanged between the bride and groom this episode are shouted through a bathroom door. 'I hate you!' screams Emily, to which Ross – as if he has mis-heard – cries back, 'And I love *you*!'

Spoilt Rachel: Despite already having ruined Ross's wedding, Rachel continues to think Ross is in love with her. She con-fronts Monica with the evidence of the name-swap just as Monica is about to hunt down Chandler for some more illicit nookie. Consequently, Monica's advice to Rachel is rather blunt: 'He's married. *Married*. If you can't realise that, I can't help you.' 'You're right,' admits Rachel, 'you can't help me.' Then she walks off more determined than ever to speak to Ross.

Freaky Monica: Most of Monica's freaking comes from her trying to deal with her affair with Chandler. 'I blame London,' she explains ('*Bad* London,' agrees Chandler, smacking a roast chicken with a spoon). Monica convinces herself that their fling is merely a by-product of being in a foreign country. With Chandler in agreement, she decides that the affair should end when they return to New York . . . but we all know how well they stuck to *that* plan.

The Chick and the Duck: Returning home, Joey goes to Monica's before telling everyone he's going to his apartment to check on the chick and the duck. Delighted with this idea, Phoebe says she'll go too, until Joey points out that she must have seen them all the time, having been left with the job of caring for them while he was away. Phoebe immediately decides to go home instead, leaving us to wonder just how underfed the poor birds are by now.

Parents – Who Needs 'Em?: Mrs Geller, who is never short of a cutting comment, decides that the marriage of Ross and Emily is 'worse than when he married the lesbian'. She does, however, feel guilty. 'Is it all our fault?' she asks her husband, 'are we bad parents?' 'Yes,' snipes a drunken Stephen Waltham as he walks past. Andrea Waltham, on the other hand, seems quite pleased with the outcome. She calls Ross 'monkey' (a term of endearment, it would seem), and tells him, 'I think you're absolutely delicious.' Watching this, her husband complains, 'I'm *right here*,' before dragging her away with a casual 'Come on, bugger face.'

The Story So Far: Of course, courtesy of Ross's mother we are reminded of his first failed marriage to Susan the lesbian, and his long-term crush on Rachel. Rachel also mentions how she escaped from her wedding to Barry by crawling out of the ladies' window – just like Emily does in this episode. Monica and Chandler made love seven times before deciding that it was wrong. We're reminded of Joey's promise to Phoebe not to eat meat, and Joey points out that they've been away for four days. Oh, and Phoebe's still pregnant (although Lisa Kudrow had given birth in the gap between filming seasons four and five).

The Ballad of Ross & Rachel: Just for once, Ross actually *isn't* obsessing over Rachel, though no-one will believe him now. 'She's just a friend, that's all,' he tells Emily's father, and that is his attitude towards her for the entire episode. Rachel, meanwhile, is running round convinced that, because of Ross's slip of the tongue, she is still in with a chance. At one point she gets Phoebe on the phone and explains why she thinks Ross is still in love with her: 'Ninth grade. The obsession starts . . .'

Generation X: *My Giant* (Michael Lehmann, 1998) starred Billy Crystal as an agent trying to get a very tall Romanian into the movies (Crystal made a guest appearance in 'TOW The Ultimate Fighting Champion'). Note that the airline Ross is using just happens to be Virgin, owned by Sir Richard Branson, who appeared in the previous episode.

The Last Word: A great start to a great season, the only shadow of anything unfunny being Ross's misery – a state that increases in intensity, while decreasing in humour, over following episodes. Monica and Chandler's awkwardness – and extreme horniness – is brilliantly carried off by a sharp script and excellent acting from Cox and Perry, while Kudrow launches the first broadside in a campaign which will make her the funniest actor this year.

502

'The One With All The Kissing'

Writer: Wil Calhoun
Director: Gary Halvorson
First US transmission: 01.10.98
First UK transmission (Sky One): 14.01.99

Guest Cast: James Michael Tyler (Gunther), Zen Gesner (Dave)

Summary: Rachel returns from Greece, and tells an apologetic Ross not to worry as she had a wonderful time. But once Ross has left, she reveals to Monica that she hated her holiday and is still desperately in love with Ross. Chandler stands up to leave the apartment, giving Monica a passionate kiss before he goes, only realising as their lips disengage that neither Phoebe or Rachel know about the two of them. Thinking quickly, he wrestles the other two women into tender lip-locks and walks out as if nothing unusual has happened.

Going over the events in London and Greece, Rachel decides that she has made a terrible mess of her life and agrees to let Monica make all her decisions for her. Within hours, this plan seems to pay off as Rachel lands herself a date. But Rachel's evening out ends abruptly when she returns to her apartment to find Ross, dejected and alone. Finally, Rachel takes her decisions back into her own hands and confronts Ross with the fact that she still loves him.

Chandleresque: Joey bursts in on Chandler and Monica in the bath, to find out if his flatmate would like some takeaway chicken. Monica quickly hides by submerging herself, leaving Chandler alone in a sea of bubbles with a glass of wine in hand. 'I've had a very hard, long day,' he explains to a surprised Joey. After he has been chastised for snogging everyone, a delighted Chandler wonders what might have happened if they had been caught having sex. 'Do you know anything about women?' Monica asks him. His reply is a simple, honest 'No.'

Phoebisms: Phoebe's still put out that her friends got to go to London while she stayed, pregnant, in New York. When Rachel is railing against her disastrous love life, she blames London. Phoebe agrees, somewhat forcefully: 'London *is* stupid!' And we find out that, at some point, someone was crazy enough to let Phoebe make all their decisions for them but, as she explains, 'I'm not comfortable having that kind of power and control over someone's life.' But it seems that someone else is . . .

Freaky Monica: The split second after Phoebe has refused to handle Rachel's decisions for her, Monica, ever the control freak, chips in, 'I'll do it!' In the bath, once Joey has left them in peace, she tells Chandler that she would have liked some chicken. She submerges herself once more as Chandler calls Joey back in to place an order that includes Coke. It's at this point that Monica does *something* painful to Chandler under the water, and he corrects the order to Diet Coke. At least now he knows which she prefers. Later, the gang meet in Central Perk and Monica shows off her photos of London. As Rachel handles them carelessly, she begins to freak out quietly: 'Honey, sweeties, by the edges . . . edges . . . fingers . . . smudgy fingers!' In retaliation, a fed-up Rachel licks the photos. Things only get worse for poor Monica when Phoebe, still angry that she couldn't go to London, starts to draw herself on to all the photos. Ever the pragmatist, though, when she hears about Emily returning Ross's roses, she suggests making potpourri out of the remains.

Poor Ross: As Ross is explaining why getting back in touch with Emily is so important to him, he says, 'She's my wife. Rachel is my wife, you know . . . Emily! *Emily* is my wife!

Man, what *is* that?' His very romantic gesture – sending 72 long-stemmed red roses to Emily – eventually results in him receiving a box of 72 red roses cut up into mulch. While we obviously sympathise with Ross, we also begin to see his scary side as he rounds on Chandler for mentioning that Emily outran him at the airport: 'Hey, she's FAST, OK?!'

Slow Joey: Having witnessed Chandler's embraces with the girls, Joey thinks his luck could be just as easily in. When Monica is banging on the locked door of her apartment, desperate to stop Rachel telling Ross she still loves him, Joey appears in the corridor and says, 'I'll kick that door in, if you give me a little sugar.'

Gunther is . . .: Monica, vetting potential new love interests for Rachel, first turns to Gunther. 'I mean,' she says, 'he's nice, he's cute.' Rachel momentarily looks at him in a new light and begins, 'Yeah, I guess Gunther is . . .' She doesn't finish, though, as Monica spots a much more buff specimen at a different table. Once Rachel has spoken to this new guy and arranged a date, Gunther calmly goes over, holding up a sign reading 'We reserve the right to refuse service to anyone' and tells him to get out.

Cool Britannia: The gang are still high on their visit to London; remembering a cabbie called Angus; a pub called The Wheatsheaf and the refreshing qualities of Boddingtons bitter. Quoth Joey: 'I'd *walk* back to London for another frosty one of those bad boys.'

Dinosaurs ROCK!: Rachel's trying to talk to Ross, explaining that some people have told her it may be stupid to say what she is about to say. Ross knows just what she means: 'Once at work, I thought carbon dating was –' 'Ross,' Rachel interrupts, 'I'm *really* trying to tell you something here.'

The Ballad of Ross & Rachel: Rachel is still cut up about Ross and Emily and just can't get over her love for him. When she finally tells him that she's still in love with him, Ross is bowled over. Although it's momentarily icky, they both see the funny side of the whole situation – the marriage to Emily included ('Hey, Ross,' he mock-asks himself, 'where's the missus? I dunno!') – and agree to leave it at that. This is a nice watershed for their relationship, which leads to a string of

episodes relatively free of the bitching that occasionally
marred the last two seasons.

The Story So Far: This episode is set two weeks after 'TO
After Ross Says "Rachel"'. In total, Ross has known Emily for
72 days. Ross does 'the manoeuvre' that he introduced in
'TOW Joey's New Girlfriend'.

The Last Word: A lovely episode, where the soap-opera angst
of Rachel's agony is nicely balanced against Chandler's
new-found passion. Phoebe has some great moments, especially leading up to the cliffhanger where her waters break. If
Joey is sidelined, it's hard to notice among the sharp lines and
crackling performances.

503

'The One Hundredth'
(a.k.a. 'The One With The Triplets')

Writers: Marta Kauffman & David Crane
Director: Kevin S. Bright
First US transmission: 08.10.98
First UK transmission (Sky One): 21.01.99

Guest Cast: Giovanni Ribisi (Frank Jr),
Sam Anderson (Dr Harad), Debra Jo Rupp (Alice),
Patrick Fabian (Dan), Iqbal Theba (Joey's Doctor),
T. J. Thyne (Dr Oberman), Brenda Isaacs-Booth (Nurse),
Heidi Beck (Delivery Room Nurse)

Summary: The gang rush Phoebe to hospital, as the surrogate
mother prepares to give birth to her brother and sister-in-law's
three children. Considering the many pitfalls of giving birth,
the actual event goes off without a hitch, except that her doctor
has had an accident and is forced to send a wacky replacement.
As Phoebe's contractions begin, Joey appears to be suffering
too. Phoebe assumes they are sympathy pains, but Joey soon
discovers that he actually has kidney stones and he must
undergo a particularly painful 'birth' himself.

While all this is going on, Rachel – her priorities sorted as
ever – has arranged dates for her and Monica with two nurses.
When Chandler hears about this, he feigns a lack of concern to

Monica. But, as time goes on, the two of them begin to realise how deeply they feel for each other.

Having carried the triplets inside her for nine months, Phoebe is reluctant to part with them and wonders if Frank Jr will let her keep one of them.

Chandleresque: Chandler's obvious jealousy at Monica's date with Dan, the nurse, is one of the highlights of this episode. When he finally meets his rival, he challenges him: 'So, Dan. Nurse, not a doctor, huh? Kind of girlie, isn't it?' Dan then explains he's only nursing to pay his way through medical school, and that 'it didn't feel girlie during the Gulf War'. Chandler is suitably cowed by this, and gets his come-uppance later. While Phoebe's ultrasound scan had shown that little Chandler was a boy, the truth is revealed when the baby is born and he is actually a *she*. Frank Jr rushes out to the waiting friends and screams, 'Chandler's a girl!' 'Oh, God,' moans Chandler, 'kindergarten flashback.' Later still, he checks with Phoebe that they are going to keep the name Chandler for the youngest girl. 'It's kind of a masculine name, don't you think?' he argues. Phoebe just replies, 'It works on you.'

Spoilt Rachel: Rachel wants to know all about giving birth, and asks Phoebe, 'So does it really hurt as bad as they say?' Phoebe, wise to Rachel's delicate-flower constitution, replies, 'Yeah. You won't be able to take it.'

Slow Joey: Joey's brought along a camcorder to video the birth for the children to watch later in life. At one point, he jams it up Phoebe's skirt and when she asks what he's doing, Joey claims, 'I've got to get the "before" shot.' Later, he points the camcorder at the day's newspaper, then asks the girl baby to turn away. He reveals a copy of *Playboy* hidden inside the pages of the newspaper and says to the boys: 'This is how naked women looked the month you were born.' When Rachel announces to Monica that she's got them dates with two cute nurses, Joey smiles and sighs, 'Oh, my . . .' They point out to him that they are *male* nurses but he answers, 'Not in *my* head.' Rachel says that she has arranged to go down to the canteen with them to get some jello and Joey growls in a filthy voice, 'There's always room for jello . . .' He then claims he can make anything innocent sound rude by using the same

voice, proving it with 'Grandma's chicken salad'. When he has
been diagnosed with kidney stones, his doctor explains the
methods they could use to remove them, getting as far as
saying they could go 'up the urethra' before Joey interrupts.
'Nothing is going up. Up is not an option. What's a urethra?'
When Monica whispers the answer to his question, he just
stares at the doctor and screams, 'Are you crazy?'

Phoebisms: Phoebe is plainly terrified by the idea of a painful
childbirth. When Joey asks her for a pre-birth camcorder
message to the babies, she looks into the lens and says, 'Hi,
kids . . . can't wait to see you. Please don't hurt me.' As her
agitation increases, she lashes out at Ross who assures her that
the fact that her doctor is Fonz mad is not a problem: 'That's
easy for you to say,' she snaps, 'I don't see three kids coming
out of *your* vagina.' 'Can I tell you a little secret?' Phoebe asks
Rachel when they are alone. 'I want to keep one.' 'Oh,' Rachel
moans, hand to her head, 'I'm going to be on the news.'
Phoebe goes on to explain that she would, 'hate to miss an
opportunity just because I didn't ask.' Kudrow does a fine job
here of balancing Phoebe's desperation to keep her children
with a sure knowledge that the answer is going to be no.

Just Plain Weird: Phoebe's doctor, Dr Harad, is deeply
obsessed with the Fonz, otherwise known as Arthur Fonzarelli,
lead character in the 70s US sitcom *Happy Days*. Phoebe is
very unhappy with the idea of this madman being in charge of
her birth: 'I don't want someone down there telling me I'm
dilated-a-mundo!' He seems very pleased to announce to a
worried Phoebe that the kids are being born on the Fonz's
'half-birthday', before switching the television on to a re-run
of an old *Happy Days* episode. When Rachel innocently comments that she always liked Mork, an icy silence descends and
the doctor states, 'Fonzie met Mork. Mork froze Fonzie.' It's
only through some quick thinking and fast talking that Rachel
manages to undo this grave insult.

Generation X: Somehow, Frank Jr gets the word 'Lamaze',
the birthing method, muddled with 'Mazda', the car. Phoebe
calls the just-graduated replacement Dr Oberman 'Dougie', in
reference to the 80s show *Doogie Howser, MD*, in which a
whizzkid teenager becomes a doctor. Sam Anderson (Dr Harad)

plays Dr Jack Kayson and Iqbal Theba plays Dr Zagerby in *ER* (see also 'TOW Two Parts', Part 1). Patrick Fabian (Dan, the nurse), played Spencer in the soap *Time of Your Life*, and Jerry in *Providence*, two series yet to make it over to the UK. See also **Just Plain Weird**, above.

The Story So Far: We're reminded why Phoebe's pregnant in the first place throughout this episode. Phoebe corrects the nurse who asks which of her friends is the father of her babies by pointing out that the father is her brother (and Rachel tells her that she's going to miss seeing people freaked out by that revelation, which suggests she's done it on numerous occasions before). Frank Jr, keen that Alice is present for the birth, asks Phoebs if she can do him a favour and 'hold them in'. Phoebe snaps back: 'Sorry, Frank. I'm kind of in the middle of the last favour you asked me to do.' As agreed in 'TOW Rachel's New Dress', Frank and Alice call their children (in order of birth) Frank Jr Jr, Leslie and Chandler, despite the surprise development that baby Chandler's actually a girl. And Phoebe reminds the babies of the little chat they had when they were just eggs in a Petri dish ('TOW The Embryos'). We see Chandler almost do his celebration dance again, but Monica stops him before it's even begun (and see the next episode for the ultimate Chandler victory dance).

The Last Word: Since 'TOW the Birth' has already been used, we're left with the clever-clever title of this episode, the 100th in the series' run. It gets about as schmaltzy as you would expect, as Phoebe gives birth to – then gives up – her brother's triplets. The cuteness of these events is offset by some great physical comedy with Ross being forced to sit with Joey while his kidney stones pass, and by Chandler and Monica facing up to their level of commitment to each other. The episode ends with Phoebe's saccharine-sweet, yet very sad, speech to her nieces and nephew; making them promise that they will always consider her their favourite aunt, Phoebe reminds them, 'I know Alice's sister has a pool, but you lived *in* me.'

504

'The One Where Phoebe Hates PBS'

Writer: Michael Curtis
Director: Shelley Jensen
First US transmission: 15.10.98
First UK transmission (Sky One): 28.01.99

Guest Cast: Helen Baxendale (Emily), Gary Collins (Himself),
Sandra Thigpen (The Stage Manager),
John R. McLaughlin (the PBS Volunteer)

Summary: Rachel catches Monica – who is waiting for Chandler – lying naked and alluring on her bed; Monica claims that she was waiting for a man from work that she has started dating. Monica lets Rachel know that he is the best sex she has ever had, and it isn't long before Chandler discovers this and makes a meal out of basking in the glory. Monica, however, is not too pleased at his indulgent revelling.

Joey's agent has landed him a job, telling him he's going to co-host a Public Broadcast Television telethon. When he gets there, however, he discovers that he's actually just an operator, taking viewers' pledges. Hearing about Joey's new gig, Phoebe reveals that she can't stand PBS (the Public Broadcasting Service) and she and Joey soon end up arguing about the value of good deeds. Joey is adamant that there is no such thing as a selfless good deed, so Phoebe sets out to prove him wrong. In among all this, Emily finally phones Ross and the newlyweds begin to talk about patching their relationship up. Initially, Emily is unwilling to move back to the States, but relents when Ross points out that he can't move to England without his son, Ben. Emily is prepared to come to live in New York to work on the relationship, on one condition – that Ross agrees never to see Rachel again.

Slow Joey: His argument with Phoebe over the altruism of good deeds reaches new heights of surrealism: 'All people are selfish,' he tells Phoebe. 'Are you calling me selfish?' she asks. 'Are you calling you people?' he retorts (Chandler's face during this exchange is superb). Phoebe describes why she is unwilling to lose the argument with Joey: 'I just gave birth to three children and I will not let them be raised in a world where Joey is right!'

Phoebisms: During the first argument with Joey, he asks her, 'You know the deal on Santa Claus, right?' to which she just answers 'yeah'. Later, she checks with him what he meant. 'That he doesn't exist,' Joey confirms. 'Right,' she says; and then, as Joey walks off, a look of absolute terrified desolation crosses her face. In the search for a selfless good deed, Phoebe lets a bee sting her so that the bee can 'look tough in front of his bee friends'. When Joey tells her that the bee probably died afterwards, Phoebe is foiled again. When Ross is looking for answers to the Emily/Rachel dilemma, he turns to a Magic 8-Ball, which Monica dismisses as a toy. 'Oh, it's not a toy,' gasps Phoebe, showing deep respect for its powers of prediction. In a last-ditch attempt to prove Joey wrong, she gives $200 to the hated PBS pledge drive. She explains that she was using the money to save for a hamster. Joey says, 'Those things cost, like, ten bucks.' 'Not the one I had my eye on,' Phoebe answers.

Chandleresque: Matthew Perry wheels out Chandler's weird victory dance once more, as he discovers that Monica thinks he is 'the best sex she's ever had'. Monica is quite right to not want to have sex with him after he's performed those revolting hip movements! When he finally tries to patch it up with Monica, his attempts at reconciliation cast more light on his hitherto unsuccessful sex life: 'I was nothing before you, call the other girls and ask. Which wouldn't take long.'

Scary Ross: Ross and Joey are thrown out of the cinema because Ross was talking loudly on his mobile phone. 'I had to *talk* loud because the *movie* was *loud*,' he shrieks, failing to realise that using a phone in a cinema for whatever reason should be an executable offence.

Freaky Monica: When Joey arrives at Monica's dressed in his tuxedo, Chandler leaps up, points at him, and screams, 'Vomit tux! No, no, vomit tux!' Monica is about to ask how the suit got its name, but then realises she just can't bear to find out. When Chandler tells her that they've used her pan as a receptacle for the duck's vomit, she knows exactly in which catalogue (and on what page!) a replacement can be found.

Joey's an Actor: Indignant, he explains to the woman who is showing him to his phone at the PBS telethon, 'I was Dr Drake Ramorey!' 'There's your phone, doctor,' she deadpans back.

The Chick and the Duck: Chandler returns to his apartment and flies into a panic when he sees the birds watching a recipe for duck on the Cooking Channel. Later, Monica comes to Chandler's looking for a broiling pan he had borrowed from her. 'We used it when the duck was throwing up caterpillars,' he apologises.

Cool Britannia: Ross, on the phone to one of Emily's relatives in England says, 'I don't care if I said some other girl's name, you prissy old twit!' – thereby summing up a great deal of the attitude of the series towards the Brits.

Magna-Doodle: 'EVIL JOE' is scrawled on the Magna-Doodle, surrounded by flames of damnation, presumably courtesy of Phoebe.

The Ballad of Ross & Rachel: Poor Rach. Before Ross has had a chance to explain to her what Emily wants done if Ross is to get her back, she is telling him to 'just fix whatever it is she wants fixing'. Emily then calls while Rachel is still in Ross's apartment and, without letting Rachel realise, he tells Emily that he's willing not to see Rachel ever again. Pleased that her friend is going to get his wife back, Rachel gives Ross a big hug. But just see the look on Ross's face.

Generation X: PBS is a non-commercial television service that aims to 'enrich the lives of all Americans through quality programs and education services that inform, inspire and delight'. It's funded purely by pledge drives, such as the one in this episode. It's famous for broadcasting the best of British television in its *Masterpiece Theatre* slot, and for being the home of *Sesame Street* since it began thirty years ago.

Rachel describes a waiter from Monica's restaurant as 'an unthreatening Ray Liotta' in reference to the star of *Field of Dreams* (Phil Alden Robinson, 1989), *Goodfellas* (Martin Scorsese, 1990) and *Unlawful Entry* (Jonathan Kaplan, 1992). Gary Collins is a familiar face on American TV having been the host of *Hour Magazine* from 1980–1988.

The Magic 8-Ball is, like Monica's dice in 'TO In Vegas', a way of foretelling the future by blind chance. Inspired by the luck one needs to clear a pool table with an 8-ball in the way of a clear shot, the Magic 8-Ball has a clear window on one side in which phrases appear that can answer life's mysteries with a frightening accuracy. Apparently. Ross had arranged to go to the cinema with Rachel to see *How Stella Got Her Groove Back* (Kevin Rodney Sullivan, 1998), which stars Angela Bassett, and was based on the popular novel by Terry McMillan.

The Story So Far: Shortly after her mother committed suicide, Phoebe wrote to *Sesame Street* for consolation. All she got back was a keyring, which, as she explains, was no use at all: 'By that time, I was living in a box. I didn't have keys!' We've already seen the effect *Sesame Street* has on Phoebe in 'TOW Old Yeller Dies'. There's a lot of catching up to do for this episode. Not only are we reminded of recent events (the name mix up at the wedding and the disappearance of Emily), but there are also apposite mentions of Ross's son Ben, Ross's ex-wife Carol and her wife Susan.

The Last Word: Some great performances from Lisa Kudrow and Matthew Perry (doing *that* dance) provide the laughs, while the final scene between Ross and Rachel brings on the sadness. Rachel's ignorance of her own self-sacrifice is heavy with bitter irony, and Ross's supposedly final hug is heartbreaking. Joey's telethon antics aren't the best thing about this episode, but they do at least make a great springboard for Phoebe's hunt for the selfless good deed.

505

'The One With The Kips'

Writer: Scott Silveri
Director: Dana deVally
First US transmission: 29.10.98
First UK transmission (Sky One): 04.02.99

Guest Cast: Christopher Liam Moore (Hotel Clerk)

Summary: Tired of sneaking around all the time to be together, Monica and Chandler decide to take a romantic weekend away in a hotel. They hit a snag, though, when room after room is not up to Monica's high standards and the two end up having a row. For a couple of days afterwards, the two of them bicker, finally making up just minutes before Joey uncovers their secret.

Ross finally tells Rachel that he has agreed to Emily's demand that he doesn't see his ex-girlfriend any more. Rachel thinks that maybe her time in the group has come, and so plots with Phoebe to run away and create a new group of friends.

Chandleresque: Monica and Chandler's bad weekend starts when Chandler finds an exciting live car chase on television just as Monica finds a dirty glass in the bathroom. Their trek for a perfect room goes on and on, with Chandler trying to catch another bit of the chase on each room's TV set. Eventually, when they are each blaming each other for their bad time, Monica decides to lay the blame at the feet of someone else entirely: 'How about the idiot who thought he could drive from Albany to Canada on half a tank of gas?' Chandler, offended to the core, warns her, 'Do not speak ill of the dead.' He then puts his foot in it when he tells her to 'Relax, Mom!' 'What did you say?' she demands angrily. 'I said, "Jeez, relax, Mo*nnn*",' he replies, realising his terrible mistake. After their return to New York, Joey tells Chandler that the hotel had phoned saying that they'd found an eyelash curler in his room. 'Yes,' he whimpers, confused and scared of discovery, 'that was mine.' 'I figured you'd hooked up with some girl and *she* left it there,' Joey says. 'That would have made more sense,' Chandler agrees, prompting Joey to ask in all seriousness: 'Were you, or were you not on a gay cruise?' When Chandler says to Monica that he thought their fighting meant their relationship was over, she's surprised at his fatalistic attitude. She explains to him: 'If you give up every time you have a fight with someone, you'd never be with anyone longer than – *oh* . . .!' and suddenly understands why Chandler has spent so much time single.

Freaky Monica: When she finds a glass in the bathroom with lipstick marks on it, she justifies moving to another room by noting, 'Who knows what else they didn't change.' They move to over ten rooms before they finally find one she is happy with. Later, as the gang play Mad Libs (see **Generation X**), Monica explains a personal philosophy: 'If we follow the rules, it's still fun *and* it means something . . . Rules are good. Rules help *control* the fun!'

Poor Ross: It seems that events concerning Emily and Rachel have finally driven him to drink. Or at least, the popular antacid remedy Peptobismol.

Slow Joey: Another example of fine Italian–American logic, as Joey reveals the contents of his survival kit hidden in Monica's room. 'Condoms?' asks Chandler. 'You don't know how long we're going to be in here,' Joey explains, 'we might have to re-populate the Earth.' When Monica praises the seeming perfection of her hotel, she points out the little chocolates on the pillows. 'You should live with Joey,' Chandler tells her. 'Rolos *everywhere*.' As if to prove the point, Chandler later sits on a Rolo in his apartment. When, to cover up the reason for their row, Monica lies to Joey about Chandler stealing money from her purse, Joey makes the startling realisation that while he constantly finds himself without twenty dollar bills, Chandler always has lots (which would have nothing to do with Chandler earning more than Joey, of course).

Spoilt Rachel: Rachel receives a letter telling her that her little dog Lapou has died. When she starts crying, Phoebe rushes up to her to see what's wrong. 'It's Lapou,' Rachel tells her. 'I know it's la poo right now,' Phoebe says in comfort, 'but it'll get better.' When Ross tells her that he plans to cut her out of his life on Emily's wishes, Rachel grabs her coat and walks to the door. 'What are you doing?' Ross asks her. 'Storming out,' she says. 'Rachel, this is your apartment,' he points out. 'Yeah,' she spits, 'well, *that*'s how mad I am!'

Phoebisms: As a ploy to remove themselves from the storm about to hit between Rachel and Ross, the gang pretend that they're going into Monica's room to flip her mattress. 'So I'm thinking, basically we pick it up and *then* we flip it,' Joey bluffs. 'That's better than *my* way,' says Phoebe. She spoils the game of Mad Libs for Monica by inserting her own name in every one of the blank spaces (see **Generation X** below). As she leaves to prepare for her and Rachel to leave the group, she says goodbye to Ross, then out of earshot whispers 'For *ever*.' She's never really liked him, has she?

The Story So Far: Chandler once told Rachel about Kip, his old roommate (first mentioned in 'TOW The Dozen Lasagnes'), who it's revealed Monica dated for a while. When they broke up, the others promised that they would all remain friends with him, but eventually he was left out of the group (and, as we already know, he eventually married someone else and left). This is the fate Rachel fears will befall her. Joey refers back to Ross and Rachel's big fight in 'TO The Morning After', where the rest of the gang were trapped in Monica's room for the night. Rachel tells Ross that she suffered a nosebleed when her grandfather died, and of course this is the first (and presumably last) time we hear of Rachel's family dog Lapou.

The Ballad of Ross & Rachel: This episode, Ross has to tell Rachel that he cannot see her any more if his marriage is to survive. But, he says, it's a little while until Emily arrives, and so they can see each other until then. Rachel, deeply pissed off, replies, 'Oh, that *is* good news, I think that's the best news I've heard since Lapou died!' 'What would *you* do?' Ross asks her. 'Well,' she replies, 'for starters, I would have said the right name at my wedding.'

Generation X: Both Chandler and Monica claim to have seen Donald Trump, the famous millionaire and Manhattan property developer. Mad Libs is a crazy game where you substitute words in a passage of text to create a wacky new meaning. We guess you have to be there.

The Last Word: The best moment in this episode comes at the very end, when – putting together a couple of pretty incriminating clues (Donald Trump waiting for an elevator at *both* Chandler's conference and Monica's catering fair, and Monica bemoaning the loss of her eyelash curler after Chandler's hotel had phoned to say one had been found in his room) – Joey uncovers Monica and Chandler's affair. The mad panic shared by the three involved is as nothing, however, to what chaos will come in 'TOW Everyone Finds Out', but it is a hilarious prelude nonetheless. Rachel and Phoebe's plotting to create a splinter group of friends, despite making up only a couple of lines, is one of the funniest things here also. And, while Monica and Chandler deal with their first argument, Ross and Rachel face up to a life without each other, adding a bit of gravitas to create a strong, rounded episode.

506
'The One With The Yeti'

Writer: Alexa Junge
Director: Gary Halvorson
First US transmission: 05.11.98
First UK transmission (Sky One): 11.02.99

Guest Cast: Helen Baxendale (Emily), James Michael Tyler (Gunther)
and introducing: George Newbern (Danny)

Summary: Rachel and Monica, on a hunt for the 'little round waffle maker', head down to the basement of their apartment block, where all their useless old bric-a-brac is stored. While down there, the lights cut out and the girls are seemingly ambushed by a giant of a man with straggly hair, a bushy beard and a pickaxe in hand. Rachel attacks him with a canister of insecticide and they make their escape.

Phoebe meets the gang in the coffee shop, excited that her mother has handed her an heirloom that used to belong to her grandmother. When she opens the box, she is horrified to find that she's been given a mink coat. For days, she wrestles with her conscience, unsure of what to do to dispose of the reprehensible item of clothing. She rants and raves against the injustice of little fluffy animals being used to clothe humans, until she finally puts on the coat and realises just how good she looks in it.

Ross and Emily's reconciliation continues. Ross gets rid of all his old furniture, saying that Emily would rather have new things for their new life together – but Monica points out that she's getting rid of anything Rachel has touched. Emily then persuades Ross to sell his old apartment so they can buy somewhere new, miles away from the village. Happily, Ross does all this, until he realises just what a wedge she is driving between him and his friends, particularly Rachel. Finally, during a fraught phone conversation, he breaks it off with Emily.

Rachel discovers that the yeti she 'fogged' is in fact her new neighbour Danny. After she has apologised to him – in all his hairy glory – she later bumps into him with short hair and no beard. She doesn't recognise him at first, and Danny dismisses her as someone who judges people simply on appearances. Outraged, she attacks him for sticking to his initial judgement of her as a shallow person, arguing that she at least changed her opinion of him when he saw that he wasn't, in fact, a yeti. Seemingly impressed with her verve, Danny abruptly invites her on a date.

Phoebisms: She keeps a knife hidden in her boot – obviously not a lady to tussle with late at night. She tries to comfort Ross about the disastrous wedding: 'When my friend Sylvie's husband said someone else's name in bed, she cursed him and turned his thingie green.' Though Phoebs is initially horrified by the gift of a fur coat, once she's actually put it on, she falls instantly in love with it. 'It's the best thing I've ever had wrapped around me,' she says, 'including Phil Huntley.' When Ross asks her why she's wearing fur, she blurts, 'Let's get some perspective, people. It's not like I'm wearing a seeing-eye dog coat!' (Or, as we Brits call them, 'guide dogs'.) She also prepares an 'I'm So Sorry' song for Ross after they've all told him that they're worried he's doing the wrong thing by changing his life for Emily. We never get to hear it, although Phoebe accuses Monica of stealing its lines when she tells Ross they will support him, 'Whatever you decide, whatever you do.'

Spoilt Rachel: It's love at first sight for Rachel – not with Danny, but with Phoebe's new coat. When Phoebe tells her that she's planning to have the coat cremated by her friend Chris, Rachel complains, 'If you destroy a coat like this, that is like a crime against nature . . . Pfft. Not nature – *fashion*!' When the newly shorn Danny makes his snap judgement of Rachel, deciding she is shallow and bases her opinions on appearances, he is basing his own on the fact that she is carrying a bundle of department store carrier bags. She complains that she might have gifts for underprivileged children in the bags but when he asks if she does, all she can say is, 'If kids like to play with pretty pants . . .'

Slow Joey: As the gang help pack Ross's things, the clumsy Joey begins to reminisce about the happy times they've had in his apartment. He points to a shutter saying, 'Remember when I ran into this thing and it kind of knocked me out a little?'

Freaky Monica: 'If you want the little round waffles,' she tells Rachel as they pick through the detritus in the store room, 'you've got to wait till I find the little round waffle iron.' Evidently, nothing else will do.

Chandleresque: He manages to completely freak out Phoebe when he suggests that most clothes are made by poorly paid, badly treated Filipino kids. When he realises that this might drive Phoebe towards a life of nudism, he hastily says, 'That didn't happen. I made that up!' Emily tells Ross that they're moving uptown, far away from his friends and a good trek from the museum. Ross tries to convince himself it's a great idea, saying that, as he now has a long train journey to and from work, he's 'been given the gift of time'. 'Last Christmas, I got the gift of space,' says Chandler. 'We should get them together and make a continuum.'

Joey's an Actor: Joey interrupts Monica and Chandler's canoodling and they ask why he's not at his audition. 'I'm sorry if I'm not a middle-aged black woman,' he replies, 'and I'm sorry if *sometimes* I go to the wrong audition.'

Gunther Stalks: Ross tries to put up flyers advertising the sale of his furniture in Central Perk, but Gunther stops him. When Ross says that other people do it, Gunther simply states, '*You* can't.' Gunther then finds out that he is selling the furniture on Emily's instructions, as Ross is getting rid of basically all the things Rachel has been near. Immediately, Gunther snaps up this unrepeatable offer.

Magna-Doodle: There's just a big, black 'WHY?' scrawled on it, which is possibly Joey's reaction to Monica and Chandler's little secret.

Ugly Naked Guy: He makes a return appearance, and Phoebe confesses: 'I really missed that fat bastard.'

Generation X: When Joey tries on Phoebe's coat, Chandler bitingly chimes, 'You're on in five, Miss Minnelli' – a reference to the actress and singer, and her penchant for big fur coats. The way Phoebe keeps her knife in her boot is possibly a nod to fellow cab driver, Travis Bickle from *Taxi Driver* (Martin Scorsese, 1976). George Newbern (Danny) played the boyfriend/husband in the remake of *Father of the Bride* (Charles Shyer, 1991) and was a regular in the medical drama series *Chicago Hope*.

The Story So Far: Danny lives at No. 15 in the same block as Monica and Rachel. Joey's already met him, but their first meeting with him is in the basement. When Rachel picks up her mail, there's a sign that says the manager of their block can be found at No. 16 (Mr Treager's apartment?). Phoebe once dated a guy called Phil Huntley who was 'fine', and has a friend called 'Crematorium Chris' . . . who works at a crematorium. Not surprisingly, Ugly Naked Guy hasn't been seen since the gang tried to wake him with the Giant Poking Device.

The Last Word: Phoebe is great as she emotionally wrestles with the joys of fur and Rachel finally meets her match in Danny, the first man she's ever met who's totally dismissive of her. Ross finally gets to the heart of Emily's problem – that she can no longer trust him, which sets up the problems that are to intensify for Ross over the following episodes. This is one of the last times we actually feel sorry for Ross, before he becomes a complete pain in the ass.

507

'The One Where Ross Moves In'

Writers: Perry Rein & Gigi McCreery
Director: Gary Halvorson
First US transmission: 21.11.98
First UK transmission (Sky One): 18.02.99

Guest Cast: Gregory Sporleder (Larry), James Michael Tyler (Gunther), George Newbern (Danny), Doug Benson (Tom)

Summary: Ross's marriage is officially over, his old apartment's sold on and Emily's cousin has kicked him out of the apartment he was subletting to Ross. Joey and Chandler suggest that he can stay with them until he finds somewhere new, but don't reckon on just how annoying it might be to live with someone like Ross. As his habits begin to get on their nerves, they try to push him into taking the first apartment going.

Monica's restaurant is checked out by Larry the health inspector, who Phoebe instantly falls for. They begin to date, and Phoebe initially gets off on the power Larry has as she watches him close down restaurant after restaurant. But when

Central Perk comes under Larry's scrutiny, Phoebe finally realises that he's threatening to close all the places she loves and so reluctantly lets him go. Rachel, meanwhile, gets to know Danny a little better. While he is innocently treating her like any other neighbour, she reckons that he is attracted to her and his seeming indifference is merely a ploy in a relationship power game. Helpless, Monica looks on as Rachel's plot to gain the upper hand in this non-existent relationship just embarrasses her more and more.

Spoilt Rachel: Unaccustomed to not getting exactly what she wants, Rachel manages to convince herself that Danny is just playing hard to get to make her interested in him. It's truly cringe-worthy to watch her decide that he's not inviting her to his house-warming party because he actually *wants* to invite her, and then to see Rachel turn down the invitation by pretending that she's going to a 'regatta gala'. Her self-possession reaches its height when she is inadvertently cruel to Danny's friend Tom. She thinks Tom has been sent as Danny's 'wingman', when in fact he is genuinely interested in meeting her. Painful or not, this story gives us possibly Rachel's funniest line in the show – 'Balls flying all over the place' – when Monica is trying to work out whose court the ball is in.

Slow Joey: Chandler watches as Joey sniggers at something in the pages of *National Geographic*. 'Are you looking at naked tribeswomen?' he asks, not unreasonably. Joey says that he's actually looking at a picture of a pig: 'Look at the knobs on it!' When Ross complains that his lack of apartment is beginning to make him feel like a nomad, Joey sniggers to himself again. Chandler explains to Ross, 'He thought you said "gonad".' When Joey and Chandler are trying to get Ross to look at the 'apartments to rent' section of the newspaper, Joey snatches away the 'international' section, which Ross wants to read. 'I'm Italian,' he shrugs at Ross's scepticism. It's not like it's not a pleasure Ross and Chandler both indulge in later, but when Chandler first sees what Joey has done with Ross's boxes, he is a little disapproving: Joey has made a little fortress out of them. The child inside Joey comes out later when he plays with a clockwork crocodile – much to the annoyance of Ross, who is trying to work.

Phoebisms: As she tells Monica when she first meets Larry at the restaurant, 'I'd let him check out *my* kitchen floor!' Impressed by the deductive abilities he uses in the course of his inspection, Phoebe suggests that Larry should have his own detective show: 'Then I could be your sidekick, Voonda.' Superstitious as ever, at the dinner table later she takes a pinch of salt and throws it over her left shoulder.

Chandleresque: Both he and Joey realise that maybe letting Ross move in wasn't such a good idea when they hear the new answering-machine message: 'You're fake-laughin' too, right?' asks Joey. 'Oh, the tears are real,' Chandler says with a fixed grin. When he and Joey try to persuade Ross to move into a completely unsuitable, tiny apartment, Chandler is gripped by a terrible guilt. When Ross asks him if he really thinks it's the perfect apartment, Chandler can only whimper, 'Kitchen-slash-bathroom . . .' Chandler arrives home at the end of the episode to find Joey (with cowboy headgear) and Ross (Red Indian) playing in the box fort. Joining in, they give Chandler a frilly bonnet. 'Isn't this a woman's hat?' he asks. 'Dude, stop talking crazy,' says Joey, 'and make us some tea!' – a task which Chandler excitedly embarks upon.

Freaky Monica: When Larry tells her that her restaurant isn't 100% perfect due to a Section Five violation (whatever that is!), she tells him, 'I wrote the book on Section Five.' Wryly, Phoebe suggests, 'You should really read that book you wrote.'

Poor Ross: Being the good friends that they are, Chandler and Joey ask Ross to let them know when he's feeling better so they can make fun of his outrageously windswept hair. But really, this is not so much 'Poor Ross' as 'Poor Joey and Chandler', when their living space is invaded by Ross, his boxes and his irritating habits, including the pincer-like movement, which means 'quieten it down'. Grrrr. At one point, with glee, Ross plays the new answering-machine message to his mortified roommates; to the tune of 'We Will Rock You', Ross sings, 'We will, we will . . . *callyouback*!'

Gunther takes the bins out: . . . and runs straight into Larry, who tells him that rubbish should only be carried through the back of the shop. Phoebe narrowly manages to persuade Larry not to cause any more trouble, urging Gunther to 'Go, go, go!'

Magna-Doodle: Now that it's an all-boys hangout, someone – presumably Ross – has amended the Magna-Doodle to read: 'NO GIRLS ALLOWED'. Later, there's just a big smiley face.

Boys Will Be Boys: Joey is annoyed that Ross taped over his *Baywatch* tape with a documentary on bugs. 'What if it had been porn?' he asks Chandler, visibly distressed by the possibility.

Generation X: Ross hideously abuses Queen's anthem 'We Will Rock You'.

The Story So Far: We are reminded that Chandler and Ross shared a room at college when Chandler comes across Ross's air purifier in their lounge. 'All I heard for four years through college was "*mmm* . . .",' he moans.

The Last Word: A lovely, sparkly script, which barely lasts two seconds without another joke, and the cast rises to it perfectly. Ross is on the cusp of becoming an annoying freak, but at least his descent into madness is used here to great comic effect. Phoebe's infatuation with Larry is priceless, and Rachel gets a brilliant line that completely sums up what it's sometimes like to come on to someone new: 'I see him in the hallway, we flirt, I'm all "hahahahahaha!". Nothing.' And we've all been there . . .

508
'The One With The Thanksgiving Flashbacks'

Writer: Greg Malins
Director: Kevin S. Bright
First US transmission: 19.11.98
First UK transmission (Sky One): 25.02.99

Guest Cast: Morgan Fairchild (Nora Bing), Michael Winters (Doctor), Christina Pickles (Judy Geller), Elliot Gould (Jack Geller), Alec Mapa (Housekeeper), Douglas Looper (Paramedic), Joshua Preston (Young Chandler)

Summary: The gang, sated by a delicious dinner at Monica's, relax and talk about Thanksgiving's past. Rachel seems terribly keen to hear the story of Monica's worst Thanksgiving ever, but Monica is very reticent on the subject. While they all try to get to the heart of Monica's secret, we are treated to a tour through the friends' Thankgivings past . . .

Freaky Monica: The young, and extremely virginal, Monica refers to sex as the woman 'giving her flower' to the man. Rachel can't stand this euphemism, and adds to Monica, 'A guy's thing is not called his 'tenderness'. *Believe* me.'

Chandleresque: 'Relieving past pain and getting depressed is what Thanksgiving's all about,' Chandler tells his friends, and in this episode we finally get to see first hand just why he thinks so. Chandler admits that he once 'rushed the stage at a Wham! concert'. Bemused, Ross adds, 'I can't believe you let George Michael slap you.' When he lets slip to Monica that he loves her, she gets all excited, saying, 'You said you love me. I can't believe this!' Panicked, and in classic Chandler style, he stammers, 'No, I didn't!'

Poor Ross: 'Am I more thankful for my divorce or my eviction?' Ross wonders, filling the audience in on events of recent episodes. In 1988, he comes home with wonderful news about a new woman in his life: 'Her name is Carol . . . and she's on the lacrosse team *and* the golf team. Can you believe it?' he gasps. 'She plays for both teams!' You'd *better* believe it. Chandler complains that the events of 1988 led to him being called Sir Limpsalot round campus. 'I came up with that,' says Ross, proudly. Joey replies, 'You're a dork.'

Phoebisms: When Joey complains that he has no past lives, Phoebe just pats him on the head, telling him, 'Course not, sweety. You're brand new.' In 1992, she seems rather pleased that she's being visited by a disembodied voice, only to discover it's Joey with his head up a turkey. Phoebe wants to tell a Christmas story at one point, but it's vetoed by the others: 'Mine had a dwarf that got broke in half, but whatever . . .'

Slow Joey: Despite everyone else being stuffed to the gills by Monica's dinner, Joey still claims, 'I need something sweet.' He then goes on to give thanks for the autumn they are having: 'The other day . . . this lovely Fall breeze came in out of nowhere and blew this chick's skirt right up. Which reminds me, I am also thankful for thongs.' He continues this line of conversation, praising the heavenly nature of this type of underwear, 'It's not so much an underpant as it is a feat of engineering.' In 1992, Monica tries to get the turkey off his head, saying, 'I'm going to spread the legs as wide as I can.' Predictably, Joey's response is simply to giggle. Finally, his plan to scare Chandler backfires on him when he sees Monica wearing the turkey and runs screaming from the building.

The Chick and the Duck: After the revelation about his toe, the duck wanders past a depressed Chandler. He sneers at the bird, 'Oh, I'm a duck. I go quack, quack. I'm happy all the time.'

Magna-Doodle: Someone has drawn a tattoo-style heart with wings with the number 327 on it, and the word 'Bye' underneath.

Parents – Who Needs 'Em?: When Monica finally decides to start eating properly and refuses second helpings, her father congratulates her mother: 'Well, Judy, you did it. She's finally full.' After Rachel's cosmetic surgery in 1988, Jack Geller tactlessly crows, 'Wow! *Love* your new nose!'

Generation X: In 1987, Chandler sports a hairdo redolent of those in the contemporary band A Flock of Seagulls. One year later, he and Ross are done up as if they've walked straight off the set of *Miami Vice*, the drug-busting, Florida-based, show starring Don Johnson. Chandler mentions he once went to a Wham! concert (see 'TOW All The Haste'). As the knife falls directly towards Chandler, we once again hear the shower-music from *Psycho*. Michael Winters (Chandler's Doctor) played Judge Herbert Spitt in a few episodes of *Ally McBeal*.

The Story So Far: Another big one. We see Chandler's mother again ('TOW Mrs Bing'), we're reminded of Chandler's father's sexuality, first alluded to in 'TOW Underdog Gets Away', and we finally get to see the 'Flock of Seagulls' haircut mentioned in 'TO After The Superbowl – Part 2'. Chandler first met Monica and Rachel in 1987. As we know that Chandler was nine years old when his parents split up, and we learn that this happened in 1978, Chandler is now 29 years old. We discover that, thanks to Monica dropping a knife on his foot in 1988, he is missing a toe from his right foot. We get to see 'Fat Monica' and Rachel's old nose, and Rachel tells Monica that she's been dumped by her boyfriend, Chip (see 'TOW The Prom Video') in favour of Nancy Branson (despite the fact he'd already cheated on Rachel with Amy Welch – see 'TOW The Cat'). It was a couple of flippant comments from Chandler that inspired Monica to be a chef and to lose all that weight. By 1988 she'd slimmed down and Rachel had also had a nose job.

There's more on Ross's ill-fated musical career (see 'TOW Chandler Crosses The Line') – he was in a band with Chandler, and they wrote a song called 'Emotional Knapsack'. Joey got his head stuck up a turkey while Phoebe still lived with Monica ('TOW The Flashback' seems to contradict this, though). Among the new information here, we learn that, at college, Ross and Chandler used fake IDs with the names Clifford Alvarez and Roland Chang respectively. In two of her former lives, Phoebe was a field nurse during both the American Civil War and World War I. Tragically, and somewhat messily, during both wars she lost an arm as a result of an enemy attack. Note how, in the flashbacks to the turkey incident, the cast have hairstyles and are wearing clothes just like they did in the First Season – and Chandler has the goatee he had in 'TOW The Flashback'.

The Last Word: This unusual episode is one of the series' best ever, with the non-stop comedy roller-coaster suddenly throwing a brilliant surprise ending at you (Chandler's inadvertent admission that he loves Monica). Best of all, there's lots of the 80s 'Fat' Monica and big-nosed Rachel, who are always good for a laugh. Throw into the mix the embarrassing posing of college boys Ross and Chandler, turkeys on heads, bizarre Phoebe flashbacks and Joey's discourse on female underwear, and you've got a bona fide classic.

509
'The One With Ross's Sandwich'

Writer: Andrew Reich & Ted Cohen
Director: Gary Halvorson
First US transmission: 10.12.98
First UK transmission (Sky One): 04.03.99

Guest Cast: Michael Ensign (Dr Ledbetter), Scott Mosenson (Teacher), Jennette Robbins (Cynthia), Alexia Roberts (Female Student)

Summary: With Ross feeling increasingly under the weather following his second divorce and his eviction, it only takes one tiny thing to push him over the edge. Someone at work has eaten his sandwich. Phoebe helps him by composing a threatening note to ward off other potential food thieves, but this backfires when people at work start getting very wary of him. He is called before his boss, Dr Ledbetter, who reveals that he was the one who ate the sandwich in the first place. When Ross finds out that Ledbetter didn't even finish it, throwing away the leftovers, he finally flips. Ledbetter sends him to a psychiatrist, who signs Ross off from work for an indefinite period.

Chandler and Monica have to enlist the help of Joey to keep their relationship a secret when Rachel finds a pair of underpants behind the cushions of her sofa. His support goes to extreme lengths, covering for one thing after another, until he finally looks like the filthiest of filthy-minded perverts.

Rachel, meanwhile, joins Phoebe on a course of literature classes, but her heart's not really in it, much to Phoebe's annoyance. Finally, Rachel accepts that she should stop going, so Phoebe has to find a new classmate . . .

Slow Joey: Chandler and Monica use Joey's reputation as someone a little free with his affections to cover up for their own indiscretions. When Chandler's underwear is found on Monica's sofa, Joey intones, 'I'm Joey. I'm disgusting. I take my underwear off in other people's homes.' Later, Joey comes home as Monica and Chandler are about to video themselves having sex. Joey's date sees the candles-and-camera set-up and runs a mile, but not before her loudly expressed disgust has alerted Rachel to the goings on. She is appalled, thinking the camera is Joey's, but he just explains, 'I'm Joey. I'm disgusting. I make low-budget adult films.' He turns the tables on Monica, though, when the weight of evidence against him just becomes too perverted to cope with. He tells them that he and Monica had sex in London, and that she's been after him ever since. 'I'm Monica,' she reluctantly explains. 'I'm disgusting. I stalk guys and keep their underpants.' In the course of covering for his friends, he tries to bargain with Monica, saying he will make himself look bad for their sakes, 'but you do it with me once.'

Phoebisms: 'You gotta scare people off,' she tells Ross, when she hears his lame attempt at a note warning people not to eat his sandwich, 'I learned that living on the street.' She then scribbles something on a piece of paper, which all the gang lean in to read. Gasping with horror, they all immediately back away from the note. 'Phoebe,' comments Monica, 'you are a bad ass!' Agreeing, she tells them, 'Some day, I'll tell you about the time I stabbed a cop . . . well, he stabbed me first!'

Spoilt Rachel: She's late to her first literature class, and is remarkably honest in her excuse: 'I'm sorry I'm late, I left late.' When she turns up to the second class having not read the text, she apologises to Phoebe by saying, 'I accidentally read something else . . . *Vogue*!' When she realises that Phoebe was in the classes for her own self-improvement, a rather shocked Rachel admits, 'I just wanted to have fun.'

Freaky Monica: When Rachel leaves the class, Phoebe conscripts Monica as her new study buddy, but it all goes horribly wrong when the ever-keen Monica starts to turn the classes into torture sessions. 'I know! I know! I know!' she is seen to yelp at one point, only for the teacher to sigh, 'Monica, you asked the question.' She rushes into the class at one point to tell the other students that she's persuaded the teacher to give them all a test the following week. 'Tests make us all better learners,' she explains, before realising how she can make it all even more fun: 'Oh, yeah! We should have essay questions!' Finally, to avoid embarrassment by association, Phoebe has to disavow all knowledge of her friend.

Poor Ross: Apart from the whole rage problem, more of Ross's essential wussiness is revealed. When he excitedly announces that his new nickname is 'Mental Geller', Monica says, 'The best you had in high school was "Wet-Pants Geller." Piqued, he argues, 'That was the water fountain!'

Joey's an Actor: When Rachel discovers a woman's razor in Joey's bathroom, he explains that he's using it because he's playing a woman in a play. Rachel then helps him shave his legs – Monica is impressed that he even did the tricky bits round the ankle.

Dinosaurs ROCK!: We see a plaque outside Ross's place of work, reading 'Museum of Prehistoric History'.

Magna-Doodle: Someone's drawn a pretty space scene on the board this episode, complete with ringed planet and a sweeping comet.

Generation X: Chandler cracks a joke based on The Carpenters' 'Top of the World', and Otis Redding's '(Sittin' on the) Dock of the Bay', and later notes how Ross's suggestion for Phoebe's 'hands off' note sounds like a dainty line from the musical *Annie*. The first book on Phoebe's course is *Wuthering Heights* by Emily Brontë, which is a story of forbidden love and secret assignations (so not at all like Monica and Chandler's relationship then), and later they're asked to read *Jane Eyre*, written by Emily's sister, Charlotte.

The Story So Far: The downhearted Ross gives us a quick info-dump at the start of the episode: 'I'm 30 years old, I'm going to be divorced twice, and I just got evicted.' Phoebe tells Rachel that she never went to high school. Ross's boss, Dr Ledbetter, also appears in 'TOW Everyone Finds Out'.

The Last Word: This marks the last time we can really find Ross's rage problem funny, as in following episodes his strange behaviour becomes unbearable. The other distractions here are pure delights, however: Rachel and Phoebe at the literature classes, and the brilliant storyline about Joey covering for Chandler and Monica by making himself out to be some sort of perverted freak. The convoluted explanations when Joey finally shifts the blame to Monica, making the rest of the gang believe they had sex in London and Monica has been stalking him ever since, are brilliantly tortured.

510
'The One With The Inappropriate Sister'

Writer: Shana Goldberg-Meehan
Director: Dana De Vally Piazza
First US transmission: 17.12.98
First UK transmission (Sky One): 11.03.99

Guest Cast: June Gable (Estelle), Julie Lauren (Krista),
George Newbern (Danny), Tom Bailey (Bob),
Lee Arenberg (The Man), Robyn Pedretti (Ginger)

Summary: The newly unemployed Ross begins to grow

seriously bored, until he finds a new project – encouraging Joey to write his own screenplay. As Ross's extreme regime of work continues, Chandler begins to worry that he is being too hard on Joey and tries to make sure Joey spends time having fun too. Finally Chandler and Ross lock horns over what Joey should do with his time, inspiring Joey to write an all-too-poignant resolution to his screenplay.

Phoebe finds a new way to fill her days – as a collector for a charity. However, she finds that a lot of citizens don't respect the charity quite as much as they should, dropping all sorts of rubbish into her collecting bucket. Cue the return of 'Street Phoebe'.

Monica, exasperated by Rachel's imagined relationship game with Danny, decides to step in and arrange a date between the two of them. Things go swimmingly until Rachel meets Danny's sister, Krista, and is terribly worried by how close they seem . . .

Slow Joey: Ross tells him that he is frustrated at having nothing to do, saying, 'I've already been to the bank, the post office *and* the dry cleaners.' Joey is surprised: 'Dude, you just described seven days' worth of stuff.' He tells Ross that he must adjust to being unemployed, but Ross asserts that he's 'on sabbatical', to which Joey replies, 'Hey, don't get religious on me!' His crowning glory is the script he writes for Monica and Rachel to re-enact. Rachel: 'God, Tiffany, you smell great.' Monica: 'Why don't you come closer where you can really appreciate it?' At this point, they both flick through the remaining pages and, disgusted, refuse to play any further part.

Chandleresque: Phoebe arrives at Central Perk, ringing a bell and asking, 'Guess what?' Chandler looks at her and, in typically dry fashion, replies, 'The British are coming?' Voicing the thoughts of most of the audience, Phoebe just says, 'Oh, you and your ways . . .' At one point, Chandler is annoying Joey by playing a game where he has to flick a Ping-Pong ball into a bowl using only a desert spoon. Joey begs him to make it harder by moving the bowl further away but, when he does, Chandler completely misses, sending the ball flying out of sight. 'You suck,' Joey says, 'but at least you suck at a man's game.' When Joey writes him into the script where he apologises to Ross for being a jerk, we get another dig at Chandler's distinctive speech patterns when he has to speak the line: 'Could I *be* more sorry?'

Phoebisms: When the rudeness of the people she meets while fundraising begins to get her down, she decides to get tough: 'I'm going to go back to being "Street Phoebe",' she says (and just look at the previous episode to see how tough that can be). She does, however, give the qualifier, 'I can't go totally back, because "Street Phoebe" wouldn't be friends with you guys . . .'

Freaky Monica: Having seen Danny and Krista tussling with each other, Rachel asks Ross and Monica if they ever did anything similar. They say they did, and Monica proudly proclaims, 'I was undefeated.' Laughing, Ross says, 'Well, you weighed two hundred pounds!' before saying he'd be too strong for her nowadays for her to win. Angered by this, the competitive streak in Monica takes over: 'You wanna go for me right now? 'Cos I'll take you out right now, buddy!'

Poor Ross: When Chandler finally loses patience with Ross taking control over Joey's career, he comes back into the apartment after having seen some children playing around outside and says, 'Do you want to give *them* a project, ruin *their* day?'

Joey's an Actor: Joey visits his agent, the glorious Estelle, because he's just lost out on another audition. 'You're just going to say no again,' she reckons, 'but . . . gay porn?'

Dinosaurs ROCK!: In Joey's apology script, Ross has to read the line 'I am one sorry polontologist.' Well, at least he tried.

Magna-Doodle: A blunt reminder: 'Shop'.

Generation X: Joey loses a role to actress Talia Shire, best known for her role in The Godfather trilogy, directed by her brother, Francis Ford Coppola. Ross tries to persuade Joey to write the screenplay by offering the example of *Good Will Hunting*, the film written by and starring Matt Damon and Ben Affleck.

The Story So Far: More mentions of fat Monica and 'Street Phoebe', the fact that Rachel doesn't have a brother and a brief recap of Ross's current situation, but it's more or less business as usual.

The Story So Far: When seen alongside recent events, nothing much really happens in this episode, though it's quite entertaining nonetheless. Fireball, Ultimate Fireball, and 'Gonna-Need-Stitches' Ball give a very funny insight into how Chandler and Joey spend their spare time, and Ross brings a few jokes into the mix by feeling at a very loose end. Danny and his sister are truly creepy, the best scene between them being the cake-eating in Central Perk, but the highlight of the episode is the tag scene at the end, where Rachel and Monica begin to act out Joey's lesbian porn script.

511
'The One With All The Resolutions'

Teleplay: Suzie Villandry
Story: Brian Boyle
Director: Joe Regalbuto
First US transmission: 07.01.99
First UK transmission (Sky One): 18.03.99

Guest Cast: Sara Rose Peterson (Elizabeth Hornswaggle),
Jack Allen and Charlie Allen (Ben)

Summary: It's just turned 1999, and the gang make sweeping New Year's resolutions. Phoebe decides she wants to become an airline pilot, while also helping Joey with his resolution – to learn guitar. Monica resolves to record the year in photos, while Ross decrees that he's going to try something new every day. Chandler is bet $50 by Ross that he won't make fun of anyone, a challenge pushed to its limits when Ross starts dating someone called Elizabeth Hornswaggle while wearing tight leather trousers. Rachel's self-control is put to the ultimate test, however, when she tries to keep her resolution. She has been challenged not to gossip any more, but when she accidentally discovers Chandler and Monica's affair how can she possibly keep it to herself?

Slow Joey: Carefully orchestrating the midnight kisses to enable Monica and Chandler to be together, he pairs off with Rachel. They kiss for perhaps an inappropriate length of time, before he asks, 'So, that do anything for you?'

Poor Ross: 'No divorces in '99!' he cries as midnight strikes. When it's pointed out that his divorce to Emily hasn't *quite* been finalised yet, he amends it to, 'Just the one divorce in '99!' The whole sequence in Elizabeth's bathroom is wonderfully played by Schwimmer, with Ross's panic increasing as he first tries water, then talc, then lotion to slide his leather trousers back on. His comedy 'Wild West' swagger, which he develops when he learns that Ben thinks of him as a cowboy, is a delight as well.

Phoebisms: 'Do you want to play guitar?' she asks Joey. 'Then don't touch one!' she yells, summing up her bizarre teaching method. She even sniffs his hands at one point: 'strings . . . pick!' she says accusingly. She first has to pass on to Joey the secrets of the chords before he is allowed near an instrument, only she doesn't know the real terms for the chords, preferring to name them after the shapes her fingers make while playing: bear claw, turkey leg, old lady, tiger, dragon and iceberg. She seems quite sure that her resolution to fly a jet plane can be easily realised: 'I figure if I hang around there long enough, someone's bound to leave one of those planes unattended.'

Freaky Monica: Mon's determination to photograph every important event leads to her stopping at nothing for the perfect shot, even if it's of Joey and Phoebe arguing fiercely over guitar tuition. Ross is a little over-sensitive when she takes some flash photos of Ben, accusing her of trying to blind his child.

Spoilt Rachel: Although it is slightly too similar to Chandler's ordeal, Rachel's inability to spread gossip is hilarious. We actually love her gossiping; her comment on the botched boob job ('They were like *this*!' she says, her fingers pointing in opposite directions) is wicked.

Chandleresque: Chandler's frustration at not being able to make fun of his friends is really pushed to the limit. Watching Phoebe teach Joey the guitar, for example, he comments on her unorthodox style, 'Some might find it amusing. I, myself, find it regular.' When Ross explains he has bought leather pants because he likes the smell – saying, 'I've never owned a really good-smelling pair of pants before' – Chandler's pain is positively palpable. We also discover what Monica's nickname for him is: 'Mr Big'.

Magna-Doodle: Someone's drawn a picture of a nice coffee cup.

The Chick and the Duck: Joey doesn't want to hear Rachel's gossip, tired enough of keeping Monica and Chandler's secret, so sticks his fingers in his ears and starts shouting to block out her words. She storms off, and Chandler walks in, sees Joey – still in the same position – and picks the chicken up and puts it in front of Joey's face. It begins to furiously flap its wings, terrifying the life out of Joey when he finally opens his eyes.

Joey's an Actor: He wants to learn guitar because he feels it's about time that he was able to do at least one of the things mentioned on his résumé.

Generation X: Phoebe derides the song 'Bad Bad Leroy Brown' (made famous by Frank Sinatra, among others) as typical guitar lesson fare. And Chandler, his resolve finally collapsing, criticises Elizabeth Hornswaggle by adroitly suggesting that she's a character from *Fraggle Rock*, the 1980s series from Jim '*Muppets*' Henson.

The Story So Far: Brief reminders of Ross and Rachel's relationship, and Ross's divorce from Emily. But, of course, the biggest progression in the ongoing story here is Rachel's discovery of the affair between Monica and Chandler.

The Last Word: At last, Monica and Chandler's secret begins to fall apart, leading to some of the funniest moments this season. Rachel confronting Joey with what she thinks she knows, with him not letting on what he knows until she tells him what she thinks she knows, both of them, of course, knowing that the other one knows what they think each other knows . . . Well, it's a beautiful scene, anyway. Ross's sojourn in Elizabeth's bathroom is wonderful slapstick (with a real slap, for good measure), and Phoebe's guitar lessons are a treat too.

512
'The One With Chandler's Work Laugh'

Writer: Alicia Sky Varinaitis
Director: Kevin S. Bright
First US transmission: 21.01.99

First UK transmission (Sky One): 25.03.99

Guest Cast: Maggie Wheeler (Janice), James Michael Tyler (Gunther), Sam McMurray (Doug), Lise Simms (Kara)

Summary: Chandler takes Monica to one of his work's parties, and she watches agog as he puts on a fake laugh to suck up to his boss, Doug. Although she tries to play along, Monica begins to find herself losing respect for her boyfriend. Things come to a head at dinner at Doug's house, when Chandler refuses to laugh at Doug's bad jokes, only to watch himself fall out of favour with his boss.

Rachel confronts Monica with what she has learned about her relationship with Chandler. Monica flatly denies it all, and Rachel begins to feel hurt that her friend is lying to her. When she overhears how much keeping the secret is hurting Monica as well, however, she decides to respect her friend's decision.

A lonely and depressed Ross mopes through the streets of New York after he hears that Emily plans to get married to someone else. On his wanderings, he bumps into Janice, Chandler's ex, and the two of them start to date. But Ross's endless moaning becomes even too much for Janice to bear.

Slow Joey: For his upcoming game with his boss, Chandler needs to borrow a tennis racket off someone, as when he lent his to Joey, he went down to Central Park and 'thought it would be fun to hit rocks at bigger rocks'. After Ross has taken his rage out on the scone (see below), Joey points at it and innocently asks, 'Is anyone going to eat that?' It is also revealed later that he once got stuck in their apartment block's garbage chute, though God alone knows how.

Phoebisms: She tries to persuade Ross not to get too angry about Emily's new marriage, by pointing out that it's in the past. 'Are you still mad about the Louisiana Purchase?' she asks. When it is later revealed that Ross has been out with Janice, he says, 'I know what you're thinking.' Quickly, Phoebe says, 'You two would have *very* hairy children.'

Spoilt Rachel: She seems determined that Monica *will* confirm her affair with Chandler, because it is her *right* to know. She corners Monica into a forced girlie gossip but Monica is still not forthcoming, asking instead if Rachel has anything she wants to tell her. 'If there was,' Rachel mutters in reply, 'I wouldn't tell *you*.'

Chandleresque: As Monica is complaining that hanging around with 'Work Chandler' is making her lose respect for him, watch Chandler's face – someone *respects* him? But Monica later states that she thinks 'Work Chandler' is a 'suck-up.' Chandler, affronted, yelps, 'OK, because you said that, I'm not putting out tonight!'

Freaky Monica: 'Competitive Monica' returns for the tennis-doubles game with Chandler's boss and his wife. As Doug and Kara pant, exhausted, on the other side of the court, Mon turns to Chandler and boasts: 'Those birds are brown, basted and ready to be carved!' Chandler explains to her that they have to lose to avoid upsetting his boss. Uncomfortable with this, Monica agrees to 'take it down to 95 per cent, but that's the best I can do'. Disgusted at Chandler's deliberate poor show, she ends up smashing his racket.

Poor Ross: 'Man, can't *anything* go right in my life?' he ponders at one point. Well, obviously not if he engenders the following reaction from Janice: 'I believe that the sun has set on our day in the sun.' This is Janice *dumping* someone? She explains that Ross's endless whining about his problems is putting her off. 'So you're saying,' Ross says, a horrible realisation dawning, 'that I've become so whiny that I annoy *you* – Janice? Oh . . . My . . . God!'

The Chick and the Duck: Phoebe mediates a row between the two birds on Joey and Chandler's kitchen counter. The duck is quacking away, apparently explaining his grievance to Phoebe, only to be interrupted by a cluck from the chicken. Phoebe snaps at him, 'You'll get your turn!' A great bird-based moment helped by Kudrow's earnest portrayal of Phoebe's eccentricities. Ross gets momentarily angry that the duck has defecated all over the bitter letter he had written to Emily, but then suddenly sees the bright side of this misfortune. Later, Joey and Phoebe are seen racing the birds in a hunt for a 'tasty treat', for a $40 stake.

Magna-Doodle: A smiley reminder: 'Joey call Kim'. A series of further notes show that a few other girls are expecting call-backs from Joey too.

Cool Britannia: At the opening of the episode Ross buys a scone at Central Perk as he announces to his friends that Emily is planning to get married to someone else. He takes the scone, places it on the table and then, bashing it with his fist to accent each syllable, shouts, 'Stupid British snack food!'

Generation X: There is a shameless plug for the Warner Bros. film *You've Got Mail*, the Meg Ryan/Tom Hanks romantic comedy on release in the US at around the same time this episode was broadcast. Trying to calm Monica during the tennis match, Chandler says, 'Easy, Martina' – a reference to past Wimbledon women's champion, Martina Navratilova. (It's interesting to note that Navratilova was as competitive as Monica. She was determined to win more titles than her rival Chris Evert. They both managed to achieve eighteen Grand Slam titles before their retirements.) The tennis sequence serves (no pun intended) to remind us that Matthew Perry was one of the top junior tennis players in Canada.

The Story So Far: While trying to get Monica to admit to her relationship with Chandler, Rachel tells Monica that when they were in high school, she made out with James Farrow even though she knew Monica liked him. Janice still believes Chandler is in Yemen ('TOW All The Rugby') and Ross tells her the whole potted history of his love life. Chandler's boss was first seen in 'TOW The Ultimate Fighting Champion'.

The Last Word: Hooray! Janice is back, and this time with a nice twist. Her final break-up with Ross is lovely, with her getting all overemotional, and then there's her priceless 'two down, one to go' implication to Joey. The fake laughs of both Monica and Chandler are great fun, but her final actions when she sees just why Chandler creeps to his boss end up seeming just a little too twee and cheesy. Rachel overhearing the conversation between Monica and Chandler is genuinely sweet, however, as is her almost tearful hug when she congratulates Monica on her 'new job'.

513
'The One With Joey's Bag'

Writers: Seth Kurland (teleplay),
Michael Curtis (story)
Director: Gail Mancuso
First US transmission: 04.02.99
First UK transmission (Sky One): 01.04.99

Guest Cast: Bob Balaban (Frank Sr), Daniel Hagan (The Casting Director)

Summary: Joey's up for an audition for the role of a fashionable man, so he turns to Rachel for some style advice. She manages to sell him the idea of a shoulder bag which, although Joey first thinks it's a bit feminine, he soon carries everywhere with him. While the other boys are convinced the bag is just a ridiculous purse, Joey's determined that it's going to 'bag' him the role.

Phoebe receives a shattering shock when her grandmother dies while they are shopping for groceries. At the memorial service, Phoebe is showing the guests to their seats when a man arrives announcing that he's Frank Buffay, Phoebe's long-lost father. Although her sudden interest in him scares him away, she chases after him and fools him into thinking she's the executor of his dead mother-in-law's will. She arranges a meeting with him to reveal the truth and a cautious reconciliation is begun.

Monica and Chandler decide that they should share massages, but when she – the self-proclaimed queen of massage – starts to knead Chandler's shoulders, he screams out in agony. How can he break it to her that she is, in fact, the world's worst masseuse?

Freaky Monica: 'I give the *best* massages,' she claims, but Chandler's pained appraisal says otherwise. When the rest of the gang start to complain that she's actually not that good at massage, she claims that she 'used to give them to Rachel all the time before she got allergic'. Chandler tries to reassure her, 'You don't have to be the best at everything,' causing Monica to screech: 'Oh my God, you don't know me *at all*!' Chandler tells her, though, that 'If anyone was looking for the best *bad* massage . . . they'd have to go to you,' adding that she would be the outright winner if there was an award for the worst massage. 'So maybe they could call the award "The Monica"?' she asks, finally calming down.

Chandleresque: He tells Joey about his dilemma over Monica's massages, and Joey suggests that he just tell her that he doesn't like them. Showing typical self-awareness, Chandler argues, 'For the first time in my life, I'm in a real relationship. I'm not going to screw that up by telling the truth.'

Scary Ross: When he discovers that Phoebe is staying (at least slightly) calm about running into the father who abandoned her, Ross explains how he'd react in a similar situation: 'I'd walk in there. I'd be like, "Yo! Dad! You and me, outside, now!"' He then admits, 'I kind of scared myself,' to which Monica replies, 'Well, at least you scared someone.' This sudden fierce burst from Ross can probably be attributed to the reason for his ongoing anger management therapy.

Phoebisms: She comforts herself over her grandmother's death by saying with some certainty, 'It's not like I'm never going to see her again.' Just when you think Phoebe's referring to the day she will die and join her grandmother in the afterlife, she adds, 'She's gonna visit.' She claims not to be angry at her father, but the evidence during her meeting with him contradicts against this. She poses as the executor of her grandmother's estate, and takes Frank through her 'official forms' (a bundle of screwed-up paper from the bottom of her handbag), posing accusatory questions that he feels as uncomfortable answering as she seems to be when asking them.

Slow Joey: Rachel shows him the bag, and Joey, although initially reluctant, says it's strange how a woman's bag looks good on him. 'Exactly,' says Rachel, 'unisex.' 'Maybe you need sex,' he says, 'but I had sex a couple of days ago.' With amused patience, Rachel explains, 'No, Joey. U-N-I sex.' 'Well,' smiles Joey, 'I ain't gonna say no to that!' When he is given a pair of 3-D glasses at the memorial service, he waves his hand to and fro in front of his face. 'It's like it's coming right at me!'

Joey's an Actor: When he wears a top hat, he explains that 'I'm up for the part of this real cool, like, suave international guy, a real clothes horse.' A top hat is, it seems, his idea of *haute couture*.

Just Plain Weird: The guests at the memorial service are each given a pair of 3-D glasses, although we never find out why.

The Story So Far: There's a wonderful occurrence in this episode, and it happens off-stage. When Frank Buffay announces his name to Phoebe for the first time, the studio audience gasps, immediately realising that it's Phoebe's father; the one who deserted her, her sister, her half-brother and their mother(s). There was no reminder of this in the episode up to this point, which just goes to show how familiar the audience is with Phoebe's past. In their later meeting, we also get a reminder that Phoebe's Mum Lily died 17 years ago, and Phoebe's twin, Ursula, pops up again (see 'TOW Two Parts'). The sweetest moment is when it's revealed that Frank used to sing a song to baby Phoebe that was clearly the inspiration for her classic 'Smelly Cat'.

The Last Word: With very little prelude, a new chapter in Phoebe's life begins, and ever so moving it is too. Avoiding the saccharine of other American sitcoms, Phoebe's gentle, nervous reconciliation with her father is genuine. Bob Balaban's portrayal of Frank Sr as a bumbling, reluctant, and even guilt-ridden father is just perfect, and we can only hope we see more of him one day.

514
'The One Where Everyone Finds Out'

Writer: Alexa Junge
Director: Michael Lembeck
First US transmission: 11.02.99
First UK transmission (Sky One): 08.04.99

Guest Cast: Michael Ensign (Dr Ledbetter)

Summary: A sad day as Ugly Naked Guy packs his stuff, apparently moving out. It strikes Ross that maybe he can move into his apartment. He, Phoebe and Rachel head over the street to check the place out, and – through the window – Phoebe witnesses Monica and Chandler 'doin' it'. Her loud panic alerts Rachel, but she calms her down just in time to prevent Ross from finding out about his sister's affair.

As Ross takes increasingly extreme steps to secure Ugly Naked Guy's apartment, Rachel and Phoebe decide to have some fun with their new-found information. Phoebe pretends to hit on Chandler, much to his flattered confusion. When he tells Monica about it, the only reason she can see for Phoebe's actions is that she has found out about their relationship. In retaliation, she forces Chandler into a romantic liaison with Phoebe. Before long everyone knows that everyone knows – except Ross – and Monica and Chandler are adamant that he mustn't know. But from his new apartment window, Ross spies Monica and Chandler together and flies into another uncontrollable rage . . .

Spoilt Rachel: Another focus on Rachel's love of gossip, when Phoebe asks her how much she knew about Monica and Chandler. Phoebe begins to realise all the times when they were sneaking off to have sex, and Rachel confirms this with a gleeful, 'Doin' it. Doin' it. *Phone* doin' it.'

Phoebisms: She seems pleased for Monica and Chandler, with a small proviso: 'I think it's great. For *him*. She might be able to do better.' When she and Rachel start to plan their attack against Monica and Chandler, Phoebe decides, 'I would use the strongest tool at my disposal – my sexuality.' And use it she does. In her stunning seduction of Chandler, she proceeds to do the strangest, but strangely sexiest, dance you'll ever see.

Slow Joey: After a dizzying build-up of trying to work out the state of play over who knows what concerning Chandler and Monica's relationship, Phoebe suddenly realises, 'They don't know that we know they know we know.' She turns to Joey and adds, 'You can't say anything.' Blankly, he replies, 'Couldn't if I wanted to,' which pretty much sums up poor Joey's position in this episode. He's not comfortable with the game Rachel and Phoebe want to play, but one suspects it has less to do with morality than it does with the fact that it's confusing the hell out of him. He's terribly excited at the prospect of Ross moving in over the street: 'We could do that phone thing, where you have a can and we have a can and it's connected by a string . . .' Chandler deflates his plans by pointing out that they could, in fact, use a real phone. Rachel offers a concise analysis of Joey's wide-ranging interests: 'If I wanted something from Joey, I would strike up a conversation about sandwiches, or my underwear.' We also find out that Joey likes sleeping with Hugsy, his 'bedtime penguin pal', whom we see Joey cuddling later as things just get too much for him.

Poor Ross: Ugly Naked Guy's apartment is obviously prime real estate, as Ross has to fight off many contenders to win the contract. While other potential tenants send Ugly Naked Guy a pinball machine and a mountain bike, Ross plumps for the somewhat lame (small) basket of mini-muffins. He does, however, come up with the masterstroke of joining Ugly Naked Guy in his nakedness, thereby securing the property for himself.

Chandleresque: When Monica asks him just how he got so cute, Chandler explains his fortunate ancestry, 'Well, my grandfather was Swedish and my grandmother was a tiny little bunny.' Joey gives Phoebe some advice as she embarks on her game of seduction: 'Show him your bra. He's terrified of bras – can't work 'em.'

Freaky Monica: Her obsessive need to win really knows no ends. As she is egging Chandler into the seduction of Phoebe, she insists that he must go as far as he needs to, because 'My team always wins!' 'At *this*?' he asks, agog.

Dinosaurs ROCK!: Justifying his naff bribe of muffins for Ugly Naked Guy, Ross says, 'Someone sent us a basket at work once, and people went crazy for those little muffins.' He then adds, dreamily, 'It was the best day.' Chandler just mutters, 'Your work makes me sad.'

Ugly Naked Guy/Cruelty to Animals: We finally see him, if only from the back, although he still doesn't get a line. There's a rather disturbing mention of Ugly Naked Guy's sadly departed pet: 'Poor cat never saw that big butt coming.'

Magna-Doodle: Someone's drawn a pretty picture of two people skiing and snowboarding.

The Story So Far: Ross's boss, Dr Ledbetter, previously appeared in 'TOW Ross's Sandwich'. This marks the last appearance of Ugly Naked Guy, and we get references to his gravity boots ('TOW The Evil Orthodontist').

The Last Word: The phrase 'with hilarious consequences' has become something of a cliché when talking about farcical comedy mix-ups, but this episode writes the book on those very hilarious consequences. And that old befuddling 'I know you know'/'I know you know I know' trick is used to mind-bending effect. Just try not sympathising with Joey! The highlight of this whole year comes in the face-off between Chandler and Phoebe, both determined to 'win', but neither wanting to go through with it. And after all the hilarious consequences comes the *pièce de résistance*, as Chandler admits to Phoebe, 'I can't kiss you, because I'm in love with Monica.' A real masterpiece.

515

'The One With The Girl Who Hits Joey'

Writer: Adam Chase
Director: Kevin S. Bright
First US transmission: 18.02.99
First UK transmission (Sky One): 15.04.99

Guest Cast: Willie Garson (Steve), Soleil Moon Frye (Katie),
David Dalton (Guest #1), Linde Gibb (Guest #2), Stephon Fuller (Guest #3)

Summary: Joey's got a new girlfriend, Katie, who's developed a really cute habit of punching him playfully on the arm. Although his friends find it hard to believe, Joey insists that it's really, really painful. Eventually, he decides he cannot take it any more, so he swathes himself in six sweaters and prepares himself to break it off. Before he can, however, Rachel ends up getting in a tussle with Katie and finds out just how excruciating that cute little habit actually is.

After his initial anger, Ross rather warms to the idea of Chandler and Monica being together – just as Chandler begins to get cold feet. The others make idle talk of their future wedding and baby making, but this terrifies the commitment-phobic in Chandler. This, in turn, leads to a huge argument with Monica and he begins to fear that, unless he takes some drastic action, their relationship might be over.

Ross, meanwhile, is finding it difficult to make friends with his new neighbours. Steve, the president of the residents' association, greets Ross just after he has moved in and asks him to pay $100 towards the retirement present for the block's handyman, Howard. Ross, not unreasonably, refuses, and makes himself instantly unpopular with the other residents. Phoebe tries to make the others see that he's a nice guy, really, but this only leads to further disaster.

Scary Ross: Is there comedy in mental illness? We don't think so. As the episode unfolds, we are expected to sympathise more with Ross, but it's sometimes hard to do so. The double-use of the line 'My best friend and my sister? I cannot believe this!' (first in anger, then in elation) could have been amusing. Whether through Schwimmer's overacting or just some quirk of direction, it doesn't quite come off, leaving an impression of Ross as a deeply unstable personality. He doesn't handle the first meeting with Steve terribly well either and continues to behave like a klutz at Howard's retirement do, leading us to believe it when he says that, 'the whole building hates me. A little kid spat on my knee.' Having said all that, Steve's attitude towards Ross is unnecessarily hostile, especially when he stops referring to him by name, choosing instead to call him by the number of his apartment: 'Go back to 3B, 3B!'

Phoebisms: She arrives at Ross's new apartment with some typically strange housewarming gifts: 'Salt, so your life always has flavour. A loaf of bread, so you never go hungry. And a scented candle for the bathroom, because . . . well, you know.' Phoebe really starts to enjoy herself at Howard's retirement party, having chipped in $100 for his gift so she could be 'The exotic generous stranger'. But she ruins it all when she tries to explain to the partygoers why they shouldn't judge Ross on first impressions. She goes round the room, explaining what she thought of people when she first met them, 'Kurt: abrasive drunk. Lola: *mind-numbingly* stupid,' she says, then points at a young woman and an old man who are together. 'Gold digger. Cradle-robbing perv.'

Chandleresque: 'You want babies! You have baby fever!' he yells at Monica, panicked by the prospect of a real relationship. 'Why don't we turn the heat down on this pressure cooker?' he wails, pushing Monica just that little bit too far.

His apology for the argument – to get down on one knee – is pure Chandler over-reaction, though it is terribly sweet.

Magna-Doodle: Someone, no doubt the mischievous Joey, has scrawled a love heart on the Magna-Doodle this episode. Inside it lies the inscription: 'C.B. 4 M.G.'.

The Ballad of Ross & Rachel: Stupid, stupid Ross. At the end of the episode, the gang all poke fun at Chandler for trying to say sorry to Monica by proposing marriage. Ross pushes it too far, however, when he turns to Rachel and says, 'Remember that whole "we were on a break" thing? Well, I'm sorry. Will you marry me?' and sees that no-one – but no-one – finds it funny.

Generation X: At Ross's lonely party, he listens to Fatboy Slim's 1998 smash hit 'The Rockefeller Skank'. Joey's girlfriend, Katie is played by Soleil Moon Frye, famous in the States as the child-star of the sitcom *Punky Brewster*.

The Story So Far: This episode is a direct continuation from the previous one, so there's a lot of filling in on Monica and Chandler, and who knows about them, in the first few minutes. Chandler says that he and Monica have been together for at least four months. Monica's ex-boyfriend Richard is mentioned, as is the reason for their break-up: that he did not want to have more children. Oh, and Ross now lives in apartment 3B, Ugly Naked Guy's old place.

The Last Word: Here comes whiny Ross again. While we can see his point over the retirement present, watching him go through more crap becomes tiresome. At least Phoebe's efforts to save his reputation are amusing, but Schwimmer is milking the maudlin Ross just a little too much at this point. The opening scenes, where he confronts Chandler and Monica, are just terrifying. Joey's dilemma brings a few smiles, though, and Katie is undeniably 'cute', but equally scary. The examination of modern relationships played out between Chandler and Monica is surprisingly mature and honest, and not a little funny when Chandler is completely freaking out. This episode does have some good points, but these are outweighed by its unpalatable elements; some of which are truly tasteless.

516
'The One With The Cop'

Writers: Gigi McCreery & Perry Ryan (teleplay),
Alicia Sky Varinaitis (story)
Director: Andrew Tsao
First US transmission: 25.02.99
First UK transmission (Sky One): 24.04.99

Guest Cast: NiCole Robinson (The Smoking Woman),
Mark Fite (The Salesman), Aloma Wright (The Saleswoman)
and introducing: Michael Rapaport (Gary)

Summary: Phoebe finds a New York Police Department badge under the cushion of a chair in Central Perk. Though her friends tell her she should return it to the police, she begins to get a kick out of pretending to be a cop. She's finally caught out when she flashes the badge at its real owner, Gary, but before he can stop her, she throws it to the ground and makes a run for it. Gary traces her to her last known address (Monica's apartment) and turns up, not to arrest her but to ask her out on a date.

After witnessing Monica and Chandler sweetly completing a crossword together, Joey dreams that Monica is his girlfriend. Although he is initially worried that he is falling in love with her, his friends convince him that he is just yearning for a similar closeness with someone else. Following their advice (to become friends with a woman before going any further), he ends up getting terribly close to a woman – and her roommate. Ross, meanwhile, has bought a new sofa for his apartment, but he refuses to pay the exorbitant delivery charge. It's up to him, with the help of Rachel and Chandler, to get it up the stairs to his home. But the sofa is way too big for the staircase.

Slow Joey: Monica and Chandler are trying to solve a crossword and foolishly ask Joey for help on a clue. 'What's a six letter word for red?' Chandler asks; Joey replies: 'Dark red.' When he dreams of doing his own crossword with Monica, the clues are a little easier: 'Three letter word. Not dog, but . . .' When it is suggested that he get to be friends with a woman before he takes it to the next level, he immediately tries to hit on Rachel (with the famous 'How *you* doin'?' line) – simply because she's the first female friend he sees. When he tries the

'I want to be friends with you' tack on a woman, he boasts that he 'suddenly became irresistible to her . . . and her roommate.' When Monica reminds him that he was actually seeking closeness, not sex, he replies, 'Closeness, schmoseness. There were three of us, for crying out loud!' There's also a very strange moment when Joey, alarmed by the sudden arrival of Gary, seems to believe that eating pizza is illegal.

Chandleresque: When Phoebe finds the badge, he cracks a joke about how he is surprised because Central Perk doesn't serve doughnuts (the US police, of course, being notorious – at least in comedy shows – of doing nothing but eating doughnuts). When no-one laughs, he asks Phoebe, 'Can you discover the badge again? I think I can come up with something better than that.' Monica and Chandler seem deviously frisky when it is revealed that Chandler currently has a tape measure in his bedroom (anyone remember 'Mr Big'?).

Phoebisms: She's quite looking forward to taking the badge back to the police station, as she'll get the chance to check their 'Ten Most Wanted' list. 'My friend Fritzy's been number 11 for, like, ever,' she says, 'so this could be her year!' When she's playing with the badge, she revels in being able to say things like, 'NYPD. Freeze, punk!' with some authority, later admitting she's, '*totally* drunk with power'. Later, Gary admits to checking out her police record, commenting, 'You've done some pretty weird stuff.' And don't we know it?

Freaky Monica: 'Monica is freakishly strong,' Chandler tells us. Yep, and just keep an eye out for her handshake in the next episode.

Poor Ross: He really believes that a decent sofa is what he needs to pull the chicks. When he is alone, he sits on it and, patting the space next to him, croons, 'Come here to me. No, no, *you* come here to me.' As Rachel points out, though, it's not a magic sofa.

Magna-Doodle: Early in the episode, the message 'JOEY, YOUR AGENT CALLED' appears on the Magna-Doodle, to be replaced later by a giant target.

Just Plain Weird: Although Gary seems very sweet and all, and Phoebe likes him very much, are we really to trust someone who does something creepy like trace a woman through her finger prints? And then take an in-depth look at her police record?

The Ballad of Ross & Rachel: The sofa salesman is very sceptical that Ross could ever have gone out with someone as attractive as Rachel. Indignantly, he tells him, 'Not only did we go out, we did it 298 times.' Classy.

Generation X: Chandler refers to John Steinbeck's *Of Mice And Men* when he calls Joey 'Len', to *Bambi* when discussing Joey's use of the word 'meadow', and puts an interesting spin on Martin Luther King's famous speech: 'I kinda have a dream . . . I don't want to talk about it.' When Gary rumbles Phoebe, she intimates that she works at the 57th Street precinct, asking him, 'Do you know Sipowicz?', a reference to Dennis Franz's character in *NYPD Blue*. Gary throws a reference from the same show back at her, mentioning 'that kid from *Silver Spoons*', the 1982–6 NBC sitcom that starred *NYPD Blue* actor Rick Schroder. Michael Rapaport traditionally plays the ordinary, not-so-bright guys in films like *Copland* (James Mangold, 1997), *Mighty Aphrodite* (Woody Allen, 1995) and *Beautiful Girls* (Ted Demme, 1996).

The Last Word: An ordinary episode, but in the very best sense of the word. The cast are on top form and every scene has at least one laugh-out-loud moment. Surprisingly, Ross's sofa is the source of much of the hilarity, especially when he tries to return it to the shop after he has hacked it in half. Joey trying to fight against his true nature is funny too, but it's Phoebe who once again steals the show, making a meal of being a 'fake undercover whore'.

517
'The One With Rachel's Inadvertent Kiss'

Writers: Andrew Reich & Ted Cohen
Director: Shelley Jensen
First US transmission: 18.03.99
First UK transmission (Sky One): 29.04.99

Guest Cast: Michael Rapaport (Gary),
Samantha Smith (The Window Woman), Steve Ireland (Mr Zelner),
Marc Goldsmith (The Man), Devyn La Bella (The Little Girl),
Ralph Manza (The Old Man)

Summary: Rachel's excited because she's got an interview for a new job at Ralph Lauren. As her interviewer, Mr Zelner, reaches past her to open the door, she thinks he's leaning in for a kiss. Rachel kisses him, but then realises that she has read the situation all wrong. When she turns up for the second interview, she has been nervously chewing her pen and it has left ink on her lip. She goes into the office and Zelner taps his own lips to bring Rachel's attention to the mark on hers; but she thinks he's pushing his luck by asking for another kiss, and lays into him. Later, when she realises her mistake, she is utterly mortified and begs for another chance at an interview. This time, despite inadvertently grabbing for Zelner's crotch, she gets the job.

Joey, while watching Ross's antics from Monica's window, spies a 'Hot Girl' in the same apartment block as Ross. They flirt across the street, and Joey decides to go over and find her. When he gets there, he finds his calculations are all off, as he ends up knocking on Ross's door. After a few more attempts, he finally figures out where she lives and heads over to properly introduce himself. But, when he gets there, he finds Ross once again. While he thinks he's got the wrong apartment again, the truth is that Ross is round at her house – on a date.

Monica begins to get competitive (again) when Phoebe talks all the time about how much sex she and Gary are having. Monica feels she needs to prove to her friend that her relationship with Chandler is as hot as Phoebe and Gary's. While Chandler is more than happy to go along with this in the short term, he has to tell her some home truths before Monica will finally calm down.

Freaky Monica: Phoebe tests Rachel's handshake technique in preparation for her interview. Monica wants a go too, but when she grabs her hand, Phoebe yelps, 'Oh my God, what did I ever do to you?' 'Did I squeeze it too hard?' Monica asks. 'Well,' says Phoebe, 'let's just say I'm glad I'm not Chandler.' When Phoebe inadvertently suggests that Monica's relationship with Chandler is no longer 'hot', Monica gets instantly – and violently – defensive. 'Oh God,' Phoebe whispers, 'I woke the beast.' Monica goes to Chandler and starts demanding a hot relationship – but for all the wrong reasons: 'We have *got* to beat them . . . We've got to go upstairs and have a lot of sex to prove them wrong.' After a particularly steamy session, she says, 'Phoebe and Gary are *so* going to hear about this at dinner.' Then she tells Chandler, 'You're the best,' to which he replies, 'No, you're the best.' Contemplating this, she agrees, 'I *am* the best.'

Chandleresque: 'I gotta check out this hot girl,' Chandler says when he hears about Joey's latest find. Then he realises his mistake, turns back to Monica and says, '*There* she is!' He wants to hold a policeman's gun, but Gary is reluctant to let him. 'What could happen, I –' he manages, before he splashes coffee all over the place, proving Gary's point. Later at dinner, Gary gives him a police badge as a present. Chandler flashes it then announces, 'Officer Bing's gotta 10–100 . . . That's pee-pee.' When he finally manages to talk Monica down from her crazy competitiveness with Phoebe, he realises they've swapped places, saying, 'You just freaked out about our relationship! I'm the relationship king, and you are the crazy, irrational screw-up!' He begins to jig about. 'Woo-ha-hoo!' he cries, before realising what he's doing. 'And now we're back.'

Poor Ross: He's behaving like a lunatic too, performing little mimes in his lounge for his friends in Monica's apartment opposite. 'Is he doing his shark attack bit yet?' Monica asks Joey, just as it begins. Then Joey reports, 'Ross is doing his watching TV bit.' Monica looks, but says that he is actually watching TV. But we find out that he's just pointing the remote control at a dead television set. The sad man.

Slow Joey: He tries to mime his famous 'How you doin'?' to the Hot Girl, with some success.

Spoilt Rachel: When she returns depressed about her appalling performance at the interview, Joey offers her a hug to cheer her up. As they embrace, he sees a familiar face through the window behind them: 'She's back,' he cries happily. 'Hot Girl's back!' Self-centred as ever, Rachel replies, 'Well, I'm not totally back yet . . .'

Phoebisms: The minute Gary leaves, she turns to Monica and admits, 'Oh God. Oh, I miss him so much . . . He's like this little puppy dog, but a really tough one who shoots bad guys.' She's got it bad, but it's just a shame that bad guys aren't the only things he shoots . . .

The Story So Far: When 'Hot Girl' meets Ross, she immediately identifies him as 'the guy who wouldn't chip in for the handyman'. But at least she agrees that it wasn't fair for him to be asked.

Generation X: To appease Ross's desperate need to perform for his friends, Monica and Rachel stick photos of their faces to two life-sized cardboard cut-outs of Pamela Anderson and Yasmine Bleeth, stars of Joey and Chandler's favourite show, *Baywatch*. One of Ross's favourite mimes is his 'Shark Attack' from Jaws (and it *is* surprisingly accurate!).

The Last Word: Once again, it's just another week in the life of the friends, with no earth-shattering occurrences, and it's all the more pleasant for it. Monica's rivalry with Phoebe is great fun, and the resolution (when Chandler tells her that the closeness and stability they have is just as exciting as lots of hot sex) is ever so sweet. Joey's abject pain at being unable to track down the 'Hot Girl' is hugely entertaining, as is Rachel's catalogue of woes in the course of her job interviews. Great, solid stuff.

518
'The One Where Rachel Smokes'

Writer: Michael Curtis
Director: Todd Holland
First US transmission: 08.04.99
First UK transmission (Sky One): 06.05.99

Guest Cast: Jane Sibbert (Carol), Megan Ward (Nancy),
Judy Kain (The Casting Director), Jim Wise (Kyle),
Jack Allen and Charlie Allen (Ben),
Matt Weinberg (Raymond) **and introducing:**
Joanna Gleason (Kim Clozzi)

Summary: While walking with his father in Central Park, Ben is spotted by a talent scout and put forward for an audition for a television advert. Joey is initially piqued that Ben got a chance so easily, but then realises he could run for the part as Ben's dad. Problems arise, however, when – because he looks so different – the casting director says that Joey can't play Ben's father. Joey is paired with another boy, while a different actor plays Ben's father. Whichever pair is best will make it through to the final production, but Joey begins to get cold feet about competing with his friend's son.

Rachel starts her new job and, although she's getting on well, begins to get a bit annoyed that she is being left out of some major decision making. Her boss smokes, as does her colleague, and Rachel can only watch as they nip off for cigarette breaks, during which they continue to make plans for their work. Rachel soon decides that if she can't beat them, she'll have to join them . . .

Slow Joey: He decides to try his new card trick on Chandler, asking him to pick a card from the deck. While Chandler still holds the card, Joey takes another, shows it to him and asks, 'Is that your card?' When Phoebe suggests to Monica that they jointly plan Rachel's party, Monica squeals, 'I'd *love* to do it together,' to which Joey just sniggers to himself. Ross tries to explain possible reasons why Joey is jealous of Ben's success: 'I think, subconsciously–' 'Woah!' Joey interrupts. 'You lost me.'

Chandleresque: Rachel has to start smoking if she wants to join in with the planning meetings in her new office. 'It's like I'm being punished for not having this disgusting, poisonous habit,' she claims. 'Yeah,' sighs Chandler, dreamily, 'it is the best.' When Rachel finally takes up the evil weed, Chandler immediately notices: 'There's something different . . . Oh my God, you smoked! . . . You look happy and sick.' Rachel admits that she does feel like throwing up, but Chandler tells her, 'You've got to push past this, 'cos it's going to get *so* good.'

Freaky Monica: At the first planning meeting for Rachel's party, she tells Phoebe that she has prepared 'a sketch of the cake' and 'some sample menus', before handing her 'an alphabetised list of all my CDs. I've highlighted the ones that go really well with my food.'

Phoebisms: 'Monica is going to rue the day she put me in charge of cups and ice!' she cries. Phoebe carries through this threat by going all-out in her area of responsibility: 'Cup hat, cup banner, cup chandelier, and the thing that started it all – the cup!' She also offers a bewildering array of ice: dry, crushed, cubes and – Chandler's favourite – snow cones.

Joey's an Actor: He manages to secure himself an audition for the advert that Ben is up for: 'Turns out one of the casting ladies has seen me in a play, so I steered clear of her.' When Ross, Joey, Carol and Ben are at the final audition, Ross says to Joey, 'This is so nerve-racking, how do you do this?' 'Fortunately,' he replies, 'I don't get many call-backs.' When Carol asks him, 'Is it a good sign that they asked us to hang around after the audition?' Joey continues to demonstrate his lack of actual experience: 'Who knows?'

Magna-Doodle: A message for Joey: 'Carla wants you to call her!!'

The Story So Far: We're reminded of Ben's lesbian mother, and of the fact that Chandler is an ex-smoker. Of his career, Joey warns Ben, 'One day you're Dr Drake Ramoray [his character in *Days of Our Lives*], the next day you're eating ketchup right out of the bottle.' Rachel points out that her birthday comes after Chandler's (see 'TOW Unagi').

Generation X: Joey mentions that Raymond, the ace child actor he is paired with, has starred in an advert with 'the cartoon tiger', a reference to Tony, the advertising mascot of Kellogg's Frosties. They're *grrr* . . . Oh, you know the rest.

The Last Word: Another fun episode in a strong run, with by far the best laughs coming from Rachel's new work place and her nicotine dilemma. Chandler wallows in his fond memories of smoking, bringing some choice lines to the show, while Phoebe raises a giggle with her ideas for the party. The Ross and Joey stuff is strong, but isn't Schwimmer overacting again?

519
'The One Where Ross Can't Flirt'

Writer: Doty Abrams
Director: Gail Mancuso
First US transmission: 22.04.99
First UK transmission (Sky One): 13.05.99

Guest Cast: Kristin Datillo (Caitlin),
Lilyan Chauvin (Grandma 'Noni' Tribbiani)

Summary: Joey's grandma comes over to Monica's to watch his latest big part in *Law and Order*. Thankfully, the old Italian lady doesn't speak a word of English, so when something terrible happens, he is able to share his panic with his friends – his scenes have been cut from the show. When he lost his job on *Days of Our Lives*, it apparently nearly killed his grandma and now he's worried that if she doesn't see him on *Law and Order*, it might do the same. But, in a surprising show of quick-thinking, Joey manages to come up with a plan to save the day.

Ross decides that he would like to get to know Caitlin, their pizza delivery woman, better and tries to flirt with her. Unfortunately, his flirting abilities are less than first rate, and he just ends up embarrassing himself more than anything else. Rachel decides that someone's going to have to step in if he's ever going to get a date.

It's Chandler and Monica's ten-month anniversary, and he has managed to secure them a table at an exclusive restaurant. He suggests to Monica that she wear the earrings he bought for her, so she goes to Phoebe, to whom she lent them, and asks for them back. Phoebe's let Rachel borrow the earrings, but Rachel's lost one of the pair and Monica is going to freak when she finds out . . .

Freaky Monica: 'I'm not allowed to borrow her stuff,' says Rachel, and we see why. When Phoebe sheepishly takes the blame for losing one of the earrings, Monica tells her that it's OK and gives her a hug. Seeing this, Rachel thinks it will be OK if she tells the truth and owns up. Angrily, Monica snaps, 'That is *exactly* why I do not lend you stuff.'

Poor Ross: He gets two chances to really flirt with Caitlin. In the first, he says how much he likes eight-year-old boys (Caitlin having complained that her new haircut makes her look like one). In the second, he ends up telling her how they put a smell in domestic gas so you can tell if there's a leak. *Sexy*!

Phoebisms: 'Ross,' she asks after his second failed attempt at flirting, 'what else do they add smell to?' And she's genuinely interested. At one point, she converses fluently with Joey's grandmother. When she is asked, 'You speak Italian?', she just shrugs and says, 'I guess so!'

Chandleresque: Joey tries to tell his grandmother that his big scene is coming up. Chandler asks, 'If you said, "Big lima bean bubbling up," would she know the difference?' Phoebe reveals that Chandler has a jewellery box (although she doesn't have time to ask why). His conversational gambit with Joey's grandmother is a treat: 'So . . . you're old and small . . .' When Monica has to wear a different pair of earrings, she is nervous that Chandler's going to notice they're not the ones he bought. He just says they look lovely, turning aside to say to Ross, 'Thanks for picking out the earrings, man.'

Slow Joey: Rachel explains to Caitlin that the reason they 'have seven people and ten pizzas' is because Ross wanted to call her over to flirt with her. Caitlin says, 'Oh, I thought you had Joey there.'

The Chick and the Duck: Caitlin sees the duck when she delivers a pizza to Chandler's apartment, and asks where the chicken is. 'Oh, he's in the back,' Chandler explains. 'The duck pissed him off. He said that eggs came first.' The duck is also used in a gripping hostage situation, when he interrupts Joey's camcorder *Law and Order* insert.

The Ballad of Ross & Rachel: Ross seems uncomfortable around Rachel when he's talking about his feelings for Caitlin. 'Ross, we broke up two years ago,' she points out. 'You've been married since then. I *think* it's OK if we see other people.' Sardonically, Rachel agrees that Ross's flirting skills are second to none: 'We met, you flirted and then – *bam!* – nine years later, you had me!' Chandler asks Rachel if Ross's flirting with women when they were going out ever bothered her. 'No, no,' she says, 'it bothered me when he *slept* with other women.' These are, without doubt, the finest lines in the episode, and it makes such a change that Rachel and Ross's difficult history can be used in a truly funny way.

Magna-Doodle: The board features an artistic interpretation of the Manhattan skyline at night.

Boys Will Be Boys: Chandler explains to Monica the differences in psychology between a woman and a man flirting: 'When you flirt with a guy, you think, "I'm just flirting, no big deal." But the guy is thinking, "Finally, someone who wants to sleep with me!"' Monica asks, 'And this goes for all guys?' Chandler confirms, 'All guys that are awake.'

The Story So Far: Chandler tells Ross that he's been dating Monica for ten months now.

Generation X: When he notices his scenes have been cut from *Law and Order*, Joey tries to fool his grandma into thinking that he's currently on screen. But she immediately recognises the other actor as Sam Waterston, Executive Assistant District Attorney Jack McCoy from the series. She also points out – in broken English – that he starred in the feature films *Crimes and Misdemeanours* (Woody Allen, 1989) and *Capricorn One* (Peter Hyams, 1978). ('She doesn't know "hello",' Chandler points out, 'but she knows "*Capricorn One*".') Chandler once camcordered himself performing David Bowie's hit 'Space Oddity' (a number five hit in 1969, it reached number one in the UK charts when it was reissued in 1975). 'Oh, the humanity!' Chandler quotes the famous words of a news commentator on the footage of the 1937 *Hindenburg* disaster (the *Hindenburg* was a luxury transatlantic airship, the accidental destruction of which – killing 35 of the passengers and crew – marked the end of the use of airships as commercial passenger liners. Funny how no-one banned boats after the *Titanic*, but there you go . . .).

The Last Word: For an episode to be set almost entirely within the two apartments is not unusual, but when it works, it shows off the great interplay between the characters brilliantly. This is one such episode, with some classic and, for once, entertaining bitching between Ross and Rachel; some lovely Monica and Chandler exchanges; and some great moments from both Phoebe and Joey. Ross's chronic awkwardness is thankfully used to comic effect, and the sequence where he talks to Caitlin about smelly gas is the highlight of the episode.

520

'The One With The Ride Along'

First US transmission: 29.04.99
First UK transmission (Sky One): 20.05.99
Writers: Shana Goldberg-Meehan & Seth Kurland
Director: Gary Halvorson

Guest Cast: Michael Rapaport (Gary), Helen Baxendale (Emily)

Summary: Gary agrees to take Ross, Joey and Chandler along in his car while he is on duty. When they hear what they think is a gunshot, Joey dives to cover Ross – in fact, he's making sure his delicious sandwich is safe. Ross gains a whole new outlook on life, while Chandler is outraged that Joey would save Ross instead of him.

While fetching some things from Ross's apartment, Rachel hears Emily leaving a message on Ross's machine. She is due to marry her new beau in the morning, but can't stop thinking about Ross and wants him to call her. Rachel and Monica discuss whether they should tell Ross about the message, but during their conversation accidentally delete it. Finally, Rachel decides that Ross has a right to know that Emily called – but not the right to call her back.

Chandleresque: He's terribly eager to join Joey and Ross on the ride-along, but Gary asks him, 'Really? You? . . . It's kind of dangerous.' 'Well, I like danger,' Chandler sniffs. Gary then says they'll do the ride-along today, if they're all available tonight. Suddenly scared, Chandler says, 'You didn't say it was going to be at night-time.'

Slow Joey: During the ride-along, they stop at a shop which Joey claims 'makes the best sandwich in the world', which contains the frankly unappetising concoction of meatballs, melted cheese and marinara sauce. Then, when Chandler tries to check the smell of the sandwich, Joey bats him off, saying, 'Half the taste is in the smell. You're sucking up all the taste units!'

Freaky Monica: She decides to sort out her and Rachel's photo collection, dividing them into categories. 'And then what I've done,' she explains, 'is I've cross-referenced them by subject. So, if you're looking up, say, birthdays and dogs, you get photo 152.' This is a photo of Rachel's dog Lapou, who can also be found under 'Dogs and dead.' 'I need some cash,' she tells Rachel as she's heading over to Ross's. 'While you're at Ross's, if you see any lying around . . . I don't do that!' When she finds out about the message from Emily, she argues that it should be erased, saying, 'I love [Ross] and I don't want to see him get hurt. Doesn't that give me the right to control – help him?' Rachel tries to explain how it should be up to Ross to decide what to do, to which Monica responds, 'If you're going to be totally rational about this, I can't argue with you.' At the close of the episode, the gang are discussing what they'd be like in a war situation. 'Man, I'd be great in a war,' Monica decides. 'I'd make general before any of you guys!'

Phoebisms: When they're discussing war, she says, 'I'm a pacifist, so I'm not interested in war. But you know what? When the revolution comes, I will have to destroy you all.' And she means it too.

Poor Ross: He's sitting in the front during most of the ride-along, claiming that it makes him 'Gary's partner'. As Chandler says, 'When you say "partner", it doesn't sound cop. It sounds gay.'

The Story So Far: Mention is once again made of Lapou, Rachel's deceased dog (see also 'The One With All The Kips'), as is the story of Rachel leaving her husband-to-be Barry at the altar. And, of course, we gets some brief recaps of Emily's marriage to Ross, and Rachel's attempt to stop it.

Generation X: A passing reference is made to Frank Serpico, a New York policeman who famously blew the whistle on some of his corrupt colleagues. His life was recorded in a book titled *Serpico* by Peter Maas, and he was played by Al Pacino in a biographical feature film of the same name (Sidney Lumet, 1973). John Herschel Glenn Jr, the first man to fly faster than sound (in 1957) and the first to orbit the Earth (in 1962), is also mentioned.

The Last Word: Where the last few episodes have been ordinary and all the better for it, this episode is ordinary in the 'nothing special' sense. The ride-along storyline is just silly, and Ross's *carpe diem* mentality is just not funny. Neither of these things is explored terribly deeply, which might explain why they seem so inconsequential. The debates between Monica and Rachel over Ross's right to know about the message from Emily are the highlights here. But, again, there doesn't seem to be any reason – dramatic or comic – for her phoning in the first place. Next!

521
'The One With The Ball'

Writers: Greg Malins (teleplay),
Scott Silveri (story)
Director: Gary Halvorson
First US transmission: 06.05.99
First UK transmission (Sky One): 27.05.99

Guest Cast: Michael Rapaport (Gary), James Michael Tyler (Gunther),
Victoria L. Kelleher (Woman #2), Antoinette Spolar (Woman #1)

Summary: Ross and Joey start throwing a ball and, before they know it, find they've been doing it for over an hour. They decide to continue for two hours, then longer, and then Monica gets involved. Meanwhile, Rachel decides to treat herself to an expensive pedigree cat; the same kind as the lovely, sweet, cuddly cat her grandmother used to have. Rachel's cat, however, is distinctly unlovely, sour, and vicious and she soon decides to get rid of it.

Gary tells Monica that he's going to ask Phoebe to move in with him. When Phoebe finds out, she's very alarmed and asks Chandler – as the resident commitment-phobic – to try and persuade him that it's a bad idea. Chandler fails, however, and Gary goes ahead and asks her. Phoebe tries to refuse, but is so distressed by how deflated Gary seems, that she eventually agrees to go through with it. Gary begins to cotton on to the fact that she's a little reluctant and so confronts her, asking if she really wants to live with him. Giving it some more thought, she decides that it *is* a good idea after all. But, when they wake up on their first morning together, Gary casually shoots a twittering bird outside the window and Phoebe decides that their relationship is over.

Spoilt Rachel: Monica is shocked: 'You spent $1000 on a cat when you owe me three hundred?' 'Well,' says Rachel, 'I was going to let you play with it.'

Freaky Monica: She *slightly* overreacts when she gets an allergic reaction to Mrs Whiskerson during the ball-throwing game. Her eyes filling with tears, she screams, 'My vision has been compromised!' She enthuses about the game, referring to the participants as 'Team Monica', then saying, 'all right, we can work out that name later.'

Chandleresque: When he hears that Gary is going to ask Phoebe to live with him, Chandler begins to panic: 'It's fast! It's so fast!' 'Relax,' Monica tells him, 'it's Phoebe, not you.' He visits Gary at work to persuade him not to ask Phoebe, saying that they 'should have a talk, man to . . . well, me.' Monica doesn't want him to join in the ball game, claiming that he's 'a dropper', an opinion proved in the brilliant sequence under the closing credits.

Slow Joey: He believes that neither Long Island nor Staten Island are actually islands. When Ross and Joey miss lunch because of the ball game, he reckons, 'That's the first time I've ever missed a meal.'

Phoebisms: Rachel has to take to wearing oven gloves to protect herself from Mrs Whiskerson. When Phoebe sees her carrying the cat she yelps, then apologises, 'I'm sorry, the oven mitts really freaked me out.' When Gary accuses her of not looking hard enough for an apartment, he shows her all the suitable ones advertised in the paper that she has claimed to have read. Although it's a lie, her excuse is believable – for Phoebe: 'Are these for rent? I thought people were just bragging.'

Gunther Loves Animals: He pays $1500 for Mrs Whiskerson, telling Rachel she's welcome to come and visit her any time she likes. He then turns to Ross and asks him whether it is actually a snake.

Cruelty to Animals: 'Why is it inside out?' Ross asks about Rachel's new cat. 'That's not a cat,' says Joey. Mrs Whiskerson ('Well, what am I gonna call her?' says Rachel. 'Fluffy?') is a hairless sphinx cat, and is also the highlight of this episode. It cost her $1000 in cash, but countless millions in Savlon: when she tried to get it to play with a piece of string, 'it just flipped out and scratched the hell out of me'. At various other points, Mrs Whiskerson is mistaken for a hand, a sick baby, and 'a minion of the Antichrist'. There's also the poor bird that inadvertently becomes the catalyst for Gary and Phoebe's break-up.

Dinosaurs ROCK!: While throwing the ball back and forth,

Ross tells Joey an 'interesting' story about some fossils. Joey just says, 'Maybe this should be more of a quiet game.'

Magna-Doodle: A pretty picture of a UFO flying through space.

Generation X: Rachel once had a crush on Shaun Cassidy, member of The Partridge Family (from the TV series) and teen idol. He never had a hit in the UK, leaving his stepbrother David to do most of the work on this side of the Atlantic. We're not entirely sure whether that's a good thing.

The Story So Far: Chandler tries to persuade Gary that living with his girlfriend is a bad idea, but he seems totally sold on it, saying it is wonderful to be around the person you love all the time. 'Were your parents happy or something?' Chandler wonders, referring to the break-up of his mother and his gay father.

The Last Word: Rachel's cat is wonderful and for a while you wonder how much fun could be had if it was kept on, like Marcel or the chick and the duck. But then you realise, having enjoyed the extreme density of jokes about the animal, that if its inclusion were to be stretched out it might not continue to be so funny. Mrs Whiskerson does, however, make this episode. The ball game's a good laugh too (especially the way it ends) and the Gary and Phoebe storyline is sweet – the abrupt ending is a masterstroke.

522
'The One With Joey's Big Break'

Writers: Wil Calhoun (teleplay),
Shana Goldberg-Meehan (story)
Director: Gary Halvorson
First US transmission: 13.05.99
First UK transmission (Sky One): 03.06.99

Summary: Joey's excited to have been cast as the lead in a new movie being filmed in the desert outside Las Vegas. While everyone is very happy for him, when Chandler finds out that Joey won't get paid unless the film is a success, he begins to think that Joey's guilty of deluding himself. As they

set out on their road trip across the US, Chandler accidentally
lets slip that he thinks that Joey might be wasting his time.
They have an argument, and Chandler remains in New York.
When Joey reaches the set, he finds out that the movie hasn't
received enough financing and is not going to be filmed. In
order to save face and not let Chandler know that he was right,
Joey takes a job as a centurion host at Caesar's Palace.

Rachel's caught an eye infection, but is terrified about
seeing a specialist. Monica finally persuades her to get over
her irrational fears, and she is given some eye drops to clear
the infection. But she is still reluctant to use them.

Ross, meanwhile, has done something to upset Phoebe, only
she won't tell him what it is he's done . . .

Slow Joey: As Rachel is flickering her infected eye, Joey
notices and thinks she's winking at him. So, without for one
minute wondering why she might be flirting with him, he
winks right back at her. As he and Chandler set off for Las
Vegas in the taxi, Joey, who is driving, says, 'I'm getting
pretty tired, you might have to take over soon.' Chandler
points out that they've only 'been driving for a half-hour'.
Chandler thinks it might be a good idea to send Joey a gift to
apologise for not having faith in his movie, but doesn't know
where he can find just the right thing: 'I wonder where I could
get a basket of porn?'

Chandleresque: Monica mentions Richard (who was an
optometrist) in relation to Rachel's eye infection, and Chandler
says, 'That's all I ever hear – Richard, Richard, Richard!'
Monica points out, 'Since we've been going out, I think I've
mentioned him twice.' 'All right,' Chandler says, 'Richard,
Richard!' It's a clever move to highlight his irrational jealousy
over this man, as it's instrumental in the plot of the next
episode.

Phoebisms: She appears to be a one-woman tourist guide to
the weird sights of America. She tells Joey that he can find 'a
man in Illinois with a beard of bees' on the north route to
Vegas, or 'a chicken that plays tic-tac-toe' on the south route.
When Ross wonders if it was him saying Phoebe's hand-
writing was 'childlike' that has put her in a bad mood with
him, she says that, actually, 'That made me feel precious.' She

finally realises what it was that caused the friction between them: 'We were playing chess,' Phoebe says, 'on the frozen lake . . . And then you took off your energy mask and you were Cameron Diaz . . .' before realising the slight possibility that this was in a dream.

Freaky Monica: Rachel, who is tackled by Monica at one point, says, 'Oh my God, you really *are* freakishly strong.' (See 'TOW A Cop'.) At the opticians, she shows Dr Miller that she is perfectly able to read the smallest letters on the board. 'Very good, Monica,' he says. 'You know where they are.' And indeed she does, as she grabs a lollypop out of a nearby drawer.

Poor Ross: He gives Joey $20 to put on black 15 at the casino, but Joey just pockets the money, clearly not intending to bet at all. When the gang are trying to figure out why Phoebe is in a mood with Ross, Monica asks, 'Is it because he's always correcting people's grammar? *Whom. Whom* . . . Sometimes it's just who!' Rachel wonders, 'Did you beat him at a board game? He turns into such a baby when he starts to lose.'

The Story So Far: Monica's eye specialist ex-boyfriend Richard is mentioned and we learn that Phoebe keeps her grandmother's ashes in her taxi ('TOW Joey's Bag'). There's also a welcome return for the Gellers' special way of 'giving the finger' without actually having to give the finger (see 'TOW Joey's New Girlfriend').

Joey's an Actor: His starring role is in a film called *Shutter Speed*, which seems to be some sort of supernatural thriller.

Generation X: Cameron Diaz is revealed as Ross's true identity in Phoebe's dream. Diaz made her feature film debut in 1994's *The Mask* (starring Jim Carrey and directed by Chuck Russell). She has also starred in feature films such as *There's Something About Mary* (Bobby and Peter Farrelly, 1998) and opposite Jennifer Aniston in *She's the One* (Edward Burns, 1996). Monica mentions the De La Soul song 'Me, Myself and I' (a number 22 hit in the UK in 1989) and America's 'A Horse With No Name' (number 3 in 1972) plays as Joey arrives in the Nevada desert.

The Last Word: The pace of the last few episodes continues, bringing us more of the usual fun in preparation for the

following week's big Vegas blow-out. Rachel's terror of anything to do with eyes is superb, as is the way the whole gang
wrestle her to the floor in order to administer her eye drops.
Phoebe's behaving reassuringly kookily, and the argument
between Joey and Chandler gives us some good dialogue. A
very nice scene setter for 'The One In Vegas'.

523
'The One in Vegas'

Writers: Andrew Reich & Ted Cohen and
Greg Malins & Scott Silveri
Director: Kevin S. Bright
First US transmission: 20.05.99
First UK transmission (Sky One): 10.06.99

Guest Cast: Thomas Lennon (Randall), Jeanette Miller (Elderly Woman),
James Paradise (Casino Boss), Rick Pasqualone (Croupier),
Todd Glass (Airplane Guy), Baillie Gerstein (Tourist),
Lisa Jamie Cash (Flight Attendant), Rojai Holloway (Security Guard),
Frank Novak (Gambler), Gabi Simson (Woman Dealer),
Nina Mann (Attendant)

Summary: As a one-year anniversary present, Monica buys
Chandler and herself a pair of tickets to Las Vegas, so they can
have a weekend away and visit Joey – who they still think is
working on a film out there. Overhearing their plans, Phoebe
invites herself and then, before they can stop her, she invites
Ross and Rachel too. When they are alone, Monica tells
Phoebe that she bumped into and had lunch with her ex,
Richard, but doesn't plan to tell Chandler about it, because it
meant nothing at all. But on the plane to Las Vegas, Phoebe
accidentally lets the secret slip and Chandler and Monica end
up falling out.

Back in New York, Rachel decides to follow Phoebe's
advice and spend an evening naked in her own apartment. Ross
spies her from across the road, and assumes that she's tempting
him in for a night of passion. When he finds out she wasn't, he
is terribly embarrassed. On their flight to Las Vegas, they have
a competition to see who is the more easily embarrassed,
which finally leaves Rachel with a black ink moustache and

beard on her face. Arriving in Vegas, Rachel discovers that the ink on her face won't come off. Distraught, she insists that she cannot leave her hotel room and demands that Ross stays with her to keep her company. The couple spend the evening playing cards, spitting macadamia nuts across the room, and getting horribly drunk on the mini bar.

Phoebe finally persuades Monica to make it up with Chandler. Once they do so, they go down to the casino to play craps. Monica seems freakishly lucky with the dice and, getting carried away by the excitement, Chandler says if she rolls a hard eight (two fours) again, they will get married that night. Although the roll is slightly botched, they agree that it is a hard eight, and they set out to an all-night chapel.

When Monica and Chandler arrive at the chapel, they're told to wait as another couple are getting married before them. Just as they are wondering if they really are ready for this, the doors of the chapel swing open and out stagger a drunken Ross and Rachel, the new Dr and Mrs Geller . . .

Spoilt Rachel: She can't be bothered to answer her own phone, asking Phoebe – the only other person there – to do it for her. When Phoebe accuses her of being lazy, she makes up the lame excuse that 'All the people in the entire world that I would want to talk to are right here.'

Slow Joey: He has scratched his PIN number (5639) on to a cash machine in New York. He thinks he knows why Roman soldiers had the crest on the top of their helmets: 'They would scrub the floor with it, they'd use it to brush the mud off their shoes . . .' They would even, Joey reckons, use it to clean the underside of their horses. When Joey's given a chip for $100 as a tip, he tells Chandler that he's going to turn it into millions on the gambling tables. Chandler wishes him luck but Joey replies, 'I do not need luck, I've worked this through.' Talking about the millions he'll make through his identical hand twin, he dreams of living in a 'hand-shaped mansion', saying that Phoebe can live in the thumb. He tests Rachel's level of sobriety by asking her, 'How you doin'?' She smiles at him and replies, 'I'm doin' fine, baby. How *you* doin'?' He turns to Ross and says, 'Don't let her drink any more.'

Phoebisms: Arriving in Las Vegas, Phoebe gets excited when she is handed a token for a 99-cent lobster meal. Monica points out that she doesn't eat any meat, but Phoebe claims, 'For 99 cents, I'd eat *you*.' When Joey tells her that he has found his identical hand twin, she seems to be the only one impressed, saying, 'Oh, you're so lucky.' Left alone in Joey's room, she tries on his centurion helmet and obviously likes it, saying, 'I really should start wearing hats.' When she gets into a fight with the old woman who haunts her slot machines, they attract the attention of a security guard. She tries to make him believe that the old woman 'sells drugs to kids', but the guard tries to throw her out. 'I won't go back!' she screams, thinking he is arresting her. 'I won't go back to that hellhole!' Phoebe uses her 'Philangi' alter ego again (see 'TO After Ross Says Rachel'), this time giving a first name (Regina) and claiming that she is 'a business woman in town . . . on business'.

Chandleresque: Chandler reminisces about the time before he was Monica's boyfriend, when he was just 'your annoying friend Chandler'. Phoebe states, 'Now you're just *my* annoying friend Chandler.' When Ross gets excited about his tickets to the Van Gogh exhibition, Chandler accuses him of being an art lover. 'Is that supposed to be an insult?' Ross asks. 'I don't know,' Chandler mumbles, 'I'm very tired.' Later, Monica meets him in the casino hall as he is carrying his bag out of the building. She persuades him to stay, then takes the bag and notices that it's empty. 'I wanted to make a dramatic scene,' he explains, 'but I hate packing.' Monica won't get married without 'something old, something new, something borrowed and something blue'. He says he has a condom that he's owned since he was 12 – that's old. ('That'll work,' says Monica, and he replies, 'I don't think so.') He solves the borrowed, new and blue things in one fell swoop, by getting Monica to shoplift a brand new blue sweater. He tries to sing the Wedding March to Monica, but can only remember the American graduation song.

Freaky Monica: Monica feels that her and Chandler's anniversary justifies dreaming up cheesy names for the celebration, such as 'plane-iversary', 'Anni-Vegas-ry', and 'An-Nevada-versary'. When Chandler proposes marriage at the craps table, the other patrons whoop with excitement. 'Shut up!' she yells, holding out her arms to – very effectively – silence them. 'This just got interesting.'

Poor Ross: As he watches Rachel dance naked round her apartment, he begins to think that maybe she is enticing him over the road for sex. 'Oh, Dr Geller! Stop it!' he thinks to himself. When he goes over, he shames himself totally by kicking off his shoes and informing Rachel, 'This is just about tonight. I don't want to go through with this if it raises the question of us.'

The Story So Far: Monica's ex, Richard, is mentioned, as is the one-time relationship between Ross and Rachel. Ross reveals that his grandma was a whizz on the slot machines. 'That's how she paid for my dance . . . karate lessons.' 'Dance karate?' asks Phoebe. He explains that 'It's a deadly, but beautiful, sport.'

Generation X: There are name checks for American fitness guru Richard Simmons and actor and quiz show host Richard Dawson. Rachel, while naked, sings Donna Summer's 1976 number four hit 'Love to Love You, Baby'. We also hear 'It's Not Unusual' by Tom Jones, 'Danke Schön', as sung by Vegas showstopper Wayne Newton, 'Everybody Loves Somebody' by Dean Martin, 'Viva, Las Vegas!' by Elvis Presley and Henry Mancini's theme from the *Pink Panther* movies. Phoebe thinks her slot machine rival might be one of the 'Mole People', a possible reference to the villains faced by The Fantastic Four in the first issue of their Marvel Comics series.

The Last Word: Though this hour-long special was made as two separate episodes, we've taken the decision of lumping them together as one, because that's how it was broadcast and billed in the listings magazines, which makes for a bumper entry here. Ross and Rachel steal this episode with their brilliant battle on the plane, each trying to embarrass the other (Rachel tipping the water into Ross's lap is probably the finest moment). While the argument between Monica and Chandler is engaging, it's really the good old Ballad of Ross & Rachel that we care about here for the first time in a long while. It's so nice to go back to caring about both these characters, instead of wishing they'd just grow up.

Just like last year's name mix-up, this year's cliffhanger is wedding-based and guaranteed to raise a gasp of utter surprise. While we're just beginning to think that the end of the season is going to focus on Chandler and Monica appearing to get marriage fever, enter Ross and Rachel with the biggest shock imaginable. Joey's meandering story about his 'hand twin' is just nonsense and while Phoebe similarly potters through the episode at least her rivalry with the old woman is thoroughly entertaining. But, like all the very best episodes of *Friends*, it's the romances that really grab our attention. And just *how* will Ross get out of this? Well, maybe he won't . . .

Sixth Season

1999–2000

23 Episodes

601

'The One After Vegas'

Writer: Adam Chase
Director: Kevin S. Bright
First US transmission: 23.09.99
First UK transmission (Sky One): 13.01.00

Guest Cast: Bill Stevenson (Rick), Nina Mann (The Attendant),
Rick Pasqualone (The Croupier)

Summary: Ross and Rachel wake up in bed together after their wild, drunken night. Neither seems able to remember how they got there, but both insist that nothing could have happened. It's only later, when their friends remind them, that they realise that, in a drunken stupor, they got married. Ross suggests they simply get an annulment, until Phoebe points out that this will be his third failed marriage. Ross tells Rachel he doesn't want to get the marriage annulled, leaving Rachel furious.

Having finally been told that the movie he'd been working on has been cancelled, Joey decides to go back home, forgetting that he'd borrowed Phoebe's cab to get to Las Vegas in the first place. Unwilling to drive back on his own, Joey convinces Phoebe to travel back with him, but Phoebe finds that this is just an excuse to get her to drive the car all the way while Joey sleeps.

Monica and Chandler separately realise that they're not ready for marriage, but can't find the right time to tell each other how they feel for fear of appearing as if they're not still in love. Back home, Chandler comes up with the perfect compromise . . .

Poor Ross: We can perfectly understand Ross's dilemma, even if we can't condone his actions. As Phoebe rather tactlessly puts it: 'You love divorce so much you're probably gonna marry it! Then it won't work out, so you're gonna have to divorce it, divorcing guy.' No-one wants to be a three-time divorcé (or even 'two-times-divorced-and-an-annulment'), but his behaviour towards Rachel is nothing short of childish. There have been many times when it's been difficult to distinguish who's actually being the more selfish between these two, but in this instance it couldn't be more clear-cut.

Slow Joey: Sitting impatiently at the breakfast table, Joey moans to Chandler that he's been waiting ages for a waitress to take his order. Chandler points out that the breakfast is buffet service. Joey takes this as a sign to 'win back' the money he lost by eating his way through the buffet. When Chandler reveals to Joey his insecurities about getting married, Joey advises him to just 'Tell her she's not marriage material,' as that's what most girls have said to him in the past. And when Ross suggests that he and Rachel get an annulment, Joey is concerned: 'Ross! I don't think surgery's the answer here.' However, it's Joey who points out the obvious to the newly-weds, who are shocked that they were allowed to get married when they were so drunk: 'Most people who get married in Vegas are drunk!'

Phoebisms: Phoebs seems more than a little concerned to discover that a Las Vegas marriage certificate is valid everywhere, not just in Vegas itself as she'd previously believed. Watch Lisa Kudrow's performance as the drunken Phoebe – a real scene-stealing moment!

Spoilt Rachel: Despite the stupidity of Ross's suggestion, Rachel does at least consider it for a second when he suggests that if they stay married she could keep all the wedding presents. When she finally convinces Ross that they can't stay married, she asks him in all seriousness, 'Is there any such thing as an annulment shower?' Good one.

Generation X: The music we hear as Joey drives the cab is Bernard Herrmann's haunting theme from *Taxi Driver* (Martin

Scorsese, 1976). Before he falls asleep again, we hear Joey sing an excerpt from 'I Wanna Rock And Roll All Night' by Kiss, and later he tries to woo Phoebe with his rendition of David Bowie's 'Space Oddity'. In the credits, all the regular cast-members are credited with the additional name of 'Arquette' in reference to Courteney Cox's recent marriage to actor David Arquette (who played Ursula's stalker in 'TOW The Jam').

The Story So Far: As Phoebe and Joey play a round of 'Twenty Questions', Phoebe guesses instantly that Joey is thinking of a meatball sub sandwich; as we know by now, Joey's favourite food is sandwiches, by a mile. When Monica symbolically gives Chandler a key to the apartment, Chandler notes that the door to the apartment hasn't been locked in five years [she learned her lesson after 'TOW Underdog Gets Away'].

The Last Word: 'This is not a marriage!! This is the world's worst hangover!' Once again the difference between all the potential couples on the show is underlined. Joey and Phoebe pair off once more, though other episodes make more of this. With their insecurities and obsessions, Chandler and Monica are bound to be forever trying to second-guess each other, but the fact that they love each other, understand each other and care about each other's feelings goes some way to prove that they're clearly perfect for each other. Much of the visual comedy in this episode comes from the way they instinctively behave like they're the newlyweds, including Chandler carrying Monica over the threshold and Rachel throwing a bouquet that automatically lands in Monica's hands.

Conversely, Rachel and Ross seem destined to be forever moving in opposite directions, despite the cards that fate is dealing them. Ross's reaction is predictable, but one can't help wondering just how far the writers will go before we all tire of Ross's self-centred, clinical logic trampling over the feelings of the very people he claims to love the most. Listen to the audience's reaction when Chandler asks Monica to live with him; their clear excitement at this development should tell the writers that we're most happy with *Friends* when the characters fight against the world, not against each other.

602
'The One Where Ross Hugs Rachel'

Writer: Shana Goldberg-Meehan
Director: Gail Mancuso
First US transmission: 30.09.99
First UK transmission (Sky One): 20.01.00

Guest Cast: Ross Glass (Russell, Ross's lawyer),
Alex Kapp Horner (Stephanie), Tembi Locke (Karin),
Janelle Paradee (Meg)

Summary: Ross confides in Phoebe that he lied to Rachel about getting the annulment. Phoebe is furious, but as she feels she's special being the only other person who knows about the deception, she agrees not to break his confidence. She does, however, vow to break Ross's fear of being forever tarnished as the 'Three Divorces' guy. Spotting three women sitting in Central Perk, she drags Ross over and asks them if Ross's failed marriage ratio might put them off seeing him as a potential date. To Ross's disbelief, they all agree that the divorce issue wouldn't be a problem, but that the fact that he is so obviously in love with Rachel might.

Chandler and Monica worry about how to break the news about them moving in together to their respective flatmates. Joey takes the news very badly, and it takes a great deal of effort on Chandler's part to convince his best friend that things will still be the same. Rachel, on the other hand is overjoyed. It seems she hasn't realised that when Monica said that Chandler would be moving in, she meant that Rachel would have to move out. Monica finally tells Rachel the truth and is horrified by how easily Rachel takes the news. Eventually, Monica confronts her, and learns that Rachel is having no difficulty with this development simply because she doesn't actually believe it's going to happen. But when she realises how serious Chandler and Monica are, Rachel is distraught.

Phoebisms: Trying to reassure Ross that his tombstone won't label him as being the guy with three divorces, Phoebs tell him that she intends her epitaph to read: 'Phoebe Buffay. Buried Alive.' Note how, being a good feminist, she corrects herself,

having used the word 'girl': '*Woman*, sorry'. When Joey speculates that maybe he and Phoebe should 'hook up', she
reassures him by saying that they will . . . after Chandler and
Monica get married, become filthy rich and then split up,
Phoebs marries Chandler for the money, Joey marries Rachel
and they have beautiful kids, at which point Phoebe and Joey
will ditch their partners and get married. That way they get all
of Chandler's money *and* Rachel's kids (thanks to Rachel's
drinking problem). Phoebe won't elaborate regarding Ross's
future beyond 'we have words and I kill him'. Harsh, but it
could be fun.

Poor Ross: The thought of having yet another marriage under
his belt begins to push Ross further over the edge (and you
thought he was bad last year!). After one of the women at the
coffee shop suggests that maybe he still has feelings for
Rachel, he flips out: 'This is crazy! I mean, yes . . . yes, Rachel
is my good friend and I . . . I have loved her in the past. But
now she is just my wife!' Yeah, that'll convince them. Even
his divorce lawyer thinks he should undergo therapy. As he
tries to muster the courage to confess to Rachel that he still
hasn't got the annulment, he asks his friends to tell her some
bad news so his doesn't sound so bad.

Chandleresque: Trying to calm an emotional Joey, Chandler
(perhaps unwisely, considering his proximity to Monica) says:
'I promise you, the minute Monica and I break up I'm moving
right back in with you!'

Spoilt Rachel: Some people face life-threatening illnesses,
some (mentioning no names) are onto their third divorce, but
for Rachel, her 'worst day ever' seems to come about simply
because her boss at work gets her name wrong. She has no idea
how bad her day might have been if Ross hadn't been such a
wimp and actually got the annulment as he'd promised.

Freaky Monica: When Rachel becomes the third person to
mistakenly guess that Monica is trying to tell her she's pregnant, Monica declares: 'No, but I'm throwing this shirt away!'

Just Plain Weird: As Ross freaks out at the women in Central
Perk, one of the women comments how she wouldn't date him
because he seems a little creepy, but one of her friends can't
help confessing: 'I am so attracted to him right now.' Having

said that, she previously admitted that she has a history of fancying the wrong guys.

Magna-Doodle: Someone has scrawled a tropical island on the guys' message-board-cum-art-gallery.

Generation X: Rachel and Monica sing a few lines from the theme tune to *Three's Company* (and if you need that reference explaining you obviously haven't been reading this book in the right order).

The Story So Far: Chandler tells Monica that Joey never allowed him to have a gumball in the apartment: 'When it comes to sweets, he's surprisingly strict.' Ross has, we learn, used the same divorce lawyer the previous two times, which, Chandler notes, must surely qualify him for a discount this time round.

The Last Word: With Ross slowly becoming even more unbearable, Rachel facing the prospect of moving home for only the second time in her life and Chandler and Monica moving in together, the series format does seem to be drifting slowly away from the light and fluffy *Friends* of Series One. Certainly, it's hard to equate the monster in this episode with the shy, shell-shocked and loveable Ross who won us all over in 'TOW Rachel Finds Out'. Especially with what Rachel's about to find out here. Is Ross right? Is this all 'Nevada's fault'? Well if you can't wait to find out, flick forward a few pages.

603
'The One With Ross's Denial'

Writer: Seth Kurland
Director: Gary Halvorson
First US transmission: 07.10.99
First UK transmission (Sky One): 27.01.00

Guest Cast: James Michael Tyler (Gunther),
Brooke Boisse (The Potential Roommate)

Summary: Rachel accepts that if she's going to move out she'll need somewhere to live. She asks Phoebe if she can move in with her, but Phoebe shocks her (and everyone else) by claiming that she has no room, due to the existence of the hitherto unmentioned 'Denise'. Joey offers to help Rachel, but it's clear to her that it's all just a ploy on Joey's part to see her naked. Ross gives Rachel a contact number for one of his colleagues whose apartment has just become available, but when this falls through, he offers Rachel his spare room. This, of course, does little to dissuade Phoebe from her belief that Ross is still in love with Rachel, as does the news that he still hasn't told her they're married.

Chandler and Monica debate what to do with Rachel's room when it becomes spare. Both have very fixed ideas on what they'd like to do with it, but somehow Monica cannot incorporate Chandler's dreams of a games room (complete with an original Space Invaders arcade machine) with her ideal guestroom. Soon their debate develops into a full-blown argument. Maybe Rachel won't have to move after all . . .

Phoebisms: Phoebe tells Ross that apparently, ninety per cent of a women's pheromones come out the top of her head, which is why women are shorter than men – so that men can smell their hair and fall in love with them. Now we don't know if that's true, as we're not scientists, but it certainly sounds true enough to confound Ross. Passing over the revelation about her roommate Denise for a second, watch how Phoebe tries repeatedly to steal Ross's cookie and his coffee as she tries to convince him he's still in love with Rachel. She eventually makes a grab for his magazine, clearly using it as a decoy so she can get both the cookie and the drink. When she claims she's trying to move a pencil through sheer willpower, and Rachel just hands it to her, the joy with which Phoebe cheers 'It worked!' is matched only by the wry smile that Rachel gives, as she realises that, sometimes, it's worth knowing Phoebe just for moments like this. As if she couldn't get any better, Phoebs sings a gross song about how she discovered a 'Little black curly hair' in her bed, and then suggests that if the patrons at Central Perk want to receive e-mails about her upcoming shows, then they should give her money so she can afford to buy a computer. Genius!

Scary Ross: Explaining to Phoebe how he just happened to notice that Rachel's hair smelled of coconut when he hugged her, Ross insists that this does not mean he still loves her, 'Maybe it means I have feelings for coconuts!' he cries, exasperated. After he learns that Chandler and Monica might not be moving in together after all, he takes a greater than normal interest in their life just so Rachel will move in with him. But when he suddenly realises that living with Rachel will be a big mistake he completely flips out, screaming at Chandler and Monica: 'DON'T DO IT!!!' As Chandler notes: it's enough to put you off ever wanting share with Ross, at least.

Slow Joey: Joey tells Chandler that he's just missed a phone call. When Chandler asks who it was from, Joey replies, impatiently, 'I don't know! How about, "Thanks for taking the message." Jeez!' before storming out. His roommate requirements, as listed in his ad are perfect Joey: 'Wanted: Female roommate, non-smoker, non-ugly.' This is, however, nothing compared to his interview technique for the prospective roommate. Having successfully made it to a second interview, the poor woman gets rejected because, in Joey's 'Word Association Game' she links 'Doggy' to 'Kitten' instead of . . . well instead of something else.

Freaky Monica: As part of her pitch to Chandler for her dream guest room, she suggests they could display some comment cards for people to write messages saying how much they enjoyed staying there. Seeing Chandler's look of amazement, she claims not to have thought much about the idea, though we just know she's dreamed of this since she was a child.

Chandleresque: Defending his desire for an arcade machine in Monica's collection of antiques, Chandler claims: '[This] is why Asteroids is perfect! It's the oldest game!' When he sees how Monica has marked out a space for his reclining chair, Chandler cries, in mock horror: 'Oh my God! Someone's killed Square Man!'

Dinosaurs ROCK!: After telling Rachel about the potentially vacant apartment of his work colleague, Ross tells her, 'Don't thank me! If you want to thank something, thank the volcano that erupted thousands of years ago, killing but perfectly preserving an entire civilisation.' Even in a situation like this, Ross just can't help himself.

Gunther's There For You, Rachel: Hearing that Rachel might be on the move, the platinum-haired one offers Rachel his place. When Rach asks him where he's moving to, Gunther can only reply with a lame, 'I don't know'.

Generation X: Both Space Invaders and Asteroids have recently been updated for a new generation, but they have little of the charm of the original arcade smashes.

The Story So Far: We hesitated to include this, but apparently Phoebe had a roommate called Denise, though as she has never been heard of before, and she's unlikely to be heard of again, we suspect she's a figment of Phoebe's overactive imagination. Ross mentions a work colleague called Warren, but as he's going on a dig for two years, we probably shouldn't mention him either.

The Last Word: He's predictable, but Joey's persistence is his charm. Maybe one day, Rachel will succumb to him and he'll finally see her naked. Somehow we doubt it, though. Ross is equally eager to get Rachel to live with him, though it's not altogether clear why. Has Ross officially lost it, making decisions that he subconsciously knows are bad for him?

604

'The One Where Joey Loses His Insurance'

Writers: Andrew Reich & Ted Cohen
Director: Gary Halvorson
First US transmission: 14.10.99
First UK transmission (Sky One): 03.02.00

Guest Cast: June Gable (Estelle), Ron Glass (Russell),
Christopher Darga (The Director), Kim Harris (Casting Director #1),
Joe Everett Michaels (Casting Director #3), Rick Fitts (The Professor),
Ian Meltzer (Alex), Michael Naughton (The Student),
Matt Bellner (The Crew Member)

Summary: Ross gets a trial post as a lecturer at New York University (NYU). He practices his first speech on his friends but suffers their usual derision and lack of interest which only helps to make him more nervous. Monica and Rachel decide to sneak in to his lecture only to discover that he's taken to using a fake English accent to hide his nerves.

Back at Monica and Rachel's, Rachel is packing for her big move. Monica notices that some of her possessions are 'mysteriously' appearing in Rachel's boxes. When she confronts her roommate, Rachel merely claims the things were hers, causing the girls to fall out. Just as the girls reach a compromise, Rachel gets a call from Ross's lawyer, who tells her that as Ross hasn't come back to him regarding the divorce he's assumed they've decided to make a go of the relationship. A furious Rachel goes to see her "husband" at work . . . right in the middle of a lecture!

Scary Ross: Trying to diffuse Phoebe's insistence that he's still in love with Rachel, Ross turns it back on her and accuses Phoebe of having lustful thoughts about her: 'You're obsessed with her! It's always, "Ross, what are you gonna do about Rachel?" "Ross, why are you moving in with Rachel?" "When are you gonna confess your secret marriage to Rachel?" You want her!' Evidence, if it were needed, that Ross has never really recovered from his ex-wife leaving him for another woman. Fortunately Ross's new job is a much greater success, thanks largely to his fake accent. Strangely, since the collapse of his marriage to Emily, Ross seems unable to let go of her Britishness – hence the accent popping up throughout this episode, usually when he feels under great stress.

Phoebisms: Phoebs once again steals the opening scene by casually blurting out that Ross and Rachel are still married. Once she's certain she's given Rachel the ultimate fright, she tells her she's 'just kidding', much to Rachel's relief. As she passes a stunned Ross, Phoebe mutters 'Saved *your* ass.' Smart!

Joey's An Actor!: When the Screen Actor's Guild notifies Joey that his health insurance has lapsed due to his lack of work, he realises he must get some more auditions. Enter his agent – the glorious Estelle – who, it is revealed, has been bad-mouthing Joey because she thought he'd left her agency. Quickly doing some damage-limitation, Estelle gets Joey a load of auditions just as – surprise, surprise – he injures himself lifting weights. Some might think having a hernia is a hindrance to selling dog food or breakfast cereal, but not Joey. Fortunately Joey lands the role of a dying man and puts his hernia to good use by frightening his on-screen son and making him cry (after 37 takes!).

Dinosaurs ROCK!: Ross tries out his speech on sedimentary rock formations on his friends (prompting Phoebe to guess that the speech will kill her).

Just Plain Weird: A psychic tells Phoebe that she'll be dead by the end of the week and Phoebe believes her as she previously predicted that she would have triplets (although she *did* say that one of them would be black). Strangely enough, though, it's the psychic who ends up dead. Maybe she had the cards upside down.

Magna-Doodle: Another aquatic one – two fish swimming about happily.

Generation X: One of the products Joey is asked to advertise is 'Purina One Dog Chow', a real product and an outrageous example of product placement!

The Story So Far: Rachel attended NYU (see 'TOW The Fake Monica') where she was in the 'Kappa Kappa Delta' sorority.

The Last Word: OK, so it's really predictable that Joey will fall ill just as his health insurance expires, but it's worth it, if only because it gives us another chance to see Estelle (who really should be in it more often). Joey's auditions have traditionally been a source of great merriment, but his seedy 'Hey, Timmy, I've got a surprise for you' comes close to topping the 'Holden McGroin' scene from Season One. Just as it looks like Joey's hilarious gurning and groaning are going to steal the episode, Ross runs away with it with his superb 'Hallo Raychall!' Ross calls his newly acquired fake accent British, but we'd call it more Australian – God knows what the Australians would call it ('Crap', probably). Thankfully Rachel's fake Indian accent is a real treat!

605

'The One With Joey's Porsche'

Writers: Perry Rein & Gigi McCreery
Director: Gary Halvorson
First US transmission: 21.10.99
First UK transmission (Sky One): 10.02.00

Guest Cast: Conchata Ferrel (The Judge), James Michael Tyler (Gunther),
Kevin Ruf (The Porsche Owner), Charity Nicole James (The Woman),
Shane Nickerson (Guy #1), Dennis Singletary (Guy #2),
Steve Pierce (The Passerby)

Summary: After Rachel discovers that Ross didn't get their
marriage annulled, she refuses to take any more of his moaning
and arranges for them to have an annulment. But when their
meeting with the judge breaks into another of their customary
rows, the bickering newlyweds are told that getting a divorce is
the only way they'll ever undo the mess they're in. Ross concedes defeat and picks up the divorce papers. But once they're
signed, Rachel reveals that she has something Ross needs to
know – she's remembered that getting married was, in fact,
her idea!

Joey finds a set of keys for a Porsche. When he locates the
car they match, he can't help but pretend that the Porsche actually belongs to him – even when the car's owner finally turns
up. Unable to give up the dream, Joey buys himself a
whole Porsche-branded outfit. Meanwhile, Phoebe persuades
Chandler and Monica to help her baby-sit for Frank and Alice.
But when Chandler foolishly swallows a toy gun (!), Phoebe is
left to care for the infants alone. Things are going well for a
while. That is, until they begin to play 'hide-and-seek' with
her . . .

Chandleresque: As Chandler's said before, it's all a matter of
timing. As Ross tries to explain his actions by repeating how
he wanted to avoid a third failed marriage, Chandler asks
incredulously, 'At what point did you think this was a *successful* marriage?' before checking, 'just for my own piece of
mind, you're not married to any more of us are you?'

Freaky Monica: When she lets slip that she has a whole cupboard full of car-cleaning equipment, Monica confesses that

she once saw a really dirty car outside her apartment and felt compelled to clean it. And six others.

Phoebisms: When she tells Rachel that her roommate isn't expected back until 26 December, Rachel jokes that maybe Denise is in fact Santa Claus. Phoebs laughs along, but then comes to the startling realisation that Rachel might be right. As Monica, Chandler and Phoebs change the babies' nappies, each doing a different job, Monica jokes that this is how they set the plates at the restaurant; Phoebe looks at 'her' baby and says, 'Well this is not what I ordered.' As baby Leslie plays, Monica wonders aloud at what age it is babies stop being able to get their legs behind their head. When Phoebe boasts that she still can, Monica asks her why she's still single.

Gunther Drives: When Joey asks Gunther if the Porsche keys belong to him, Gunther deadpans: 'Yeah, that's what I drive. I make four bucks an hour; I saved up for 350 years.' Sharp.

The Ballad of Ross & Rachel: So now Rachel knows – she's still married to Ross. Ross claims he would have told her some time – 'When?' asks Rachel, 'after the birth of our first secret child?!' Rachel's retribution is astounding; when she and Ross seek an annulment from the judge, Rachel claims their marriage is unconsummated, due to Ross being mentally unstable, an intravenous drug-user and, er, gay. This might have worked, had Ross not let pride get in the way and blurt out that not only is he none of these things, but that their former relationship was indeed consummated – 'like bunnies'. After Ross's outburst, the judge is, not surprisingly, unwilling to grant them an annulment, leaving divorce the only alternative. Once Ross has picked up the divorce papers, however, Rachel confesses that she has been able to piece together the events of 'that night' and has remembered that this whole mess is probably her fault. Ross thought it would be funny to eat lots of grapes, while Rachel thought it would be funnier if they got married. They compromised – they got married and *then* ate lots of grapes. Considering the circumstances, Ross is remarkably calm about it all, revealing a sensitive side that hasn't been seen for far too long.

The Story So Far: This story carries on where the last episode left off (so how come everyone at Monica's has had time to change?). Phoebe claims that her (imaginary) roommate has left town, so Rachel moves in. Ross tactlessly reminds Rachel about the time(s) he said 'We were on a break' ('TO The Morning After' and many others), the time she flew to London to break up his wedding ('TOW The Wedding') and the time she confessed her love for him after he was already married ('TO After Ross Says "Rachel" '). Going on an aside Chandler makes, we can assume there was a Coach Ruben at his High School. Ross and Rachel spent their drunken wedding night at Pizza Hut enjoying their free 'Newlywed Special' (not the first time Ross has celebrated a wedding at that fine establishment – see 'TOW The Worst Best Man Ever').

The Last Word: 'I know I divorce a lot of women . . . never thought I would be divorcing you.' This is one storyline we're all probably glad to see the back of. Though we all pictured Ross and Rachel one day being married, this was not how any of us imagined it would be. Strangely, this is, perhaps, the perfect outcome, with Ross being supportive and forgiving of Rachel, even though he can't resist pointing out that it's all her fault ('Don't push it!' she warns). It's been very easy to knock Ross, over the last year or so, but here he almost makes up for it. And Rachel could so easily have kept quiet and no-one would have ever known how culpable she is. Bravo, both of you.

Joey's plot, however, is clearly designed to give the poor lug something to do. Matt Le Blanc tries his best, but even he can't raise our interest in this silliness.

606
'The One The Last Night'

Writer: Scott Silveri
Director: David Schwimmer
First US transmission: 04.11.99
First UK transmission (Sky One): 17.02.00

Summary: It's time for Rachel to move out of Monica's and for Joey to face the responsibility of paying the bills alone. Realising that his unemployed friend might find the transition difficult, Chandler offers to loan Joey some money to cover the first few bills. Joey refuses, insisting that he will never take charity, so Chandler is forced to devise other ways to give him money. First he plays Joey at foosball, but thanks to a fluke shot, Chandler ends up winning. Then he challenges Joey to a game of Blackjack, but Joey claims it's 'not his game'. Chandler finally finds inspiration to create an entirely made-up game, which he calls 'Cups', which is designed to ensure Joey can win enough money for at least the first few months' bills. Unfortunately, Joey is so excited at his 'beginner's luck' with 'Cups' that he challenges Ross to a game . . . and loses all his money. In desperation, Chandler gives Joey $1,500 in exchange for his giant porcelain dog before heading off to get his money back from Ross.

Despite the fact that she's supposed to be moving, Rachel hasn't even begun to clear her bedroom yet. Tricking Monica into helping her is fairly easy, but coping with the realisation that this marks the end of an era isn't and soon the girls are in floods of tears. Phoebe tries to cheer them up by asking them to think of things they won't miss about each other, but of course, this just escalates into a vicious row about how much the girls hate each other. In exasperation, Phoebe announces that she doesn't want Rachel to move in with her, as she doesn't want to hate her the way Monica obviously does. Monica finds herself defending Rachel to ensure she has somewhere to move to, only to realise that she will miss her after all.

Slow Joey: On being shown their monthly phone bill, Joey shrieks. Chandler points out that the number he was balking at is just their phone number.

Chandleresque: When Joey loses the foosball match, kicks the table in frustration and breaks it, Chandler notes wryly that 'that's why only the little fake men are supposed to do all the kicking'.

Phoebisms: When Phoebe announces that it's her birthday, Monica corrects her. 'What a mean thing to say!' cries the clearly confused Phoebe. 'I would *never* tell you it's not *your* birthday!'

Poor Ross: Trying to get out of helping Monica pack Rachel's things, Ross tells her he is looking after Ben. When she reminds him that she can see right into his apartment and so will know if he's lying, Ross acts appalled: 'Do you think I'd just use my son as an excuse? What kind of father do you think I am?' Presumably the kind of father who makes a fake son out of a pumpkin and then doesn't notice that its 'head' has fallen off.

Spoilt Rachel & Freaky Monica: When Monica discovers that Rachel hasn't even begun to pack the contents of her room, Rachel manages to diffuse the situation with some amazingly quick thinking; telling her that she knows how good Monica is at packing and thought she might enjoy it. Monica is, of course, overjoyed at Rachel's thoughtfulness, even down to apologising for not getting her anything in return, and promptly gets stuck in. Good one, Rach!

Thanks to Phoebe's suggestion that they should think of things they dislike about each other to make the parting less painful, Monica claims that Rachel moves the 'phone pen' and never passes on any telephone messages. In retaliation, Rachel asks her who she ever missed a message from, pointing out that she only ever gets calls from her Mum and Chandler before mentioning that Monica's obsessive-compulsive cleaning drives her to clean the toilet 'seventeen times a day . . . even if people are on it!' This is the catalyst for another marvellous bitching session: Imitating Rachel, Monica asks if her sweater is too tight: ' "No?",' she cries in mock-surprise. ' "Oh, I'd better wash it and shrink it!".' Then, underpinning the central thread running through the entire history of the programme, Monica crows: ' "Oh my God, I love Ross! I hate Ross! I love Ross! I hate Ross!" ' Not to be out-done, Rachel replies with a vicious jibe at Monica's inability to find a boy-friend: ' "I guess I'll just stumble across the hall and sleep with the first guy I find in there!" ' This is, evidently, going too far and Monica storms out. Rachel may have won the battle, but considering she's about to move out it's an empty victory. Phoebe convinces Monica to apologise, but when she discovers that Rachel has decided not to move it's gloves off again. Get out Phoebe, while you still can!

Generation X: The director of this episode is a newcomer called David Schwimmer. We think he made an encouraging

debut, though we'd hate him to give up his day job (and for
those that still haven't worked it out, it is *that* David
Schwimmer).

The Story So Far: We learn here that Ross has often claimed
that he gave up a career as a professional basketball player to
become a palaeontologist. Rachel finds a pair of roller-blades
on top of her wardrobe that Monica doesn't recognise, so presumably they aren't the same pair Monica had to wear at the
Moondance Diner (see 'TOW The Chick. And A Duck').

The Last Word: So finally it happens; Rachel leaves Monica's
place to start anew . . . with Phoebe. Some might question the
purpose behind moving Rachel out – after all, that now means
that half the regular cast now live apart from the other half.
Time will tell if the move was a wise one, but it at least gives
us a sweet, emotional episode that allows everyone to shine
except Ross (who's hiding from Monica at his apartment).

607
'The One Where Phoebe Runs'

Writers: Conchata Sherry Bilsing-Graham & Ellen Plummer
Director: Gary Halvorson
First US transmission: 11.11.99
First UK transmission (Sky One): 24.02.00

Guest Cast – Introducing: Elle MacPherson (Janine LaCroix)

Summary: New roommates Phoebe and Rachel are settling
into their new life together. Rachel invites Phoebe to come
jogging through Central Park with her, but is shocked to discover that Phoebe runs like a Muppet. Making excuses that
she's hurt her ankle and can't jog with Phoebs any more,
Rachel secretly continues to jog alone – until Phoebe catches
her. Rachel is forced to confess that she finds her friend's style
of running too embarrassing. Phoebe explains that she just runs
like that because it's more fun that way. Rachel isn't convinced until, some time later, she tries Phoebe's way and discovers just what Phoebe meant.

Joey has finally got a new roommate, Janine, though the fact
that she's an extremely beautiful dancer leads his friends to

suspect that he hasn't exactly been strict in his vetting process. Joey confesses that he can't wait to start dating her until Monica spells out to him just how complicated that might make things. Joey suddenly becomes terrified that his natural sexual magnetism might ruin things with Janine.

Having finished unpacking all of his things, Chandler makes the biggest mistake of his life – he tries to clean Monica's apartment, not realising just how impossible it will be to put everything exactly where it was. When it finally dawns on him just how impossible this is, he begins to prepare himself for Monica's wrath . . .

Poor Ross: Ever the geek, Ross bores everyone with his story about a book he's been reading in which it's theorised that by the year 2030, there'll be computers that will be as capable as a human brain, enabling people to download their memories and the . . . *zzzzzzzz* . . . Yeah, Ross. Right.

Freaky Monica: When Rachel describes Phoebe's running as a cross between The Six Million Dollar Man and Kermit the Frog, Ross tells her that Monica used to have such a crush on him and used to kiss his poster every night. Only after Rachel admits that she did that too does Monica reveal that her crush was on the frog, not the biomechanical super-hunk.

Phoebe: Phoebs continues her run of larceny by stealing the show once more. Summing up her attitude to life, she explains to Rachel the joys of just letting go and being more 'free': 'Didn't you ever run so fast you thought your legs were gonna fall off?' she asks, '. . . like when you were like running towards the swings or running away from Satan?' Seeing the confused look on Rachel's face, Phoebe explains that Satan was her neighbour's dog, though past experience tells us that she could so easily have meant the devil.

Generation X: Elle MacPherson – a.k.a. 'The Body' – is an international supermodel and actress who had small roles in, among a few others, *Sirens* (John Duigan, 1994) and *Batman & Robin* (Joel Schumacher, 1997). Rachel compares Phoebe's running to both *The Six Million Dollar Man* (who was always shown running in slow motion, apparently to accentuate his immense speed – go figure!) and Kermit the Frog, the most famous of Jim Henson's Muppet creations.

The Story So Far: Janine LaCroix is from Australia and she works as a dancer – none of which Joey asked her at the interview. Joey once dated a girl called Donna (not, we're guessing, the same Donna mentioned in 'TOW Chandler Can't Remember Which Sister'). Monica reveals that Chandler once had 'something' that required medicine – and we're glad she doesn't get the chance to explain what it was. Ross reminds us of all those photographs Monica has been taking in the last year (see 'TOW All The Resolutions').

The Last Word: Another good mix. Of note is the main storyline regarding Phoebe's running technique. Huge credit to Phoebe, who is much braver than us. We tried this, running through Regent's Park in London. Or at least, we *went* there, but then chickened out.

608

'The One With Ross's Teeth'

Writers: Andrew Reich & Ted Cohen (story),
Perry Rein & Gigi McCreery (teleplay)
Director: Gary Halvorson
First US transmission: 18.11.99
First UK transmission (Sky One): 02.03.00

Guest Cast: Joanna Gleason (Kim), Ralph Lauren (himself),
Elle MacPherson (Janine), Missi Pyle (Hillary)

Summary: Phoebe drops by at Rachel's office to use her company's photocopier. Returning the copy-card to Rachel, Phoebe tells her that she's just made out with Ralph Lauren himself. Rachel is shocked – but that doesn't stop her passing this information on as gossip to her boss, Kim, in a bid to make her like her. It works – Kim tells Rachel that it's the best gossip she's heard all year. But when Phoebe fails to recognise a photo of Ralph Lauren, and describes the guy she made out with, Rachel realises that it wasn't Ralph Lauren, but Kenny, 'The Copy Guy'. Worse, Kim has checked and only one copy card was used that day – Rachel's – and now Kim is convinced that not only has Rachel bedded Ralph Lauren but that she's trying to sleep her way to the top.

. . . and while Joey and Chandler try to avoid an inevitable slide towards the feminisation of their masculinity, Ross overdoses his teeth on a whitening gel that leave them unnaturally bright.

Chandleresque: Chandler calls round to Joey's and 'introduces' himself: 'I just moved in next door and I was wondering if you would be interested in battling me in a post-apoplectic world for control of the galaxy's last remaining energy source?' Only Chandler could reference a coffee ad and the plot of a million videogames in one go.

Poor Ross: When Ross asks his sister to set him up with her assistant chef at work, Rachel can't help but ask if the woman already has a wedding dress. When he shows his new glowing-white teeth to the gang, Chandler asks nervously: 'What was wrong with your old . . . *human* teeth?'

Slow Joey: Noting the many changes Janine has made to his apartment, Joey complains that when he goes to the bathroom 'My towel is not on the floor where I keep it. It's up here on some hook. And . . . smells different.' Janine explains why: 'It's *clean*.' 'Yeah,' continues Joey, 'well, it *feels* different.' 'It's *dry*,' counters Janine. He also reveals that he mistook Janine's potpourri for 'chips'. Euch.

Boys will be . . . Girls?: After insisting that flower-arranging, making potpourri and enjoying the look of nice pictures are too feminine, Chandler can't understand how he has hurt Joey's feelings. Joey tries to explain: 'It's not what you said. It's the way you said it . . .' before he realises what he's just said. 'Oh My God!' he cries in horror. 'I'm a woman!'

Generation X: One of the pictures Janine puts up in the apartment is by celebrated Australian photographer, Anne Geddes, who specialises in pictures of babies and cute children (check out her website at www.annegeddes.com). Native New Yorker Ralph Lauren has been one of the biggest names in fashion for over thirty years.

The Story So Far: Rachel reminds Phoebe that she changed jobs a year ago (see 'TOW Rachel's Inadvertent Kiss'), while Rachel's boss, Kim first appeared in 'TOW Rachel Smokes'. At her restaurant, Monica has an assistant chef called Hillary. Ross implies that Monica used to put make-up on him when he was 13 (but see 'TOW The Metaphorical Tunnel' for an alternative explanation). Ross tells his date that he came to New York for college and points out that Ben is now 5 years old.

The Last Word: It has to be said, Joey's discovery of the joys of potpourri ('like summer in a bowl!') is a joy to behold, as is Chandler's u-turn in helping Monica with her hemming, having just berated Joey for allowing Janine to feminise his life. But it's Ross's teeth that are bringing the biggest laughs here – Phoebe's terrified panic ('Demon!! DEMON!!') being just one of many hilarious reactions to yet another stupid decision by Ross. His attempts to conceal them from his date only help build up the tension until they are finally revealed in all their radioactive glory in her dark-lit living room. Horrifying! Meanwhile, Rachel's gossiping finally catches up with her and she's forced to do some quick thinking. It's a shame that Rachel can't work anywhere where the boss doesn't have a problem with her, but we think Kim is a fine replacement for her last boss, Joanna, and look forward to some more bitchy asides from her.

609
'The One Where Ross Got High'

Writer: Greg Malins
Director: Kevin S. Bright
First US transmission: 25.11.99
First UK transmission (Sky One): 09.03.00

Guest Cast: Elle MacPherson (Janine),
Elliott Gould (Jack Geller), Christina Pickles (Judy Geller)

Summary: Jack and Judy Geller are joining their daughter and her friends for Thanksgiving dinner. Chandler is excited by the prospect of them seeing him and Monica happy together, but Monica admits that they don't know he's moved in. She hasn't told them yet because, she confesses, they loathe him. Understandably upset by this news, Chandler endeavours to make a good impression with the Gellers. Despite being charming, trying to laugh at Jack Geller's lame jokes and generally sucking up to them as best he can, Chandler makes little headway – until he learns that way back in college Ross told his parents that Chandler smoked pot, which is why Mr and Mrs Geller hate him. He and Monica try to make Ross tell his parents the truth, but he's too distracted by the news that he and Joey have been invited to spend Thanksgiving drinking with Janine and her dancer friends. The guys are desperate to rush through their dinner and spend time with the hot babes. All they're waiting for is the dessert, a trifle made by Rachel from a traditional English recipe . . . or two.

Poor Ross: Proving here just why he is such a sad loser, Ross tries to think of whom he can blame his pot-smoking on, now that he's forced to confess to his parents that it wasn't Chandler as they'd previously believed. When Monica tells him to tell the truth, he asks her: 'Who should I say tricked me into doing it?' Such behaviour would be unforgivable, but it *was* Ross who asked everyone to pretend to enjoy Rachel's disastrous dessert to spare her feelings, thereby balancing things out a little.

Freaky Monica: Considering her tendencies to be a little 'control-obsessive', Monica shows remarkable trust and kindness in allowing Rachel to make the dessert and not prepare an alternative 'just in case'. However, when Rachel asks her how long it takes before the butter is done cooking, Monica tactfully tells her, 'It's done about two minutes before it looks like that.'

Phoebisms: OK, we know she's ditsy, we appreciate she can be a little weird at times, but how can she possibly see Jack Geller as a 'dream hunk'. However, she manages to get out of eating Rachel's dessert quite effectively when she points out that it contains meat, a no-no ingredient for a veggie like Phoebs.

(Not So) Slow Joey: When Rachel complains about the intense heat in Joey's apartment, Joey asks her if it made her want to walk around in her underwear. She replies with a shocked 'no!' prompting Joey to run back over there muttering, 'Still not hot enough.' He's not just a pretty face, eh?

Cool Britannia: Still punishing us for inflicting Emily on Ross, the writers have another pop at those strange British customs, in this case, the trifle (is that really so *exclusively* British?). Trying to get her head round the concept of putting beef and peas in a trifle (before the truth is revealed), Rachel muses that 'mincemeat pie' is an English dessert: 'these people just put very strange things in their food, y'know.' We suspect confusing 'minced meat' with the *mincemeat* (*fruit*) that goes into mince pies was a fatal flaw in her argument there.

Boys Will Be Boys: When Ross refers to Janine's friends as 'Sweet Potato Pie', Joey scolds him: 'Dude, they're not objects . . .' before adding 'Just kidding!'

Parents – Who Needs 'Em: Hearing a rapid succession of revelations slightly fazes Judy Geller, who rightly points out, 'That's a lot of information to get in in 30 seconds!' Still, it all helps to prove, to Judy and Jack at least, just how great a person Chandler really is, putting up with the lot of them.

The Ballad of Ross & Rachel: Dragging Rachel aside to let her know about her mistake with the trifle, Rachel misunderstands his hesitance and assumes he's going to ask if they can get back together again. She claims that she suspected this might happen, what with him being alone at the moment. Ross points out that she is also alone, but Rachel callously spells it out for him: 'I live with Phoebe. I mean you're *alone*, alone.' Ross, however, takes this development rather well, seeing it as just another piece of bad news he can get out of breaking that evening.

Generation X: Chandler mentions Sidney Poitier, star of *Guess Who's Coming To Dinner* (Stanley Kramer, 1967). The game that Ross and Joey are playing on Chandler's PlayStation is *Twisted Metal 2*. Jacques Cousteau, who Phoebe claims popped up in her dream, was an undersea explorer and TV presenter. He died in 1997.

The Story So Far: When Chandler claims he'll win Monica's parents over just like he won her over, she says, 'I don't think you'll ever get my parents that drunk' (see 'TOW The Wedding – Part 2'). Janine reveals that she can't cook. Monica's decision to allow Rachel to prepare the dessert without having a back-up plan is probably motivated by the events in 'TOW The 'Cuffs'. Chandler tells Jack Geller that his father stars in a gay burlesque show (first alluded to in

'TOW The Boobies'). Joey bemoans the single layer of jam in Rachel's weird trifle (see 'TOW The Jam'). And of course, we learn that during the spring break of his first year at college, Ross was caught smoking marijuana by his parents. He quickly blamed the smell on Chandler, claiming he had just jumped out of his window. Ever since, Jack and Judy have disliked Chandler. Monica also tells them that it was Ross who stole Jack's issues of *Playboy* and not the mailman that Jack got sacked. Monica broke their porch swing when she was still fat, and in all this we also learn that the Gellers had no idea that Ross lost his job at the museum a year ago (see 'TOW Everyone Finds Out') or that he married Rachel ('TO In Vegas', as if you need reminding of that) . . . and got divorced. Again.

The Last Word: 'This is great. Another Thanksgiving with nothing to give thanks for!' Like *The Simpsons* and their Halloween Specials, *Friends* always makes Thanksgiving something special and this is no exception. Obviously, being Thanksgiving, the plot must revolve around a food disaster and a revelation or two (or three). Rachel cooking more than toast is a novelty and it's a shame that two pages of the recipe book she's using have stuck together, as the trifle and the shepherd's pie both individually look stunning. Together, however . . . yuck! There's a nice run of excuses from everyone – except Joey – trying to get out of eating it. Chandler's decision to eat it on the balcony just as a bird apparently swooped down and stole it is perhaps the most far-fetched of the lot, while Monica's claim that she wants to 'eat it in the bathroom so she can look at it in the mirror' is the weakest. Fortunately, Joey is unperturbed: 'What's not to like? Custard? Good. Jam? Good. Meat? *Good*!' As for the revelations, well maybe it's a slight repeat of the exposition scenes in 'TOW Phoebe's Husband' and 'TOW Chandler in a Box' but as they're two of the best episodes ever, why not?

610

'The One With The Routine'

Writer: Brian Boyle
Director: Kevin S. Bright
First US transmission: 16.12.99
First UK transmission (Sky One): 16.03.00

Guest Cast: Elle MacPherson (Janine), Patrick Bristow (The Stage Manager),
Lex Medlin (The Tall Guy), James Michael Tyler (Gunther),
Sandra Plazinic (Dancer on Platform), Sybil Azur (The Dancing Girl)

Summary: Joey is finding it difficult living with Janine as he realises just how attracted to her he really is. So when Janine invites him to be her dance partner on a pre-recorded New Year's Eve TV Special, Joey takes this as a sign that he should ask her out. But Janine also invites Monica and Ross, which suggests that Janine didn't mean the invitation to be a romantic one. Monica and Ross are more excited by the prospect of achieving their lifelong dream, having been fans of the *Dick Clark New Year's Rockin' Eve* since they were children. But when they reach the set they are disappointed to find that the director is unwilling to allow them on camera. Meanwhile, Joey's attempts to get closer to Janine are thwarted when she is selected to dance with another guy. If he wants to be with Janine in time for the New Year countdown, he's gonna have to fight dirty . . . and if the Gellers want to be on TV, then maybe they'll have to resurrect their old High School dance routine!!

While Monica is out of the apartment, Chandler catches Phoebe and Rachel tearing her apartment apart looking for their Christmas presents. They explain to Chandler that they need to know what scale of present Monica has got them so they can shop for something of a similar value. Chandler is initially appalled but is soon persuaded to lend a hand. They eventually find the presents. Can Chandler convince the girls not to open them before Monica gets back?

Freaky Monica: Ross's surprise at seeing Monica allow other people to decorate her Christmas tree is borne out when we see that she's only let them do the side that no-one will see – it's her perfectly decorated side that will be visible.

Poor Ross: Lecturing his friends, Ross compares the Christian festival Christmas to the Jewish Hanukkah, explaining that elements of the Jewish festival date back 4000 years, which, Rachel snipes, must have been around the same time that Ross started telling his story.

Chandleresque: Joey, describing his feelings for Janine, tells Chandler how he wants to 'feed her grapes and brush her hair'. Chandler asks him: 'You are aware that she's not a monkey, right?' When he learns that the girls have searched his old apartment for Monica's presents, Chandler becomes concerned that they might have found some stuff at the bottom of his wardrobe. Realising that his secret, whatever it might be, is out, Chandler clicks his fingers and cries, optimistically, 'That did not just happen!' Yeah, Chandler, that'll work.

Spoilt Rachel: As the Gellers geek out at the thought of dancing at the Dick Clark Special, Chandler asks Rachel why she's laughing. 'Well,' she says, pointing to Ross, 'I used to date him, but,' now pointing to Monica, 'you're still going out with her!'

Slow Joey: In all seriousness, he asks Ross when the New Year Special is due to air.

The Chick and the Duck: Phoebe tries to elicit help from the feathered friends to find Monica's gifts, but Chandler is scornful, saying it'll only work 'if the presents are hidden south for the winter'.

Generation X: The dreydel is a spinning top, a traditional gift for Jewish children during Hanukkah. Dick Clark is the TV king of seasonal specials, as mentioned in 'TOW The Monkey'. Patrick Bristow cameos in *Austin Powers: International Man of Mystery* (Jay Roach, 1997) as a tour guide, but is probably best known for playing Peter in the sitcom *Ellen*. Rachel calls Chandler 'Linus' in reference to Charlie Brown's oft-disappointed idealist friend from the 'Peanuts' comic strips. This reference is continued when, in the final scene, Monica boasts that she can catch Ross, only to dodge out of the way at the last minute, just like Lucy used to do to Charlie Brown. At the party, we hear Robbie Williams' version of 'I Wouldn't Normally Do This Kind of Thing', and the song playing while Ross and Monica do 'The Routine' is 'Trouble With Boys' by

Loreta (maybe this is why Ross gets so many strange looks!).
We also hear a version of the traditional New Year chorus,
Auld Lang Syne.

The Story So Far: Rachel tells everyone about the time back
in High School when Ross tried to kiss her, then claimed
he only did it because he needed chapstick. Monica has presumably used the same hiding place for her Christmas presents
since she first moved into the apartment (and no-one has ever
found them – until now).

The Last Word: All words fail us. Monica and Ross's performance must go down in history as one of the most glori-
ously awful dance routines ever – and we bet you've all tried
to copy it. That, Joey's water-fight solution to his problematic
love rival and the climactic kiss all add to a hugely enjoyable
show. A nice comment from Joey, too, as he returns from the
premature New Year's countdown ridiculing 'all that Y2K
panic'. OK, so he's two weeks early but didn't we all make the
same comment the morning after the real thing?

611
'The One With The Apothecary Table'

Writer: Brian Boyle
Director: Kevin S. Bright
First US transmission: 06.01.00
First UK transmission (Sky One): 23.03.00

Guest Cast: Elle MacPherson (Janine)

Summary: When Rachel buys an apothecary table from a
well-known chain store, Monica warns her that Phoebe won't
want it in her apartment. She explains that Phoebe hates
mass-produced furniture, preferring her possessions to be
unique and have a history to them. Rachel decides to tell
Phoebe a huge lie, creating a fictional history to make her table
appear to be one of a kind. Typically, Ross ruins everything
when he buys a table identical to Rachel's.

Though things seem to be going well with Janine, Joey is
shocked to learn she doesn't particularly like Chandler and

Monica. Trying to make them all get on, Joey only exacerbates the situation and Janine moves out.

Spoilt Rachel: The way Rachel manages to completely con Phoebe by playing on her lack of education is actually quite cruel, but it also goes to show that, despite her college education, she's still as ignorant as Phoebe in certain matters. When Phoebs asks her what period the table is from, Rachel claims, simply: '. . . it's from Yore. Like the days of Yore'. She then leads her to believe it's from a magical place called 'White Plains' (when in fact that's just where the store is located, 25 miles north of Manhattan). A large ornamental birdcage is passed off as having belonged to 'Early Colonial bird merchants'. Evidently, Rachel is only aware of a few time periods. In addition to 'Yore' and 'Colonial' she can only come up with 'Yesteryear', though that might say as much about American history in general as Rachel's knowledge of it.

Phoebisms: Despite the fact that Phoebe is famous for her strong principles, it's good to see more evidence to suggest that she's more flexible and forgiving than she lets on. In the past we've seen her eat meat, wear a fur coat, donate money to the one TV channel she hates, and now become as obsessed with high-quality mass-produced furniture as Rachel. Making it all seem Rachel's fault for blackmailing her is just the masterstroke though.

Slow Joey: When Rachel criticises a fruit bowl of Phoebe's, Joey is upset, claiming that he was the one who made it for her. But Chandler challenges him on this, and Joey explains that he 'made it' out of a fruit bowl he found in the garbage.

Dinosaurs ROCK!: Hoping to cheer Joey up, Ross invites him to watch a lecture he's giving on erosion theories. Amused by the concept of his attending one of his friend's boring lectures, Joey laughs out loud.

Generation X: Pottery Barn is a chain of stores in the USA, a little like IKEA in that they only sell furniture exclusive to their chain. You can probably work out the beginning of Chandler's joke about the cow, but if you need it explaining, there's a slightly more graphic version of it in the film *Kingpin* (Bobby & Peter Farrelly, 1996).

The Story So Far: Rachel has yet to notify the post office of her change of address, meaning she hasn't paid any of her bills since she moved out. Joey reminds Monica and Chandler about when they first got together and he helped them keep their relationship a secret. Monica learns that he only did that because Chandler paid him $200. Apparently this all lasted for six months.

The Last Word: As we all know, the relationships between the *Friends* regulars are superbly crafted. Monica's obsessive neatness contrasts with Rachel's laziness; Phoebe's weirdness and Joey's sexual confidence both play off Ross's attention to detail and Chandler's insecurity over relationships. Each of the characters oppose and complement any of the other characters in the set, so inevitably, any time a new character is brought in, they are doomed not to last. While it's nice to see Joey living with Janine, we're so used to this kind of character failing to go the distance by now (Paolo, Julie, Richard, Emily . . .) that it's hardly worth taking the time to get to know them. However, that doesn't mean that the writers shouldn't bother trying to give the character some personality anyway. Maybe this is down to MacPherson's inexperience or lack of range, but we doubt anyone was seriously expecting her character to be around for long.

612
'The One With The Joke'

Writers: Andrew Reich & Ted Cohen
Director: Gary Halvorson
First US transmission: 13.01.00
First UK transmission (Sky One): 30.03.00

Guest Cast: James Michael Tyler (Gunther), J. D. Lewis (Customer), Joeanna Sayler (Woman at the Table), Matthew Mullany (Patron)

Summary: Ross sends a joke to *Playboy* magazine and is thrilled when they print it. But when Chandler reads the joke he's a little annoyed, claiming that he made the joke up in the first place. The girls, meanwhile, become obsessed with jealousy when a flippant question reveals that, hypothetically, Phoebe would prefer to date Rachel than Monica. And, tired of being unable to pay his bills, Joey is forced to accept a less-than-glamorous job.

Poor Ross: Explaining to Phoebe why he was writing to *Playboy*, Ross tells her that 'they print jokes, interviews, hard-hitting journalism. It's not just about the pictures.' 'That didn't work on Mom,' interrupts Monica, 'it's not going to work on us.'

Chandleresque: When Chandler and Monica hear a noise coming from their living room, Chandler suggests it might be 'the sound of Ross climbing into my brain and stealing my thoughts.'

Freaky Monica: Trying to explain why she would pick Rachel instead of Monica, Phoebs tells the uptight friend that she considers Monica a little 'high maintenance'. Monica denies this and orders her to produce a list for her to go through 'point by point'.

Joey Was An Actor: Joey confesses to Monica that he feels embarrassed that he's had to take a job at Central Perk, 'I mean, I was an actor and now I'm a waiter. It's supposed to go in the other direction.'

Gunther Stalks!: Trying to bump up the benefits of working at Central Perk to Joey, Gunther lets slip that 'you get to stare at Rachel as much as you want'. When Joey appears surprised by this, Gunther explains it away as another way of saying 'flexible hours'.

Generation X: 'Behind the Music' is the music biography series on the music channel VH-1. The edition Chandler wanted to watch with Joey was the one that told the story of platinum-album-selling Heart, who had a few major hits in the late 80s, including 'Alone' and 'These Dreams'. With the sister duo Ann and Nancy Wilson at the band's core, they are recognised as the biggest female-led hard rock band ever. *Playboy* was founded by Hugh Hefner (or as Ross calls him, 'The Hef').

The Story So Far: From this episode, Joey is now employed at Central Perk as a waiter. Gunther tells Joey that he has his hair dyed (and you thought he was a natural albino, didn't you?). Ross was 'outed' as a *Playboy* reader in 'TOW Ross Got High'.

The Last Word: Another one where everyone is actually quite nasty to one another. Chandler and Ross fight over who wrote this joke about a monkey doctor, the girls fight over which one of them would make the best hypothetical lesbian girlfriend, which one's a pushover and loads of other trivial stuff. Just as we begin to suspect this episode has no redeeming features, Joey tells Rachel that he's lost his low-paid job at Central Perk. Rachel, who is usually the most selfish of the gang, rushes to her friend's aid and demands that Gunther gives Joey his job back. OK, so where Rachel's concerned Gunther's a bit of a pushover, but she's the only one, bar Chandler, who seems to have noticed how important this job is for Joey. He is seriously struggling to make ends meet, something that is all but glossed over thanks to all the other stuff.

613
'The One With Rachel's Sister'

Writers: Seth Kurland (story),
Sherry Bilsing & Ellen Plummer (teleplay)
Director: Gary Halvorson
First US transmission: 03.02.00
First UK transmission (Sky One): 06.04.00

Guest Cast: James Michael Tyler (Gunther), Susan Yeagley (Woman #1),
Jeffery David Brooks (Male Patron), Lex Arquette (The Customer)
and introducing: Reese Witherspoon (Jill Green)

Summary: Monica is sent home sick from work. Chandler tries to get her to relax, but Monica, convinced 'sickness' is another word for 'weakness', refuses to give in and instead tries to seduce Chandler. Meanwhile, Rachel's sister, Jill, comes to town after her father cuts off her allowance. At first, Rachel is excited by the prospect of helping Jill start a new life of independence, but when Phoebe tells her that she thinks Ross and Jill fancy each other, Rachel freaks out.

Slow Joey: Having witnessed Joey accurately divide up his friends' bill at Central Perk, Chandler notes wryly: 'This coming from the man who couldn't split our 80 dollar phone bill in half.'

Phoebisms: Perhaps trying a little too hard to remind us just how weird Phoebe can be, an early scene shows her emptying her hand-bag of a whole load of strange items, including a fairground-style goldfish in a bag. When Jill asks sarcastically who made Rachel 'queen of the world', Phoebe exclaims 'I'd *love* that job!'

Spoilt Rachel: Not only does she completely steal Phoebe's (joke) idea for 'apartment pants', but when Rachel learns of the possibility of Ross and Jill hooking up, she goes into a self-obsessed overdose. 'I don't really like it when Ross goes out with anyone,' she confesses to Phoebe, 'but my sister – isn't that, like, incest or something? Oh my God, and they're gonna have sex! Oh! Oh no what if he marries her too?! Oh this is just terrible!' All this from Phoebe's claim that there might have been a 'spark' between them. Strangely, for someone desperate to stop her sister from dating her ex-boyfriend, Rachel does a remarkable job of 'selling' him to Jill when she claims he's not her type: 'What, handsome is not your type? Smart? Kind? Good kisser? What, those things aren't on your list? Ross is a great guy! You would be lucky to be with him!' We do love her lame attempt to convince Jill not to overachieve too soon: 'You do remember what happened to the little girl that tried too much too fast don't you?' 'What?' 'She . . . she died, Jill.'

Gunther's A Hard-Ass: Gunther is forced to deduct money from Joey's wages for all the free food he's been giving away to beautiful women. OK, so it might be against company policy to use muffins as bribes, but we think Gunther's just jealous of Joey's luck with the ladies.

Families – Who Needs 'Em?: A chip off the old block for certain, Jill is a terrifying parody of Rachel. In a phone call not too dissimilar to the one Rachel made in the first episode, Jill threatens her father: 'I'm gonna hire a lawyer, and I'm gonna sue you and take all your money. Then I'm gonna cut *you* off!' When Rachel asks her what their father said to that, Jill moans, 'That he wouldn't pay for my lawyer!' Jill is, if anything, even more spoiled and ruthless than Rachel; when Ross asks her how she could afford all the clothes she's bought, Jill boasts that she learned her father's credit card number when she was fifteen years old. As with Rachel six years ago, Dr Green's credit card seems to play a major role in Jill's attempt at making it on her own.

The Story So Far: Rachel first mentioned having a sister back in 'TOW The Dozen Lasagnes', but we learn here that she actually has two; the 'bitter' one lives in Poconos, and Jill is the younger, 'spoiled' one. Monica claims she hasn't been sick in three years [when she was heartbroken over Richard in 'TOW The Princess Leia Fantasy'].

Generation X: A Pashmina, for all those who were wondering, is a type of shawl and not, as Ross guessed, a rug.

The Last Word: When all of the friends are together at Monica's and there's a knock at the door, watch as each of them counts off each other in their heads – if they're all together, who would be calling for them? Rachel's younger sister makes her first appearance – and what an appearance she makes! Reece Witherspoon is superb, frighteningly close to how we remember Rachel in the early days, but without the supportive peer group. One wonders if Rachel might have become the only daughter her father respects without the help of her friends; going on Jill's behaviour, it's unlikely.

614
'The One Where Chandler Can't Cry'

Writers: Andrew Reich & Ted Cohen
Director: Kevin S. Bright
First US transmission: 10.02.00
First UK transmission (Sky One): 13.04.00

Guest Cast: Reese Witherspoon (Jill Green), James Michael Tyler (Gunther), Larry Joe Campbell (The Fan), Douglas Looper (The Vampire), Lisa Kudrow (Ursula)

Summary: Concerned that Ross has slept with her sister, Rachel is ecstatic to learn that he merely bored her rigid with a slide show of his favourite fossils. Before she can relax completely, however, Ross tells her that he thinks Jill might actually be interested in him as she's agreed to go on another date with him – on Valentine's Day! Rachel finally cracks and confesses that she can't cope with the thought of him dating her sister. Ross reluctantly agrees not to see her again. Jill, however, is furious that her sister is intent on running her life for her, and sets out to seduce Ross out of spite.

Monica discovers her boyfriend is an emotionless robot, and Phoebe discovers she's a successful porn star. You'd think she'd remember something like that!

Slow Joey: It's revealed that Joey has, for some time, been sneaking into Monica's apartment to steal her food, and both Monica and Chandler *know* he does it.

Chandleresque: Joey is horrified to learn that Chandler didn't cry when Bambi's mother died. 'Yes,' Chandler observes with just a pinch of cynicism, 'it was very sad when the guy *stopped drawing the deer*!' Joey refuses to drop this and tries to provoke Chandler into crying, suggesting that he might be upset by the sight of a three-legged puppy. Chandler agrees that he'd be sad, but not enough to cry. 'OK,' tries Joey, 'what if the puppy said "Help me Chandler. All the other puppies pick on me".' Chandler can't be moved, however, simply crowing: 'Cry? I just found a talking puppy – I'm rich!'

Freaky Monica: Her vivid hypothetical vision of her life with Chandler is wonderfully manipulative, demanding whether he would cry when they have their first child, or when their child leaves home, or if she died after a long illness and, as he was writing the eulogy, he found a note from her telling him she'll always be with him. When Chandler fails to crack after this emotional tale, Monica flips: 'What is wrong with you? . . . You can't shed a tear for your dead wife!! Now, I left you a note from the beyond!'

Poor Ross: The local kids are persecuting Ross with games of 'knock and run'. Also, despite the fact that Jill appears to be fascinated by Ross's slide show, she is actually lying – badly – just to get at Rachel, who never managed to fake interest to this degree.

Spoilt Rachel: Rachel is furious that her younger sister thinks she's jealous of her. 'I mean, who does she think she is – Princess Caroline?' Monica is a little surprised: 'You're jealous of Princess Caroline?' she asks. 'Do I have my own castle?' Rachel replies, as this explains everything.

Ugly Naked Couple: Though Ugly Naked Guy moved on a year ago, Rachel spies on an old couple two apartments over from Ross. She doesn't go into detail, but there's enough movement over there to force Chandler to ask if they're using a swing.

Dinosaurs ROCK!: After showing Jill his collection of fossil slides (!), Ross tells Rachel that he was certain Jill was giving him 'the vibe'. 'Right,' says an incredulous Rachel. 'Was it the "Please don't show me another picture of a trilobite" vibe?'

Gunther's a Dirty Pervert: The Peroxide One freely admits to having seen Phoebe's porn films – yet he still fancies Rachel more?!!

The Ballad of Ross & Rachel: Thought this category was closed? Well think again. Despite the fact that Rachel has asked him not to date her sister, Ross finds himself trapped between a War of the Greens when Jill sets her sights on him merely to wind up Rachel. Ross tries to explain the situation to Rachel. Once he's managed to calm her down he tells her that he did in fact kiss Jill, but then he stopped ('Well thank you for taking your tongue out of my sister's mouth long enough to tell me that!' screams Rachel). But Ross goes on to explain that the reason he stopped kissing Jill was because if things progressed it would mean he would no longer have a chance of getting back with Rachel. He admits that he doesn't think that they ever *will* get back together, but that he'd hate to think that they never *could*. Rachel is speechless, realising what a sweet thing her ex-husband has done for her. Chandler, who has been watching this little drama unfold, suddenly bursts into tears. 'I just don't see why those two can't work things out!' he sobs.

The Story So Far: Joey reminds us of the time Chandler snogged Joey's sister (see 'TOW Chandler Can't Remember Which Sister'). Phoebe claims that she watched Bambi (David Hand, 1942). Chandler claims that his parents didn't want to attend his parents' evening in first grade so he took Janitor Martin instead. Aww. Rachel tells Jill there's a guy called 'Bob' who works in the Human Resources department at Ralph Lauren. Ursula has a tattoo on her ankle (though it might be a temporary one). Joey's reaction to the porn film reminds us that, way back in 'TOW Two Parts' he dated Ursula and remains the only one who can see a sexual difference between the twins.

Generation X: Monica, Phoebe, Joey and Chandler watch *ET The Extra-Terrestrial* (Steven Spielberg, 1982). With this being another episode containing porn-spoofs there are lots of references to real films: *Toy Story 2* (John Lasseter et al, 1999), *Lawrence of Arabia* (David Lean, 1962), *Buffy The Vampire Slayer* (though Buffy originally appeared in a film, it's probably the later TV show that they're spoofing), *Inspector Gadget* (again, it was a film at the time this was broadcast, but it's the TV show that people remember) and *Nosferatu* (F.W. Murnau, 1922). Chandler alludes to The Tin Man from *The Wizard of Oz* (originally a book by L. Frank Baum, but it's the film everyone . . . OK, you get this already). As you all know, Ursula was originally a character in *Mad About You*. *Mad About You*'s final episode, 'The Finale Frontier' (broadcast May, 1999), set 20 years in the future, confirms that Ursula Buffay had a lucrative career in the porn industry, after which she became the governor of New York State!

The Last Word: Another episode to feature a whole video shop's worth of fake porn spoofs – *Lawrence of A Labia*, *Sex Toy Story 2*, *Inspect Her Gadget* and the absolute best – *Buffay: The Vampire Layer*, in which 'Buffay' battles a vampire called (wait for it) NosferaTOOL! As with 'TOW The Free Porn', some fans felt the porn references were a little crude. We, however, laughed our heads off. Phoebe's reaction as she walks in to see 'herself' in a porno ('Oh my God – what am I doing?!') is classic Phoebe, but it's also sweet that only Joey finds it difficult to watch the film when he thinks it's Phoebe doing . . . what she's doing, yet when they discover it's actually Ursula he's suddenly *very* interested. The plotline about Chandler being incapable of crying does seem a little strange – especially when we remember such episodes as 'TOW The Giant Poking Device' and 'TOW Chandler in a Box', which showed that, though he might be unable to cry, he is still one very emotional guy.

615 / 616

'The One That Could Have Been', Parts 1 and 2

Writers: Greg Malins & Adam Chase and
David Crane & Marta Kauffman
Director: Michael Lembeck
First US transmission: 17.02.00
First UK transmission (Sky One): 20.04.00

Guest Cast: Kristian Alfonso (Hope Brady), Kevin Spirtas (Dr Wesley),
Jane Sibbet (Carol Willick), Pat Finn (Dr Roger),
James Michael Tyler (Gunther), Cacey Riggan (The Nurse),
Jessica Hecht (Susan Bunch), Mitchell Whitfield (Barry Farber),
Paul Gleason (Jack), Larry Cox (Arthur), Lisa Calderon (The Woman)
and introducing: Cole Mitchell Sprouse (Ben)

Summary: Hearing about the divorce of her ex-best friend and her ex-fiancé, Rachel begins to wonder if her life might have been different if she had actually got married to Barry instead of jilting him at the altar. This prompts the gang to all consider how their lives might have been had certain things happened. Ross tries to imagine what it would be like if he and Carol hadn't split up; Phoebe fantasises about life as a hyper-stressed stockbroker; Chandler pictures himself as a writer; Joey wishes he was still the star of *Days of Our Lives*; Monica remembers what it was like being enormously fat.

Poor Ross: It's another 'pick on Ross' session with the friends. Hearing Rachel's news about Barry and Mindy's divorce, Joey immediately berates Ross. When Phoebe explains that it's someone other than Ross getting divorced, Joey apologises saying, 'Sorry. I hear divorce I immediately go to Ross.' Ross asks his friends to imagine what his life might have been like if his ex-wife, Carol, hadn't realised she was a lesbian. Joey typically misses the point: 'I can't. I keep seeing it the good way.' And when Ross tells them all that he was doing a lot of 'kara-tay' towards the end of his marriage as a release valve for all his pent-up physical energy, Chandler speculates that maybe the problem was that he insisted on pronouncing the word as 'kara-*tay*'.

Phoebisms: She claimed that at one time she believed that everything that rhymed must be true, hence if she had worked with stocks, she'd have to live in a box, and only eat locks, and have a pet fox . . .

Slow Joey: It's handy that Joey can't remember who Barry and Mindy are, as it gives the writers the chance to explain their relationship to the audience.

Spoilt Rachel: Explaining her back-story with Barry, she brushes off the fact that he cheated on her with her best friend: 'That just means that he was falling asleep on top of her instead of me.'

Buy, Buy, Sell, Sell: Alternative-Phoebe, the hard-assed stock-broker, rules her staff with a rod of iron: 'It's OK,' she reassures an unfortunate employee. 'You're allowed one mistake,' only to add: 'Just kidding, you are, of course, fired.' A new employee doesn't even get to have their own name – Phoebe informs the poor girl that she'll be addressing her as 'Joan'.

Flabby Monica: The return of Fat Monica allows Courteney Cox to play the blushing virgin, as opposed to the bossy Monica we're used to. When Rachel tactfully asks if Monica has lost weight, Mon gushes: 'You are so sweet to notice! Yes, I lost three and a half pounds!'

Joey IS An Actor!: . . . and in this universe a particularly successful one as well. As Alternative-Rachel doesn't work (leaving all that to her husband), she gets to watch every episode of *Days Of Our Lives* and immediately recognises the mega-famous Joey Tribbiani. A star of such magnitude needs an assistant – which he finds in the more-than-capable form of Chandler. Joey's list of tasks for his out-of-work friend include dropping off his dry cleaning, collecting his vitamins (and, Chandler jokes, teaching him how to spell vitamins) and wearing in his new jeans, prompting Monica to note that Chandler is Joey's 'bitch'.

Generation X: Kiristian Alfonso and Kevin Spirtas do actu-ally play characters in *Days of Our Lives*. Pat Finn was a famil-iar face on the Chicago comedy circuit, having been a member of the ImprovOlympia team (which also included Jon Favreau and Chris Farley). Along with his twin brother Dylan, Cole Mitchell Sprouse has already tasted stardom thanks to his appearance as an abandoned kid in the Adam Sandler comedy *Big Daddy* (Dennis Dugan, 1999). Chandler refers to Archie

Comics, which have been running in one form or another since the early 40s. Crammed with family decency and All American values, they tell the story of Archie Andrews, an ordinary high school guy who tackles day-to-day problems.

The Story So Far: Ben is now played by Cole Mitchell Sprouse (well if his mother can change faces, why not?). Barry and Mindy have now filed for divorce. Mentioned in the 'Pilot' episode, Barry was first seen in 'TOW The Sonogram At The End', and last popped up, unsurprisingly, in 'TOW Barry and Mindy's Wedding'. It's tricky tying any of this episode to the 'real' past, but as the Gellers and Rachel hadn't seen each other for a while in 'Pilot', it's safe to guess that they last saw each other in 1987, the day after Christmas, at Sean McMahon's party. Ross reminds Rachel that that night he played her one of his songs, 'Interplanetary Courtship Ritual'. Alternative-Rachel confides in Monica that she wishes she and Barry could be 'on a break', reminding us of Ross's catchphrase from the Third and Fourth Seasons, while Fat Monica once again refers to her virginity as her 'flower', as she did in 'TOW The Thanksgiving Flashbacks'. Monica is now 30 (unless Rachel is just rounding up), and Phoebe is 31, which means that we've passed their 30th birthdays and no-one even mentioned it. As Joey is still Dr Drake Ramoray in this universe, he still has the raining window-pane and the giant ceramic greyhound, who we learn here is called Pat. It's good to see that even in this universe, Carol and Susan find each other – well, good for them at least, but not for Ross, obviously.

The Last Word: OK, so we've skimped on the review for these two episodes, but in honesty every other line is a corker. As you can probably tell, we love *Friends* for its strong continuity, and when the writers know their back-history well enough to mess around with it, as they do here, and when a series has the savvy to redo the title sequence just for a parallel universe episode you know that you're in for a treat. Using clips of the alternative characters as if they're from previous episodes in the same universe is a nice touch, as is getting Mitchell Whitfield (Barry) back for just one scene (plus a bonus clip in the titles). *Buffy The Vampire Slayer* did something similar this year, but it was nowhere near as effective – or funny – as it is here. Well done!

617

'The One With Unagi'
(a.k.a. 'The One With The Mix Tape')

Writers: Zachary Rosenblatt (story) & Adam Chase (teleplay)
Director: Gary Halvorson
First US transmission: 24.02.00
First UK transmission (Sky One): 27.04.00

Guest Cast: Louis Mandylor (Carl), Jill Matson (The Receptionist),
Ron Recasner (The Doctor), Mongo Brownlee (The Instructor),
Maggie Wheeler (Janice – uncredited voice only)

Summary: Phoebe and Rachel have signed up for a self-defence class. Their enjoyment is short lived, however, as Ross begins to bore them about his expertise in Karate thanks to a concept he calls 'Unagi'. Joey, meanwhile, is desperate to earn some extra cash and approaches the university with regard to donating some 'body fluids'. However, he learns that the only research project still running requires sets of identical twins. Joey sets about training up a fake twin to help him earn $2,000 of research money.

During all this, Chandler and Monica prepare for a belated Valentine's evening. Monica has hit on the idea that they should show their love for each other by exchanging gifts that they have made themselves. Having struggled for days to think of anything suitable, Chandler finally gives Monica a tape of romantic songs that he found at the back of his closet while an embarrassed Monica gives Chandler a 'bunny-sock' that is quite clearly the work of Phoebe. To make amends for failing to make anything herself, Monica works overtime on making Chandler's favourite meals, buying him expensive gifts and treating him in ways that only a lover could know how. But then, Monica plays Chandler's tape and discovers who *really* made it . . .

Scary Ross: Where's all this 'Kara-tay' come from recently? As Ross tries to teach Phoebe and Rachel the importance of 'Unagi', the girls simply ridicule him, pointing out that Unagi is a type of sushi. He spends the remainder of the episode jumping out at them unexpectedly, terrorising them just to make his point – that they need to beware of attack from strangers. When the girls pin him to the ground and refuse to let him free unless he admits they are 'Unagi' ('It's not something you are!' he pleads lamely. 'It's something you have!'), he insists that he's only allowing them to hold him so that he doesn't hurt them. Eventually, he joins the girls' defence class just so he can ask their instructor for advice on how to attack them. The instructor's facial expression tells Ross that this might not be a good idea, but Ross goes further, asking him if maybe they could attack the women together. The closing scene, where Ross, thinking he's attacking Phoebe and Rachel instead jumps out on two other unsuspecting women, just goes to show that there is something dangerously wrong with this man.

Slow Joey: Early on, Joey berates himself for blackening in his teeth on one of the three remaining portrait photos he has left. Only Joey could possibly wish for a twin when he's standing in a room filled with Joseph Tribbiani lookalikes.

Generation X: Australian kick-boxer Louis Mandylor apears as Carl – Mandylor has appeared in a number of films, such as *Jane Austen's Mafia* (Jim Abrahams, 1998), usually as a 'heavy'. Chandler's – er – Janice's mix-tape includes renditions of Rodgers and Hart's 'My Funny Valentine' and Jerome Kern's 'The Way You Look Tonight'. Though Frank Sinatra's version of the latter song is the best known, it's recently enjoyed a resurgence in popularity thanks to the versions sung by Tony Bennett and by Dermot Mulroney in the Julia Roberts romantic comedy *My Best Friend's Wedding* (P.J. Hogan, 1997). Joey reminds Monica that he once lost out on an audition for Minute Maid (the orange juice). Pat Sajak hosts *Wheel of Fortune* in the States, Alex Trebek hosts *Jeopardy!* and Chuck Woolery hosts *The Dating Game*. Oh, and Unagi *is* a type of eel.

The Story So Far: Echoing what most of us thought at the time, during the First Season, Ross says to Joey: 'Hey, remember when I had a monkey . . .? What was I thinking?' Joey remembers how he has previously made money by offering himself for medical experimentation (see 'TOW Rachel Finds Out'), and Phoebe reminds us again that she used to live on the streets. As this episode is set two weeks after Valentine's Day (i.e. the beginning of March) and as Monica reminds Chandler that his birthday is a month and a half away, we can assume that his birthday is in mid-May (and see also 'TOW Rachel Smokes'). Monica cooks one of Chandler's favourite meals – macaroni cheese (or, as it's also known, Canadian food). And of course, the voice we hear on the mix-tape is that of Chandler's ex-girlfriend Janice.

The Last Word: Well, despite the fact that this is another 'we can't help but hate Ross' episode, it actually hangs together quite well. It's good to see the girls getting the upper hand with Ross on a number of occasions, though we might question the wisdom of making a joke out of what is really harassment. Our favourite moment though, is when Monica plays the tape that Chandler gave her only to hear the inimitable voice of Janice screeching from the tape deck. We're thankful that one of our favourite semi-regulars, Maggie Wheeler has been able to contribute to the season, even if it's in an uncredited voice-over. And of course, it's typical that even her voice can ruin things for Chandler. God only knows what Janice would do if she knew Chandler was dating Monica and that he hadn't moved to Yemen after all!

618

'The One Where Ross Dates A Student'

Writer: Seth Kurland
Director: Gary Halvorson
First US transmission: 09.03.00
First UK transmission (Sky One): 04.05.00

Guest Cast – Introducing: Alexandra Holden (Elizabeth)

Summary: Ross learns that he has an admirer in one of his classes. He's aware that, while it's not against the rules to date a student, it is certainly frowned upon. But when the student asks him out for a date, pointing out that next semester he won't be her tutor any more, Ross can barely contain himself. They begin to date, even though Ross is nervous of what the other lecturers might think about him dating a student. Quite rightly, it seems, as he learns from one of his colleagues that such a relationship could be grounds for dismissal.

Joey discovers that a woman who went to college with Chandler is directing a forthcoming Al Pacino movie. Playing on his friend's better nature, Joey persuades Chandler to ask the woman out so he can put in a good word for the unemployed actor.

Slow Joey: As Ross describes why dating one of his students would be a bad idea, Joey muses, 'When you're 90 . . .' but he's quickly interrupted by Ross: 'I know. When I'm 90 she'll be, like, 80 and it won't seem like such a big difference.' But that wasn't Joey's point. 'What I was going to say,' he continues, 'is when you're 90 you'll still have the memory of what it was like to be with a 20-year-old.'

Spoilt Rachel: Emerging from Monica's bathroom, Rachel asks if she can use Monica's phone to check on her messages. Chandler questions why she thought of this while she was on the toilet. She quips, 'Yeah sure, nature called, she wanted to see who else did.' It's then that she discovers that her apartment has been gutted by a fire. When a sympathetic fireman asks if the girls have anywhere to stay, Rachel misinterprets his concern and rounds on him: 'Look pal, I am not in the mood to be hit on right now!' Adding '. . . but if you give me your number I will call you some other time.'

Freaky Monica: Having volunteered to give Rachel somewhere to stay after the fire, Monica is very apologetic for the mess in her spare room . . . only to unveil an obsessively neat guest room. When Phoebe comes to stay, Monica comments on a strange smell coming from Joey's apartment and offers to bake a pie just to cover it up.

Generation X: Alexandra Holden also appears in *Drop Dead Gorgeous* (Michael Patrick Jann, 1999). Chandler compares Joey to the autistic mathematics genius played by Dustin Hoffman in the movie *Rain Man* (Barry Levinson, 1988).

The Story So Far: Chandler took a mime class at college – or as he calls it a 'movement' class, and went on one date with Dana Keystone, who is now a movie director. It would appear Monica got her own way as to what her spare room would be used for – Hotel Monica (see 'TOW Ross's Denial'). Despite requests from Phoebe to swap, Rachel now lives with Joey and Phoebs is at Hotel Monica's.

The Last Word: Well we came down pretty hard on Elle MacPherson earlier on in this season, but isn't Elizabeth just cute as a button? Her eagerness for Ross, her confidence (shown in the way she pretends she's not interested in him now she's got her 'A' grade) and the way she encourages Ross to break the rules is definitely bringing out the best in the man.

619
'The One With Joey's Fridge'

Writers: Seth Kurland (story),
Gigi McCreery & Perry Rein (teleplay)
Director: Ben Weiss
First US transmission: 23.03.00
First UK transmission (Sky One): 11.05.00

Guest Cast: Alexandra Holden (Elizabeth), Scott Paetty (Sebastian),
Chris Kennedy (Patrick), Josh Cox (Eldad), Jim Bentley (Professor Friesell),
Hunter Cochran (Guy #1)

Summary: Despite the fact that he and Elizabeth need to keep their relationship secret from the other university staff, Ross proudly shows off his new girlfriend to his gang. Though they gently mock the age gap between the two, Ross's friends are actually very pleased to see him so happy. Ross tells them that as Elizabeth is young, it means their relationship is taking its time, something he's very pleased about. But then Elizabeth brings up the subject of spring break. Before she can elaborate, they are interrupted by another tutor and Elizabeth is forced to make a quick excuse and leave. Ross suspects that Elizabeth was about to ask him to go away with her for spring vacation and, concerned that she's taking things just a little too far too soon, he tries to get her to back off a little. But when she explains that she was just letting him know that she'd be gone for a few days, Ross is both relieved and embarrassed. Then, of course, he begins to worry about what she might get up to while she's away.

Rachel has been asked to attend a charity ball with the Ralph

Lauren team. She asks her friends to find her a suitable date, but she is completely unprepared for the way her friends suddenly become competitive over their proposed dates for her. Monica and Chandler pitch a guy from Chandler's work; Phoebe puts forward an ex-massage client of hers (who, she says, has an excellent body). As the friends battle for the right to choose Rachel's date – even to the point of frightening off a guy that Rachel has in fact chosen for herself – Rachel realises that it would be much less hassle if she attended the ball alone.

Spoilt Rachel: Telling her friends about the charity ball she's supposed to be attending, Rachel says it's in aid of 'either trees or disease', blaming her vagueness on the fact that Ralph Lauren 'mumbles a lot'. Monica challenges this, suggesting that Ralph mumbles only when Rachel's not paying attention. 'Yeah. It's weird,' replies Rachel, innocently. After the event, when she's again asked what the ball was in aid of, Rachel can only say 'a disease'.

Slow Joey: Joey's ancient fridge has broken down, but he can't afford to get it fixed, so he tries to get each of his friends to share the burden – with little success. Trying to get Rachel to shoulder half the cost of the repairs, Joey tells her that the fridge is almost as old as he is and he's never had any problem with it until she moved in with him. 'What does that tell you?' he asks confrontationally. 'That refrigerators don't live as long as people?' suggests Rachel. He then turns his attentions to Chandler's wallet. Trying to explain why he should pay for a fridge even though he doesn't live there any more, Joey asks him to think of it as if they were a divorced couple and Joey had been given custody of their child. 'Suppose the kid dies and . . . and I gotta buy a new kid . . .' he begins, but it's clear that this analogy is getting a little complicated so Joey resorts to a more blunt tactic: 'Give me $400!' Not surprisingly, this approach is also a failure. Having also tried to get Ross to foot the bill by pushing him against the fridge and accusing him of breaking it, Joey is becoming desperate. He simply tells Phoebe that *she* broke his fridge and owes him $400. Surprisingly, Phoebe seems quite content with this up until the moment she realises that, technically, Joey still owes her $600 for sending out happy thoughts on his last ten auditions.

Panic-stricken, Joey asks if she could just call it even, which Phoebe generously agrees to. Poor Joey.

Chandleresque: Boasting about the man she's picked for Rachel, Phoebe tells Chandler and Monica that he has a chin dimple – or as Chandler calls it a 'face ass'. Knowing that her guy has a fantastic physique, Phoebs asks if the couple have seen their guy's body. 'No,' confesses Chandler, 'our guy is just a floating head.' As the three become more and more competitive, Chandler boasts that their guy 'smells *incredible*'. Momentarily distracted by this admission, Monica asks her boyfriend: 'Do you want our guy to be *your* guy?'

Poor Ross: Once again the target of some serious ribbing from his friends, Ross takes it all in his stride. Chandler starts the ball rolling, asking if it's a school night and Elizabeth has a lot of homework to do. Rachel suggests that Elizabeth is young enough to celebrate her birthday at 'Chuckie Cheese' and Monica asks if she can order her cookies early from the young girl. Only Phoebe fails to see the subtlety of their jokes, asking quite spitefully, 'OK, um, what is she? Like twelve?' before realising that she might have gone just a little too far.

Magna-Doodle: Two surfers riding the waves.

Generation X: *Field & Stream* is a magazine that pitches itself to people who enjoy hunting and fishing – Rachel has quite clearly never read an issue in her life, but it seems to have been a successful way of chatting up Sebastian. 'Sebastian', as Chandler notes, was also the name of Alexandra's moggie in the Hanna Barbera cartoon series *Josie and the Pussycats*.

The Story So Far: Jim Bentley (Professor Friesell) played one of Ross's fellow tour guides at the museum back in 'TOW Phoebe's Uterus'. Joey claims that his parents bought his fridge soon after he was born (though it looks remarkably like the fridge Chandler already owned before Joey moved in with him). In 1981, when he was just thirteen, Joey spent spring break at the Hotel Corona, on Daytona beach. Despite the obvious enjoyment that they get from ribbing Ross about his young girlfriend, no-one seems to have noticed how much of a hypocrite Monica is being – watch 'TOW The Ick Factor' to see why.

The Last Word: Traditionally, throughout the history of the series, the other actors have worked hard to carry a scene only for Matthew Perry or Lisa Kudrow to be awarded a single killer punch line that ends the scene on a high. While this is undoubtedly because of Kudrow and Perry's good sense of timing, it does mean that the efforts of the other actors, notably LeBlanc, tend to get ignored while the glory goes to the person who delivered the last line. But increasingly in recent episodes, Aniston is being given the comedic last word, as exemplified by her triumphant storming out of Central Perk only to storm back in again to get some hair tips from one of the terrified prospective dates. As the Ross and Rachel storylines are slowly pushed aside to make way for the romance between Chandler and Monica, it's good to see that the writers haven't excluded Schwimmer and Aniston in the way one might suggest the writers did with other characters when Ross and Rachel dominated the series.

620
'The One With Mac And C.H.E.E.S.E.'

Writer: Doty Abrams
Director: Kevin S. Bright
First US transmission: 13.04.00
First UK transmission (Sky One): 18.05.00

Summary: As Joey rehearses with his friends for a forthcoming audition, he begins to suffer a crisis of confidence. Is he really cut out to be an actor? Despite his fears, his friends convince him he'll be OK. But when Chandler forgets to pass on the message that Joey's audition has been brought forward, the friends begin to remember times when they've let each other down in the past.

Chandleresque: As he enjoys a game of foosball, Joey ponders out loud how weird it would be to see a full-sized version of the game. 'As crazy as *soccer*?' Chandler suggests, reminding his Italian friend of the sport that *is* actually a full-sized version of foosball.

Freaky Monica: Rubbing salt into the wound over Chandler's distress at forgetting to pass on the message to Joey, Monica reminds him that this is why she always has a pad with her, in case she needs to write anything down.

The Chick and The Duck: Chandler tries to reassure his feathered buddies that it's not his fault he doesn't see them as much as he used to, blaming it on the fact that Monica has an allergy towards them – or that she simply hates them. The birds seem emotionally distressed by this news.

The Story So Far: Joey does his 'pretending-he-messed-up-the-audition-but-really-it-went-well' joke that he continues to think fools everyone – and even more surprisingly it often does. The show that Joey is rehearsing for is 'Mac and C.H.E.E.S.E.', in which he plays 'Mac Macaveli', a detective with a robotic sidekick known as 'Computerized Humanoid Electronically Enhanced Secret Enforcer' – or C.H.E.E.S.E. for short. It's entirely coincidental that the show is named after Chandler's favourite food. Trying to make up with Joey, Chandler buys a 'Joey Special' from the Pizza place. That's two pizzas, as first revealed in 'TOW Ross's Wedding, Part 1'. In the flashbacks, we see Joey's explanation of 'smell-the-fart' acting from 'TOW The Lesbian Wedding', plus Joey's performance in the musical 'Freud!' and his announcement that he'll be Al Pacino's butt double, both from 'TOW The Butt'. We see Chandler getting all flustered over his W.E.N.U.S. from 'TOW The Stoned Guy'; Monica's disturbing job interview from 'TOW The Prom Video'; Rachel bitching about her new job in 'TOW Rachel's Crush'; Phoebe confessing that Rachel's boyfriend Paolo tried to seduce her, from 'TOW The Dozen Lasagnes'; Ross completely losing it, in 'TOW Ross's Sandwich'; Chandler mocking Joey's bracelet gift in 'TOW The Prom Video'; Chandler confessing to Joey that he kissed Kathy in 'TOW Chandler Crosses The Line'; Chandler discovering that Joey has let a burglar clear their apartment, from 'TOW The Cat'; Joey setting Chandler up on a double-date – with Janice, from 'TOW The Candy Hearts'; the revelation that Joey's tailor is a 'very bad man', from 'TOW Ross's New Girlfriend'; Ross and Rachel breaking up for good in 'TOW The Jellyfish'; Monica and Rachel arguing over Jean-Claude Van Damme, from 'TO After The Superbowl, Part 2'; Joey wearing all of Chandler's clothes from 'TOW No-One's

Ready'; Joey and Chandler missing each other's company, from 'TOW Eddie Moves In'; and a load of clips of Chandler and Joey hugging – and if you think we're going to spend all day checking out every single one of them then you're nuts.

The Last Word: This episode was largely a series of clips, which some fans felt cheated by, but it serves as a nice reminder of all the different relationships and events from the past. If nothing else, they must have saved enough money to afford the episodes with Bruce Willis in them. We think it's shameful, and we certainly wouldn't repeat whole passages from a book just to save time, as our review for 'TOW The Invitation' proves.

621

'The One Where Ross Meets Elizabeth's Dad'

Writers: Scott Silveri (story), David J. Lagana (teleplay)
Director: Michael Lembeck
First US transmission: 27.04.00
First UK transmission (Sky One): 18.05.00

Guest Cast: Bruce Willis (Paul Stevens),
Alexandra Holden (Elizabeth), June Gable (Estelle),
Andrew Bilgore (Wayne), Brad Koepenick (The Producer)

Summary: Elizabeth has invited Ross to meet her dad, Paul, a prospect that fills Ross with dread. Ross asks his friends to help him by saying nice things about him to Paul, but he needn't have bothered as Paul has already made his mind up about him – and he's not impressed. Rachel, however, puts a lot of effort into making Ross look good, though, as Ross discovers, this largely entails Rachel making out with Elizabeth's dad.

On the set of *Mac and C.H.E.E.S.E.* Joey immediately comes into conflict with Wayne, the creator and operator of C.H.E.E.S.E., his robot sidekick on the show. At first, Joey thinks that, seeing as he's the star, he'll be able to have Wayne removed from the show. However, he later learns that Wayne is the only one who knows how C.H.E.E.S.E. works and, thanks to his earlier run-in with him, it's now Joey whose job is on the line. When he tries to reach a compromise with

Wayne he learns that there are still some skills that Wayne doesn't have that Joey can teach him – specifically the ability to attract women. Joey agrees to give Wayne lessons in return for Wayne letting him stay on the show.

Chandleresque: Spotting Phoebe examining two books, Chandler asks her if she's judging them by their covers, 'Because you're really not supposed to do that.' When, trying to flatter Phoebe, Chandler calls her 'the Queen of Everything,' Phoebe responds by saying, cattily, 'Thank you – so are you,' prompting Chandler to moan to Monica: 'I *told* you I should not wear this colour'.

Poor Ross: Everyone is still baiting him about having a very young girlfriend. Having agreed to stick with him when he meets Elizabeth's dad, Monica adds, 'We know how tough those parent/teacher conferences can be.' When he finally meets Mr Stevens, Ross tries to lighten the mood with a joke. 'Two guys go into a bar,' he begins. 'One of them is Irish.' 'I'm Irish,' Paul interrupts, bluntly. '. . . and the Irish guy wins the joke!' interjects a quick-thinking Ross. When Rachel, desperately trying to salvage something out of her botched PR attempt, claims that Ross learned something from each of his marriages, Paul quips: 'How to make the next one even shorter?'

Phoebisms: Phoebe claims that she's written fourteen books, telling Chandler that as she's the only one who's read them they've all been very well-received. She tells Monica and Chandler that her new book will be about relationships, about how 'none of it matters when the people really love each other.' When Chandler and Monica kiss, she adds, under her breath: '. . . and how people will believe anything you tell them as long as it's a compliment.' The couple later discover that much of Phoebe's book concerns the relationship between 'Marcia' and 'Chester'. Through some amazingly adept investigations that border on telepathy, Monica and Chandler deduce that the book is actually about them, so Monica threatens to write a book about a woman called 'Phyllis'. 'Ooh,' cries Phoebe, 'I have tasted my own medicine and it is *bitter*!'

Joey's An Actor!: Joey's Agent, the glorious Estelle, makes another welcome appearance, to tell Joey that she's got him an audition in a series, but that the actor who has the part doesn't know he might be fired.' Then she drops the bombshell – it's the lead in a series, *Mac and C.H.E.E.S.E.* When Joey points out to her that he *is* the lead in *Mac and C.H.E.E.S.E.*, Estelle can only utter an 'Uhh-ohh'.

Just Plain Weird: Chandler and Monica have a minor row over the brand of toilet paper Monica has bought. Chandler asked her to get the kind with a baby on the front as the one with the little girl, for some reason, freaks him out!

Generation X: Famous action-movie star Bruce Willis was persuaded to make a guest appearance by Matthew Perry, who he worked with on the film *The Whole Nine Yards* (Jonathan Lynn, 2000). Willis is said to have donated his entire fee for these episodes to charity. It's been noted that C.H.E.E.S.E. bears more than a passing similarity to Johnny 5 from the *Short Circuit* films.

The Story So Far: Elizabeth's father, Paul, is a lawyer. Elizabeth's mother died shortly after she was born, so she was raised by her father, which probably accounts for why he's so defensive for her (though in our experience, most fathers are the same!). Paul's sister also died young. Joey lets slip that the only thing he knows how to do on a computer is finding porn, and that's only because that's the first thing that pops up on Chandler's computer. Rachel reminds us that Ross dated her little sister (maybe this is where he got a taste for younger women?). She also tells Paul and Elizabeth the story of how Ross volunteered to take her to the prom when her date had stood her up (as seen in 'TOW The Prom Video'), which Paul quickly puts into perspective: 'So Ross was in college, and decided to jump at the chance to take a young girl to her high-school prom.' Ross tells Paul about his ex-wife, Carol, and their son, Ben, but Rachel also lets slip that both she and Emily were also married to him once (though she admits that her marriage to Ross was just a 'big drunken mistake').

The Last Word: Bruce Willis!!! A major coup for the production team, and it's nice to see them playing along with Bruce's public image – largely inspired, we suspect, by his character in *Armageddon* (Michael Bay, 1998) – only to undermine it in the next episode to great effect. It's also interesting that it's now so long since the broadcast of 'TOW The Prom Video', one of the most popular *Friends* episodes ever, that the writers feel it's OK to show a cynical response to events that we all thought were so beautiful. As Rachel says, 'I definitely did not see that one backfiring!' Some clever playing with our assumptions and our understanding of the characters here, a trait that runs through the remainder of this season.

622
'The One Where Paul's The Man'

Writers: Brian Caldirola (story),
Sherry Bilsing & Ellen Plummer (teleplay)
Director: Gary Halvorson
First US transmission: 04.05.00
First UK transmission (Sky One): 25.05.00

Guest Cast: Bruce Willis (Paul), Alexandra Holden (Elizabeth),
Merrin Dungey (The Museum Official), Ilia Volok (The Dry Cleaner),
Susie Park (The Dry Cleaner's Wife), James Michael Tyler (Gunther)

Summary: Joey strives to get his photograph back on the Wall of Fame at his local dry cleaners but the owner refuses to believe he's in a new TV show. Fortunately, a woman who works there is more open to Joey's charms. Unfortunately, she's the dry cleaner's wife!

Elizabeth takes Ross up to her grandmother's old log cabin in the woods so they can spend some time alone. Unfortunately, Paul decides to take Rachel there too. As Ross tries to hide in Paul's bedroom, he overhears Paul psyching himself up for a night of passion with Rachel. When Paul finally catches Ross trying to sneak out of the cabin, Ross is forced to confront him. He reveals to Paul that he witnessed his little 'display' earlier. Ross successfully blackmails Paul into allowing him to continue seeing Elizabeth.

The girls visit a museum and learn that weddings are performed there, though there's a two-year waiting list. Rachel and Phoebe convince Monica to put her name down, figuring that if, after two years, she's engaged to Chandler, she won't have to wait, and if she's not she can just cancel it. This seems to make sense at the time. But later on, a woman from the museum calls Monica at home to tell her there's been a cancellation and that her wedding to Mr Bing can be brought forward. Monica isn't home to take the message. Chandler, however, is, and when Monica finally gets home it's to an empty apartment . . .

Phoebisms: Phoebe tells her friends that a client of hers has given her three tickets for an exhibition at a museum. She adds that she feels bad that three of her friends will have to stay behind. Chandler and Joey quickly volunteer to give up their tickets, only to learn that it's actually an exhibition of 'photographs of lesbian love scenes interspersed with video games and free sandwiches.' Which, cruelly, are Joey's three favourite things (in reverse order, obviously).

Dinosaurs ROCK!: Trying to ridicule Rachel for dating Paul, and pointing out that the age gap is much greater than between him and Elizabeth, Ross chides, 'Looks like I'm not the only one interested in fossils, huh?' Rachel maintains the upper hand by saying that all his comment has done is remind everyone that Ross *is* interested in fossils.

Generation X: You might just recognise Ilia Volok from his role as a Russian in Harrison Ford's dull action flick *Air Force One* (Wolfgang Petersen, 1997) – which *is* offensive, and not just to Russians. Joey refers to Jim Belushi – a.k.a. James Belushi, brother of John, and star of such films as *Salvador* (Oliver Stone, 1986), *K-9* (Rod Daniel, 1989) and *Curly Sue* (John Hughes, 1991). The concept of Joey asking for his photo to be up on the wall of the local dry cleaners is inspired by a similar struggle at the centre of *Do The Right Thing* (Spike Lee, 1989). Matt Lauer is a host of NBC's *Today* news programme. As he tries to sex himself up, Paul sings 'Love Machine, Pt. 1,' by The Miracles.

The Story So Far: We're reminded that Joey used to be in *Days of Our Lives*. In all his excitement, Joey forgot to tell Gunther that he'd quit Central Perk, which is fortunate, as Gunther was going to fire him anyway.

The Last Word: As Monica calms a panicked Chandler, aware of his fear of commitment, we all breathe a sigh of relief. They are a great couple, and none of us want Chandler's immature fear of commitment to ruin anything. So of course it must have come as quite a shock to people when it's revealed that, in fact, Chandler has conspired with Phoebe all along, and that the whole point of her trip to the museum with Monica was to see if she'd want to be married there because – BIG SHOCK – it's Chandler that wants to rush Monica up the aisle! With Chandler finally recognising how much he loves Monica and, as a consequence, overcoming his absolute dread of marriage, surely nothing can come between them.

But there's still some way to go before this particular run of episodes is over . . .

623
'The One With The Ring'

Writers: Andrew Reich & Ted Cohen
Director: Gary Halvorson
First US transmission: 01.06.00
First UK transmission (Sky One): 25.05.00

Guest Cast: Bruce Willis (Paul), Oliver Muirhead (The Jeweller),
Brian Dunkleman (The Customer), Janet S. Blake (Jeweller #2)

Summary: Though things are going OK with Paul, Rachel can't help wishing he'd open up a little for her. But when she tries to get him in touch with his feelings she opens the floodgates and Paul dissolves into a sobbing, emotional mess. Chandler, meanwhile, is desperate to keep his intended proposal from his friends so that he can surprise Monica, but his behaviour is causing suspicion. As Phoebe seems to be in collusion with Chandler, Ross asks her if she can shed any light on the problem, but Phoebe isn't much help as she leads him to believe Chandler is sulking because Ross and Joey didn't invite him to a recent Knicks game. In retaliation, Joey and Ross decide to stop being friends with Chandler.

With little help from Phoebe, Chandler finds the perfect ring for Monica – a snip at $8,000. Realising he doesn't have his credit card with him, Chandler asks Phoebe to 'guard' the ring while he nips home. Passing time, Phoebe tries out all the other jewellery in the store, and when another man buys the ring Chandler wanted and leaves the store, Phoebe tries to follow him – triggering the store's heavy security gates in the process. She and Chandler eventually trace the man who bought the ring and manage to trade him another ring for it. Chandler is so excited by what he's planning to do that he breaks the news to his friends. All he has to do now is find the right moment to propose to Monica . . .

Chandleresque: Flicking through a jeweller's catalogue, Chandler and Phoebe discuss what type of ring he should get Monica. 'Should I get her a Tiffany cut or a Princess cut or a . . .' he asks as he turns the page, 'aaah! Paper cut!!' Telling Phoebe why he's confided in her, Chandler claims it's 'Because I trust you, you're one of my best friends, and you walked in on me when I was looking at ring brochures.' Phoebe then says that it's one of the benefits of not knocking before she walks in, though she wishes he hadn't been sitting on the toilet at the time, something Chandler can only agree with. Later, a sobbing Paul asks Chandler if his father ever hugged him as a child: 'No,' replies Chandler defensively, 'Did he hug *you*?' Paul tells him that he's upset because he misses his father. 'Well, you can see my dad in Vegas kissing other dads,' Chandler suggests unhelpfully.

Spoilt Rachel: Tired of Paul's emotional drowning, Rachel flips out: 'Y'know, the only person who would want to listen to this is a mental health professional! And then it's only because they get paid $100 an hour! Do you know how much money I could've made listening to you? $2,000! And do you know when I figured that out? While you were talking!' Very harsh. Very true.

The Story So Far: We can guess that at one time, Rachel was invited to a slumber party where she fell asleep and a girl called Sharon Majesky put Rachel's hand in some warm water which made her pee in her sleeping bag, something Rachel is still clearly bitter about. Paul, meanwhile, remains deeply traumatised by his childhood nickname of 'Chicken Boy'.

The Last Word: Stand-out moment in this episode is the sight of Phoebe trapped inside the security cage at the jewellers, brandishing a musket. But where is Monica in all this? One brief appearance? Well don't worry, she gets a lot more to do in the season finale.

624 / 625

'The One With The Proposal', Parts 1 and 2

Writers: Shana Goldberg-Meehan & Scott Silveri (part 1),
Andrew Reich & Ted Cohen (part 2)
Director: Kevin S. Bright
First US transmission: 18.05.00
First UK transmission (Sky One): 08.06.00

Guest Cast: Tom Selleck (Richard), Alexandra Holden (Elizabeth),
Steve Hytner (Mr Thompson), John Apicella (Mr Bowmont),
Natasha Pearce (Zoe), Tori McPetrie (Sarah),
Amil Raman (The First Dorm Guy), Jacqueline Schultz (Lisa),
Tony Nichols (The Maître'd), Alexandra Margulies (The Waitress),
Steven Harad (Emil Alexander), Hunter Cochran (The Second Dorm Guy)

Summary: Ross's friends shed some doubt on his relationship with Elizabeth as they admit that their constant ribbing of him has some basis in truth, namely that they're all worried that the age gap will prove to be a problem. Ross dismisses this as nonsense, confirming his belief that Elizabeth is very mature for her age. But when he finds himself caught in the middle of a water-balloon war between Elizabeth and some frat guys, Ross realises that their relationship doesn't have much of a future and breaks up with her.

Invited to another work's charity event, Rachel brings along Phoebe and Joey. It's a silent auction – where bidders write down their offers and the highest bid wins. Not wishing to get caught out with a prize she can't afford, Rachel deliberately bids low. Joey however, misunderstanding the rules of an auction, 'guesses' the right amount for a sailing boat and finds himself lumbered with a bill for $20,000. Rachel manages to persuade the next highest bidder to take on the boat instead, but by then Joey has fallen in love with the idea of having a boat and refuses to let it go.

Chandler is finally ready to propose to Monica. He's taken her to her favourite restaurant, selected some expensive champagne and is about to reveal the ring when Richard, Monica's ex-boyfriend turns up unexpectedly. Monica invites him to join them, thereby spoiling the moment for Chandler. When he and Monica return home, their friends are all excited, thinking he's already 'popped the question'. As Chandler tries to warn them that it didn't happen (to avoid spoiling his planned surprise for Monica), Monica grows suspicious. The only way Chandler could possibly keep her off-track and maintain his surprise is if he pretends that, instead of wanting to marry her, he's completely against the idea of commitment (he has, after all, had 30 years of practice). This certainly puts Monica off the track . . . but it also seriously puts her off Chandler.

Richard pops by to see Monica at her restaurant. He tells her that he regrets letting her go, that he still loves her and that, if she'll have him, he wants to marry her and have children with her. Monica tells him that he's too late, that she's with Chandler now. Richard apologises, but tells her that he'll only give up on her if she's certain that Chandler will give her the same things he can offer her. Monica is confused and very upset. After Joey, playing along with Chandler's plan, tells her that Chandler is never going to marry, Monica blurts out that Richard wants her back, and that she's seriously considering it. Joey immediately rushes to find Chandler and warns him to put an end to his 'surprise' plan and get Monica now before Richard does. Chandler rushes over to Richard's apartment and explains that he'd planned to propose to Monica until he'd shown up. Richard encourages him to find Monica and never let go. When Chandler returns home, however, Joey tells him that Monica has packed her bags and gone to her parents . . .

Poor Ross: Ross describes Chandler's engagement ring as the most beautiful one he's ever seen. Rachel can't help herself: 'Yeah? Well, you should know. You've bought, like, a billion of 'em.' Ross however, gets the last word: 'Yeah, *you* didn't get one.' After Ross admits that he doesn't think he and Elizabeth have a future together, Chandler warns him: 'If you're not careful you may not get married at all this year'. Yeah, *he* can talk!

Phoebisms: At the auction, Phoebe takes advantage of the free bar and tries to justify it by claiming she's helping the kids. When Rachel asks how drinking herself stupid is 'helping the kids', Phoebe states: 'Because the more I drink, the less there is for the kids to drink.'

Chandleresque: Asking Ross about his relationship with Elizabeth, Monica begins: 'All jokes aside . . .' Chandler is startled: 'All jokes aside? I didn't agree to that!' He later introduces himself to Richard's date thus: 'I'm Chandler; I make jokes when I'm uncomfortable.' His attempt to put Monica off the scent certainly makes one of them feel uncomfortable, especially when he begins to describe the sex-life of swine: 'A pig can have, like, a hundred sexual partners in a lifetime,' he boasts, 'and that's just an ordinary pig, not even a pig that's good at sports!'

Slow Joey: 'I don't know why the kids need a youth centre anyway!' moans Joey at the charity benefit. 'They should just watch TV after school like I did, and I turned out fine!'

Freaky Monica: Mon confesses to Richard that getting over him was the hardest thing that she's ever had to do. 'And I never let myself think about you,' she asserts. Richard seems a little taken aback by the harshness of her claim, but we all know this is just her defences kicking in. Later, she tells Richard how disgusted she was by Chandler's 'pig-sex' anecdote, a feeling that Richard believes is fair. 'Fair?' Shrieks Monica. 'Please don't even talk to me about "fair"! "Fair" would've been you wanting to marry me back then! Or "fair" would've been Chandler wanting to marry me now! Believe me, nothing about this is *fair*! Nothing! Nothing! Nothing! Nothing!' Later on, when Chandler comes to see Richard, he instantly knows that Monica has been there thanks to the incriminating evidence of a glass of scotch on the rocks – with a twist, on a coaster!

The Ballad of Ross & Rachel: You'd think Rachel would learn her lesson. Having discussed with Phoebe the idea of having a back up, should she still be single by the time she's 40, she hits on the idea of choosing Ross. Ross?! She's already dated, dumped, married and divorced him – does this not tell her anything??

Generation X: Chandler stumbles through a paraphrasing of the Pledge of Allegiance of the United States. Richard quotes from the visionary prose poem 'The Prophet' by Kahlil

Gibran. Joey's new nautical look reminds Rachel of the popular (in the US, at least) musical duo The Captain and Tennille. And in the last scene of the season, we hear 'Wonderful Tonight' by Eric Clapton.

The Story So Far: Phoebe and Joey are introduced to Mr Thompson, the head of Rachel's department. Phoebe points out that Ross is twelve years older than Elizabeth, confirming his age as 32. Monica notes that Richard has grown his moustache back (see 'TOW Monica and Richard Are Just Friends'). Monica and Richard reminisce about the time they almost got caught in the Gellers' bathroom by Monica's parents (see 'TOW Joey Moves Out'). Chandler claims he once caught his mother and father having sex with the same man.

The Last Word: If you've read the summary of this episode without knowing what happens, then hopefully by now you're wiping a tear of disbelief from your face. How could Chandler and Monica get so close and then lose it all because of Chandler's plan to pretend he would never marry her and the surprise return of Richard?

Well of course, that's not how the episode ends. Chandler comes home to find the apartment bathed in candlelight. Monica is standing there in the darkness and, as she gets down on one knee she stumbles through a proposal, but she's too emotional and she begins to cry. Chandler's crying too, but he manages to make what will probably go down in history as the most perfect proposal ever. Finally, after six years, two of the friends are to be married. It might not be the couple we all thought it would be way back in 1994, but it's certainly the ending we all hoped for.

Of course, with the spotlight shining all too often on Ross and Rachel over the years, it's easy to forget that Monica and Chandler were always meant to be together. Remember how, way back in 'TOW The Birth', Chandler suggested that, hypothetically, he and Monica could get married if they were both single by the time they reached 40? Remember how Monica asked in all seriousness why he didn't think she'd be married by the time she was 40? Maybe in the future, Phoebe and Joey will finally get together – there have certainly been some very unsubtle hints that this is how they both want to end up. And despite everything that's happened between them, it's too soon to give up hoping that there's a future for Ross and Rachel. But for now, it's the turn of Chandler and Monica. Let's raise a glass to the happy couple!

At the beginning of this season, it looked like this could well be the last ever episode of our favourite sitcom, hence an ending that offers closure for all the characters and hope for the future. However, scant days before the US transmission of this season's stunning finale, Warner Bros. announced that the entire cast have signed for an additional two years. President of Entertainment for NBC, Garth Ancier, was quoted as saying that NBC 'anticipate upcoming strong seasons from a "must see" cast and a producing team that's still at the top of their game'.

We couldn't agree more. Roll on the next two years.

References

Although we used many different sources in our research, we must acknowledge the excellent book by David Wild (*Friends* which looks at the First Season) and the three publications by Penny Stallings (covering up to the Fifth Season). These books provide insight into behind-the-scenes on the show as well as containing some rather nice pictures of the cast at work.

Friends on the Internet

As one might expect, there is a huge amount of interest in *Friends* on the World Wide Web; shrines dedicated to individual cast members, discussion groups and e-mailing lists all showing their love for the show.

The official website at **www.warnerbros.com** is a great site that links to Warner Bros.' TV, films and cartoons. It's very US-centric but fun nonetheless.

Many websites carry transcripts of the episodes – pretty much all of these are taken from The Friends Script Index, which was started by Guineapig and later taken over by Eric Aasen. Eric's 'The One With All The Scripts – The Complete Friends Script Index' was an absolute godsend in the creation of this book (you can find this superb site at **www.thecfsi.com**). Eric's site also contains some excellent fan fiction and is without a doubt one of the best on the Internet.

In addition, there's the **'Friends Episode Guide'** page, (**www.friends-tv.org/epguide.html**) created by Andy J. Williams and maintained by Darcy Partridge, which you might want to check out. There's a similar site for all you francophiles at www.fanfr.com while British fans might want to dip into Rob 'JustcallmeRob' Wilson's UK Friends site, which can be found at www.cynic.demon.co.uk. In addition to a list of Channel 4 transmission dates, Rob also carries a link to the 'Friends Mailing List', which is a friendly, informal e-mail group who discuss (but don't limit themselves to) all the latest rumours, merchandising and general points of interest for the average fan. They're a lovely bunch of people, so don't be scared – sign up today!

Oh, and the world would be a much darker and ill-informed place if it weren't for the incredibly hard-working people at **www.imdb.com**. If you've ever wanted to know just how many films contain the word monkey* for example, here's the place to look.

---

* 98 at the last count.